P9-CMQ-410

PRAISE FOR
NETGUIDE
THE BEST GENERAL GUIDE
TO THE INTERNET

"The liveliest, most readable online guide yet."
—*USA Today*

"A valuable guide for anyone interested in the
recreational uses of personal computers and
modems."—Peter H. Lewis, *The New York Times*

"The best attempt yet at categorizing and organizing all
the great stuff you can find out there. It's the book
people keep stealing off my desk."
—Joshua Quittner, *New York Newsday*

"*NetGuide* focuses on the most important aspect of
online information—its content. You name it, it's
there—from erotica to religion to politics."
—Lawrence J. Magid, *San Jose Mercury News*

"*NetGuide* will keep you from wandering around
aimlessly on the Internet, and is full of good ideas for
where to pull over."—*Forbes FYI*

"Thanks to Wolff and friends, the cyberswamp may just
have become a little less murky."
—*Entertainment Weekly*

"One of the most complete, well-organized guides to
online topics, from photography to the Church of Elvis,
you'll find it here."—*PC Magazine*

"The *TV Guide* to Cyberspace!"
—Louis Rossetto, editor/publisher, *Wired*

Your Personal Net Series available from Dell

NETGUIDE
NETSTUDY
NETSPORTS
NETSCI-FI
NETMONEY
NETDOCTOR

net sci-fi

A Compendium of the Best Science Fiction on the Internet

A Michael Wolff Book

A Dell Book

Published by
Dell Publishing
a division of
Bantam Doubleday Dell Publishing Group, Inc.
1540 Broadway
New York, New York 10036

NetSci-Fi, NetSpy, NetCollege, NetStudy, NetDoctor, NetMarketing, NetVote, NetJobs, NetGames2, NetTravel, NetTaxes, NetMusic, NetGames, NetChat, NetMoney, NetTech, NetSports, Your Personal Net, the Your Personal Net Logo, NetBooks, NetHead, NetSpeak, NetBest, and CyberPower are trademarks of Wolff New Media LLC. The Net Logo, What's On in Cyberspace, and YPN are registered trademarks of Wolff New Media LLC. The trademark NetGuide, created by Michael Wolff & Company, Inc., is now owned by CMP Media, Inc., and is used under a license from CMP. The book *NetGuide* is an independent publication not affiliated with CMP or any CMP publication.

The trademark Dell® is registered in the U.S. Patent and Trademark Office.

ISBN: 0-440-22423-3

Printed in the United States of America

Published simultaneously in Canada

October 1997

10 9 8 7 6 5 4 3 2 1

OPM

WOLFF NEW MEDIA

Michael Wolff
Publisher and Editor in Chief

Kelly Maloni
Executive Editor

Stevan Keane
Editor

Research Editor: Kristin Miller
Senior Editor: Dina Gan
Production Editor: Donna Spivey

Art Director: Stephen Gullo
Associate Art Director: Eric Hoffsten
Assistant Art Director: Jay Jaffe

Editor of *NetSci-Fi:* Deborah Cohn

Associate Editors: Molly Confer, Lev Grossman, Hylton Jolliffe, Bennett Voyles
Staff Writers: Henry Lam, Wendy Nelson, Stephanie Overby
Copy Editor: Sonya Donaldson
Editorial Assistants: Jennifer Levy, Vicky Tsolomytis, Eric Zelko
Production Assistants: Alex Fogarty, Jackie Fugere, Amy Gawronski
Intern: Keith Hays

Executive Vice President: James M. Morouse
Vice President, Marketing: Jay Sears
Advertising Director: Michael Domican
Advertising Sales: Eric Oldfield
Marketing Assistants: Nicholas Bogaty, Amy Winger

WOLFF NEW MEDIA LLC

Michael Wolff
President

Alison Anthoine
Vice President

Joseph Cohen
Chief Financial Officer

Special thanks:
As always, Aggy Aed

TABLE OF CONTENTS

FAQ

Frequently asked Questions about the Net and NetSci-Fi

The following is a genuine transcript of a series of questions put to the NetSci-Fi team by a recent visitor identified only as "The Visitor"...

1. Your planet is interesting to us. You are interesting to us. We are intrigued by the recent acceleration of your technological growth. But tell us, in your publication, *NetSci-Fi*, what do you mean by the words "the Best SF on the Internet"?

A few things actually, but let's start simply. The Internet, AKA cyberspace, is big. Really big. And very full. Put it this way. There's a show called *The X-Files* which is kind of popular. Now suppose you wanted to find the best *X-Files* Web sites. You would probably begin by using a search engine. You would type "X-File" into Alta Vista and up would come a list of 20,000 entries. At a conservative estimate, and allowing for download time, you may want to allow ten minutes to examine each site. Which means you would need to spend more than four solid months reading them before you could begin to choose which you thought was the best. At NetBooks we've done it all for you. We have the staff, we have the will, and we have the time. All you have to do is turn to the *X-Files* section, read what we thought, then add the URLs you'll find there to your bookmarks.

2. This is very impressive. But tell us, what do the abbreviations "Sci-Fi" and "SF" stand for?

We use both "Sci-Fi" and "SF" on the cover because although most of this planet accepts that "Sci-Fi" is an abbreviation of "Science Fiction" (a generic term used to describe a wide range of imaginative entertainment, and hence the reason why the book is called *NetSci-Fi*), there are those who take a more expansive view. They prefer "SF," which stands for "speculative fiction." Non-partisan souls that we are, we say, "hey, let's use both abbreviations."

3. Ah, an example of your infamous "humanity." So, how are we to find our way around this thing you call "book."

For experienced netsurfers it's as easy as moon pie. If you already know the genre, show, book, character, or author you're interested in, just turn to the *NetSci-Fi* index. If you know nothing of the Internet, or, if you will forgive me, have just arrived from another planet, then you may wish to browse the book section by section. Accordingly, the book is divided into nine sections.

• Center of the Universe
• Sci-Fi Screen
• Star Trek
• Sci-Fi Literature
• Cyberpunk
• It Came From Comics
• Sci-Fringe
• Sci-Fi Games
• New Worlds

4. Enough! Do not try our patience! What distinguishes one section from the next?

Let's take it from the top, shall we? **Center of the Universe** is where you will find sites that have been created by true devotees, with links to almost every subject in the sci-fi universe. If you fail to find a scif-fi page that grabs your attention when you begin at one of these pages, you may be forced to conclude that SF just isn't your cup of tea.

All the same, you may want to drop by **Sci-Fi Screen** just in case. There you will find the best Web sites of the best SF movies and TV ever made. And scattered through the chapters are longer pieces dedicated to the masters of the genre, directors like Stanley Kubrick and Edward D. Wood Jr.

Star Trek is a section unto itself because *Star Trek* is a world unto itself. If the Net hadn't been invented, it would eventually have been introduced as a plot device in perhaps the most successful science fiction franchise ever. *Trek* is so successful that its owners are extremely protective of its iconography. As you might notice, we have taken pains not to intrude upn their dominion.

Sci-Fi Literature is an introduction to the geniuses who crafted brave new worlds in literature, and is followed by **Cyberpunk**, the recent, thrilling literary movement and fascinating subculture that has inspired some of the worst films ever made. Following that, **It Came From Comics** is a roundup of the sci-fi worlds which began in issues of comics like *Batman* and *Akira*, and which have spawned TV shows, movies, and empires of poseable action figures.

Sci-Fringe is where the dark corners of imaginative fiction receive the full illumination of the Net. You might be surprised at the mental wattage that powers its beam. Fantasy, Horror, Cult, the Paranormal and the films of Lloyd Kaufman receive special attention here. This is followed by **Sci-Fi Games**, an arena for those who have read, understood and absorbed the rules of other worlds and who want to test their new skills against like-minded adversaries.

Finally, **New Worlds** is where our SF is tested against the predictions of our generation's professional futurists. From Faith Popcorn to Alvin Toffler online is the best place to see their ideas digested and revisited.

5. Your explanation has pleased us. But we crave more data. What is this Net of which you speak?

The Net is the electronic medium composed of millions of computers networked together throughout the world. Also known as cyberspace, the Information Superhighway, or the Infobahn, it comprises four types of networks—the Internet, a global, non-commercial system with more than 30 million computers communicating through it; commercial online services, such as America Online and CompuServe; the set of discussion groups known as Usenet; and the thousands of regional and local bulletin board services (BBSs). Although the most common use of the Net is the exchange of email, the past year has seen the development of increasingly sophisticated methods for displaying and sharing information. More and more, the Internet refers to the World Wide Web, and more and more the Web unites all the diverse locations and formats that make up the Net. To traverse this medium you will, of course, need a computer and a modem.

6. Connection is now a priority. Tell us, what computer and modem would we need?

Most new computers are sold with everything you need. But let's assume you have only a bare-bones PC. In that case you'll also need to get a modem which will allow your computer to communicate over the phone. So-called 14.4 modems, which transfer data at speeds up to 14,400 bits per second (bps), are standard. You should be able to get one for less than $100. But 28,800 bps modems are fast replacing them, and prices are dropping rapidly. Next, you'll need a communications program to control the modem. This software will probably come free with your modem, your PC, or—if you're going to sign up somewhere—your online service. Otherwise, you can buy it off the shelf for under $25 or get a friend to download it from the Net. Finally, you'll want a telephone line. If *that's* still not fast enough, you can contact your local telephone utility to arrange for installation of an ISDN line, which allows data to be transmitted at up to five times the speed.

7. And what kind of account?

You'll definitely want to be able to get email; certainly want wide access to the Internet; and perhaps want membership to at least one online service.

Here are some of your access choices:

Email Gateway

This is the most basic access you can get. It lets you send and receive messages to and from anyone, anywhere, anytime on the Net. Email is quickly becoming a standard way to communicate with friends and colleagues. (Yesterday: "What's your phone number?" Today: "What's your email address?") Email gateways are often available via work, school, or the online services listed here.

Online Services

Expensive, yet ubiquitous, these services offer a wealth of options for the cybersurfer. Online services are cyber city-states. The large ones have more "residents" (members) than most U.S. cities—enough users, in other words, to support lively discussions and games among their membership, and enough resources to make a visit worthwhile. They generally require special start-up software, which you can buy at any local computer store or by calling the numbers listed in this book. (Hint: Look for the frequent starter-kit giveaways.) AOL and CompuServe, the largest online services, both provide access to many of Usenet's more than 10,000 newsgroups, email gateways through which you can subscribe to any Internet mailing lists, and access to the World Wide Web (WWW). America Online is even incorporating links to Web sites in its own forums. The cyberwalls are tumbling and the easy-to-use online services are making the Internet accessible to millions of technophobes.

Internet Providers

There are a growing number of full-service Internet providers (which means they offer email, Usenet, FTP, IRC, telnet, gopher, and WWW access). In practical terms, the Internet will take you to the SF site of your choice; subscribe to a mailing list that can satisfy your thirst for *Trek* discussion; or locate a newsgroup which can help you find that elusive filk artist. Dial-up SLIP (serial line Internet protocol) and PPP (point-to-point protocol) accounts are currently the most popular types of Internet connections, replacing the text-only access of the standard dial-up accounts with significantly faster access and the ability to use point-and-click programs for Windows, Macintosh, and other platforms.

BBSs

BBSs range from mom-and-pop, hobbyist computer bulletin boards to large professional services. What the small ones lack in size they often make up for in affordability and homeyness. Unfortunately, the scenic by-roads are becoming obsolete, as the information highway continues to expand. On the other hand, many of the large BBSs are as rich and diverse as the commercial online services. BBSs are easy to get started with. If you find one with Internet access or an email gateway, you'll get the best of local color and global reach at once. You can locate local BBSs through the Usenet discussion groups alt.bbs.lists and comp.bbs .misc, the BBS forums of the commercial services, and regional and national BBS lists kept in the file libraries of many BBSs. Many, if not most, local BBSs now offer Internet email, as well as live chat, and file libraries.

Direct Network Connection

The direct network connection is the fast track of college students, computer scientists, and a growing number of employees of high-tech businesses. It puts the user right on the Net, bypassing phone connections. In other words, it's a heck of a lot faster. If you're downloading hundreds of articles on alien abductions or trying to follow a Net simulcast of a symposium on crop circles, you'll need this kind of connection speed.

8. Email? Run that one by us again.

With email, you can write to anyone on a commercial service, Internet site, or Internet-linked BBS, as well as to those people on the Net via email gateways, SLIPs, and direct-network connections.

Email addresses have a universal syntax called an Internet address. An Internet address is broken down into four parts: the user's name (e.g., wolff), the @ symbol, the computer and/or company name, and what kind of Internet address it is: **net** for network, **com** for a commercial enterprise—as with Your Personal Net (ypn.com) and America Online (aol.com)—**edu** for educational institutions, **gov** for government sites, **mil** for military facilities, and **org** for nonprofit and other private organizations. For instance, the address for one of the main writers of this book, whose mystery is matched only by her Stakhanovite output, would be soverby@ypn.com.

9. The Web. Explain.

The World Wide Web is a hypertext-based information structure that now dominates Internet navigation. The Web is like a house where every room has doors to a number of other rooms, or an electronic magazine where elements on the page are connected to elements on other pages. Words, icons, and pictures on a page link to other pages, not only on the same machine, but anywhere in the world. You have only to click on the appropriate word or phrase or image, and the Web does the rest. In a snap you'll be beamed from The Sci-Fi Channel home page to the *Planet of the Apes*. All the while you've FTPed, telnetted, gophered, and linked without a thought to case-sensitive Unix commands or addresses.

If you know exactly where you want to go on the Net and don't want to wade through Net directories and indexes, you can type a Web page's address, known as a URL (uniform resource locator). The URL for the Alien Exploratorium, for example, is http://area51 .upsu.plym.ac.uk/~moosie/ufo/ aexplo.htm. On some Web browsers, such as the latest version of Netscape Navigator, "http://" is not required.

10. Graphical Web browsers? What are these things?

With the emergence of new and sophisticated software like Netscape Navigator (**http://www.netscape.com**), the Web looks and sounds the way its architects imagined—pictures, icons, appetizing layouts, downloadable sound clips, and animation. Some commercial services have developed customized Web browsers for their subscribers. Web browsers are more than just presentation tools. Most of them allow netsurfers to see all kinds of sites through a single interface. Want to read newsgroups? Need to send email? Interested in participating in real-time chat? You can do it all with your browser.

11. And these newsgroups?

There are many places in cyberspace where netsurfers can post their opinions, questions, and comments, but the most widely read bulletin boards are a group of over 10,000 "newsgroups" collectively known as Usenet. Usenet newsgroups are global, collecting thousands of messages a day from whomever wants to "post" to them. Newsgroups are the collective, if sometimes babel-like, voice of the Net—everything is discussed here. While delivered over the Internet, Usenet newsgroups are not technically part of the Internet. Smallish service providers that have news feeds sometimes store only a few hundred newsgroups, while most Internet providers and online services offer thousands. (If there's a group missing that you really want, ask your Internet provider to add the newsgroup back to the subscription list.)

The messages in a newsgroup, called "posts," are listed and numbered chronologically—in other words, in the order in which they were posted. You can scan a list of messages before deciding to read a particular message. If someone posts a message that prompts responses, the original and all follow-up messages are called a thread. The subject line of subsequent posts in the thread refers to the subject of the original message. For example, were you to post a message with the subject "There are aliens in my office interrogating me" to alt.alien.visitors, all responses would read "Re: There are aliens in my office interrogating me." In practice, however, topics wander in many directions. Popular newsgroups generate hundreds of messages daily. To cut back on repetitive questions, newsgroup members often compile extensive lists of answers to frequently asked questions (FAQs). Many FAQs have grown so large and so comprehensive that they are valuable resources in their own right, informal encyclopedias (complete with hypertext links) dedicated to the newsgroup's topic.

12. Mailing lists?

Mailing lists are like newsgroups, except that they are distributed by Internet email. The fact that messages show up in your mailbox tends to make the discussion group more intimate, as does the proactive act of subscribing. Mailing lists are often more focused, and they're less vulnerable to irreverent and irrelevant contributions.

To subscribe to a mailing list, send an email to the mailing list's subscription address. Often you will need to include very specific information, which you will find in this book. To unsubscribe, send another message to that same address. If the mailing list is of the listserv, listproc, or majordomo variety, you can usually unsubscribe by sending the command **unsubscribe <listname>** or **signoff <listname>** in the message body. If the mailing list instructs you to "write a request" to subscribe ("Dear list owner, please subscribe me to…"), you will probably need to write a request to unsubscribe.

Once you have subscribed, messages are almost always sent to a different address than the subscription address. Most lists will send you the address when you subscribe. If not, send another message to the subscription address and ask the owner.

13. And telnet, FTP, gopher? Can you explain?

Telnet

When you telnet, you're logging on to another computer somewhere else on the Internet. You then have access to the programs running on the remote computer. If the site is running a library catalog, for example, you can search the catalog. If it's running a live chat room, you can communicate with others logged on. Telnet addresses are listed as URLs, in the form **telnet://domain.name:port number**. A port number is not always required, but when listed it must be used.

FTP

FTP (file transfer protocol) is a the way to copy a file from another Internet-connected computer to your own. Hundreds of computers on the Internet allow "anonymous FTP." In other words, you don't need a unique password to access them. Just type "anonymous" at the user prompt and type your email address at the password prompt. The range of material available is extraordinary—from archives of journal articles to collections of anatomical images. Since the advent of Web browsers, net-surfers can transfer files without using a separate FTP program. In this book, FTP addresses are listed as URLs, in the form **ftp://domain.name/directory/filename.txt**. And here's a bonus—logins and passwords aren't required with Web browsers.

14. So the addresses will look *how* exactly?

All entries in *NetSci-Fi* have a name, review, and address. The site name appears first in boldface, followed by a review of the site. After the review, complete address information is provided. The name of the service appears first—**WEB** to designate the World Wide Web, **AMERICA ONLINE** to designate America Online, and so on. The text following the service tells you what you need to do to get to the site—sometimes just a simple URL, sometimes something more complicated. When you see an arrow (→), this means that you have another step ahead of you, such as typing a command, searching for a file, or subscribing to a mailing list. Bullets separate multiple addresses, which indicate that the site is accessible in more than one way.

If the item is a Web site, FTP site, telnet, or gopher, it will be displayed in the form of a URL, which can be typed in the command line of your Web browser. FTP and gopher sites will be preceded by **URL**, while telnet sites, which cannot be launched directly through a browser, will be preceded by **TELNET**. If the item is a mailing list, the address will include an email address and instructions on how to subscribe (remember—the address given is usually the subscription address; in order to post to the mailing list, you will use another address that will be emailed to you upon subscribing). IRC (Internet Relay Chat) addresses indicate what you must type to get to the channel you want once you've connected to the IRC server. Entries about newsgroups are always followed by the names of the newsgroups.

In an online service address, the name of the service is followed by the keyword (also called "go word"). Additional steps are listed where necessary.

In addition, there are a few special terms used in addresses. *Info* indicates a supplementary informational address. *Archives* is used to mark collections of past postings for newsgroups and mailings lists. And *FAQ* designates the location of a "frequently asked questions" file for a newsgroup.

15. You have intrigued us. The knowledge we garner from this visit shall assist us in our future plans for the Earth. Meanwhile, where might we learn more about your planet using "the Net"?

As it happens, we at NetBooks are charting the whole range of human existence as it is represented online. We probably have exactly what you're looking for. Try one of these for size: *NetChat, NetGames, NetSports, NetMusic, Fodor's NetTravel, NetVote, NetJobs, NetMarketing, NetTech, NetDoctor, NetStudy, NetCollege, NetGuide, NetShopping, NetKids, NetLove,* and *NetMoney*.

With *NetSci-Fi* we have taken another step towards clarifying the content of the Net for newcomers intimidated by its sheer volume. For each subject covered we have selected what we consider to be the best sites, the Click Picks. These are listed at the beginning of each chapter. That should make life on earth a little easier for you. And by the way, you may want to take a look at *NetSpy* before you drop by again. The green complexion, the antenna, and the ray gun are a bit of a giveaway, you know.

PART 1

Center of the Universe

THE SPACE STATION

CYBERSPACE IS A DANGEROUS place to go exploring. It's full of uncharted territory, unstable wormholes, and really strange inhabitants. Travelers might even conclude that there's a conspiracy by a galactic superpower to make it as disorganized as possible: we're so busy wandering aimlessly, we won't notice as they melt our brain cells and take our DNA for their ungodly genetic experiments. Fortunately, the Net is also home to some of the friendliest sci-fi guides to be found anywhere. There are entire Web sites devoted to making online fandom easier for everyone. Whether it's a master index, a newsgroup, a mailing list, an archive of reviews, or a chatty news magazine, it's out there somewhere in cyberspace, the final frontier.

▶ CLICK PICK

rec.arts.sf.misc Anybody remember the TV series *Quark*? Where can I get a short story about mutant goat men? This newsgroup is like a deluxe pizza—it's never the same twice, but it always tastes delicious. It's not the busiest spot in cyberspace, so if you only like *The X-Files* or are deep into Robert Jordan and nobody else, there are no guarantees that anyone else cares. Pay a visit if you have an unanswerable question to post ("I was just wondering what the effect of the Earth would be if the Moon suddenly winked out of existence?") or if you seek an undending source of trivia, news, and miscellaneous knowledge from those who really know their stuff.
USENET rec.arts.sf.misc

The Science Fiction Gallery Try to imagine a site that has the scope of an index and the depth of a thesis paper. At The Science Fiction Gallery, dozens of movies, TV shows, and anime series get at least a synopsis, and at most a page-long hypertext article linking to a half dozen features. Want to know if anyone else thought *ID4* was a waste of celluloid

and Brent Spiner's indubitable talent? All the latest SF movies are reviewed here. And don't forget, the gallery is based on your interactive participation, so donate your "Ode to Barbarella" today.
WEB http://www4.onestep.com/scifi

▶ MOTHERSHIPS

Fandom Domain This is the site that will make all others obsolete. Whatever your fantasy, however fictive your science, the Fandom Domain contains links for you and your filk, er, ilk. Even if you haven't found anyone else quite like you, begging the question, "Am I really alone in the universe?" the positively exhaustive indexes of clubs and conventions will link you up with your soulmates in fandom. Read up on the genre you love best, through links to more than 35 zines online. Love Pern? Goth? *Trek*? Furries? The Good *Doctor Who*? Links to fan pages for these subgenres and many of their cousins are all here. Plus, games, art, anime, reviews, and lots more. Do not miss this site—it's almost like seeing *Star Wars* for the first time. OK, it's not quite that good, but almost.
WEB http://www.sff.net/sff/sflinks

The Sci-Fi Site The Sci-Fi Site is like visiting an SF convention and wandering from exhibit to exhibit. (Well, if each booth had a couple thousand dollars for interior design and multimedia). Over here, *Planet of the Apes* fans show off their timeline; over there, someone's giving directions to the *Trek* booths; and in the corner, a few more people are trading *X-Files* conspiracy theories. The Web masters' interest in feedback and interactivity gives things the personalized yet random feel of those conversations you stumble onto in convention center elevators.
WEB http://www.abacus.ghj.com/sci_fi /default.htm

Science Fiction Forum A heavy concentration of literature, which means there's traffic for readers of any popular author from Stephen Donaldson to William Gibson to Robert Heinlein. It also means that many of the postings are fans' notes—gushing appraisals of classic works ("Bradbury's *Martian Chronicles* is the most completely imagined science fiction novel ever"), arguments over originality (should we credit the invention of robots to Karl Capek or Isaac Asimov?), and even clarifications of picayune points in massive epics (how exactly does mind-reading work in Frank Herbert's *Dune?*). Looking to read even more sci-fi adventures? The Interactive Fiction Library (a subset of the Science Fiction Libraries) has stories, poems, and songs written by other AOL members. Plenty of people love related media, of course, and there are some fascinating discussions on film and TV. Don't expect much esoterica here: Spielberg and Lucas rule the libraries. *Star Wars* fans have packed a separate library with images, timelines, FAQs, and newsletters.

AMERICA ONLINE *keyword* scifi→Science Fiction

SF/Fantasy Literature Forums The forums collect a sketchy, haphazard, and unflaggingly energetic group of posts on various science-fiction and fantasy literature and art topics—zines, novels, filks, and magazines. "I have a good plot idea for the *X-Files*," writes one fan, and proceeds to detail a wild plot that has something to do with paranormal phenomena infiltrating TVs from the inside out, using boob tubes as transmitters for alien agendas. Give it time! Sci-fi fans can also speak their piece both on the message boards and in live conferences on the great cultural milestones of their beloved genre—*Star Wars*, *Star Trek*, *Highlander*, and even Anne McCaffrey's Pern novels—and the forums include workshops in which published sci-fi authors share their advice on writing effective speculative fiction.

COMPUSERVE *go* sflit • *go* sflittwo

SF/Fantasy Media Forums Every industry, medium, and genre has its "big players." Science fiction has *Star Trek*, *Star Wars*, *Doctor Who*, *The X-Files*, and more, all commanding a steady following in these forums. For FAQs, images, and archives of interesting discussions, head for the libraries.

COMPUSERVE *go* sfmedone • *go* sfmedtwo

> **CYBERZINES**

Dark Carnival Online Here's a classy, quality monthly with an emphasis on the dark side of sci-fi. The editors must be well-connected, because they've been recently blessed with permission to publish stories by Clive Barker, Poppy Z. Brite, and Peter Straub, to name a few. Regular departments include fiction, features (an interview with Anne Rice, for example), books, games, movies, and columns. The interface is clever, too, since each issue is available as an all-in-one issue or as part of a comprehensive index.

WEB http://www.darkcarnival.com

Neil Wallman's Film and Sci-Fi Journal Neil is an underemployed London law graduate who, in his copious spare time, reviews sci-fi films and books in droves. His wide-eyed, purist take on such topics as Doctor Who kissing an actual woman is always amusing, and he also collects the contributions of readers and fans who have weighed in on the many debates currently underway, such as the one about on-screen violence. It's difficult to find your way through the maze of the journal, but entertaining nonetheless.

WEB http://ourworld.compuserve.com/homepages/neil_wallman

OMNI Online A magazine that has, throughout its history, boldly gone where other science mags dared not go, *OMNI* is now almost entirely an online enterprise, publishing only four paper issues each year. OMNI Online is all fans have come to expect—original fiction, discussion of scientific realities behind paranormal phenomena, etc.—and lots more. The interactive capabilities of AOL are used here to their utmost, with chat rooms, message boards, libraries, and real-time interviews supplementing the considerable regular content. The Web site is similar, if less interactive.

WEB http://www.omnimag.com
AMERICA ONLINE *keyword* omni

Science Fiction Weekly An online venture that may appeal to beginning fans more than those who have found a niche in the SF universe. This slick and pretty production reviews the recent sci-fi nascences and newsmakers. The best section by far is News of the Week, with its well-written and suitably brief updates to sci-fi events, including awards and hot shows. The reviews, on the other hand, are more plot summary than critique, and some show little knowledge of sci-fi. However, for sheer elegance, this magazine deserves a place in the forefront of similar media, and many online fannish types point to it as an authority.
WEB http://www.scifi.com/sfw

SF-Lovers No, the name of this digest does not refer (specifically anyway) to the incestuous world of cyberpunk authors, Captain Kirk's seduction of green, half-dressed princesses, nor the late night action at a science fiction convention. It refers to lovers of the genre. All science fiction and fantasy themes are game, and much of the digest material comes from the rec.sf.* newsgroup hierarchy. Saul Jaffe, the moderator, speaks of the digest as a magazine, and brings a strong sense of decorum to his editorial choices. The flame-free result is really the only human way of keeping up with the hyperactive science fiction newsgroups for literature, TV, and movies. The digest is still huge, though—monthly compilations available from the immense FTP archive average about 1.25 meg.
EMAIL sf-lovers-request@rutgers.edu
✍ *Write a request*

SF-News: Mr. Data's Data An electronic news column covering the sci-fi media—from *Dr. Who* to *Star Trek*—on a monthly basis. Culls gossip, rumor, and hard news about shows from all the sci-fi newsgroups and mailing lists, offline fan clubs and newsletters, and the press. What actor will make his directorial debut

this week? Where are the plot twists of your favorite show heading? What shows are being threatened with cancellation and which are being revived?
EMAIL majordomo@stargame.org ✍ *Type in message body:* subscribe sfnews

SMASH! The Cyber-Zine! Collectors, comic book readers, and TV junkies alike will delight in the freshness of this no-frills newsmag. The home page greets visitors with the question "What's New?" in any one of six categories, including anime, cards, and science fiction. The features are especially geared to collectors and comics fans, but one much-needed section, The Dead Zone, lists all series (comics, cards, and shows) that have been recently canceled or are doomed. Science fiction (like Rodney Dangerfield) gets no respect.
WEB http://smash.mgz.com/current/html/mag/maghome/maghome.htm

▶ ARCHIVES

Giant Science Fiction Gophers Ceaseless in their pursuit of links, these sci-fi gophers have created connections to archives of sci-fi zines, the full-text of sci-fi novels, FAQs for every sci-fi discussion group on the Net, newsletters from publishing houses, convention schedules, fan club information, author biographies, image and sound clip collections, and lists galore.
URL gopher://marvel.loc.gov:70/11/employee/clubs/scific • gopher://wiretap.spies.com/11/Library/Media/Sci-Fi

The Linköping Science Fiction and Fantasy Archive For any fan looking to vent, or to find out what to read, see, or think next in the realm of sci-fi, this archive is the place to visit. Linköping collects texts, especially reviews, related to your favorite authors, books, and movies. Full versions of sci-fi newsletters and mags such as *Ansible* are gathered here, too, along with publicly available fiction, art, and guides to the genre.
WEB http://sf.www.lysator.liu.se/sf_archive

Rutgers Archive Trouble remembering that *Star Trek* episode in which people were turned into green styrofoam dice and crushed by a childish god? How about the first scene of *The Flash*? You'll find the answers here, in Rutgers' huge collection of science-fiction TV show episode guides, with entries on shows ranging from the immensely popular to the barely remembered. Annotated links to hundreds of sci-fi Internet sites organized into archives, authors, awards, bibliographies, bookstores, fandom, fiction, movies, publishers, reviews and criticism, role-playing games, television, Usenet newsgroups, and zines. The Rutgers archive also contains other documents of interest to science-fiction fans, including a UFO guide, a list of Nebula award winners, and a large archive of posts to the SF Lovers mailing list.
URL ftp://sflovers.rutgers.edu/pub/sf-lovers/Web/sf-resource.guide.html

frenzied? Then you'll appreciate this index to the sci-fi Web. Each link is listed next to the most complete annotations available (outside of this book, of course!) so there's no time wasted. Categories cover the whole SF spectrum, including more rarely-seen topics like sci-fi artists or bookstores. Old standbys like *Star Trek*, *Doctor Who*, and *Star Wars* are here as well.
WEB http://www.oneworld.net/SF

The Speculative Fiction Clearing House The SF Clearing House is aptly named. Without regard to personal preference, except for a slight lean toward the written word, John Leavitt has assembled the clearest, quickest-to-comprehend site of any of the super indexes on the Web. Looking for awards and who won them? Start here for the best and most frequently updated list.
WEB http://polarbear.eng.lycos.com/sf-clearing-house

▶ INDEXES

Beyond the Farthest Star A highly detailed list of links with minimal graphics and a ton of information, organized into sensible categories that make finding stuff quick and easy, including Organizations, TV Shows and Listings, Animation, Games, Stores, FAQs, and Zines.
WEB http://www.cs.swarthmore.edu/~binde/sf/index.html

Nathan's Fandom Page It isn't nearly as comprehensive as Fandom Domain, but it is attractive and easy to use, with topics like Fantasy (four links) and Fandom (seven links). The links favor quality over quantity, and Nathan's use of frames is intelligent. Sci-fi fans particularly interested in Filk, Megafandom (Goth), or The Artemis Society will want to visit Nathan's other Web sites devoted to these topics.
WEB http://members.tripod.com/~Aelffin/sfandom.html

Science Fiction Earth Links at One World Network Are you fannish and

▶ COLONIZATION

Cybertown You'll be glad to learn that Cybertown is populated mostly by people from Earth, probably because it's not far from this galaxy. It's a fully realized virtual community of folks looking to pretend that the Internet has literally taken over the Earth sometime in the late twenty-first century. Get a VR apartment, join in the entertainment, and generally lose yourself in a fun, role-playing Web tour, which is really what this is.
WEB http://www.cybertown.com

Planet X Transhumanism and political humor are just two of the topics that the "science fiction-obsessed" residents of Planet X love to discuss. These are netizens who—gasp—know each other well and get together in real life for yearly reunions, but new members join all the time. Head to Immigration and Naturalization Services to join the mailing list and find out the dirt. "Don't be offended" and "R.A. Heinlein and Larry Niven are Gods" is a preview of the advice you'll get. Good luck: it's a hairy planet.
WEB http://www.planetx.com/PlanetX

▶ NEWSGROUPS

alt.fandom.cons Those with any doubts about the limitless depths to which fandom can sink will find those reservations erased after a perusal of just a few of the posts in this celebration of "cons," the ultimate fan gatherings. Those who know nothing about cons—even if they are willing to learn—will find little here, other than a certain knowledge that cons attract an inside crowd. Those who have attended one, two, or umpteen cons, and don't already know about this busy newsgroup have found the ultimate handbook and insider's guide.
USENET alt.fandom.cons

rec.arts.sf.fandom This newsgroup seems to exist to prove two points: one, that fandom is a complex operation with its own history and culture, and two, that sci-fi fans like to talk about plenty besides sci-fi. The threads that don't discuss naming your cat or embarrassing typos are about fandom itself, and often involve passing on lore about con etiquette and the pre-Net days. Discussions are extremely long-winded; nearly every thread has more than a dozen posts in it, and many have more than a hundred. It's a polite, thorough, and (almost) always interesting bunch, even when they're not discussing anything to do with SF.
USENET rec.arts.sf.fandom

rec.arts.sf.marketplace Looking for *Star Wars* figures in mint condition? How about a complete set of *Star Trek* cards? If you're in the market for such wares, you've come to the right place, as long as you've got a credit card, cash, or something to trade. This is the place to visit if you want to buy, trade, or just chat about sci-fi stuff—everything from Harlan Ellison books to videos of Gene Roddenberry.
USENET rec.arts.sf.marketplace

rec.arts.sf.science Private space exploration, cold fusion, personality cloning, and other candidates for the Year 2000 edition of the Sharper Image catalog. Speculative science at its best—nowhere else outside of the physics lab do people argue as intelligently about "ways around the Heisenberg Uncertainty Principle" and other basic assumptions of modern science. The most skillful posters make the scientific seem absurd and the fictitious sound plausible.
USENET rec.arts.sf.science

Science Fiction Fandom AOL's Science Fiction Fandom board covers a broad spectrum of sci-fi topics, from general categories (the best and worst sci-fi movies of all time) to more specific concerns (How are women depicted in sci-fi? Where can you see naked footage of David Duchovny?). A friendly environment for discussion and debate.
AMERICA ONLINE *keyword* scifi→Science Fiction→Message Boards→Science Fiction Fandom

▶ MAILING LISTS

SF-Lit Some like Harlan Ellison. Some think he's an obnoxious jerk. Some question whether the Hugo awards are "just a popularity contest," and others say that of course they are. What do these people have in common? Merely a love of sci-fi as a genre, and especially as a literary genre. The conversations tend to be socio-political, too, with a discussion of why book publishers neglect sci-fi reprints or how sci-fi is sneaking into the cynical realm of American popular media.
EMAIL listserv@loc.gov ✍ *Type in message body:* subscribe sf-lit <your first name>

Spaced Sci-Fi Discussion List This list is home to a busy and intense bunch of subscribers who love to criticize everything that is sci-fi pop culture. Their focus is primarily on TV and movies, both the latest and the greatest (the original *Trek*: any more movies coming?) The discussion is generally playfully rude, but those who tread into the obnoxious zone will be flamed unmercifully. Newbies are welcomed, although most posts are by the same few list junkies.
EMAIL majordomo@branson.org ✍ *Type in message body:* subscribe spaced

PART 2

Sci-Fi Screen

VISUAL DATABANKS

SCIENCE MAY OFTEN BE HARD TO understand, but it's clear that science fiction isn't, especially when it's fed through the cathode ray or blasted from a silver screen. Then it's really simple. Just take a look at *Independence Day*. Watch as aliens stampede through gigantic plot holes! See flying saucers lock mass media in their tractor beams! Perhaps this desire to believe in the absurd lies in the fact that sci-fi removes our fears of not understanding. We never question the faster-than-light capability of the *Battlestar Galactica*, or the powers of the *Misfits of Science*. Let it never be said, however, that human beings are ingrates. Cyberspace, once a dream of science fiction, now pays homage to the genre with monumental video and cinematic sci-fi resources.

▶ CLICK PICK

The Sci-Fi Channel
As frantic as *Blade Runner*-style billboard advertising, and with a graphical interface that assumes a prior knowledge you couldn't possibly possess, this site gloriously transports you to the front lines of science fiction. Highs include Pulp, which offers excerpts from *TeknoNation*, and other great sci-fi magazines, and the BBoard Dominion Chat "will give you an opportunity to flaunt all of the useless factoids you've gathered throughout your life." Then there are the pages devoted to the shows themselves—from *The Bionic Woman* to *The Prisoner*—with elaborate multimedia pages which pay homage to your favorite, dearly departed shows.
WEB http://www.scifi.com
AMERICA ONLINE *keyword* scifi channel

▶ MOTHERSHIPS

Hyperion Science Fiction Archive A frequently updated collection of FAQs and guides related to science fiction, including the Sci-Fi TV titles list and schedule, an archive of *Lois and Clark* pictures, and an enormous collection of *Babylon 5* lists, pictures, and episode guides.
URL ftp://ftp.hyperion.com/pub/TV

The Logbook Opening with a graphics-heavy menu featuring cast members of *Babylon 5* and the three latest *Trek* incarnations, The Logbook moves to text-heavy master files of actors, directors, and writers; entries for episodes for four of the *Trek* variations, as well as *Blake's 7*, *Red Dwarf*, *Sliders*, and *Babylon 5*.
WEB http://www.uark.edu/~cbray/logbook

Sci-Fi Digest Consider *Sci-Fi Digest* if you're overcome with nostalgia for seventies sci-fi. There's news about *Star Wars*, the *Twelve Million Dollar Man and Woman* (that's six million twice), and *Planet of the Apes*. A text-only version is also available for the graphically challenged.
WEB http://cygnus.rsabbs.com/~mpinto/mj7.html

Science Fiction Episode Guides Essentially an online card catalog featuring highlights and greatest hits from the Science Fiction Repository at Rutgers, SFEG lists more than 30 noted SF shows within the Episode Guide folder. The listings are accessible by episode and broken down into brief plot summaries and info-bits (mostly cast and crew facts) that are either highly significant or useful mostly as answers to trivia questions, depending on your perspective. There is also a TV show FAQ folder, and a folder for movies. Because the movies page contains many broken links to movie home pages, the TV episode guide remains the best resource at this site.
URL ftp://sflovers.rutgers.edu/pub/sf-lovers

▶ MOVIES

A list of Sci-Fi Movies 1900-1960 From *Trip to the Moon* in 1902 to *The Village of the Damned* in 1960, this list records significant sci-fi films and their release dates for the first half of the century.

Lamentably, this page is a stand-alone, without links to other sites.

WEB http://www2.gist.net.au/~yogione /Movies.html

rec.arts.sf.movies In this forum, participants scheme to pitch ideas to Steven Spielberg, rewrite scripts for their own satisfaction, and debate the merits of any given sci-fi flavor of the month. Although discussions are dominated by issues concerning contemporary releases, you will still will find topics like "Godzilla v. Destroyer: Why!?!." Note the oft-ignored newsgroup FAQ request that Trekkies post to the appropriate *Trek* newsgroup, rather than here. To some participants' ire, William Shatner's acting, ego, and hair occasionally turn up as subjects.
USENET rec.arts.sf.movies

Sunrise Theater Intriguingly designed in the comforting colors of a cricket pavilion tea room, the Sunrise Theater is in fact a repository of all things '50s sci-fi. Membership is required, but has its unique rewards—visit the Hall of Heroes and meet Klaatu; learn the secrets of rudimentary special effects; find out about the "F" factor is. A warm bath in sci-fi nostalgia that the hardest heart could not resist.
WEB http://www.sunrise-theater.com

The WEB Science Fiction Film Page "There is nothing wrong with your computer terminal… Do not attempt to adjust the picture… We are controlling transmission… Psychotronic Cinema." Through automatically loading pages, the designers blitzkrieg these words on your screen to make you feel even more powerless over your already stubborn desktop computer. For this momentary lapse of control, you get more than 150 alphabetically and chronologically arranged reviews of sci-fi films. Movies that normally get filtered out by the human brain's quality meter, such as the TV movie *Knight Rider 2000*, and *Metalstorm: The Destruction of Jared-Syn*, find their way here. Unfortunately, the frequent one-liners offset even the camp value you may hope to derive from it.

Note that an automatic search is performed there when you press the link IMDB option for movies that correspond to entries from the Internet Movie Database.

WEB http://weber.u.washington.edu /~ataraxus

▶ **TV SHOWS**

rec.arts.sf.tv With so many different allegiances, you'd think it would be hard to make your way through the flame wars in a place like this, but it's not. Sci-fi fans can find common ground now and then, and they do, more often than not, in this freewheeling newsgroup. *Battlestar Galactica*, *Lost in Space*, *Space: 1999*—it's all fair game here (along with all likes of *Trek*, of course). But if you criticize *The X-Files*, watch out. One guy called it "a waste of time," saying the show belongs alongside *Weekly World News*. The response? Much anger against his "wild ravings." It's a good spot to talk about the shows you still love, or want to discuss, even if they were only on the air for a season or two.
USENET rec.arts.sf.tv

Science Fiction TV Series Episode Lists Lists of episodes for the current season of SF TV programs.
URL ftp://ftp.hyperion.com/pub/TV/sftv -titles

Titles of Upcoming Episodes Titles of upcoming episodes for many sci-fi shows, including *Deep Space Nine*, *Highlander*, and *The X-Files*.
WEB http://www.hyperion.com/ftp/pub /TV/sftv-sched

The Ultimate TV List: Science Fiction List Sure, this sci-fi list features *Planet of the Apes* and *The Outer Limits*, but you'll also find *Automan*, *The Powers of Matthew Star*, and their ilk, plus a complete list of invaluable links to episode guides, newsgroups, FAQs, mailing lists, and Internet Movie Guide's vast cast/credits info.
WEB http://www.tvnet.com/UTVL/sci _list.html

2001: A SPACE ODYSSEY

WHEN *2001: A SPACE ODYSSEY* was released in 1968, it's possible that no one truly comprehended the impact it would have on the genre, the film industry, and our space-age culture as a whole. The collaboration between director Stanley Kubrick and author Arthur C. Clarke led to a new dynamic in science fiction. Creators of sci-fi films and novels, as well as audiences, had to re-evaluate their views on space, artificial intelligence, technology, and extra-terrestrials. The fascination that the film has inspired over the years finds ongoing life on the Net, where sites filled with heated debate and intricate interpretation of the movie constitute a dedicated 2001 community.

▶ CLICK PICK

2001: A Space Odyssey—30 Years On
Using an interface that's heavy with graphics but light on load-in time, the site points you to everything from transcripts of HAL's conversations to "fan" mail for the site itself. Section names such as Connection, Vision, Discourse, and Interchange guide fans to interesting discussion pieces; themes and issues such as suspicion and lasting images are deftly handled. Die-hard fans will enjoy the site creator's 20,000-plus word opus on the films, their history, and their impact. "Every frame is full of imagery, every element is exquisitely positioned and lit, every visual proportion is exact. There is no denying that Kubrick got a few things wrong, but I imagine even Michelangelo got a few brush strokes out of place."
WEB http://www.peg.apc.org/~pjv

▶ MOTHERSHIPS

2001: A Space Odyssey Did you ever notice that the hibernating astronauts are shown lying in different positions at different times? Did you know that Stanley Kubrick had several tons of sand imported, washed, and painted for the production of the moon surface scenes? Explore the extensive list of movie goofs, links, clips, and trivia from the IMDB to make your journey complete.
WEB http://us.imdb.com/M/title-exact? +2001:+a+space+odyssey

2001 And Beyond The Infinite
Modemac, a member of the Church of the SubGenius, wrote this lengthy explanation of *2001* for all the people he met who didn't understand it. Read his pieces on the "Dawn of Man" and the "Jupiter Mission," as well as his continued thoughts on *2010*. The author is the type who doesn't insist he's right; he includes a page of commentary and criticism about what he's written, and the responses there are just as insightful as his original thesis.
WEB http://www.tiac.net/users/modemac /2001.html

▶ DIVERSIONS

2001 There's nothing better than a cleanly designed site with an ample collection of resources. Lucky for fans of the *2001* series, the Web master has extended this understanding of Web production to this classic sci-fi film. He has established an extensive library of images from the film, including a scene cut from the movie that featured Kubrick's two young daughters.
WEB http://www.lehigh.edu/~pjl2/films /2001.html

2001 and 2010—The Odyssey Movies
"My mind is going—I can feel it," said the computer HAL, and everyone who has ever seen *2001* remembers those words. When you feel the need to hear it again, this and a dozen other sound clips from the films are available here. Head back to the Geocities site for sound clips from movies and television shows ranging from *Aliens* to *Young Frankenstein* whenever you get the urge.
WEB http://www.geocities.com/Hollywood /1158/2010.html

THE ALIEN TRILOGY

THE *ALIEN* TRILOGY PUT A UNIQUE spin on the old story of guests who overstay their welcome and abuse their hosts. In three movies so far, Hollywood has formulated a multitude of ways for aliens to chase humans on their own spaceships and colonies, impregnate them with eggs, and kill them in darkly-lit hallways. Circumstances in each flick forced heroine Ellen Ripley (Sigourney Weaver) to assume the thankless task of killing these vicious monsters in various claustrophobic environs. Twentieth Century Fox plans to release a fourth installment, *Alien: Resurrection*, starring Winona Ryder alongside the formerly deceased Sig, for the 1997 summer movie season. So now's the time to brush up on your *Alien* lore. Know your enemy and be spared a face hug.

▶ CLICK PICK

Alien Saga "Classified documents of the Weyland-Yutani Corporation have been leaked onto the Net. Documents include detailed information on an alien species that bleeds acid and bites with two mouths…" While most pages will give you the requisite biographical information on the main characters of the *Alien* trilogy, or show the creepy reproduction cycle of the buggers, this page incorporates key features rarely found at one site alone. Scenes cut from the theatrical releases are summarized to help fill in some plot gaps. The Dark Horse Comics' *Alien* universe is detailed, revealing an expanded, more absorbing addition to the *Alien* mythos than even David Fincher's *Alien³* could offer, and the spoilers page gives the latest buzz on *Alien: Resurrection*. Get debriefed at Alien Saga before the next encounter.

WEB http://found.cs.nyu.edu/michael/alien

▶ MOTHERSHIPS

Alien FAQ Three parts film facts and one part conjecture, the giant four-part *Alien* FAQ covers the storyline, cast/production information, paraphernalia and collectibles, and discusses plot holes. You can also find a copy of an abridged version of William Gibson's unused *Alien³* script.

WEB http://synergy.smartpages.com /faqs/movies/alien-faq/top.html

Alien IV A Ripley clone? With Winona Ryder on board and Sigourney Weaver performing multiplicity 200 years after *Alien³*, 20th Century Fox has everyone sniffing for sequels. For those who have not yet heard the leaks for the fourth installment, this page will keep you up to speed.

WEB http://www.islandnet.com/~corona /films/details/alien4.html

Aliens: The Web Site The meatiest part of this Web site is the catalog of the aliens encountered so far, as well as a description of their reproductive cycles. Other parts of Aliens: The Web Site feels more like Aliens: The Vacant Room, largely because the trilogy serves as its only information source. The section devoted to "Company" technology, for instance, is restricted to androids, cryotubes, and atmospheric plants. Nonetheless, where there is no substance, there is at least style—the well-written text suitably draws you into the *Alien* universe and the design looks clean and professional. Perhaps when the potentially exciting page of 3-D VRML-rendered models fleshes out, the site may, as well.

WEB http://www.vis-con.com/aliens /welcome.html

Al's Alien Homepage Who would've ever thought to be considerate where Aliens are concerned? Unlike most others, this thoughtful Web site gave *Alien* and *Alien³* equal time with Cameron's standout *Aliens*. You can get collages of screen shots from all three movies, plus intermittent quotes. The casting page, while not a unique idea in itself, gives all the usual info and kindly includes the mugs of all the characters to jog our failing memories. There are also QuickTime movies of missing footage found on the laserdisc versions.

WEB http://ng.netgate.net/~alvaro/alien/alien.htm

Internet Movie Database: Aliens (1986)
Film reviews, quotes, images, and extensive credits for *Aliens* with an impressive but frighteningly thorough cross-reference links to each crew member's previous credits. To wit: *Aliens* stunt man Eddie Powell played a mummified guard in the 1985 Tom Cruise vehicle *Legend*.

WEB http://us.imdb.com/cache/title-exact/6247

Wierzbowski Hunters You'd remember Private Vasquez for her muscles and Private Hudson for his mouth. Private Wierzbowski, on the other hand, would barely register on your motion tracker. The online Wierzbowski Hunters, who are even lesser known than their object of adoration, dedicate themselves to this most obscure Colonial Marine by paying homage to his existence. With painstaking effort via screen shots and hastily drawn arrows usually found in NFL replays, this congregation points out the grunt in various split-second scenes you would otherwise miss. Sure enough, Wierzbowski lurks about like a key grip who accidentally wound up in the shot. This Web site is ideal for *Aliens* fans who have squeezed every tentacle of enjoyment from the film and crave more.

WEB http://www.cis.upenn.edu/~bhou/Wierzhunt

▶ **DIVERSIONS**

Alien Pictures More than 60 .JPGs are available for downloading at this index.

WEB http://ftp.sunet.se/pub/pictures/tv.film/Alien

Alien Saga Scripts for the trilogy plus an *Alien vs. Predator* script by Peter Briggs that's currently collecting dust on some producer's shelf.

WEB http://www.alaska.net/~danielh/Scripts/saga.html

EAR-chives: Aliens Four, count 'em, four *Aliens* .WAV files. The page also links to sounds from other film and television series such as *Battlestar Galactica*, no less.

WEB http://www.geocities.com/Hollywood/1158/aliens.html

Galerie von Giger With more than 100 graphics, this cybergallery might actually live up to its name. You can find original *Alien* art and more of H.R. Giger's biomechanical-styled artwork here.

WEB http://www.ucs.usl.edu/~bpd5896/gigernew.html

Japa Sound Booth: movies/aliens This page of the Japa Sound Booth offers some more *Aliens* .WAV files.

WEB http://www.iig.com.au/~cns01019/movies/aliens/aliens.htm

The MJH Doom Page: Themes You've watched *Aliens* until your eyes bled, and there's no more space left on your wall for posters. Are you tired of this passive appreciation of the *Alien* trilogy? Well, lock and load with id software's legendary *Doom* series (I and II). *Alien*-themed levels have been created for closet Colonial Marines, and can be downloaded from the FTP links at this site. Caution: the face-huggers scurry like Manhattan businessmen during rush hour. This page also offers other thematic *Doom* rooms, including one for gamers who like to shoot big purple dinosaurs.

WEB http://www.sonic.net/~mortlgrn/themes.html

Monte's Aliens Page "Well that's great. That's just f--king great, man. Now what the f--k are we supposed to do?!? We're in some pretty sh-t, now, man!" You can catch all of Private Hudson's colorful phrases, as well as those of his doomed cohorts, in this voluminous selection of *Aliens* sounds.

WEB http://xis.com/~dainjeur/aliens.html

JAMES CAMERON

DIRECTOR OF THE *TERMINATOR* MOVIES, *ALIENS*, and *The Abyss*; writer and producer of *Strange Days*; director of photography for *Escape from New York*; art director for *Battle Beyond the Stars*; and design consultant to *Android*, James Cameron is quite the sci-fi cinema renaissance man. But whatever his title, Cameron's passion is visual.

His first directing job was inauspicious—a brief stint at the helm of *Piranha II: The Spawning*—but when he directed his screenplay of *The Terminator* in 1984 he struck celluloid gold, providing a shot in the arm for the struggling sci-fi genre, and, for better or worse, making a superstar out of an Austrian bodybuilder. At the **Sci-Fi Channel's** tribute site, Cameron describes what it was about the filmmaking process that first intrigued him: "I think for me initially obviously (it was) because I, I couldn't create things. I had to just sort of go out and photograph what was there. It was the process of, of isolating that one image that made sense, that was interesting from the, you know, the entire landscape around me... and capturing that. Which is why I love the term 'image capture' now, which we use... in the digital realm." A singular lack of hubris from one who gave his initials to his greatest hero, John Connor, initials he shares with another humble groundbreaker.

From the low-budget films he worked on for Roger Corman to his multi-million-dollar spectaculars, Cameron has always aimed straight for the optic nerve. JC movies frequently feature scenes filmed in deep blues. He likes to make effective cuts. Another device of his is to bring the camera in close during fight scenes, achieving a claustrophobic effect. And Cameron often includes sequences in which a video monitor becomes the perspective of the camera. **The Biography of James Cameron** includes a complete list of his trademark tricks.

But one of the driving forces behind Cameron's movies is his use of digital effects. Those with an keen interest in the sci-fi sleight of hand will want to visit **Digital Domain**, the home page for the visual effects company co-founded by Cameron and effects expert Stan Winston.

If it's the scripts you're interested in, all the big ones are kept at **James Cameron**. And **The James Cameron Fan Page** is a virtual clearinghouse of Cameron filmdom, with information on every movie he's been involved in, unique analyses of what makes a JC film, articles and interviews, and an unsubstantiated rumors page. The Net treats Cameron well. Blockbusters with cyberthemes always get royal treatment online. And virtual flops with the same sensibilities (*Strange Days*, the movie he co-wrote with his ex-wife and the film's director, Kathryn Bigelow, for instance), have Web pages that far outshine the celluloid versions.

Launch pad

James Cameron Fan Page
http://www.soton.ac.uk/~pdc194/cameron

Biography of James Cameron
http://us.imdb.com/M/person-exact?name=James+Cameron

Digital Domain
http://www.d2.com

Sci-Fi Channel: James Cameron
http://www.scifi.com/cameron

James Cameron
http://www.cs.fsu.edu/projects/sp95ug/group2.5/cameron.html

BABYLON 5

RENEWED FOR A FOURTH SEASON, the five-year arc of *Babylon 5* now comes closer to completion. Unlike most sci-fi series, this space station-based saga is a true serial of interconnected episodes under an overarching story line. Although each episode is enjoyable as a separate story, the show's real strength comes from the cumulative power of the ongoing narrative. Now that the space epic has survived *Trek* comparisons, characters with bad hair, and a lead change, *Babylon 5*'s limited shelf life has given its growing legion of fans something else to fight for—they want to see the 1,000-year story run to the end of its fifth season. And the Internet has become one of their favorite battlegrounds. Executive Producer J. Michael Straczynski (aka JMS) is aware of *B5*'s Net presence, and often emerges online to answer fan questions and even ask for advice. If you find him, you too can post him some questions.

▶ CLICK PICK

Voltayre's Encyclopedia Xenobiologica
Having difficulty grasping the principles of twenty-third century jumpgate technology? You're not the only one. The Encyclopedia Xenobiologica, written in Babylonian character, provides answers to *Babylon 5*-related questions. From Narn's clans to the Minbari caste system, it features an extensive archive of the life-forms populating Babylon 5, their cultures, and their technology. There's even a little stellar cartography to keep those roving gangs of astronomy enthusiasts at bay, as well as one of the largest *B5* links pages available on the W3. This Web site is artfully esoteric—a gem.
WEB http://www.actlab.utexas.edu/~voltayre/enc-xeno.html

▶ MOTHERSHIPS

B5 on AOL Warner Brothers sponsors an official *Babylon 5* area on AOL with a custom graphical interface. Most of the real-time chats with the cast and crew of *Babylon 5* take place here in the Eclipse Cafe, and the message boards are very active. JMS posts here regularly, answering questions and offering information about the story and its production. New pictures, sounds, and movies are usually posted every Monday when new episodes are aired.
AMERICA ONLINE *keyword* Babylon5

Babylon 5 Residing in the virtual projects and cyberco-ops of Pathfinder, *Babylon 5*'s official Web site offers character dossiers, a picture library, video and audio clips, and the requisite links to other *B5* and science/sci-fi Web sites. If you've had enough of solitude in cyberspace, you may find other life forms via links to the BBS and live chat. This site has less to offer than you might expect from something authoritatively described as an "official" Web site. For instance, the Episode Guide is a work in progress. Even so, the site is adequate—and pretty.
WEB http://www.babylon5.com

Babylon 5 This site also claims authenticity as the official *Babylon 5* Web site. Indeed, this one resides on its own URL and is nearly identical to the one located on Pathfinder, but includes a few additional features: this week's episode synopsis, an updated Episode Guide of the first three seasons, more images, and more A/V freebies.
WEB http://www.babylon5.com/cmp/base.htm

The Babylon 5 Spoiler Junkies Page
This would-be oracle of the space opera floats tantalizing tidbits of future possibilities for *Babylon 5*. Truth, rumor, or mere speculation? You decide. Its contents were pulled from the FTP site where full spoilers from the first three seasons may be found.
WEB http://pages.prodigy.com/wildfoto/spoilers.html
URL ftp://ftp.cdsnet.net/pub/coolstuff/StarTrek/B5/press

The Lurker's Guide to Babylon 5 Any Web site with a section called "Universe" better be large. The awe-inspiring Lurker's Guide, maintained with the cooperation of series creator J. Michael Straczynski (no, the Unabomer is Kaczynski), is so extensive that even series addicts may find themselves reeling from the wealth of information. Visitors are privy to exhaustive episode summaries and analyses; descriptions of the *Babylon 5* universe, cast, and characters; and near-infinite Straczynski Q&As. Also available are links to other Web sites, as well as newsgroups, mailing lists, broadcast information, merchandising, and a convention calendar.
WEB http://www.hyperion.com/lurk/lurker.html

Robert Lentz's Babylon 5 Resources For those of you who think *Babylon 5* might be the prequel to *Leonard Pt. 6*, check out the General Information link here for a crash course on the show's premise. The rest are links that include the Lurker's Guide, the electronic press kit, and the *Babylon 5* Encyclopedia.
WEB http://www.astro.nwu.edu/lentz/sci-fi/b5/home-b5.html

The Unofficial Babylon 5 Encyclopedia An alphabetical list of the main terms, characters, planets, and plot elements from the series, with hypertext links across the encyclopedia. Jump from "Eyes," the slang term used by Earth Alliance for Internal Affairs, to the Earth Alliance itself, the political organization based on Earth that includes the Mars Colony, Jovian moons, and Orion. Plus, you'll find an episode list of *Babylon 5* episodes, with links to synopses and cast information.
WEB http://interweb.uml.edu/B5/Enc
URL ftp://ftp.hyperion.com/pub/TV/Babylon-5/b5encyc.txt

► SATELLITES

B5_jms_answers.txt Contains a selection of actual quotes by Straczynski from Usenet, GEnie, and CIS groups. The latest version of this document can be found via anonymous FTP.
URL ftp://ftp.hyperion.com/pub/Babylon-5/b5_jms_answers.txt

Babylon 5-News-Schedule This frequently-updated schedule and list of *Babylon 5* news items will keep you on top of the latest goings-on concerning the show. You'll also find good filler material for those awkward moments of silence on newsgroups.
WEB http://www.hyperion.com/b5/babylon-5-news-schedule

Babylon-5-FAQ Gives the who, what, when, where, and why of *Babylon 5*. Also helpful for newbies interested in getting *B5*-wise before venturing into Usenet.
WEB http://www.hyperion.com/b5/babylon-5-faq

History.Babylonia Are there parallels between the plot of the series and the history of Ancient Babylonia? Maybe. And maybe not. See for yourself.
WEB http://www.hyperion.com/b5/History.Babylonia

Quote Generator A script that generates a random quote from the series.
WEB http://www.cs.dartmouth.edu/~crow/b5quotes.html

Snooze's B5 Cards Say goodbye to bent corners and faded colors. With Warner Bros.'s Official *Babylon 5* Digital Trading Cards, the traditional worries of card collectors have gone the way of smallpox. Now circulating on the Internet, WB has even greenlighted their copying for noncommercial use.
WEB http://www.nu.edu/snooze/b5/cards.html

The Zocalo Tired of cutting through *Babylon 5* newsgroup debris? The Zocalo promises to serve up a fan digest without the hassles. The home page for this weekly Internet newsletter for *Babylon 5* is taking subscription requests. It also links back issues for your perusal from the Web site.
WEB http://www.indirect.com/www/katana

▶ B5 TECH

The Anatomy of a Star Fury An in-depth speculation on the design of the *Star Fury*, a space craft often seen on the series. While probably most intriguing for young fans, the original computer-generated polygonal art and tech specs (based equally on the series, the comic, and the imagination) may engage other curious fans.
WEB http://www.csun.edu/~hbcsc091/star.html

b5.techupdate.txt From mass drivers to hyperspace travel, the latest updated version of the *Babylon 5* Technical Manual will satiate tech-minded appetites. It's unadorned, unofficial, and dense as two-week-old cookies, but more accessible than its name would imply. Best suited for technophiles curious about Babylonian mechanics.
WEB http://www.dungeon.com/~sati/b5.techupdate.txt

Nemesis—Babylon 5 Vehicles It's a bird, it's a plane. Oh no! It's a Narn Heavy Cruiser! More than 50 *Babylon 5* space craft are catalogued, each with brief descriptions and corresponding screen-captures from the show.
WEB http://ccwf.cc.utexas.edu/~ifgw727/b5_sh28.htm

▶ CHAT

alt.tv.babylon-5 Less active and more off-topic than its sibling, alt.tv.babylon-5 has lots of speculation about what's going to happen next in the series. This group is crowded with cerebral sci-fi fans bent on discussing the show's philosophical foundations and the characters' psychological motivation. One lengthy thread concerned the supposed bisexuality of a certain character. Frustrated, one fan posted, "What, you haven't shut up yet? Take it elsewhere, please. This is not alt.tv.babble.religiously."
USENET alt.tv.babylon-5

Babylon 5 This AOL site makes poking and prodding easy. Its well-rounded services include easy access to Eclipse Cafe, the *B5* chat service.
AMERICA ONLINE *keyword* scifi→Science Fiction Fandom Board→Babylon 5

rec.arts.sf.tv.babylon5 Sans Straczynski, you'll still find the usual character/plot chatter, as well as serious talk about the spirituality of the Minbari and the merits of the Earth Alliance's weapon systems.
USENET rec.arts.sf.tv.babylon5

rec.arts.sf.tv.babylon5.info Features compilations of Straczynski's postings and general information. Not as much much traffic and less random than the others.
USENET rec.arts.sf.tv.babylon5.info

rec.arts.sf.tv.babylon5.moderated *Babylon 5* has had a strong Internet presence since the series began, and discussion on this group has been lively. The creation of this new newsgroup had convinced a hesitant JMS to return to Usenet and his online fans. Under a moderated environment, JMS is safe from the legal beartraps that drove him off initially, and will address rumors and answer questions, albeit not always to everyone's satisfaction. And when he is off running his show, you can rub elbows with other like-minded individuals. Good for meandering conversations.
USENET rec.arts.sf.tv.babylon5.moderated

▶ EPISODE GUIDES

B5 CW Watch and Review Episode Index In addition to episode reviews (primarily from the third season), this Web site also gauges the rising and falling karma of the characters in each episode with its Conventional Wisdom Watch. "Alien homeworld invaded, apparitions from a dead world, and rangers to the rescue. Just another day on *Babylon 5*." For this, Captain John Sheridan gets a thumbs up in "The Long Twilight Struggle." Be warned—this is not for the ill-informed.
WEB http://www.slip.net/~terman/b5/b5.html

Your Fresh Air Waiter's Babylon 5 Pages Most notable for its episode guide and an impressive bibliography of *Babylon 5*-related articles. Aside from an oblique explanation of the site name, this succinct *Babylon 5* Web site does not have a tendency to babble on. Its surgical strike of general information works mostly to your advantage.
WEB http://www.worldramp.net/~dstrauss /b5.html

FAN FICTION

Archive of Creative Works: Babylon 5 A thorough and carefully organized compendium of fan-generated *Babylon 5* apocrypha, this archive includes guesses about what's to come, an interesting collection of verses, and *B5* humor. The latter category includes a meditation on why Susan hates PSI-Corp so much and, in a piece entitled "The Parody from Hell!!!" speculation on what Captain Picard would think of *B5*.
WEB http://www.dal.net/b5

Babylon 5's Alternate Universe Functioning as a sci-fi writer's workshop in which seminars are held via mailing list, Alternate Universe draws people interested in writing about, reading about, and discussing not only the actual *Babylon 5* TV show, but also their own intergalactic variations on the show's themes. Politeness is a requirement for continued participation—no flaming allowed in this universe, comrades.
WEB http://www.anxst.com/b5

Babylon 5's Alternate Universe Creative FAQ Subscriptions to the *Babylon 5*'s Alternate Universe Creative Mailing List can be placed on this FAQ page.
WEB http://www.anxst.com/b5/cre _faq.shtml

HUMOR

Babylon 5 Humor Links to the numerous in-jokes and had-to-be-theres that you expect when you think "sci-fi." The initiated can yuck it up to a fake ad for the Turbo-Ginsu Shadowcruiser, for exam-

ple. Don't be afraid to embark, but be prepared.
WEB http://www.ugcs.caltech.edu /~nathan/humor/babylon5.html

Everything I Ever Needed to Know I Learned From Babylon 5 A humorous list of lessons learned from the show, including "Don't argue with superior beings," "Know what you want in case somebody asks," and "Don't shoot people: The paperwork is a pain in the butt."
WEB http://www.cas.usf.edu/dforms /b5everything.html

DIVERSIONS

Agamemnon's Babylon 5 Sound Site In space, no one can hear you scream— unless you live on a five-mile long space station. Passionate monologues, galactic revelations, and just plain rants have been archived as .WAV files. The selection is considerable.
WEB http://rampages.onramp.net/%7E brummett/b5.htm
URL ftp://archive.egr.msu.edu/pub /babylon5

The ISN Vids This page of the Interstellar News Network (masquerading in character as the *Babylon 5* news service) houses a decent collection of video clips from the first three seasons.
WEB http://www.mit.edu:8001/afs/athena .mit.edu/user/m/e/megoo/www/vids.html

MARKETPLACE

The Babylon 5 Shop A Citizen G'Kar latex might help sneak you into a convention, if not the station itself. This and other series paraphernalia are available for purchase at the Shop.
WEB http://www.halcyon.com/uncomyn /b5.html

Babylon 5 Trading Post Originally intended for trading card commerce (the tangible kind), it has recently been opened to all collectibles pertaining to the series.
WEB http://acm.org/~morrisj/b5cards .html

TIM BURTON

URTON'S BRAND OF SCIENCE FICTION DOESN'T look, sound, or feel like anyone else's. Each of his films gives the impression of having been made in a parallel universe. Think of the suburban castle in *Edward Scissorhands* or the dark children's puppet show *The Nightmare Before Christmas*. His is a world of spikes, shadows, and hauntings. And it is very personal.

The director's ultimate SF tribute came with the 1994 release of *Ed Wood*, a pseudo-biopic of the filmmaker widely revilved for making *Plan 9 from Outer Space*. Burton changed our minds about Wood. Through Johnny Depp, he made him a man of passion, someone who loved film so much, he would be part of it at any cost—even if it meant bringing the art form to it's lowest level.

On the Net, which is often referred to as a virtual haven for social outcasts, Burton does rather well. Web sites devoted to his films and career show many sides of the filmmaker. One fan even used Burton for a marketing project, "The Auteur as Marketing Concept." That essay led to the creation of **Dan's Definitive Tim Burton Page**, which gives an in-depth look into Burton, his films, and the hype that surrounds him. "Tim Burton is a director who has earned the status of auteur, although he is not viewed in the same category as, say, Martin Scorsese or Woody Allen. Like James Cameron, he works within genres that are not readily accepted as 'art,' but by now Burton's 'oeuvre' is so uniquely recognizable, thematically as well visually, that critics are hard put to classify his work."

The Usenet group **alt.movies.tim-burton** is clearly the hot spot on the Net for Burton chat. What is the "genius" director working on? When will new products be released? Does Burton need to worry that his current film, *Mars Attacks*, is going to be lumped in with the million other alien encounter movies being released in 1996? No, say his fans, not when he's the kind of guy who'll cast the Joker as President.

Launch pad

alt.movies.tim-burton

The Tim Burton Page
http://www.magi.com/~gray/burton.html

Tim Burton FAQ
http://www.isc.rit.edu/~elnppr/faqs/tbfaq.html

Dan's Definitive Tim Burton Page
http://www.euronet.nl/users/mcbeijer/title.html

Welcome to Halloweentown!
http://www.lm.com/~biomech/mainindex.html

BLADE RUNNER

YOU REMEMBER THE RAIN. EVEN if you haven't seen *Blade Runner* in 10 years, and have only the vaguest memory of Harrison Ford as an android hunter facing a crisis of conscience, you still remember the rain. Most writers complain bitterly about the adaption of their work to the screen, but Philip K. Dick loved Ridley Scott's adaption of his novel *Do Androids Dream of Electric Sheep?*. "It is not a hygienically pristine space colony which looks like a model seen at the Smithsonian Institute," said Dick. "No, this is a world where people live… there is kind of a gritty rain falling and it is smoggy." With *Blade Runner*, the future changed forever. Since *Blade Runner*, it hasn't changed at all.

▶ CLICK PICK

The Official Blade Runner Online Magazine A visit to the official magazine makes the complex world of Los Angeles in the year 2019 much more comprehensible. A large collection of movie stills, background information on the film's set design, and links to many other *Blade Runner* resources are available here, as well as Philip K. Dick's last interview. "The purpose of this story as I saw it was that in his job of hunting and killing these replicants, Deckard becomes progressively dehumanized," Dick said. "At the same time, the replicants are being perceived as becoming more human. Finally, Deckard must question what he is doing, and really what is the essential difference between him and them? And, to take it one step further, who is he if there is no real difference?"
WEB http://madison.tdsnet.com /bladerunner

▶ MOTHERSHIPS

2019: Off-World Blade Runner Page Although it's apparently one of the most respected *Blade Runner* Web sites out there, 2019: Off-World isn't much more than a list of links divided into two cate-

gories—stuff within Off-World itself and resources at other places on the Net. It bills itself as a growing archive of material related to the film, and features essays of varying themes, including "Is *Blade Runner* a Misogynist Text?"
WEB http://kzsu.stanford.edu/uwi/br /off-world.html

Blade Runner The site isn't much to look at—opening with a weak facsimile of the movie's logo—but the material is of primo quality. Check out the Memorable Quotes section, which offers dialog or voice-overs as text, but links to images and sound files. "The light that burns twice as bright burns half as long," indeed.
WEB http://www.uq.oz.au/~csmchapm /bladerunner

Blade Runner The Internet Movie Database entry for this "chilling, bold, mesmerizing, futuristic detective thriller" includes movie goofs, links to reviews and images, and data on almost the entire crew. (Ladies' costumer Winnie Brown, for example, also worked on such films as *Days of Thunder* and *Body Heat*.)
WEB http://us.imdb.com/M/title-exact?+ Blade+Runner+(1982)

Blade Runner An insightful, analytic essay on the film by critic William M. Kolb. The writer makes a powerful observation about the level of strength in the viewer's involvement. "You hold your breath high above the street and hang with Deckard by wet, slipping fingers until your strength is drained," he writes. A thorough review and history piece, it's illustrated with high quality artwork and images from the film.
WEB http://www.voyagerco.com/CC /sfh/bladerunner.html • http://www .voyagerco.com/CC/featured/f.blade runner.html

Blade Runner FAQ What is *Blade Runner*? What book is it based on? Is the

soundtrack available? What are replicants? This list of frequent-asked questions (and frequently-given answers) is
overseen by Australian Murray Chap-
man, and seeks both to satisfy the entry-
level curiosities of *Blade Runner* neo-
phytes and to answer questions of
diehard fans.
WEB http://www.vir.com/VideoFilm/Blade
/brfaq_0.html#TOC

Blade Runner: The Script Intercom:
"Next subject, Kowalski, Leon, engineer,
waste disposal, file section, new employees, six days." That's how it all begins.
Here's the whole script, ready to read or
download. The alaska.net version is
more detailed, with full description of the
action as it happens in the film. Just
make sure you've got enough memory in
your browser.
WEB http://www2.gol.com/users/steve
/bladerun.htm • http://alaska.net
/~danielh/scripts/bladerun.html

Blade Runner Trivia A fanatic's dream!
Religious and philosophical parallels, as
well as the symbolism of the eye are discussed here. Most exciting, however, is
the "Did You Notice?" section, which
includes everything from Pris' incept
date (Valentine's Day) to the sheet music
on Deckard's piano (Vivaldi's *Concerto
in D major for Guitar, Strings and Con-
tinuo*).
WEB http://dingo.cc.uq.oz.au/~csmchapm
/bladerunner/trivia.html

Blob Blade Runner Somewhat basic, yet
still cool, Blob Blade Runner contains,
among other oddities, a digitized image
of the Italian version of *Do Androids
Dream of Electric Sheep?*, the short
story by Philip K. Dick that became
Blade Runner. There's also a massive
audio file (570k), a movie posters
archive, and many links.
WEB http://anubis.science.unitn.it
/services/sf/BR/index.html

The Philip Kindred Dick WWW FAQ
What on (or off) earth is "wooji"? Find
out at this comprehensive look at the life
and work of Philip K. Dick, the brains

behind *Do Androids Dream of Electric
Sheep?* Included in the FAQ is information regarding his short stories, non-fiction works, and contemporaries. The
PKD Terms/Lingo section features words
such as "conapt" (condominium and
apartment), "flapple" (flying car), and
"wooji" (high-test airplane fuel used for
sniffing). There's even a list of references to PKD in popular music, from
artists such as Sonic Youth, Elvis Costel-
lo, and Ministry.
WEB http://www.users.interport.net
/~regulus/pkd/pkd-int.html

The World of Syd Mead If you wanted to
know more about *Blade Runner's* "visual
futurist" Syd Mead, here's your chance.
The mechanical designer's biography
and a summary of works are featured
here, as well as information on video
games he's helped design.
WEB http://www.undergrad.math
.uwaterloo.ca/~mcng/sydintro.html

▶ **CHAT**

alt.fan.blade-runner Is Deckard a replicant? What's going on with a sequel?
And whatever happened to Rutger
Hauer? The topics on this newsgroup
are constantly changing and full of raging debates. Ask a *Blade Runner*-related
question, and you're sure to get an
answer.
USENET alt.fan.blade-runner

**The Blade Runner File: Compilation of
Discussion About Blade Runner** Learn
about rare *Blade Runner* books, and read
intelligent debates about a universal
question: "Which is better, the book or
the movie?" with this set of late 1980s
newsgroup posts. Contributors discuss
the Ridley Scott film, including a review
of the movie's visual sense, listings of
alternate endings, and missing footage.
WEB http://kzsu.stanford.edu/uwi/br
/br-file.html

▶ **DIVERSIONS**

Blade Runner Listen up. Vangelis' score
caused quite a controversy, and the

story is retold here with surprising clarity. Both versions of *Blade Runner's* music—in their entirety—are available, as well as two video clips in .AVI format.
WEB http://BAU2.uiBk.ac.at/perki/films /brunner/br.html

Blade Runner Bootleg CD The 1993 bootleg disc of the *Blade Runner* score was a delight to fans who could hunt a copy down. This site features an in-depth look into the unofficial release, and includes .GIF files of the compact discs and booklets, selected .MPEG audio tracks, and instructions on how to FTP the entire recording in digital quality.
WEB http://brian.homecom.com/~brian /bootmusic.html

Blade Runner Sounds "Wake up, time to die" and other popular clips from the film are available on the Net. One collection was graciously uploaded by America Online users.
WEB http://SunSITE.sut.ac.jp/multimed /sounds/movies/bladerunner
AMERICA ONLINE *keyword* mms→Sound Sample Libraries→movie samples

Blade Runner Soundtrack An excerpt from an FAQ, this document explains why the haunting Vangelis theme music was unavailable for so long, and addresses the better-late-than-never release of the official soundtrack.
WEB http://www.vir.com/VideoFilm /Blade/brfaq_3.html

Blade Runner Stuff "Harrison Ford as a high-tech detective of the future," "Rutger Hauer goes to Hollywood as a futuristic warrior," "New actress Sean Young gets her first major movie role opposite Harrison Ford in futuristic love story," and "Ridley Scott, director of *Alien*, creates another masterwork, *Blade Runner*," are just a few of the parts of the investors' press kit for the film. This kit and more, including reviews from its debut, are indexed in this comprehensive list of *Blade Runner* books, periodicals, and collectibles.
WEB http://kzsu.stanford.edu/uwi/br /br-stuff.html

Filmzone: Blade Runner "Muzak this is not," writes the staff of *Film Zone* in reference to Evangelos "Vangelis" Papathanassoiu's chilling musical creation for Ridley Scott's futuristic adventure flick. Information on his techniques and instruments are provided.
WEB http://www.filmzone.com/Sound Tracks/BladeRunner.html

SEQUEL

Blade Runner 2: The Edge of Human Next stop, 2021. "Rick Deckard was last seen fleeing L.A. with the replicant named Rachel. Like all androids, she has a built-in lifespan of only four years—and Deckard is desperate to save her. He has also just discovered that Pris, whom he executed in *Blade Runner* was not a replicant after all—but was actually human…" Look inside K.W. Jeter's sequel novel for more possibilities.
WEB http://www.bdd.com/newrl /bddnewrl.cgi/10-01-95/blad2

FAN FICTION

Blade Runner: Poems/Songs Maya, a British professional who admittedly spends too much time MUSHing, is an avid poetry writer. Her works inspired by *Blade Runner*, including "Zhora: A Definition" and "Coda: The Lift Door Closes," explore the richness of emotion that the film evokes in some viewers.
WEB http://www.tcp.co.uk/~maya/br.html

RIDLEY SCOTT

I F YOU WANT TO DOWNLOAD A GENUINE RIDLEY Scott movie on the Web, take a look at **Why Macintosh?—Advertisements**. In fact, Apple's board of directors tried to kill the ad—they thought it would be too controversial—but were forced to run Ridley's mini-epic in the end because they couldn't sell a 60-second, $500,000 Super Bowl spot without taking a major loss. In fact, Apple got really lucky. Athough it was shown only once, "1984" turned out to be one of the most popular and influential commercials of the decade. Like the rest of ad-turned-feature director Scott's work, it combined the visual elements of film noir with gaudiness and planted the seeds of cyberpunk. In Scott's movies, the monster is not to blame. We are.

As with many important directors Ridley Scott's presence on the Internet is unfortunately out of proportion to his offline reputation. *Alien* and *Blade Runner* pages number in the hundreds, but there is a dearth of information on the creative force behind these projects. Apart from **Dark Horse**, a fan page dedicated exclusively to Scott, news about the director is scarce—but thankfully, always fascinating. The **Ridley Scott** page, part of a larger *Blade Runner* hubsite, is revealing about the stories behind both *Alien* and *Blade Runner*; the **Celebrity Lounge Interview** that took place in January of 1996 is an insightful retrospective of his entire eclectic career; and **The Future of our Discontents** is a riveting article dissecting Ridley's future vision in *Blade Runner*. "Ridley Scott may not be aware of it himself, but he understands our nightmares. If you doubt it, make your way over Mulholland Drive, or coast down from Griffith Observatory some night when you have nothing better to do. Try to see la Ciudad de Nuestra Señora, Reina de los Angeles without the gas flares, without the winking lights of ground effects spinners above the Harbor Freeway. If you find, as I do, that the present is overlaid by something darker, something more ominous, then you may agree with me that Scott has, in Wim Wenders's wonderful phrase, 'colonized our subconscious.' When all is said and done, this is what has always been expected of artists. We should be grateful that someone still possesses the ancient power."

Launch pad

Why Macintosh?—Advertisements
http://www2.apple.com/whymac/ads.html

The Future of Our Discontents
http://motley-focus.com/~timber/future.html

Dark Horse—Ridley Scott
http://www.mhs.schnet.edu.au/endzone/ridley.htm

Ridley Scott
http://madison.tdsnet.com/bladerunner/ridley.html

Celebrity Lounge—Interview with Ridley Scott Jan. 1, 1996
http://showbiz.starwave.com/chat/celeblounge/ridley.html

A CLOCKWORK ORANGE

ANTHONY BURGESS DID NOT CONsider his futuristic 1962 novel a masterpiece. He was even less enthusiastic about the truncated American version which removed the final chapter and about-turned its very meaning. But tapping into fear of violence, fear of the collapse of the social order, fear of foreigners (the incorporation of Russian into street slang), and good old fear of the future, Burgess created both an accurate portrayal of the mood of his times and a fairly dead-on portrait of our own. In 1971, Stanley Kubrick took the American edition and created a screen version so inflammatory it was held responsible for most of the ills that afflicted Britain during the early '70s. Appalled, Kubrick had the film withdrawn. It is still illegal to screen the movie in Great Britain. Fabulous publicity, of course, and totally deserved. With such a heritage, it comes as no surprise to find that both the book and the film are Net favorites.

▶ CLICK PICK

A Clockwork Orange Unfortunately, there isn't one all-around perfect *Clockwork Orange* site to start with, but this is the closest. It's well-designed and very orange, and it comes from the creator of the simply wonderful online Kubrick Multimedia Film Guide. There are classic sound bites from the like "No time for the ol' in-out love—I've just come to read the meter." A large number of images—everything from an interior shot of the Korova Milkbar to Alex beating on his droogs and tossing them into the water, and of course close-ups on their infamous black and white uniforms—are also available at this site. Since there are links to several other informative *Clockwork Orange* sites on the Web (some of which are profiled in this chapter), this is probably the best launch pad for an online, ultra-violent adventure.
WEB http://.lehigh.edu/~pjl2/films /clockwork.html

▶ THE MOVIE

A Clockwork Orange—Forbidden Fruit?
"It is more than 20 years since the controversial film *A Clockwork Orange* was withdrawn from distribution in the U.K. by Time-Warner at the request of its director, Stanley Kubrick. The film remains available elsewhere and is described on the box of the U.S. video as 'a dark, ironic tale of an ultra violent future.' The brutal face stares at us, filling the screen. Slowly the camera pulls back, Alex sits on the couch of the Korova Milkbar surrounded by white sculptures of naked, submissive women. He sips milk laced with drugs to 'sharpen you up and make you ready for a bit of the old ultra-violence.'" This is just the beginning of this short, but informative legal essay about the continuing repercussions of Stanley Kubrick's request to stop distributing the film in the United Kingdom. Taken from *In-House Lawyer* magazine.
WEB http://www.gold.net/users/af82 /clockw.htm

Clockwork Orange, A (1971) Once you scroll past the far-too-large image of the movie's poster, you can read several fans' versions of the plot summary. After that, there's a cast and crew list with links that look promising, but don't seem to lead anywhere.
WEB http://www.tu-harburg.de/rzt/rzt /it/film3.html

Clockwork Orange and the Aestheticization of Violence Was Mr. U-V a pomo? Alexander Cohen, a professor at the University of California at Berkeley discussed his theories about violence and movies as part of his "Cinema and Beyond" seminar. This site features the lecture notes he wrote for this particular session, including: "In moving beyond mere violence, toward ultra-violence, Alex has incorporated and mastered the post-industrial age. As a post-modern pastiche of learnedness and stupidity, he is the inside-out reflection of the enlightenment subject." The author warns that this work is not quite finished, but the essay in its online form comes across as complete.

WEB http://remarque.berkeley.edu:8001 /~xcohen/C_B/Cinema_and_Beyond _Lectures.html

▶ THE BOOK

A Clockwork Orange Not many people know that there is an unpublished version of Anthony Burgess's book, inspired by the Teddyboys, Mods, and Rockers of the time, that was written between 1960 and 1961. Learn about the origins of the book, and read about issues such as societal controls and censorship. This is a set of discussions compiled as a general guide to themes, such as Free Will vs. Predestation, expressed in various versions of *A Clockwork Orange*.
WEB http://lucy.cs.waikato.ac.nz /~butting/kubrick/censorship.html

A Clockwork Orange: Chapter 21 New York, 1962. Eric Swenson, vice-president of Norton Books, insists that the book be published without its rather disturbing final chapter. Anthony Burgess, author of said book, later develops near-homicidal feelings toward said VP. Today the complete text of *A Clockwork Orange* is now available at your local bookstore, but you can save youself a trip and read online the final twist of Alex's adventures.
WEB http://sefl.satelnet.org/~ccappuc /aco.21.html

▶ DIVERSIONS

A Clockwork Orange A haunting design—an embossed Alex peering at you from every inch of the screen—separates this site from the rest. It has a number of sound clips, images, and sadly for the *Clockwork* fan, not much more. Keep an eye out for the animated .GIFs of Alex. Little Alex beating an old man with pipe? Little Alex licking the shoe? Little Alex and two little mall tarts

lullilubbing to Beethoven? The mind reels.
WEB http://www.fsu.umd.edu/students /dhiggins/clw.htm

A Clockwork Orange Sounds "Welly-welly-welly-welly-welly-welly-well!" It may only resemble English, but it's typical droog speak. Powerful lines from the film are archived here, including the rather sweet, "This is the real weepy and like, tragic part of the story beginning, o my brothers and only friends."
WEB http://www.geocities.com/Hollywood /1158/clockorg.html • http://.link-net .com/sounds/movies/A_Clockwork _Orange

STANLEY KUBRICK

THERE'S THE FISH-EYE CINEMATOGRAPHY THAT somehow makes everything both coldly vast and unbearably claustrophobic at the same time, but otherwise, Stanley Kubrick's movies can seem as eclectic as they are magnificently original—*The Killing*, *A Clockwork Orange*, *Spartacus*, *Lolita*, *Barry Lyndon*, *Dr. Strangelove*, *The Shining*, *2001*, *Full Metal Jacket*... The topic, the narrative, the characters, and the cinematic language is completely different in every film. One strand that does stand out is the director's interest in the possibilities of science. *Dr. Strangelove* was the penultimate atomic-age film, dealing not only with fear of technology, but with neurotic fear of flesh, and a deserved fear of humankind as well. *2001* remains the defining science fiction film of our time. It changed our idea of what a sci-fi movie is about; its influence is immeasurable. *The Shining*, characteristic of Stephen King's work, is almost too terrifying to qualify as sci-fi, but as it's entire premise is based on ESP, hauntings, and paranormal experience, it can hardly escape it. And *Clockwork Orange*—besides being a tragic lesson on how influential cinema can be, and just how seriously filmmakers can take their responsibility (it was the first film in history to be banned by its director)— is a horrific masterpiece that has provided visual and visceral inspiration to artists and subcultures ever since.

Each of these films has attained enormous cult status, and that, of course, translates into an enormous Web following. All sorts of people on the Net adore Kubrick's masterpieces: film students, avid movie-goers, collectors. The **alt.movies.kubrick Research Library**, is not simply a newsgroup archive, it's the crux of all Stanley Kubrick information available online. There are essays, articles, commentaries, interviews, scripts, and press materials, and if the site lacks graphics, it packs data. As does the **Kubrick Multimedia Film Guide**, which catalogs all of Kubrick's works with images, audio clips, and links to other home pages on the Web. If you don't have time to sort through pages and pages of resources, the place to visit is the **Stanley Kubrick Quick Information Page**. Short on splash, but visibly useful, the site features a biography, filmography, information on Kubrick's upcoming projects, quotes, and trivia. If you want a mix of eye-candy and academia, check out Voyager's **Kubrick** page—it offers in-depth articles and stunning image galleries from a half-dozen films, as well as vid clips for the ones available on laser disc.

Alt.movies.kubrick is where the real fanatics converge. Here, intelligent discussion ranges from comparisons of *Dr. Strangelove* and *Independence Day* (how many of you thought Randy Quaid was gonna open that hatch manually and ride that bomb like a bull?), the remake of *The Shining*, flaws in Kubrick's works (how many of you fell asleep watching *2001* for the third or fourth time? It's OK to admit it!), the upcoming *Eyes Wide Shut* with Tom and Nicole ("My God, it's full of stars!"), and, of course, the status of the newly discarded, but not nearly forgotten, *AI*.

Launch pad

alt.movies.kubrick

The alt.movies.kubrick Research Library
http://www.netins.net/showcase/sahaja

Kubrick on the Web
http://www.krusch.com/kubrick/kubrick.html

Kubrick Multimedia Film Guide
http://www.lehigh.edu/~pjl2/kubrick.html

Stanley Kubrick Quick Information Page
http://pages.prodigy.com/Other/kubrick

Voyager: The Films of Stanley Kubrick
http://www.voyagerco.com/kubrick/kubrick.html

DOCTOR WHO

CAMEO APPEARANCES ON *THE Simpsons* notwithstanding, the time-travelling, sonic-screwdriver wielding, identity-regenerating Time Lord commonly known as The Doctor has never been huge on this side of the Atlantic. In Britain where the series ran for 20 years, he's as familiar as the Royal Family, but even the most recent, heavily-Americanized Fox TV movie starring Paul McGann failed to have much of an impact in the U.S. In cyberspace, however, Whovians are legion. If you want to know how a species that couldn't climb stairs almost conquered the universe, why Brits go "Huh, they're just Cybermen," when they see the Borg, and how second rate repertory actresses were transformed into sex symbols with a potency the ballast of *Baywatch* can only dream of aspiring to, the Net will explain.

▶ CLICK PICKS

Doctor Who Home Page Any site claiming to cover the longest running sci-fi series in history (26 seasons, to be exact) would have to be huge. One of the more interesting sections in this hub is devoted to lost and found episodes. This area has a dual function, serving as both a warehouse of information on episode retrieval and rescue, and as a headquarters for the recovery effort. Another fun feature is the *Doctor Who* necrology, listing all the alums who have passed on to that big junkyard in the sky. Rounding out the site are the *Doctor Who* FAQ, a program guide, other roles of series actors, and a current list of stations carrying the show.
WEB http://nitro9.earth.uni.edu/doctor /homepage.html

▶ MOTHERSHIPS

Behind the Sofa Bristol University's Doctor Who Society site contains a unique archive of scripts from some of the missing episodes. Nine episodes from five seasons, destroyed in the '70s when the BBC needed storage space and old TV episodes were of little value, are stored here.
WEB http://www.bris.ac.uk/Depts /Union/BTS

Doctor and Company When this site's maintainer isn't "observing Mars and awaiting the impending threat to the timeline," he's studying the *Doctor Who* series. Here he presents a sort of mini-encyclopedia of entries, including the eight doctors, the sonic screwdriver, the key to time, and, of course, celery.
WEB http://jumper.mcc.ac.uk/~chriss /doctor.html

Doctor Who A hot spot for all things *Doctor Who*, whether you're into *Who* books, the TV series, or *Who*-related conventions. Topics include *Doctor Who* autographs, *Who* books for sale, and *Who* reruns. A number of experts can be found here, and they've got strong opinions on everything from the BBC and its handling of the show to the various doctors and their companions. Yet this is a newbie-friendly spot. If you're seeing *Who* for the first time, you'll get advice on what to look for in the episodes. The libraries have some good stuff, including "Missing Without Trace," an in-depth report on the missing *Who* episodes, a file with the latest news on a U.S. revival of *Doctor Who*, a PC-based "photonovel" for the missing episode "The Tenth Planet 4," and a color .GIF of Tom Baker.
COMPUSERVE *go* sfmedia→Libraries *or* Messages →doctor who

Doctor Who Why was the first episode of "Invasion of the Dinosaurs" accidentally destroyed? Which Doctor tended to reverse the polarity a little too often? Which single *Doctor Who* episode attracted the largest audience when first broadcast on the BBC? Test your knowledge of the longest running series in sci-fi history. You may want to test your

quote recall while you're at it. This site also includes an original text adventure based on the "Pyramids of Mars."
WEB http://superior.carleton.ca/~pwigfull /drwho.html

Doctor Who Online A gathering place for AOLers with a hankering for *Who* stuff. In addition to the usual chat rooms and message boards, this forum houses a downloadable Multimedia *Doctor Who* Factfile, a TARDIS databank of graphics files, an online newsletter called *The Matrix Mutterings* and information on fan clubs in the states.
AMERICA ONLINE *keyword* doctor who

Doctor Who: Tardis Will Not Die Assertively distinguishing itself from all other *Doctor Who* sites with a mission statement claiming that the site is based on the exchange of ideas, analysis, and fan-created fiction based on the show, this is a page that's obviously in its infancy. (Web designer, take note: lose the distracting wallpaper.) It has the potential, however, to be a good resource for fans who have outgrown the less-sophisticated thrills of down-loading endless images of the various doctors and their companions.
WEB http://www.users.fast.net/~galifrey /index2.html

Dr. Who—A Brief History of Time (Travel) A good mix of old and new *Who*, this site includes a complete guide to the original show, from season one ("Into the Unknown") to season twenty-six ("Journey's End"). The Eighth Doctor page is dedicated to exploring the attrib-utes of the latest regeneration of the good doctor: "Like the Fifth Doctor, he exhibits an endearing vulnerability, but this is contrasted by a sense of urgency and decisiveness. He also demonstrates a flippant sense of humor reminiscent of, though not identical to, the Second and Fourth Doctors." And for all the lat-est in the effort to resuscitate the all-but-dead Doctor, click to the Doctor Who News Page. What were the U.S. and U.K. ratings like for the *Doctor Who* TV movie? If *Doctor Who* returns, will

Segal, McGann, Roberts, and Ashbrook all be back? Questions about what is and isn't in the works on the screen and the page are answered.
WEB http://www.physics.mun.ca/~sps /drwho.html

Dr. Who Space A dedicated list of links divided into image/sound/ftp sites, WWW sites, newsgroups, mailing lists, book and video sites, and episode guides. If you're looking for images and sounds from the Fox movie, travel to the TARDIS room.
WEB http://www.drwho.org

Into the Vortex A guide to *Doctor Who* sites in the dimension of cyberspace, this page helps out with an oft updated top five link list covering the categories of *Who* sites from around the world, including fan pages, ezines, merchan-dise, newsgroups, and mailing lists.
WEB http://orca.ucd.ie/Doctor_Who

Out of Time A nicely laid-out, slick (but not too slick) guide to *Doctor Who*—the man, the show, the myth. Fans should enjoy traveling though this time stream, written in the spirit of the Doctor's time travels. Join *Who* fans in buzzing about the character's latest incarnation and debating the merits of the eight different actors who tackled the role. For those who simply must have physical evidence of their devotion, a souvenir section is provided.
WEB http://aimservices.com/drwho

Outpost Gallifrey The home page of Los Angeles *Doctor Who* Fandom. Included are an armchair guide to *Doctor Who*, information on local Gallifrey conven-tions, details on the *Doctor Who* books, and a wee bit of *Who* humor. There's also a tribute to the late John Pertwee (the third doctor and the one who intro-duced K9, the Whomobile, and Betsy as additional *Who* kit).
WEB http://ourworld.compuserve.com /homepages/jshaunlyon

The TARDIS Databanks The Tardis Data-banks began several years ago as a

BBS. Now they've returned with a new face (much like the mutable Doctor himself) in the form of a Web site. Worth Godwin has created what amounts to a guide to the world of *Who*, with descriptions and pictures of monsters and villains, the eight doctors, and the TARDIS.
WEB http://WWW.CompCenter.Com /~Worth/DrWho

Temporal Nexus A jumping-off point for junkyard dogs looking for news, official sites, books, merchandise, fanzines, FAQs, and discussion.
WEB http://www.mcs.dundee.ac.uk :8080/~ggreig/doctor.html

The Ultimate Doctor Who Web Page Select your entry point by clicking on the icon for your preferred incarnation of the Doctor, and go from there on your tour of this functional, friendly exploration of the space-time nexus. Find info about the various Whos, explore the Ace to Zoe list of companions, or do a little time-traveling of your own by reliving the show through the episode guide. Then join in as fandom buzzes about Fox's latest incarnation of the generation-jumping doctor.
WEB http://members.aol.com/kryten /ultimatewho/who.html

The Velvet Web A vast list of *Doctor Who* links (local and otherwise) organized neatly into reviews, fiction, quizzes, feature, pictures, editorials, and convention news. This is a nice place to visit if you're the type who wants to forego the pretty pictures in order to get the maximum amount of information per second. In the words of Who himself, "I've never seen anything like it..."
WEB http://www.ex.ac.uk/cgi-bin/counter ?user=sjjenkin&file=dw.html

The Web Page of Rasilion A collection of *Doctor Who* resources that include Web pages, ftp sites, newsgroups, and mailing lists. The Cloister Room is a rotating archive of .WAV files.
WEB http://netspace.net.au/~knine /drwho.html

WhoLINK Not only does this WWW *Who* guide include links to sites devoted to clubs, conventions, fan fiction, games, merchandise, multimedia, personal home pages, and publications, it also includes near-constant updates on the latest changes to the pages included here.
WEB http://www.sky.net/~dgleason /wholink.html

The Winds of Time Each Doctor gets his own page on Randy's site, with info on each incarnation's personality and adventures.
WEB http://webpages.marshall.edu /~lilly1/who.html

▶ FANZINES

Bog Off "A journal of post-Davison Who, postmodern feminism, and post-fandom fandom." Otherwise known as the *Doctor Who* fanzine from hell, this site archives the print zine for mature (age-wise, at least) audiences only.
WEB http://www.ocs.mq.edu.au/~korman /Bog_Off/bog_off.html

Curse—A Doctor Who Fanzine Touting itself as the fan's fanzine, Curse will publish most anything they receive from *Who* watchers—fiction, essays, puzzles, quizzes, and reviews.
WEB http://hell.btc.uwe.ac.uk/Curse

Don't Shoot the Pianist What began as a small print 'zine for the MWUSDWFC (MidWestern United States *Doctor Who* Fan Club) in 1992 has been reincarnated as an online 'zine for Whoville, featuring Querty's Quintessential Quote, the most Recent DW news, a short story selection, and reviews.
WEB http://vms.www.uwplatt.edu /~williamsc

▶ CHARACTERS

The Ben Jackson Page Ben Jackson could have easily been voted the companion least likely to get his own Web page, yet here he is. Why devote an entire site to Jackson? "My answer is that of all the companions to travel on the TARDIS, he is the one I most identify with. He is a regular bloke who finds himself traveling with the Doctor," writes the creator of this virtual shrine to a fictional character. If you relate to Ben, if you want to learn cockney in ten easy lessons, or download digitized images from long vanished *Doctor Who* videos, this is a must-see.

WEB http://members.aol.com/benjacksn /cockney/index.html

The Companions' Home Page Living in the shadows of the spotlighted Doctor wasn't easy, but on this page the companions finally get their day in the sun. The Companions' Home Page honors all the sidekicks who appeared throughout the seasons, highlights a companion of the month, and updates us on what the performers are up to now.

WEB http://www.primenet.com/~dosboy /esin/index.html

Davros's Home Page Dedicated to Davros, "creator of the Daleks, destroyer of worlds, friend to all children, ruler of Skaro, world's greatest grandfather, and so much more." Though he's not the most attractive guy, there are plenty of interesting photos of the Imperial Dalek here, as well as audio files and spoilers for the newest *Doctor Who* movie.

WEB http://watt.seas.virginia.edu/~bjo5f /davros/main.htm

Doctor Who: The Other Adventures What would *Doctor Who* be like without the Doctor? You can find out at this site. This page is dedicated to fiction told in the *Doctor Who* universe that highlights the other characters—the former companions, other renegade Time Lords, space pirates, Daleks, and Dalek-hunters.

WEB http://www.zoom.com/personal /nocturne/dwoa.html

▶ NEW WHO

Broadsword A small 'zine dedicated to discussion of the new *Who* in dead-tree format. A spoiler-laden guide to the New and Missing Adventures.

WEB http://modjadji.anu.edu.au/steve /broadsword

Kate's Eight Doctor Page Links to everything you need to know about the *Doctor Who* movie, the eighth doctor, and Paul McGann, best known for playing the "I" in *Withnail and I* opposite Richard E.Grant.

WEB http://www.ocs.mq.edu.au/~korman /drwhoetc/8th.html

New Dr. Who Movie FAQ Yes, it's true. The Doctor was in again, but only for a two-hour, made-for-TV movie co-produced by the BBC and Universal Television, starring Paul McGann as the eighth doctor. This FAQ covers the details of the latest regeneration of *Doctor Who*. If you missed the airing in the U.S. in May, you can drool over images here or find a way to get a copy of the video (available only in England).

WEB http://nitro9.earth.uni.edu/doctor /FAQ/newwho.html

Save Dr. Who If you're looking for a good sci-fi cause to champion (and frankly, who isn't?), why not join the purple ribbon campaign for the saving of *Doctor Who*. While the battle for the reinstatement of this series lacks the urgency of those concerned with more recently canceled shows, the forces behind the movement are no less zealous. There are constant updates available, as well as information on how to get involved in the strategy to resurrect the Doctor—there are even purple ribbons for downloading.

WEB http://www.cris.com/~Perval/who .htm

▶ SHOW BY SHOW

Dr. Who Chronology A chronology of *Who* episodes available by season or by time period (prehistory to the far future), logged by one dedicated doctorphile. He'd only made it through season six when we visited, but he promises to keep plugging along.

WEB http://www.islandnet.com/~dascott /intro.htm

Dr. Who Guide This site sets the stage for *Doctor Who* newbies, with information on the background and setting of the series and details on the major cast members throughout the years. Episode details are also indexed by season.
WEB http://www.ee.surrey.ac.uk/Contrib /SciFi/DrWho

The Dynamic Doctor Who Ratings Page Russell and David attempt to chart the likes and dislikes of *Doctor Who* fans everywhere with this oft updated site. At press time, "Genesis of the Daleks" was still the favorite episode, with the last movie falling to 28th place.
WEB http://www.airtime.co.uk/users /type40/dynamic.html

The Two in the TARDIS An archive of everything written by the Internet *Doctor Who* review team of Joe Ogulin and Louis Singh.
WEB http://www.cnj.digex.net/~jogulin /DoctorWho.html

Ultimate Episode Guide A text-only guide to the long run of *Doctor Who*, including a brief story synopsis and list of cast members and guest stars for each episode.
WEB http://www.york.ac.uk/~socs107 /guides/doctorwho/doctorwho_guide .html

> **CHAT**

alt.drwho.creative The long-running BBC sci-fi series may be defunct, but not on the Net. *Doctor Who* fans have kept the show alive with original scripts posted to this newsgroup of fervent followers. In these episodes, as on the series, you'll find the Doctor and the TARDIS and lots of strange happenings. Some of the writers invite their comrades in Whodom to add to ongoing story lines, so you can even get a piece of the action yourself. The group focuses on the creative side of *Doctor Who*, but occasionally you'll hear rumors of revivals and questions about what stations carry the show.
USENET alt.drwho.creative

Dr. Who List Dedicated to what the Time Lords and Ladies on this list call the greatest sci-fi show of all time (shhh... don't tell the Trekkies), discussion here covers not only the 158 episodes of the original show and the latest movie, but also the appearance of *Doctor Who* in books, magazines, conventions, videos, and collectibles (Dalek salt and pepper shakers, anyone?).
EMAIL listproc@lists.pipex.com ✍ *Type in message body:* subscribe drwho-l <your full name>

rec.arts.drwho More *Who* than you'll know how to handle, from the subsequent careers of the show's stars, to the latest in *Who* publications and paraphernalia. You'll hear endless debate about rumors of a new series. Will it be yet another regeneration? Or will it be a remake of the original series? Lots of guesses, but no real answers. Some fans, apparently, have limits to their devotion. One Who-man decided to sell his *Doctor Who* scarf, which was made by a friend's mother; he was looking for the best offer ("looks like the real thing—incredibly cool for the Tom Baker look-alike"). It helps if you know the lingo for this group. These people like acronyms, especially NA (new adventures, referring to *Doctor Who* novelizations) and MA ("missing adventures," another series of books).
USENET rec.arts.drwho

> **DIVERSIONS**

Doctor Who Picture Page A new *Doctor Who* picture featured each month.
WEB http://www.canberra.edu.au/~scott /DrWho/whopic.html

Doctor Who: The Key To Time Key to time model created by Austrian sci-fi fan Brigette Jellinek.
WEB http://www.cosy.sbg.ac.at/~bjelli /Who/index.html

Doctor Who .WAV Archive Vast and amusing, this collection of *Doctor Who* sound files is worth visiting for the text alone, which includes such deathless

prose as "This is excellent news. The Earth will be destroyed," and "Dear, oh dear. Doctor, will you never learn?" Good to hear the cybermen, but not enough Daleks.
WEB http://www.iceworld.org/~mrogers/index.html

Doug's Doctor Who Sounds Page What? Sounds. Where? Here. *Who*? Yes. Sound files from each of the eight doctors.
WEB http://www.tufts.edu/~dvermes/dr_who

Gallifrey ASCII and ANSI art inspired by *Doctor Who*. Perfect for .SIGS when you're posting to Who newsgroups and mailing lists.
WEB http://incolor.inetnebr.com/rassilon/gallifry.shtml

The Umpteenth Doctor Who .GIF/ .JPEG/Etc. Page Truth in advertising perhaps, but then again, you never can have enough pics of this sci-fi classic, can you?. In addition to the aforementioned .GIFs and .JPEGs, this site includes a page of morphs of the good doctors—Sylvester to McGann and Colin Baker to Sylvester.
WEB http://www.cofc.edu/~chandlec/doctor.html

▶ QUOTES

The Doctor Who Interesting Quote List "I know that travel through the fourth dimension is a scientific miracle I didn't expect to find solved in a junkyard." "Doctor, we've got our clothes on!" Quotes from the show, divided into a number of topics, including art, destruction, Daleks, the future, history, judgment, politics, resistance, strategy, and, of course, time.
WEB http://www.mit.edu:8001/people/dasmith/Who/Quotes.html

▶ GAMES

Doctor Who Sim Everything you need to know to join the weekly *Doctor Who* Sim on AOL. Don't forget to bring your scarf.
AMERICA ONLINE *keyword* sims→Doctor Who Sim

The Who-RPG Home Page A clearing-house of information on the Who-RPG, including rule books, character record sheets, and timelines.
WEB http://www.tardis.ed.ac.uk/~type40/who-rpg.html

TERRY GILLIAM

WHEN THE PYTHONS MADE THEIR FIRST foray into film with *The Holy Grail*, runs the old story, they had to find something for the cartoonist to do. They didn't need all that much animation, Gilliam couldn't act, so they made him the director.

Six years later, Gilliam wrote and directed *Time Bandits* and effectively created his own genre, one in which flesh-and-blood people who look and speak like cartoons are entangled in plots and situations so complex and so removed from day-to-day reality it's hard to imagine someone actually thought them up. *Brazil* was the apotheosis. As the man says in the opening quote at the **Terry Gilliam Homepage**: "I've seen the world through cartoonist's eyes and what seems to be normal appear to other people to be distorted."

In the virtual worlds of the Internet, where reality is as subjective as Gilliam believes it to be offline, this is the kind of comment that can get you vilified. But he gets surprisingly few devotional pages. For perhaps the most breathless and hilariously biased account of Gilliam's life, battles with the Hollywood establishment and a handful of links, visit **The Terry Gilliam Worship Page**. For a more restrained history of the man who took on Universal Studios' Sid Sheinberg and won, who made Bruce Willis look like an actor, who afforded Brad Pitt a Golden Globe Award, and yet who still scares the pants off Tinseltown's tyrants, take a look at **Terry Gilliam Tribute**.

Launch pad

The Terry Gilliam Worship Page
http://www.ionsys.com/~gurney/terry.html

The Terry Gilliam Home Page
http://gladstone.uoregon.edu/~chrismcg/gilliam.html

UCI Retrospective
http://www.dublin.iol.ie/dff/Terry_Gilliam_at_UCI.html

Terry Gilliam Tribute
http://www.filmscouts.com/rooms95/ter-gil/index.html

GODZILLA

KING KONG'S GOT NOTHING ON Godzilla. The city-stomping, car-crushing, people-pulverizing giant lizard has loomed larger than ape-life in movie monsterdom for more than 40 years, starring in 22 feature films. Along the way, the killer *kaiju* has amassed quite a following of fans who feel that the King of the Monsters is more than just fodder for *MST3K*. If you're one of them, you'll want to visit the God of all 'Zilla sites, Mark's Godzilla Page. If you speak the radioactive reptile's native language, you'll be able to enjoy Toho Movie News. Current rumor has it that *Godzilla vs. the Destroyer* may be the last Godzilla movie. But true large lizard lovers have heard that one before, and fan pages and chat should be buzzing with a real intensity once *Independence Day* director Roland Emmerich gets his mega-budget rendering of Godzilla underway.

▶ CLICK PICKS

Mark's Godzilla Page With a record of 24-5-7, Godzilla would probably be a pretty good bet in Vegas. Win-loss stats compiled from bouts between Godzilla and every monster from King Ghidorah to Space Godzilla are just one of the things that make Mark's page the Mothra of all Godzilla sites. Mark has also culled the most recent Godzilla news (the Lifetime Achievement Award given to the mega-monster at the MTV Movie Awards), the entire movie list, QuickTime flicks, and the first official FAQ for inclusion at his shrine to the Tokyo construction industry's best friend.
WEB http://www.ama.caltech.edu/users/mrm/godzilla.html

▶ MOTHERSHIPS

Barry's Temple of Godzilla Get in touch with your inner lizard. Barry's site, dedicated to the biggest, baddest beast of them all, features a three-room photo gallery (including one devoted to Ghido-

rah, the three-headed monster), more than 20 movie reviews and posters from the original and new series, a weekly comic strip (*Godzilla vs. The Disco Monster*), film-related news, and Barry's original collection of 'Zilla trading cards, scanned in for your viewing pleasure.
WEB http://www2.pcix.com/~barryg/godmain.htm

Bob's Godzilla Shrine Welcome to Bob's Godzilla Shrine—emphasis on God. From the mouth of Bob: "Like many of you out there in WWW land, I too grew up under the watchful eyes of G. In fact, I think that children have an instinctive appreciation and knowledge of G. Many of us are turned from His path as adulthood looms over us, but down deep, even the most remote tribesmen (and tribeswomen, too) sense the reality of G. So to those of you who do not believe, I can only say you have been warned. The wrath of G is terrible indeed, as the residents of Tokyo can confirm." Bob provides fellow believers with access to his growing list of reviews of films featuring the roving reptile along with his gigantic Godzilla collection. Perhaps some of that atomic fallout drifted over Bob's way a few years back…
WEB http://ccwf.cc.utexas.edu/~rloftin/gpage.html

Chris Nickerson's Mini-Godzilla Page It's actually a mini Godzilla page, not a mini-Godzilla page, so don't come here expecting a bonsai version of the original. Instead, you'll find the latest on the American movie in the works, a filmography, a short history, and a collection of stills from the films.
WEB http://www.geocities.com/Hollywood/2063

Connie's Museum of Radioactive Reptiles The true beauty of the beast is that, unlike most major motion-picture stars, no bad movie will ever snuff out his career. If anything, they only seem to make him stronger. This museum is

dedicated to those very monster movies, from *Godzilla: King of the Monsters*, which started it all back in '54 to the "death" of the lizard king in *Godzilla vs. Destroyer*. Connie not only rates and dates the films, she provides the plots (yes, there are plots) for each. Since many of the more recent films were never released in America, you can find out how to get your hands on them (we're talking expensive laserdiscs here). You'll also find funny—although fictitious—biological and cytological secrets of the *kaiju*, formerly held captive by the Japanese government, and an exclusive interview with the monstrous movie star.
WEB http://www.sky.net/~conniegn/musem.html

Euro-Goji Home Page The only place to go online to find out about screenings, TV broadcasts, shows, and conventions which could be of interest to those seeking the big G in Europe. And apparently, there aren't many, as there weren't any events when we visited. There's also a list of Godzilla films and the Godzilla collectibles corner.
WEB http://www.xs4all.nl/~saiko/index.html

G-Force America Homepage The Japanese call him Gojira, from the words gorilla and *kujira*, Japanese for whale. We know him better as Godzilla. The G-Force America Homepage pleases patrons East and West by providing reviews of Godzilla's films, old and new, and an announcement of Kris Pasaba's Godzilla Awards for best actor—Masahiro Takashima for his portrayal of robotics expert and pilot Kazuma Aoki in *Godzilla vs. Mecha Godzilla*—and best actress—Megumi Odaka for her portrayal as psychic Miki Saegusa in all of the new generation movies since *Godzilla vs. Biollante*.
WEB http://www.public.asu.edu/~firecat

Gamera vs. Godzilla Though to many, Gamera is just a cheap rip-off of Godzilla, Eric contends that Gamera is, in fact, vastly superior. Many Godzilla fans may scream blasphemy, but to each movie-

monster maven his own. Eric makes the case for Gamera at his page.
WEB http://web.univnorthco.edu/pub/~swedberg/GamvGoz.html

Godzilla Sony's site devoted to the real monster's monster, the one who never lost his championship title, not to Megalon or Mothra or even Bambi. Download sounds and images or buy a T-shirt.
WEB http://www.ssi.sony.com/SSI/Film/Godzilla/godzilla.html

Godzilla Cast List Starring everyone from Raymond Burr—as Steve Martin, the not-so-wild and decidedly uncrazy American reporter—to Akira Takarada—as the head of the Environmental Planning Board, a man whose job gets that much tougher after each Godzilla rampage.
URL gopher://wiretap.spies.com:70/00/Library/Media/Film/godzilla.cst

The Godzilla FAQ With all the hype surrounding the allegedly "last" Godzilla film and the anticipation surrounding a huge Godzilla movie to be made in the U.S., appearances of the *kaiju* on the Internet are on the increase. Fan Chia-Ning Kao decided it was high time for an official FAQ to be created. You'll find explanations of the origins of the monster and inconsistencies in the film series, along with titillating trivia, rumors (viscous and otherwise), and links to all the online resources devoted to the radioactive reptile.
WEB http://www.ama.caltech.edu/users/mrm/godzilla/faq/FAQ.html

Godzilla Index An FTP site in Sweden full of 'Zilla pics.
WEB http://ftp.sunet.se/pub/pictures/tv.film/Godzilla

Godzilla vs. the Smog Monster Official, Unofficial Web Page!!! Official in the sense that it's the only one out there. Unofficial in the sense that it doesn't have the Toho OK. This site is devoted to one man's favorite Godzilla film, in which all the pollution on earth gathers up and creates a giant monster named Hedorah,

which gets bigger and bigger by sucking up fumes and eating mud. Hedorah learns how to fly and nearly kills all of Japan with his bodily functions. In the end, only one famous flamebreather is monster enough to put an end to the walking environmental hazard for good.
WEB http://www.sjonesc.bus.utexas.edu /peter/zilla.html

Godzilla's Playground So the German creator of Godzilla's Playground doesn't have the best command of the English language. Neither did the big guy. But, the movie monster does manage to come off remarkably well in the sound clips from *Godzilla vs. Gigan* in which he actually has three lines of English dialogue with Agilas. The site, available in Deutsche as well, rounds up all the rumors on the latest Toho film, *Godzilla vs. Destroyer.* Apparently the Big G dies and is succeeded by Godzilla Jr. Toho is touting the flick as the ultimate monster movie, the first time since 1954 they've tried to bring back horror elements to a Godzilla-film. Survey the screenshots and decide for yourself. In related news, German-born director Roland Emmerich (*Independence Day, Stargate*) was hired as director of the American version, replacing Jan DeBont (*Speed*) who wanted to spend around $120 million to make the film using CGI effects.
WEB http://members.aol.com/Gvsgigan /Gsplay.htm

Toho Movie News Unless your browser's preferences read Japanese, and you do, too, you won't get much out of this site from the Japanese studio, Toho, the folks behind *Godzilla* and other highly polished FX movies. If you can interpret this page, let us know what it's about.
WEB http://www.hankyu.co.jp/toho/movie /m-main.htm

> ▶ **MONSTER MERCHANDISE**

Creature Feature Productions Want an 8" monster to play with? Such merchandise as soundtrack CDs, posters, photos, action figures, and videos are available at this page.

WEB http://www.mindspring.com/~curtiss /cfp/cfp.html

Godzilla A teaser for Dark Horse's *Godzilla* comic book. Beginning with Issue #9, the adventures of the king of the monsters will be chronicled by Alex Cox, the director of cult films *Repo Man* and *Sid and Nancy.*
WEB http://www.dhorse.com/features /gdz/index.html

Godzilla Wars Trendmaster's current Godzilla toy line, featuring action figures, Power Up figures, motorized walking figures, and micro figures with battle sets.
WEB http://www.trendmaster.com/road /gwar/gwars.html

Revok Film Prodigies Revok is hawking several Toho films featuring everyone's favorite fire-breathing lizard, dubbed or with English subtitles.
WEB http://www.wp.com/69031/revok .html

Showcase Collectibles The models for sale, like Godzilla or Ghidorah in a Space Ball, can run upwards of $300. That's nothing compared to the original one-sheet for Ghidorah, the Three-Headed Monster, which costs $795. For something in a lower price range, stick to the toys and T-shirts.
WEB http://rampages.onramp.net /~showcase

STEVEN SPIELBERG

YOU DON'T HAVE TO BE A SCI-FI FAN TO WANT to be director-producer Steven Spielberg. After all, his touch, usually preceded by the adjective "magical," has thoroughly enchanted views of the silver screen and its smaller friend, the boob tube, for nearly 30 years, even though the man himself is only 50 years old. Spielberg's oeuvre to date includes sci-fi classics like *Close Encounters of the Third Kind*, *E.T., The Extra-Terrestrial*, and *Jurassic Park*. Most directors would sit back and rest on those laurels, but Spielberg today is as productive as ever, continually reinventing his own magic. What are the secrets of his directing success?

Start Young: Spielberg made his first feature film at the age of 16. That was in 1963. After hanging out on the Universal lot without permission for a couple of years (according to a May, 1981 **Interview with Steven Spielberg**) Steven's short film *Amblin'* got him a job there in 1969. By 1981, the **Steven Spielberg Biography** points out, he had already made *Jaws*, *Close Encounters of the Third Kind*, and *Raiders of the Lost Ark*. He was also working on a little movie about a turtle-like alien with a fondness for peanut butter candy and flying bicycles.

Surround Yourself With the Best: Collaboration is Spielberg's middle name, and his compatriots in cinema history are legendary. George Lucas ring a bell? Michael Crichton? And who could forget that ominous bass in *Jaws*? Certainly not John Williams, the composer for *Jaws* and just about all of Spielberg's other films. The beautiful **John Williams and Steven Spielberg Collaboration** site details this long and oh-so-fruitful pairing.

Capture the Imagination, But Monopolize the Mind: **The Unofficial Steven Spielberg Home Page**, with its reviews-in-brief and flashing slide show of the indelible images left on the brain for all time by Spielberg movies, is witness to Spielberg's commercial gift. Unlike those with a "The more big words and metal toys, the better" genius (like Cameron), Spielberg's ingenuity lies in his ability to remain faithful to scientific matters—aliens landing, dinosaurs living—while bringing them to the screen in a human, even childlike way. That's the "magic." Some would call it "cheese" or "syrup," but only the deranged say it doesn't work.

Repeat the Above: Which is more famous, the *Lost Ark* or the *Temple of Doom*? Semantics and hairsplitting aside, Spielberg reliably makes the best sequels around. The sci-fi community anxiously awaits the upcoming *The Lost World*, a sequel to *Jurassic Park* in which that Barbasol can is rumored to come back to life. See *NetSci-Fi*'s Michael Crichton page for a paperback preview of what's to come.

Respond to Your Fans: Like all entertainment moguls, Spielberg has a form-letter mill, churning out replies to gaga admirers. Sometimes, a certain writing style—say, one that threatens death—will get the attention of the man himself. **The Letters of Steven Spielberg and Antonin Artaud** chronicles just such a sinister correspondence.

Rediscover Yourself: Showing that he's just a baby boomer after all, Spielberg has spent the last couple of years in a heritage quest, first with *Schindler's List* and more recently by founding the **Survivors of the Shoah Visual History Foundation**, an organization devoted to preserving the memories of Holocaust victims on film. Has this self-discovery been, at its depth, a shallow one? **The Unconscious Hypocrisy of Schindler's List** would prefer that you think so.

Start a Small Business in Your Spare Time: It doesn't have to be a big business, but it must have a large vision. **Dreamworks SKG**, in which Spielberg is the "S" and Jeffrey Katzenberg and David Geffen are the "KG," promised upon its 1994 creation to be the most incredible collaboration in media history. So far, the successes have been mostly behind-the-scenes. Highly-profiled ventures such as TV's *High Incident*, have flopped. Could it be time for another pot-bellied, geranium-pushing alien to drop to Earth? Perhaps even a measly poltergeist? Mr. Spielberg, sci-fi fans are waiting.

Launch pad

alt.movies.spielberg

Dreamworks SKG
http://www.playavista.com/studio/studio.html

Interview with Steven Spielberg (May 1981)
http://www.smartlink.net/~deej7/bantha.htm

John Williams/Steven Spielberg Collaboration
http://helix.sestran.com/~accaaa/jw_spiel.html

The Letters of Steven Spielberg and Antonin Artaud
http://www.word.com/textword/gigo/mattei.html

Steven Spielberg Biography
http://www.cat.pdx.edu/~caseyh/horror/director/spielbio.html

Survivors of the Shoah Visual History Foundation
http://www.vhf.org

The Unconscious Hypocrisy of Schindler's List
http://www.spectacle.org/195/schindl.html

Unofficial Steven Spielberg Home Page
http://www.expresslane.ca/~doug/spielberg

HIGHLANDER

WHEN FRENCH, FORMER TARZAN Christopher Lambert hit the screen as Connor MacLeod in 1986, a cult was born. The compelling story of MacLeod, an Immortal with übermensch looks and morals, but mortal fears and anxieties, has inspired fans around the world. The success of the *Highlander* feature film prompted two sequels (both so disastrous that bitter fans are prone to denying their existence), a television show and an animated series. Apparently the series' running theme, "there can be only one," does not apply to the variety of *Highlander* spinoffs currently saturating the marketplace. Online, fans relive the adventures by following Connor and Duncan as they traverse dozens of decades and countries in their pursuit of The Prize.

▶ CLICK PICKS

Highlander—The Official Site This elaborate, media-rich hubsite covers the entire *Highlander* universe. One of the most impressive features is The Travels of Duncan MacLeod, which offers a shockwave map of Duncan's adventures through time. Click on your favorite period and place—1815 at the battle of Waterloo, 1750 in Eurasia, 1637 in Verona—and you'll find, not an episode synopsis, but an enlightening history lesson covering the culture and politics of the period and region. The section on the animated series includes excellent images, character profiles, and, of course, info on how to buy the action figures. If you're more interested in the film versions, you'll find tons of multimedia, production notes, and Lambert-trivia, including the reasons he was cast as Connor MacLeod in the first place—probably that convincing accent. **WEB** http://www.highlander-official.com

▶ MOTHERSHIPS

FAQ—Highlander From where in Scotland does Connor MacLeod hail? From the shores of Loch Shiel, in the village of Glenfinnan (which does exist). Many other *Highlander*-related facts are revealed here, including the inspiring fact that Glen Widen, the screenwriter of the original film, wrote the script for a course at UCLA. **WEB** http://mithral.iit.edu:8080/highlander/FAQ

Highla-L Why didn't Duncan have a scar when he got slashed? And what happens to bullets when an immortal gets shot? "I like to think that somehow their internal Quickening dissolves the bullet and heals the wound," Adam wrote. "After all, the Quickening is what makes them immies, right? "Right, I guess—although Ellis said it had already been determined that 'bullets are ejected from the wound when it heals' (that's in the TV series, at least)." Lots of Quickening theories and talk of the latest *Highlander* buzz, whether it's about a new film or the new season of the TV show. Much mulling over details, like why Kurgan's left (or was it right?) arm was always covered. **EMAIL** listserv@psuvm.psu.edu ✍ *Type in message body:* subscribe Highla-L <your full name>

Highlander "Be careful what you wish for… I'm not sure I'd want to be immortal, especially if my loved ones weren't also immortal. Then there's the boredom that sets in as you witness mortals make the same mistakes over and over again and never learning." A dedicated, philosophical group, with lots of talk on The Quickening and plot sequences. "The one thing I didn't understand about *HLII* was that they were sent here to Earth as punishment, and became immortal. Punish me! Please!" In the libraries, you'll find goodies like a performance history for Adrian Paul. **COMPUSERVE** *go* sfmedtwo→Libraries *or* Messages→Highlander

There Can Be Only One Some *Highlander* pages just pay tribute to the esteemed films and TV series. Others delve into the minds of the actors and directors, and investigate the most arcane details. Case in point—There Can Be Only One, which documents that there are three more head-butts in the Japanese version of *Highlander*, and that the American version lacks a scene in which: "Whacko Marine impaled on blade for extra time." How poetic. It's 1639, do you know where your favorite Immortal is? According to the site, Duncan was the bodyguard of an Italian Duke at that point in history. Accounting for the whereabouts and activities of Duncan since his days as a wee Scottish lad, this timeline, like the rest of this site, is extremely thorough.

WEB http://thunder.indstate.edu/h7 /cswank/.high.html

Unofficial Highlander Archive Site Very well organized and totally comprehensive, this site covers the TV series, the films, the animated series, the beer game, the conventions, the sword replicas, everything. One is pressed to imagine what Highlanderiana is lacking. There is even a hyperlink to a Glenmorangie site, if one want to study what the MacLeods drink.

WEB http://thunder.indstate.edu/h7 /cswank/.high.htmlmithral.iit.edu: 8080/highlander

▶ THE TV SERIES

alt.tv.highlander Just how does an Immortal live off the set? In the lap of mortal luxury, according to those who saw the *Lifestyles of the Rich and Famous* episode that featured Adrian Paul. Typically, topics on this newsgroup are not excessively celebrity-oriented. Besides comparing notes on the latest episode of *Highlander*, people also discuss science fiction and historical issues. An interesting post delved into the relationship between Duncan and Connor MacLeod—were they simply part of the same Scottish clan? Are they related? Get the word on the cyber-streets about the kinsman here.

USENET alt.tv.highlander

Duncan Flag Wavers International (DFW) The phrase "cult of personality" springs to mind after visiting this site. The central force behind this collective of (mostly) women is a devotion to Duncan MacLeod—his righteousness, his loyalty, his eclectic taste in clothing, and the way he swings that sword during the opening credits, his bare, lithe muscles gleaming with sweat... oh, sorry, got a little carried away there. Duncan's appeal is generously attributed to the actor who plays him on TV, and, thus, Adrian Paul—despite his unfortunate eyebrows—occupies more than one page at this site. Celebrating those who bring them joy, the DFWers proclaim their motto "Once you lose sight of fantasy, it's only a matter of time before reality will finish you off."

WEB http://www.mt.net/~satori/DFW /DFW.html

Glenfinnan Rysher Television has put together this official site with actor bios, synopses and credits for *Highlander* episodes, links to *Highlander* fan clubs, airing schedules, and lots and lots of pictures of Duncan MacLeod (played by Adrian Paul). Since it is an "official site," one should probably take the producers' claims that "Adrian has been described as a cross between Errol Flynn and Douglas Fairbanks but most of his fans liken him to a young Sean Connery," with a grain of salt. Particularly interesting is the tempered surprise with which the producers discuss how a single screenplay, unassumingly filmed, has grown into an legend replete with TV shows, cartoons, action figures, memorabilia, and a rabid band of fanatics who clamor for more.

WEB http://www.rysher.com/highlander

Highlander Chronicles The episode reviews at this site use a rating system of one to five. If the episode is really bad, the review is furnished with a Dog icon. The last episode of the '96 season reviewed merited the woofer—the complaints raised by devoted fans were: "The Ultimate DOG!! *Highlander* is by far the best show on television, however, 'Wrath of Kali' was the WORST episode,

I have ever seen!! This episode was uninteresting, slow, and who really cared about the story. Kamir was the worst evil immortal in the history of *Highlander*. I thank God for episodes like 'Something Wicked' and 'Brothers In Arms' to give us number one, an interesting story, and number two, a reason not to turn on the 10 o'clock news. Kamir gets the Ultimate Dog bastard rating." Okay, but how do you really feel?

WEB http://www.cris.com/~rhen/reviews .htm

Highlander Lust List Limited If you think Adrian Paul is easy on the eyes, you're not alone. In their letter to Adrian Paul, which accompanied the gift of a hand-embroidered shirt, the *Highlander* Lust List refers to itself as "The *Highlander* Lassies List"—afraid to admit the depth (or the nature) of their admiration, perhaps? Unfortunately for newbie groupies, this list has a ceiling of 35 members, and, as of now, it doesn't look as if any of them are about to resign their places. However, sections including the Men of *Highlander*, *Highlander* Art, Links, and a comprehensive timeline are open to all, and are all are worth perusing as long as you can handle the gender bias. These fans appreciate the male actors exclusively.

WEB http://www.unl.edu/uevents/mine /hll.html

FAQ: WEB http://www.unl.edu/uevents /mine/hill.html#faq

▶ THE MOVIES

Unofficial Highlander Movie Page This "unofficial" site is dedicated to Gregory Widen, the screenwriter who penned the original film. Its definitely not dedicated to those who wrote the sequels, since the author of this page finds them insulting and inane. But this site is no whine-session. Outfit your computer from cursor to screensaver with all things *Highlander*. Download movie stills from the European version of the film, or link to the *Highlander* newsgroup.

WEB http://www.cs.cofc.edu/~chandlec /www/high.html

▶ GAMES

The Gathering This is where role-playing Immortals meet, greet and try to sever each other's virtual heads from their virtual bodies. The second edition of this supplement explains the rules and ideas behind *Highlander* role-playing. Learn what constitutes Holy Ground, so that in the face of a stronger Immortal, you will know where your sanctuaries are. Thousands of role-players have downloaded these rules, so there are plenty of princes out there vying for the crown.

WEB http://www.itribe.net/highlander

Highlander: The Card Game When Connor MacLeod has a flashback, he can discard five cards and pick five new ones. Act out all of your fantasies of immortality through the card game—but be warned, the rules are pretty complicated, so keep the game's FAQ at hand.

WEB http://www.tcgames.com/highlander

FAQ: WEB http://www.tcgames.com /highlander/faq.rl.html

▶ MARKETPLACE

The Highlander Catalog Legions of mass-produced *Highlander* cups, videos, T-shirts, posters, and scripts are on sale here. Fine silver and metalwork items are also available, including 42-inch replicas of Duncan MacLeod's sword. But remember kids, cutting off a person's head is illegal in many states.

WEB http://www.highlander-official.com /highland/htms/hlcat.htm

▶ FAN FICTION

HLFIC-L (Highlander Fiction) Mailing List Archive An alternative to lounging on the couch, staring glassy-eyed at the boob tube, this archive holds dozens of fan-created fictional stories based on the *Highlander* universe. Now you can let your glazed eyes absorb pixels. Or, if you are really sick of screens, print out *Highlander*-based tales like "A Terrible Beauty" or "And the Memories Live Forever."

URL ftp://mithral.iit.edu/pub/highlander /HLFIC-L

EDWARD D. WOOD, JR.

TALENT—A LITTLE CAN GO A LONG WAY, BUT none can go even further. At least, that's how we understand Edward D. Wood, Jr. Nominated for no Oscars, never a winner at Cannes, and well-known for the dubious honorific "The Worst Director of All Time," Wood has supplied the punchline for countless cinema antifans ever since *The Streets of Laredo* missed theaters entirely in 1948. A part-time cross-dresser, Ed felt plenty comfortable in the angora sweaters he wore as a closet transvestite in 1953's *Glen or Glenda*. The film was meant to be a Jorgensenian exploitation flick, but Wood transformed it into a personal look at trust and mores—albeit an unbearably cheesy, truly tacky personal look. He was little known as a novelist (or as anything else in his lifetime,) but the Glenda side of Wood was also responsible for such literary classics as *Diary of a Transvestite Hooker*.

Mostly, though, Wood stuck to writing and directing films. His retinue of frighteningly poor actors is legendary, but as **Biographical Information for Edward D. Wood, Jr.** quips, "Given the dialogue they had to cope with, it's unlikely that better actors would have been an improvement." One more talented hanger-on was ex-Dracula Bela Lugosi, whose career had washed up on the beach by 1950, in part because of a morphine addiction. He appeared in many of Wood's films including 1955's *Bride of the Monster*, as a mad scientist determined to use atomic energy to create supermen. Although some would say that Lugosi's career ended long before he died, thanks to Wood and a few seconds of footage, he was able to star in a movie posthumously. *Plan 9 From Outer Space* was the flick, 1958 was the year, and the flying saucers looked a lot like paper plates on fire. (In fact, that's probably what they were.) It's Wood's most famous, and greatest film. Sadly, the title of *Plan 9* is generally followed by its unofficial subtitle, "The Worst Film Ever Made." As **Cult Film: Ed Wood** tactfully says, "Ed Wood's signature film is in a class by itself."

Wood and his film career dwindled into the subterrain of low-budget porn after that, and his subsequent films include gems like *Orgy of the Dead* (1965) and 1971's *Necromania*. In 1994, Wood's infamy expanded with the release of Tim Burton's brilliant, pseudo-biographical film **Ed Wood**. Heartthrob Johnny Depp took the title role. The Worst Director of All Time now merits fan pages like the **Ed Wood Home Page** and collector's memorabilia like the **Ed Wood, Jr. Trading Cards**. In the end, the movie that made Wood notorious again was probably seen by more people than all of his films combined. But on the Net, fans return to the source with almost Burton-free fan pages dedicated to a man who, at the very least, proved anyone with determination and a dream, regardless of skill or talent, can make a mark on Hollywood.

Launch pad

Cult Film: Ed Wood
http://sepnet.com/rcramer/exploit.htm#Ed Wood

Ed Wood Home Page
http://garnet.acns.fsu.edu/~lflynn/edwood.html

Ed Wood, Jr. Trading Cards
http://wfmu.org/Cate/Items/c11001X.html

Biographical Information for Edward D. Wood, Jr.
http://us.imdb.com/cache/person-biography/e15905

Ed Wood
http://www.euronet.nl/users/mcbeijer/edwood.html

MST3K

THE PLOT OF *MYSTERY SCIENCE Theater 3000* is totally inconsequential, but then so is Dabney Coleman, and he still manages to get a sitcom every two years, so here goes: A mad scientist (Dr. Forrester) and his goofy assistant (once Dr. Erhardt, then TV's Frank, now Mrs. Forrester) eject some poor slob (once Joel, now Mike) into space, where they force him to watch cheesy movies so they can monitor his brain. His only companions are robots that look like 8th grade science fair projects. Mike and the bots keep their sanity by shouting running commentary at the screen. Unabashedly intelligent, sometimes to the point of snobbery, *MST3K* has found a second home on the Net. MiSTies were misty-eyed (actually, more full of blood lust) when Comedy Central dumped *MST3K*, but an Internet campaign helped inspire the Sci-Fi Channel's decision to bring it back.

CLICK PICKS

Tom Servo Fan Club The Tom Servo Fan Club is terribly exclusive, you have to take a test to get in. What members actually do in this club is shrouded in mystery—the info page talks of revolution and *CHIPs*, and little else. For all the poor newbie shlubs not allowed past the red velvet rope, there is still lots to do at this site—image and video galleries, episode lists with quotes, an FAQ, a viewing schedule, and soon, an enormous, fresher-smelling episode guide. Patrick even tells you how to build your own Tom Servo, with just a gumball machine and a dream—plus about 36 other components, including toys that haven't been manufactured since 1932, and the two most feared words in the English language: "hot glue."
WEB http://sebago.internet.com/tsfc

MOTHERSHIPS

Big Ole Mystery Science Theater 3000 "Some eye creatures are born with scaly, protective covering. Others are born with hundreds of eyes protruding from fleshy knobs. Still others, like this whisper-thin fellow, are born with tight, acrylic, wool-blend turtle-neck sweaters from Chess King." As Tom Servo would say, "Hodge-ka, that's comedy!" Nearly every sketch, every song, every wacky, loony, loopy, cock-eyed moment of hilarity is painstakingly reproduced here for your reading pleasure. Oh, and there's an episode guide, too.
WEB http://www.slinknet.com/~wmorgan /mst3k.html

Croooow's MST3K Page Hey hep cats! This is where the cool kids are! It's got that kooky *MST3K* software, an episode-guide that's really "far out," the latest smooth pics and swingin' sounds, and even a crazy viewing schedule so you can invite the gang over for a wild time. Go to Croooow's Page today, and you'll be on your way to popularity in no time.
WEB http://www.together.net/~croooow /mst3k.html

Crow's Nest Crow's Nest is a magazine for people who want to show how witty and intelligent they are by foregoing zippy running commentary for analytical articles, interviews, faux-Beckett plays, and homages to John Carradine. They are witty and intelligent, but the writers are forgetting one thing—*MST3K* is palpable to the masses because its wit and intelligence comes in easy-to-swallow sound bytes. Most people let the Sappho and John Hinkley jokes go over their heads, and wait for the "Big Head" song. It just won't work, you nutty dreamers.
WEB http://www.evansville.net/~davej /crowsnest.html

Crow's NetCenter Big fuss. Little substance. Listen to the theme for Win95, join the mailing list, and download admittedly superrific *MST3K* wallpaper, then get out, quickly!
WEB http://www.servtech.com/public /crowt/mst3k/mst3k.html

Daktari Stool Named after the last invention of the only person ever to escape from the Satellite of Love, this site doesn't have much going for it at the moment, apart from a character guide nicked from the Amazing Colossal Episode Guide, some links, and a long, long, long list of Midwest References (Crow: "Chicago. Hog butcher to the world." Tom: "We're going to Iowa City to see the dead"). All the other enticing sweetmeats—classic quips, other MiSTers' home pages, and an episode guide—are under construction.
WEB http://TheRamp.net/daktari/mst3k.html

Doug's MST3K Page Only one merit badge-worthy feature here—an index of quotes from "Ahhh, 'two scoops of raisins' my ass…" to "By this time my son's lungs were aching for air." Beware: it's not exactly an A-Z index. Strangely, Doug has chosen to alphabetize by article—now what was that line where Crow goes, "A… (trained assassin, box of Good 'N' Plenties") or when Joel goes, "Are you… (going back to the factory?, pregnant with another alien bastard?)" You've got to love it when Tom Servo quips, "And…(it's off to the Laurie Anderson concert!, you think you could cut hair professionally?)"
WEB http://doorcounty.org/gibraltar/Doug/mst3k.html

The Gizmonic Institute It's just typical of the diabolic minds at work behind the Gizmonic Institute to purport to offer features like episode guides, list of lists, and vid clips when they're just linking to other people's pages. Bastards! The page also has some neat software, and a very large, blurry image of the Institute that may cause your blood vessels to rupture.
WEB http://www.geocities.com/Hollywood/3088

John's Mystery Science Theater 3000 Page Lots of MiSTy newsgroup posting, software, drinking games and other nifty gizmos to help wash down those chalky FAQs and episode guides. Substantive,

with absolutely no style. But hey, the same can be said for Cat Stevens, and everyone loves him. Well, except Salman Rushdie.
WEB http://wwwpersonal.engin.umich.edu/~jgotts/mst3k.html

Keri's Ultimate Mystery Science Theater 3000 Page This is an elaborate, deep-frame page about a subject ripe-to-bursting with comedic possibilities, and yet, it has to be one of the dullest places to go in this or any universe. Page after page of totally deadpan exposition of the players and plot (because you know character development and narrative cohesion is what makes MST3K quality television). This site may actually be too dull to mock. If our gang tried to MiST it, the best they could come up with would be "I'd rather be smelting."
WEB http://web.nmsu.edu/~kstockma/mst.html

Matt's Mystery Science Theater 3000 Page "Suggested Names for USA-Network original movies: Jeff Conaway and Shari Belafonte-Harper play a deadly game of cat-and-mouse in *Murder Most Moist*; Judy Landers is on the trail of a devious killer in *Peekaboo Lace, P.I.*; Jeff Conaway is a vigilante who stalks by night in *Dark Underpants*; Lindsay Wagner is a sexy speech therapist in *Tongue Lashing*; Chris Lemmon and Heather Locklear form a crime-fighting unit in *The Lingerie Justice Files*; Jeff Conaway and Morgan Fairchild are *The Crotchless Killers*; William Devane tracks a killer on a tropical paradise in *The Hawaii Edible-Underwear Murders*; Jeff Conaway is a crazed cult leader in *The Waco Panty Raid*; Eric Roberts is a freaked-out artist who gets more than he bargained for in *Naked Came The Nude*." Yes folks, it's the MST3K list of lists. This site also features FAQs as well as episode and "shorts" guides. And it offers its thoughts on the appropriate vengeance to be exacted upon Doug "missed-the-boat" Herzog of Comedy Central.
WEB http://www.cybercom.net/~fringe/mst3k.html

MST3K Movie Review Guide It seems like a good idea—a half dozen legitimate reviews for each movie on *MST3K*. But most are culled from video guides which take the shlock-factor for granted. Hence, the reviews are about as funny as David Spade talking about his embittered dysfunctional relationship with his father on national television. Well, at least they don't come from Michael Medved. Imagine: "*High School Bigshot* was the only movie I let my children watch this year. It was chock full of moral fortitude, with a clear message: Doing someone's homework for them is wrong. Engineering a shipping heist is wrong. Kissing a girl is wrong. The dialogue was natural and realistic, I could totally identify with the story, and Tom's full lips, well, what can you say but 'Wow!'"
WEB http://www.webcom.com/~cgould/mstcrit.html

MST3K Stuff Includes links to a few other home pages, as well as two Mac downloads—a screensaver and the famous Stack O'Love database, which includes a huge amount of information about the show (episode guide, tape cataloguer, drinking game rules, and a cookbook) and has incurred the wrath of *MST3K*'s legal representatives. An FAQ linked to the site reviews the legal situation surrounding the Stack O'Love. It's litigeoriffic!
WEB http://www.teleport.com/~lynsared/mst.shtml • http://fermi.virginia.edu/~jcp9j/canceled.html

MSTed Movie Gallery Truly cool images of movie posters and stills from the films, even lobby cards! There's also a collection of posts to the newsgroups from actual Best Brains crew—"Mike Nelson writes: Trace? Trace Bealieu? You old dog!! This is Mike!! Mike Nelson!!! God this is great! You just left my office and now here you are "surfing the nob"! This is great. God I love technology. Do other people like technology? Write to me if you like technology." There's even a personals listing for MiSTie movie characters—"Mexican wrestler seeks undead with great set of teeth. Mark of

the devil a must. Appreciation of Beethoven helpful but not necessary. Do you get turned on by doughy men in capes and tights? If so, give me a ring!"
WEB http://fermi.clas.virginia.edu/~jcp9j/mst3k.html

The Revenge of MST3K Now this is a Web page, baby! See down there in the corner, little animated Mike (or is it Joel?) and the bots are cheerin' and jeerin'! The site covers the whole cancellation threat, the movie, and the show's salavation. There's also a sound archive, and—get this, MiSTies—they got video. There's also a survey asking about your fave episode, your fave bot, your pic for a more current movie to MiST, and which talk show host should replace our beloved Mike if some kind of horrible disaster befalls him (such as a recurring role in *Caroline In the City*).
WEB http://www.iguide.com/tv/mst3k

Web Site o' Love It's Bigger Than Huge! One of the earlier and largest *MST3K* Web sites, this site includes newsletters, links to FTP sites, FAQs, and lyrics to the show's musical numbers. It's also got ratings, ratings, ratings, my friend, because at the Web Site o' Love, judgments and labeling are what it's all about.
WEB http://www.usgcc.odu.edu/~ty/mst3k/MST3K.html

▶ SATELLITES

Catchphrase Machine So you think you're smart huh? You think you know it all, don't you? OK, fanboy, where did the catchphrase "Puma? Puma!" come from? How about "I'm dead now, please don't smoke"? Then there's "Serpentine! Dodge the bullets!" Full of Pop Culture 101 quips from *The Mary Tyler Moore Show*, *Dr. Strangelove*, and *An American Werewolf in London*, this is also one of the best places to go for the references that went over your head, flew past your ear, or just sort of plopped down a foot in front of you with an air of defeat.
WEB http://www.cs.utexas.edu/users/chaput/catch.html

Gravity's Rainbow and Mystery Science Theatre 3000 One is a low-budget, middle-brow cable TV show, and the other is Pynchon's monster of postmodernism, a novel with so many twists and turns that it makes *Finnegans Wake* look like *Pat the Bunny*. So what do they have in common? Everything, according to this page. Joel, you see, is Tyrone Slothrop, the everyman trying to impersonate technology. Dr. Forrester is Pontsman, the scientist whose Faustian pact with progress sets the world on its ear. Visit this page for more insight into the merging subtext of both these cultural icons. And remember kids: TV rots your brain. But literary analysis builds character. **WEB** http://www.best.com/~rpirani /gr&mst3k.htm

MiSTied: MAKE.MONEY.FAST Have you been a victim of this infamous pyramid scam? Well, the joke's on you, sucka! For everyone who had a hearty laugh at this thing before trashing it, this page offers an inspired piece of fan fiction. Mike and the bots are in top form, and while some of the commentary reads more like *Laugh-In* than *MST3K*, most of it is right on target. **WEB** http://www-personal.engin.umich .edu/~jgotts/mst3k/mmf.html

MST3K FAQs A clearinghouse of archival material, including FAQs, episode guides, a list of lists, a shorts guide etc… It's your every fantasy, in file form. **WEB** http://www.cis.ohiostate.edu/hyper text/faq/bngusenet/alt/tv/mst3k/top.html

SHOW BY SHOW

Mike's MST3K Show Database It's revolutionary! Well, in theory. This site is in the process of building a separate page for every single episode of the show. Right now the page has only four episodes completed, but they are as comprehensive as we were led to believe. Plot synopsis, movie poster, info on actors and directors, transcripts for the sketches, quotes, and an easy reference guide—do you need this much detail? Does anybody? Why don't you

just figure out how to program your VCR instead? You can do it. We're all behind you. **WEB** http://www.missouri.edu/~c638278 /mst3k/mst3k.html

Snake Byte's Automated Episode Guide Don't miss this page's comprehensive skit, song, and riff transcripts from *Mystery Science Theater 3000*. The FTP links no longer seem to be valid, so all the promised sounds and images are a just a tease. Good ol' Snake also offers automated episode guides (for Windows) of *MST3K*, *Star Trek*, *Quantum Leap*, *The Simpsons*, and *Beavis and Butt-head*. **WEB** http://www.cleaf.com/~wmorgan /snake.html

DIVERSIONS

Audio Clips from MST3K Dozens of classics—from "The Big Head Song" to the "Uranus" series, as well as sound bytes you probably missed because you were trying to point out the wheels under the crab monsters to your boyfriend. **WEB** http://www.trenton.edu/~klett /mst3k.html

MST for the Proletariat Sound clips for the masses. Workers of the world unite! You have nothing to lose but your ability to produce marketable pop bands. **WEB** http://www.marlboro.edu/~jamdalea /mst.html

Next Sunday A.D. You want Toobular Boobular Joy? You got it. Some great images from *MST3K*'s big adventure on the big screen, an infinitesimally small sound archive, and a (not remotely) Interactive Episode Guide. **WEB** http://rio.atlantic.net/~fiser/MST3000 /images.html

CHAT

alt.tv.mst3k • alt.fan.mst3k • rec .arts.tv.mst3k • rec.arts.tv.mst3k .misc A cynical and hilarious set of newsgroups, much like the show itself. Fans of *Mystery Science Theater 3000* revel in their ruthlessness. After all, the show relies on intellectualist disdain for movies like *Invasion USA*, *The Creeping Terror*, and *Teenagers from Outerspace*. One fan, upset by recent screenings of such pictures as *Racket Girls* and *Red Zone Cuba* (they weren't bad enough?) posted a plea for "dumb Japanese monsters" and more "stupid alien movies." Newbies, beware. Post a sincere question to this group and you're asking for a flame. Plenty of talk of sci-flicks such as *Logan's Run*, *Nightfall*, and *Fire Maidens of Outer Space*. Celebrity mentions should be particularly severe, with posts judged by their level of ridicule. After Kathy Ireland was called "the dumbest celebrity," one regular wrote: "If you ever get a chance, listen to Nancy Sinatra. She makes Tony Danza and Sylvester Stallone look like Mensa members."

USENET alt.tv.mst3k • alt.fan.mst3k • rec.arts.tv.mst3k • rec.arts.tv.mst3k .misc

Mystery Science Theater 3000 A great hangout for MiSTies and MiSTics, with folders called Joel vs. Mike, Satellite of Love, Favorite Running Gags, and lots of other goodies. The quotes in the Favorite Quotes folder include "Bite me, it's fun," and "We come bearing honey-baked yams." Check out the Itchy Mango folder for an add-on story: "Create absurd situations, zany characters, and disgusting plot conveniences. In jokes—a plus. You (all of you) are responsible to keep the wacky adventures of Ms. Itchy Mango alive and kicking. Post away!" This is a raucous and fun-loving bunch. Never a dull moment—caustic comments are appreciated, nay, demanded.

AMERICA ONLINE *keyword* scifi→Star Trek/Comics/TV/Star Wars Boards→ Mystery Science Theater 3000

▶ MARKETPLACE

Artitude Apparel Home Page Get your red-hot *MST3K* T-shirts here! Tom Servo says "I'm Huge!" Crow T. Robot says "Bite Me!" Gypsy says "Join Us!" Mike Nelson says "Movie Sign!" Dr. Forrester says "I'm Evil!" And Joel says nothing, cause he quit!

WEB http://www.bpsi.net/~artitude /index2.html

Plan 10 Your dreams have come true. Plan 10 is offering *MST3K* merchandise that would make a con-fiend weep for joy. Movie posters and lobby cards for everything from the *Amazing Colossal Man* to *Giant Leeches* to *War of the Colossal Beast*. And, as if that weren't enough, Plan 10 will have you shouting "Torgo, Torgo, Torgo!" till they take all the sharp objects and lock them out of your reach. Be the first and only person on your block to own a quality Torgo T-shirt. It's flavoriffic!

WEB http://zim.com/torgo

▶ INDEXES

Index—Deus Ex Machina Scarier than *Santa Claus Conquers the Martians*! Bigger than the *Amazing Colossal Man*! Better sorted than the M&M's backstage at a Stones concert. Prepare to be shocked out of your seats! It's Deus Ex Machina, Web site of terror! Watch in horror as a mild mannered college student is impelled by an unknown force to collect dozens of Web sites, all day, all night! Is it alien mind control? A government experiment gone horribly wrong? And what is his unearthly goal? Find out, if you dare...

WEB http://sunsite.unc.edu/lunar/mst3k /mst3k.html

Klub Kattari! What makes this index special? It doesn't give the page names, so every link is a magical surprise!

WEB http://watt.seas.virginia.edu/~dak7e /mst3klinks.html

Other Science Facts Enough links to choke a cat. Organized to perfection. And no sign of Bob Vila!

WEB http://www.engr.unl.edu/~tory /mst3k.html

BRING IN DA FILK

DOES YOUR MOTHER KNOW THAT YOU FILK? It's not a word that you'd want to shout in the street. It sounds like it could have so many meanings: an expression of disgust? a handful of dryer lint? fabric made by synthetic worms? What secret hold does filk have on the sci-fi community?

According to **What the Heck is Filk Music?** and other reliable sources, filk began in the early days of sci-fi conventions. Fans would gather at science fiction conventions for "good old-fashioned folk music song circles." Rather crazed after a long day of fandom, certain fans began to crack each other up with super-silly parodies of popular tunes outfitted with new, sci-fi-themed lyrics. For whatever reason, and most probably because late-night hilarity is the best kind, this entertainment caught on. That dreadful name? Its true origin has been obscured by time, but is uniformly attributed to a mere typographical error on a pamphlet, brochure, or rejected fan 'zine article, depending on who's relating the story.

Part of the fun of filk as it is today is attempting to define it. Everyone agrees that it's much more than just singing different words to "Rudolph, the Red-Nosed Reindeer," as kids do. After all, these filkers are adults now and want to take themselves seriously. It's not that easy to find rhymes for Kirk and toupee, for instance. **Solomon Davidoff's Thesis** is one diehard fan's honest attempt to take academic filk to the Internet. "Filkers adapt, create, perform and listen to songs (grounded primarily in the modern American folk tradition) that relate to the fiction they read and view (which can be not only science fiction and fantasy books, television programs and films, but works in other genres as well), other aspects of fandom (such as convention masquerades and art shows) and to the interests and experiences of the filkers themselves (their professions, their home lives or anything else that seems to inspire a song)," he says in one giant mouthful. Filk acts as a version of fandom's oral tradition, where there are both standards and new movements open to analysis by any average musicologist.

But a genre that began with sci-fi fans, or "fen," as they sometimes call themselves, and dealt exclusively in sci-fi parodies has expanded. Is filk limited only to parodies? Should themes outside of sci-fi be allowed? Filk has grown to encompass many topics, including computers, everyday life, pets, and even filk itself. Many of the filk folks who regularly post their ideas and songs to alt.music.filk are ready to accept any kind of filk as long as it's fun, and sing any lyrics to any tune, whether original or well-known. Rabid old believers, such as one who distributed a brochure called **Down With Fake Filk** at a recent con, think the "rule" should be more stringent. But unlike some musical genres, where the rules have become defined to the point of outright exclusion, filk and filkers seem to have opened their minds (and mouths) ever wider. Perhaps this fan, in an essay called "Filk Music? What's That?" says it best:

"Filk is...

Songs inspired by science fiction and fantasy
Songs inspired by science and technology
Songs inspired by other songs
Songs inspired by life
Songs inspired by politics
Songs that bring tears of joy. Or sorrow. Or determination.
Old songs with a new point of view
New songs with an old point of view

Songs of the past as it should have been
Songs of the future

...Music!"

Launch pad

Solomon Davidoff's Thesis
http://ernie.bgsu.edu/~sdavido/index10.html

Down With Fake Filk
http://www.izzy.net/~tomsmith/shtick/fakefilk.htm

What The Heck Is Filk Music?
http://www.zubkoff.com/what-is-filk.html

THE PRISONER

THE PRISONER IS A PHENOMENON. Possibly the biggest cult series of all time (*Trek* is beyond cult). Why? Because the themes driving the show are simultaneously timely and transcendent—omniscient authority, omnipresent technology, and pervasive bureaucracy, confronted by nonconformity, lust for freedom, and rebellion. This is created to inspire thought and discussion. Thirty years after its controversial, confounding, downright brilliant finale, people are still thinking and talking about it, especially online. What would No. 6 think of the Web—much maligned technology providing a freedom of speech and debate never before possible? And what would he think of the Communications Decency Act? In the end, the door opens on its own…

slide show of the opening credits and then leads you to a map that lets you wander around Your Village. Each section of the Village contains images, sound clips , and thematic links to the outside world—The Chess Lawn links to a gaming site, The Labour Exchange links to career counseling services, The Palace of Fun has a television where you can change the channel to bring up links to other cult shows. You get the idea. The Green Dome houses the beefiest features, with image files and sound clips for No. 6 and each No. 2, and a spoilprotected slide show revealing the identity of No. 1. Attempts at escape, through land, air, or sea, prove useless, and often fatal, but they are always entertaining. **WEB** http://www.voicenet.com/~acasas /prisoner.html

▶ CLICK PICKS

The Prisoner U.S. Home Page This site is the most analytical, verbose page on the series. The Beginners Page offers an in-depth introduction to the plot and to the philosophy behind the show. The Episode Guide gives background on the production and an episode rating table. Quotes include some gems you're sure to have forgotten. But the core of the page is discussion—What does the Butler's umbrella symbolize? Did we ever find out where The Village is located? What's the deal with the glowing rover in "Free For All"? The page also houses an intensive analysis of Episode Order, the best *Prisoner* index on the Net and a very unique "Fall Out" theory. So much for "Questions are a burden to others; answers are a prison for oneself." **WEB** http://www.cis.yale.edu/~rdm/pris.html

▶ MOTHERSHIPS

Arvin W. Casas' "Village": Warning! One of the best and most entertaining *Prisoner* sites on the Net, and one of the best sites, period. Resign and enter this media-rich page, which begins with a

Joe Brae's Ultimate Village Experience An excellent page, the text is completely in character, and the features are meaty: storyboards for the Opening Scene and "The Chimes of Big Ben," a great No. 2 gallery, and three "moving .GIFs"—the prison bars closing, a bouncing rover, and the unmasking of No. 1! Opinion polls on the key questions "What is the Village?," "Did No. 6 escape the Village?," "Who is the No. 1?" etc… The answers vary wildly from allusions to real-world politics to intra-series logic games. Don't be disharmonious—add your own brilliant theories to the poll, after all, it's Your Village. **WEB** http://members.aol.com/joebrae /prisoner.htm

Kip Teague's The Prisoner Page Great for the die-hard fan, because in addition to your usual pics of No. 6 looking pissed off, it is filled with unusual features. How about a virtual tour of the Hotel Portmeirion as it stands today, or a scrapbook from annual Six of One conventions at the hotel, revamped to duplicate the Village? Looking for insightful trivia? "The number 7 is dutifully avoided in Arrival, replaced in all locations on

the Village information board and omitted entirely from the punchout boxes on No. 6's "credit card." Hmmm. There are also village maxims, links and the like, but the real finds here are the alternate episode versions and lost scenes, some of which have sound clips. Check out "Fall Out"—and then hatch a plot to break into the BBC vaults.
WEB http://www.inmind.com/people /teague/prisoner.html

The Prisoner A comprehensive page. There isn't anything here you couldn't find in another place, but it's nice to have it all collected on one site—details about Portmeirion, Six of One membership information, episode guide, an image gallery of all the No. 2s. The page in itself, seems somehow to lack the obsessive flare, but you'll find fanaticism in the pages of the archived *Free For All* newsletters: "in the end, there is something private about the *Prisoner* experience. Something I cannot articulate, and something that… for all the publications, conventions, and good fellowship… cannot, finally, be shared."
WEB http://lolita.laas.fr/~salles/prisoner .html

The Prisoner (Ireland) Straightforward and substantive, this page offers FAQs, sounds, fonts, archived issues of *Free for All Magazine*, and a sizable index to other *Prisoner* pages. This is as good a moment as any to mention a document available at many sites, including this one—The Troyer Interview—a very long, very interesting interview with McGoohan circa 1977 about the series, his politics, the show's following and everything else. Hear all your theories justified or shot down, pick up lots of trivia available nowhere else, and get some insight into the creative force behind what is probably the biggest cult series of all time.
WEB http://ios.internet-ireland.ie/hell /prisoner

▶ **SATELLITES**

alt.tv.prisoner Who's going to play No. 6 in the movie? Crispin Glover? How about Gary Oldman? One fan thinks Christopher Walken would be the right choice. Walken reminds him of Patrick McGoohan, but he admits "he's a little too psycho, and his voice is a little annoying sometimes." Obsessive fanatics will feel right at home—one person's ranting about the latest government conspiracies, one is gushing over McGoohan's performance in *Braveheart*, and another is asking for help in building a Lotus Seven in his backyard. (OK, a model in his bedroom.)
USENET alt.tv.prisoner

Beyond Books: The Prisoner This is a fun, utterly useless little page proclaiming that Beyond Books supports No. 6 in the election. It's worth a visit just to download the crystal clear "Vote No. 6" poster image. It screams wallpaper.
WEB http://www.teleport.com/~beyond /Prisoner/index.htm

King Neptune and The Prisoner Apparently King Neptune is a British citizen who's into sci-fi, particularly *The Prisoner*, and this is his small, personal take on a program that has spawned volumes of pages of analyses and criticisms. It is perhaps not the most engrossing place to visit, but you don't have to live here— just follow the links to other larger, more developed helpings of *Prisoner* coverage.
WEB http://www.york.ac.uk/~rab108 /prisoner.htm

Once Upon A Time—Prisoner Fan Club Home Page Not quite as large and official as Six of One, this fan club offers a very nice fanzine with lots of fan fiction and conspiracy theories, and in a lovely gesture, maintains a lending library where members can borrow *Prisoner* books and documents (they hold the largest collection in the world) through mail for certain periods of time, free of charge. Membership with Once Upon A Time is a lot cheaper than that with Six of One, but then, they don't throw fantastic gorgeous conventions at Portmeirion every year either.
WEB http://www.carol.net/~lawrence /ouathome.htm

Prisoner: Episode Spoilers Short episode synopses and credits information. Uninspired, but good for quick reference.
WEB http://www.presence.co.uk/milt/prisoner.html

Prisoner Images Peter Pan getting ready for a dip in the ocean? Odd people in colorful capes playing a live game of chess? A man in a top hat being dropped down a tube in an underground cavern? Pod chairs, midgets, unnecessary surgery? A very strange show indeed. Certainly the largest collection of *Prisoner* pictures on the Net. Unfortunately, you usually don't know what you've got till you see it. A description directory would be helpful.
URL ftp://ftp.ugcs.caltech.edu/pub/gifs/Prisoner

The Prisoner Front Page No panache, but a few solid features. A nice little picture tour of The Village, episode guides, newsgroup and music FAQs, the Troyer interview, and small collections of images and sounds.
WEB http://metro.turnpike.net/D/dealgan/pages/information.html

Sci-Fi Channel : The Prisoner Click anywhere of this map of Your Village—the Town Hall, the Hospital, the Citizen's Advice Bureau—to start a virtual trip through the world of the Prisoner. While other sites are full of interesting information, series trivia, and fanatics arguing about whether the butler was No. 1, or a symbol of the oppressed working class, this page is a series of links that lead in circles, rather frustrating games, and flurries of images and sounds. It has perfectly captured the atmosphere of the show. Be warned! Trying to get to any part of The Village you don't have access to sets off an orange alert, if you're lucky. If you're not, let's just say we won't be seeing you again.
WEB http://www.scifi.com/prisoner/index.html

The Unofficial Prisoner Home Page What it lacks in style it makes up for in content: Three different FAQs, the Troyer Interview, episode guides for *Prisoner* and *Danger Man*, quotes, and even a Village font for Macs. You'll also find one of the most comprehensive indexes available for the show. Be sure to take a peek at book cover scans. One of the books dares to misquote the line that everybody, even people who've never watched the show, can say backwards in their sleep, five times fast.
WEB http://www.geocities.com/Sunset Strip/4589/tp.html

The Village A hefty archive of the *Free for All* fanzine, and a small index. But it's worth the visit for sound clips not only of the opening and theme song, but for the Iron Maiden song based on the series. Remember, "music begins where words leave off." The page is also trying to save *Nowhere Man*, the UPN rip-off, er, homage, to *The Prisoner*.
WEB http://members.aol.com/theprsnr/index.html

QUANTUM LEAP

D URING ITS FIVE-YEAR RUN ON NBC (1989-1993), *Quantum Leap* jumped into the hearts of television fans everywhere. With Scott Bakula as the superintelligent (six doctorates, eleven languages, one Nobel Prize) Dr. Samuel Beckett, and Dean Stockwell as the supersexed Rear Admiral Albert Calavicci, the show took one simple science-fiction concept—a hero who time-travels through his own lifetime, inhabiting other bodies—and spun out dozens of quality playlets. Though the plots sometimes fell into formula, some of the strongest episodes insisted on the importance of American history: depictions of the Civil Rights movement and the assassination of John F. Kennedy were two of the most memorable highlights. The Net is filled with spots to travel to and learn about the series if you're new to the phenomenon, or share opinions and complex questions if you're a *QL* vet.

▶ CLICK PICK

The Accelerator Chamber You leap through time with high technology, a healthy respect for twentieth-century American social history, and a little luck. And you leap through cyberspace? with a well-designed Web site devoted to *Quantum Leap*, especially one that includes general information such as fan club listings and an episode guide. The user-friendly Accelerator Chamber even has a map of the site with feature descriptions. A Fanatics' Look at the Life of Dr. Samuel Beckett reveals that the character "could read at age 2, do advanced calculus in his head at 5, went to MIT at age 15…" Links are provided, and so is an in-depth look at the *Quantum Leap* project: "This top secret project is located in a cavern in New Mexico in 1995. By fall 1996, it's cost $43 billion of our tax dollars, with $2.4 billion a year operating funds."
WEB http://www-usacs.rutgers.edu /funstuff/quantum-leap

▶ MOTHERSHIPS

Amy's Quantum Leap Page This is the effort of one fan doing what she can to preserve and distribute small but precious pieces of her favorite show's history and essence. Amy's Quantum Leap Page makes up for what it lacks in completeness with charm and personality, not to mention a library of sound and image files, and fan fiction. There are also links to other *Quantum Leap* fanzine pages. Amy promises frequent updates, and offers such gems as this caption to a picture of Sam feeding Ziggy: "Not integral to the plot, but the man has on boxers!! :-)"
WEB http://www.sky.net/~womack /quantum.html

The Quantum Leap Efficient and thorough, with links to U.S., French, and Peruvian television schedules for *Quantum Leap*, this fan page for the show eschews graphic wizardry for speed and clarity. The links include your basic FAQ, sound and image files, a 'zine connection, and a gallery of thumbnail images introduced with a warning that it could take a long time for text-based browsers to handle the info.
WEB http://lumchan.ifa.hawaii.edu/ql /ql.html

Quantum Leap Archive Take one drink when someone makes a remark about Sam's "Swiss cheesed" memory (the words "Swiss cheese" must be used). Take two when Sam pretends to talk on the phone so he can talk to Al. Rules to the clever *Quantum Leap* drinking game are posted here. If you're not too drunk and want some archives of mailing list posts, tape lists, interview transcripts, and FAQs for the show are also featured. Don't drive after visiting this site.
URL ftp://ftp.doc.ic.ac.uk/pub/media/tv /collections/tardis/us/sci-fi/QuantumLeap

Quantum Leap FAQ Does Scott Bakula really do his own singing on the show?

Is Scott Bakula really as nice as he seems to be? If Al is a hologram, why does he cast shadows? All this and more basic information about the show that put the humanity back in time travel. The second version of the FAQ is an extended one and contains additional information about broadcast schedules, among other topics.
WEB http://www-usacs.rutgers.edu/fun -stuff/tv/quantum-leap/faql.html

Quantum Leap FTP Site *Beverly Hills 90210*'s Jason Priestley, dance diva Debbie Allen, and *America's Funniest Home Videos*' Bob Saget all appeared as special guests on *QL* during its five-year run. The Web site offers a full database of these and other guest stars, as well as sounds, fan fiction, and an annotated list of the *Quantum Leap* comic books by Innovation Comics.
URL ftp://ftp.cisco.com/ql-archive

The Quantum Leap Information Page Follow the adventures of Sam Beckett by starting at this basic home page, which includes leaps—er, links—to general information such as a brief description of the show and an episode guide. Continue your trans-dimensional journey with digitized sound bites, images, broadcast schedules, and links to other *Quantum Leap* shrines on the Web.
WEB http://earth.ast.smith.edu/~patten //ql/ql.html

Quantum Leap Quotes "We've been having some difficulty with Ziggy, he's going through mood swings. I think we need to get a girl computer and put it right next to him, one with a nice set of hard disks…" Witty and memorable sayings that once flowed from the lips of Scott Bakula, Dean Stockwell, and company, complete with the title of the episode each quote was taken from.
URL ftp://ftp.cisco.com/ql-archive/text /ql.quote

Rerun Schedules If you've wasted hours flipping through channels looking for the show, waste no more time. This rerun schedule lists showtimes for the USA

Network and the Sci-Fi Channel.
WEB http://www-usacs.rutgers.edu/fun -stuff/tv/quantum-leap/rerun-sched.html

Ziggyland A high-concept operation that purports to be the rescued "Ziggy," that was lost in cyberspace once Project Quantum Leap was scrubbed. Files currently available from this relatively graphics-free site include Did You Ever Notice (a collection of *Quantum Leap* eyebrow-raisers) and Star Crossed (an analysis of human emotions from Ziggy's point of view). Sample Ziggyism: "It amazed me to learn how far human beings would go for the cause of what they call love." Yeah, yeah, it's a many splendored thing, whatever.
WEB http://www.lookup.com/Homepages /76852/ziggy.htm

► CHAT

Quantum Leap One of the regulars got worried when one of her comrades started to take this "leaping" business a bit too seriously. "You are aware that this is just a TV show." she wrote. The response? "What do you mean by 'just a TV show.' Is your brain swiss-cheesed:) It's real! Isn't it?" Lots of arguing and analyzing of individual episodes. In the libraries, you'll find a listing of *QL* fanstuff, a file on "the people, places, or things you won't see Sam 'leaping' into," and the *Quantum Leap* Episode Index.
COMPUSERVE *go* sfmedia→Libraries *or* Messages→Quantum Leap

► FAN FICTION

alt.ql.creative Let your imagination run wild—and into another era—with stories based on the TV show. Fans post their *Quantum Leap* stories here, where they find a small but devoted audience. If you're not into writing your own fiction, read the stories posted, such as "Ace," in which Sam finds himself as a World War I fighter pilot. Aside from the stories, there's a fair amount of discussion about the series and the rules of "leaping."
USENET alt.ql.creative

DAVID CRONENBERG

DAVID CRONENBERG IS NOT AN ACQUIRED taste. You either love him for his perverse fascinations or you loathe him for them. But that's just received wisdom talking. For as his appearances on the Net demonstrate, Cronenberg inspires feelings a little more complicated than that. His films, after all, are very much about what happens when repulsion and attraction overlap.

While the comprehensive **David Cronenberg Home Page**—the mutant-child of a devoted fanatic—is the only page dedicated entirely to Cronenberg, there is a plethora of think-pieces, articles, essays, and interviews with the man scattered around the edges of cyberspace, just waiting to suck in the idly curious. An interview with Cronenberg and fellow human oddity William Burroughs reveals what they find repulsive—from accidentally shooting your wife (Burroughs, of course) to Jerry Lewis (the disturbed duo do not share the opinions of French people in this regard). In **Word Sound Vision**, Cronenberg explores the idea of viral film: "viral filmmaking sounds like filmmaking as a disease, art as a disease, but also as something that embeds itself in your genetic structure, your chromosomal structure, and in that strange way becomes part of you even though it's not." Accompanying interviews with Cronenberg compatriots old (Deborah Harry) and new (J.G. Ballard) shed a glimmer of light on the infectious one's obsessions.

Traveling deeper still into Croneberg's psyche is a five-part theory paper entitled **Technology's Body: Cronenberg, Genre, and the Canadian Ethos,** which proposes that much of Cronenberg's narrative motivation and his entire visual subtext stems from his place of birth. "Cronenberg inherits, and with unusual clarity, what Northrop Frye calls Canada's 'garrison mentality.' This is a distinct sense of the space of human habitation characterized by an extreme 'edge-consciousness,' an anxious concern with boundaries, walls, thresholds, houses, and 'the interface between self and other.'" Which is as sound a rationalization for being a freaking wierdo as you might ever come across.

Launch pad

David Cronenberg Home Page
http://www.netlink.co.uk/users/zappa/cronen.html

Word-Sound-Vision
http://www.kgbmedia.com/wsv/index.html

Technology's Body: Cronenberg, Genre, and the Canadian Ethos
http://www.netlink.co.uk/users/zappa/cr_testa.html

RED DWARF

THE MOST BRILLIANT ACCOMplishment of the writers of *Red Dwarf* was making the single most ludicrous, complicated backstory in the history of television vaguely comprehensible in a 30-second soundbite: "This is an SOS distress call from the mining ship *Red Dwarf*. The crew are dead, killed by a radiation leak. The only survivors were Dave Lister, who was in suspended animation during the disaster, and his pregnant cat, who was safely sealed in the hold. Revived three million years later, Lister's companions are a life form who evolved from his cat, and Arnold Rimmer, a hologram simulation of one of the dead crew. I am Holly, the ship's computer, with an IQ of 6,000. The same IQ as 6,000 PE teachers." Or 6,000 times the IQ of most of the people who put up *Red Dwarf* fan pages. Here follow some exceptions.

▶ CLICK PICK

David's Smegi Page-A-Rooni As well-designed as the Cat's wardrobe, as big as the curry stain down Lister's shirt, as informative as Holly (actually more so, thankfully), and with almost as many features as Kryton—even without the groinal socket. OK, so the site ripped off all the sounds, images, and video from the Queeg site, but, as the Cat would say, style is the important thing. It does provide its own FAQ and a timeline taking us from the birth of Chu Ch'ang-lo Kuang Tsung to the End of Time Itself, which the Inquisitor has visited and doesn't much like. Script for every episode are available in HTML. But the coolest thing here is the inconsistencies page, with thousands of nit-picks. They even nit-pick the smeg-up video! **WEB** http://www.ozramp.net.au/~rocky /rdwarf.html

▶ MOTHERSHIPS

Anna's Red Dwarf Page It doesn't look like much, but hey, its better than a kick in the bread tray! Actually, this is quite a good page, with a number of exclusive features, mostly culled from the mailing list. The Famous Penguin List includes all the friends and relatives of the infamous Mr. Flibble now working in the Entertainment Industry (Chilly Willy, Feathers McGraw, The penguins in the N'Ice commercials…). You've got the usual fabulous quotes—"RIMMER: This is a nightmare. I'm on the run from the fascist police with a murderer, a mass murderer and a man in a bri-nylon shirt. I'm a piece of flotsam, jetsam human wreckage sputum bag who smells like a yak latrine, and now my best flashing mac is about to be splattered with an android's brain. I'm after you with the gun." Then there's the someone's-got-way-too-much-time-on-their-hands *Red Dwarf* Joke Count. And finally there is a bit of fan fiction that combines *Red Dwarf* with the *X-Files*. Sometimes people boldly go where they should not. **WEB** http://www.docs.uu.se/~annaer /reddwarf.html

Craig's Red Dwarf Page About as interesting as the mold growing in Lister's coffee cup. All you'll find is an episode list, the theme song (in text), and a petition begging Chris Barrie (Rimmer) to stick through all the episodes of season seven, which other pages say he's already agreed to do. **WEB** http://www.iinet.net.au/~craigjp /reddwarf.html

Getspacho Soup For newbies only. The page offers an in-depth introduction to the series and characters, links to other *RD* pages, and a detailed summation of Rimmer's cataclysmic faux pas. One word to the site author—lose the black on black text, smeghead, we can't read a bloody thing! **WEB** http://www.together.net/~rphillip /reddwarf/index.html

Greg's Red Dwarf page Cool Starbug animation, episode guides with scripts,

dozens of sound files, character profiles with quotes, and pics. Just one problem—you can't turn the smegging background music off! It's the theme song played on a 1974 Casio Jr.
WEB http://www.adam.com.au/~ghaywood /reddwarf.htm

Krosis' Red Dwarf Pagearoonie Step onto the Express Lift (patent applied for) for a tour of *Red Dwarf*. First level: Quote of the Week—"KRYTEN: The poor devil scrawled it in his death throes, using a combination of his own blood and even his own intestines. RIMMER: Who would do that? LISTER: Someone who badly needed a pen." Second Level: *Red Dwarf* FAQ—Under Construction, please remain in the lift. Third Level: Guides to the RD Books and Videos—be sure to check out Better than Life, where we find our heroes (and the git) living in their dream worlds (and you know how scary their dreams are!). Fourth Level: Episode Scripts—go back to the first episode, it's still bloody funny (even in the late eighties, Grant and Naylor managed to keep their sense of humor). Fifth Level: Mailing list info. Sixth Level: Personnel files on the boys. It reads like a *Playboy* centerfold, but thankfully they keep their clothes on. Seventh Level: Links. The cute borg at the end is Krosis of Borg. See what kind of costumes you get when you spend $1 million an episode instead of £30 and a tub of Nutella?
WEB http://www.louisville.edu/~atjewe01 /reddwarf.html

Lister's Pile 'O Smeg This is the best *Red Dwarf* index in the universe.
WEB http://www.afn.org/~afn15301 /dwarf.html

Mutton Vindaloo Beast Red Dwarf Page With one important exception, every link on this page is to the Queeg site. The exception, however, makes this page a must-see—the entire script to the never-aired American pilot. It actually has a few good jokes (most of which were yanked from the original), but in general you'll applaud the network for letting it die prematurely—the writers had the gall

to cut the "everybody's dead Dave" sequence.
WEB http://www.geocities.com/Silicon Valley/7439

Queeg's Red Dwarf Archive This is where the other site authors dip their sticky little hands to get multimedia files and everything else that they're too lazy to create themselves. There are hundreds of files in this archive. If it has anything to do with vindaloos and swimming certificates, it's here—reviews, bios, birthday lists, space corps directive lists, fan fiction, even the *Red Dwarf* fish list which documents every fishy moment, word or action in the entire series. But, you say, it's about as stylish as Dwane Dibbly, about as entertaining as Hammond Organ music, about as funny as Henny Youngman. But that's the point, innit? It's Queeg, right, so it's efficient and humorless, see?
WEB http://www.queeg.crater.com

Red Dwarf A lovely selection from the *Red Dwarf* Logbook, offering crew profiles ("Cat: Hobbies are looking good, eating, sleeping, games—very partial to Junior Angler Soap Sud Slalom and Unicycle Polo Playing"), and documenting poignant reflections ("Lister on being the last human alive: Don't have to queue for bus. Can leave toilet seat up. Am best guitarist in universe. Unlikely now to be called for jury service"), exciting adventures ("Rimmer: Esperanto Evening Class—*Bonvolu alsendi la pordiston-lausajne estas rano en mia bideo*"), insightful poetry ("When it's done in Zero-G, Sex is fun for you and me / But what can be a tragedy / Is visiting the lavatory"), and Space Corps directives ("Space Corps Directive No. 592—In an emergency situation involving two or more officers of equal rank, seniority will be granted to whichever officer can program a VCR"). Want more, don't you? Well, milado, you'll have to buy the book.
WEB http://www.webcom.com/reeduk /dwarf

Red Dwarf on AOL There are a few things here worth the unending headache involved in any aspect of using AOL. It's got all the stuff you can find on the WWW (scripts, FAQ, episode summaries, sound clips) but also an enormous fan fiction archive, a rather amusing collection of mailing list digests, and a selection of fan poetry that will leave you all twingly: "For KK—Shall I compare thee to a shami kebab? Or raw onions on cornflakes, Maybe poppadoms with curry sauce? Nay, next to thee all these pale, And lose their flavor. You are the spice I crave. And the love I need. You are my KK." and "Rimmer's Ode to Yvonne McGruder—Yvonne / Yvonne, I gave / Her one." Two major flaws—first, there is only a general sci-fi chat room where Dwarfers will probably get into virtual pub brawls with Trekkers who take themselves too seriously, and second—the goits didn't get any smegging images!

AMERICA ONLINE *keyword* britscifi→ Red Dwarf

Red Dwarf Shoals "Across the sands of time comes the mystic tale of a man, simple and honest... but enough about that smeg; let's talk some *Red Dwarf*!" A few very odd, totally original offerings for die-hard Dwarfers—a script, replete with songs, for the first act of *Red Dwarf On Ice*, a very useful television guide that tells you where and when the show is playing across the world, and a page dedicated to The Holy Sisterhood of Second Technician Arnold J. Rimmer, Bsc, Ssc., where the diciples swear to "burn our puncture repair kits; He shan't need them with us!" Frightening doesn't begin to describe it.

WEB http://www.uea.ac.uk/~u9504133 /Pages/Shoals/Red_Dwarf.html

Silicon Heaven—The Red Dwarf Guide It ain't Fiji, but it does hold a couple of very nice features. It offers a great A-Z dictionary of all the terms in the show (it's still growing) from Ace to Fuchal Day, Nodnol to Scrumping, and Jim Bexley Speed to Z-shift. And it houses what seems to be the only functioning *Red Dwarf* FAQ, full of such fascinating Q&As as—"Who is Gordon Bennett?" Suffice it

to say that, "Today, Bennett's name is used as an expression of disbelief in England, and is essentially a euphemism for God."

WEB http://www.cityscape.co.uk/users /ij88/rdguide.html

▶ CHAT

alt.tv.red-dwarf Given the mentality of the show, it's no surprise that this group wombles on about everything from the destruction of the buffalo to weevil-infestation in modern America. A conversation about the origin of "smeg," led to a lengthy, flame-filled argument about the differences between smegma, semen, and sebum. "Are there any reported incidents of sex on *Red Dwarf*?" one soon-to-be-sadly-disappointed viewer asked. "You see, I only want to watch it if there are." For those interested in the more serious side of this un-serious group, you'll find lots of discussion of Brit slang and talk about whether American fans can understand the class nuances of the relationship between Lister and Rimmer. For those interested in mercilessly taunting anyone who brings up anything remotely serious in this newsgroup, door prizes are offered.

USENET alt.tv.red-dwarf

The Red Dwarf Mailing List Dwarfers who sign up for this ML are dubbed Listers (get it? get it?), and are invited into a close-knit circle of friendly weirdos who discuss the unusual character development of old goal-post head (in that he's actually developing some character), debate why they kept dog food on a ship that didn't allow animals, and make attempts to meet face to face for *Red Dwarf* fried egg and chutney sandwich parties because their significant others are going to stab them in the head if they're subjected to another nanosecond of "CAT: Fish! COMPUTER: Your fish today is trout almondine. CAT: Fish! COMPUTER: Your fish today is trout almondine..."

EMAIL listproc@lists.pipex.com ✍ *Type in message body:* subscribe reddwarf <your full name>

STAR WARS

A GOODY-GOODY FARM BOY WITH an electric stick. A princess with a danish stuck on each side of her head. A space bum with a mutant carpet for a best friend. A tin comedian with a trashcan for a sidekick. All pitted against an asthmatic caped freak with a calculator stuck to his chest. What were they thinking? What were we thinking? Who cares! From the first frame, we knew this was the one. We knew that *Star Wars* was destined to become the undisputed king of sci-fi filmdom. Online, fans can download scripts for all three films and get the scoop on the prequels, amass closets full of collectibles, and immerse themselves in role-playing adventures. Right now, as you read this, in a cyberspace galaxy as close as your PC, the battle between good and evil rages on.

▶ CLICK PICK

Star Wars Home Page at UPenn Since you learned the most important date in the *Star Wars* calendar this decade, you have been preparing for President's Day 1997. You can proudly quote most of the dialogue from the holy triptych. You can understand every word Yoda says. But can you explain hyperspace travel, do you have a catalog of missing scenes from the trilogy, and do you know what the actor who played Boba Fett looks like? This huge (and we mean Jabba-the-Hutt-mongous) site will supplement your Jedi skills. *Star Wars* news, scripts of the trilogy, images and sound files, information on *Star Wars* collectibles, guides to *Star Wars* role-playing games, nitpicking and bloopers lists, trivia, Lucas Arts pages, and a comprehensive FAQ are all here. Altogether now, "The Force is strong in this one."
WEB http://force.stwing.upenn.edu:8001/~jruspini/starwars.html

▶ MOTHERSHIPS

David Jansen's Star Wars Page Once upon a time, this was a personal *Star Wars* home page, but it is now one of the most complete lists of Lucas-related materials on the Internet. In addition to links to all major *Star Wars* Web sites, the Jansen page contains some material of its own, most notably .GIFs captured from the *Star Wars* computer game and a "fortune cookie" program that generates random quotes from the trilogy. How random? How about this from C3PO's abashed explanation to Han in *Return of the Jedi*: "I'm rather embarrassed, General Solo, but it appears you are to be the main course at a banquet in my honor."
WEB http://www.strw.leidenuniv.nl/~jansen/sw.html

David's Star Wars Hub If there's a bright center to the online *Star Wars* galaxy, David's *Star Wars* Hub is it. Follow the terrific graphics to a gold mine of Internet resources, linking you to image servers, sound files, fiction, comic books, computer games… the list goes on. Suffice it to say that it's a Bantha-sized heap o' stuff. Unique to David's Hub is his Forceful presentation of some awesome starship blueprints and his server for collectible *Star Wars* cards. And if you've been hunting all over for a TIE Interceptor Pilot action figure, the free listings on the Jawa Trading Post might help you find what you're looking for.
WEB http://161.32.228.104/david.htm

Echo-Base: Online Star Wars Fanzine No more waiting outside your mailbox for your latest fix of *Star Wars* information from various print publications; Echo-Base offers the latest scoops online, and in a fairly timely fashion. This information-rich, if graphically listless, 'zine features interviews with *Star Wars* book authors, reviews of recent merchandise, convention coverage… anything involving our favorite band of intergalactic freedom fighters. Readers are invited to submit works, and similarly interesting results are yielded through

the 'zine's regular polls. One such poll found that fans would like those rumors that had Kenneth Branagh portraying the young Obi-Wan Kenobi in the upcoming films to be true.
WEB http://members.aol.com/pfletzer/echobase.htm

Hose Beast's Star Wars Page Billing itself as a catalog-in-process, this *Star Wars* index already seems as large as the Death Star (the second, unfinished one). Hose Beast has worked harder than a Jawa in a junkyard to amass an array of literature—from early screen-play drafts to humor articles like "Every-thing I Know I Learned from *Star Wars*." There are also links to the role-playing game, theoretical technical information, and plenty of online fan fiction. The vol-ume of *Star Wars* vs. *Star Trek* stories is truly astronomical, and it's no surprise that the Empire usually creams the Fed-eration.
WEB http://www.break.com.au/~hbeast/3-1-txts.html

The New Star Wars Homepage Ever notice that the opening scroll of *Star Wars* titles it *Episode IV: A New Hope*? Parts I through III are ever-so-slowly getting closer to production, but in the meantime, LucasFilm is re-releasing the original trilogy in theaters—with pumped-up sound, revised special effects, and extra scenes of previously cut (or never-filmed) footage, including the infamous "two-legged Jabba" scene from *A New Hope*. From this address, shameless *Star Wars* fans can keep track of new-movie rumors while watching a ticker tape countdown of the days until the release of *Star Wars: The Special Edition*. The linkage is top-flight, con-necting you to complete information on deleted scenes and the Boba Fett home page.
WEB http://www.ilinkgn.net/users/robster/default1.htm

rec.arts.sf.starwars Much talk about *Star Wars* toys and the next trilogy. Would you buy a Darth Vader carrying case for $200? No? Well, someone will.

One thread was titled, "Why hasn't Luke gotten laid yet?" "I think it's about time," Anton wrote. "Heck, I bet even the Wookie sneaks out for a little nookie. Luke gets the award for being the most sexually repressed hero ever." But, soap-opera-like worries aside, this is a sci-fi savvy group of regulars with lots of Star Wares. When the conversation veers from Obi-Wan and Luke, it often turns to *Star Trek*, with Corey contending a battle between the *Enterprise* and the *Star Destroyer* would be "very close" while Joshua trashes transporters as "the most contrived and moronic devices, ever." Hey, try and say that in rec.arts.startrek.fandom, bud!
USENET rec.arts.sf.starwars
FAQ: WEB http://bantha.pc.cc.cmu.edu:1138/INFO/faqrass.html

Star Wars If you're in the *Star Wars* message area and you see a topic on the best movie ever made, don't say it's *Jurassic Park*. Sure, these fans like Spielberg and those awesome special effects, but *The Empire Strikes Back* rules here. Got it? "I mean, I can sit down and watch *ESB* a thousand thou-sand times and still be awake," one *SW*-lover said. "I watch *Jurassic Park* three times and I'm out cold." Sometimes it seems like everyone in this place has watched *Empire* a "thousand thousand times." That doesn't mean these fans limit themselves to movie-watching. Other active topics include *Star Wars* books and toys. Rumors about new *Star Wars* films get discussed at length, as you'd expect. In the libraries, you'll find a complete *Star Wars* chronology, a dis-sertation on Jedi grammar, and a Yoda start-up screen, among other goodies.
COMPUSERVE *go* sfmedia→Libraries *or* Messages→Star Wars

Star Wars Maintained by Michael Sher-man at Carnegie-Mellon, this general site includes info on all three films in the original trilogy, as well as sounds, pic-tures, movie scripts, and news clippings about upcoming LucasFilm projects.
WEB http://www.cs.cmu.edu/afs/andrew.cmu.edu/usr18/mset/www/starwars.html

Star Wars Standing head and shoulders above all other sci-fi action movies, George Lucas's 1977 film and its two sequels forever changed the habits and expectations of movie audiences worldwide. In the AOL *Star Wars* discussion, fans fret over rumors of new Wars films ("The only thing definite about this movie is that nothing is definite"), point out inside jokes in other Lucas efforts (in *Indiana Jones and the Temple of Doom*, there's a nightclub named for Obi-Wan Kenobi), and bemoan the diminished employment prospects of *Star Wars* star Mark Hamill ("Time has not been kind to Hamill… and neither was Corvette Summer"). Except for the occasional dig, this message board is one big love-in that embraces Luke Skywalker, Darth Vader, Princess Leia, Han Solo, et al.
AMERICA ONLINE *keyword* scifi→Science Fiction→Star Wars Fan Forum→Message Boards

Star Wars at 20th Century Fox A long time ago in a galaxy far, far away (actually, in your local video stores), 20th Century Fox Home Entertainment released digitally remastered videocassette editions of the *Star Wars* trilogy and advertised it on the Web. Fortunately, by using officially sanctioned graphics (and lots of them), 20th Century Fox has created much more than just an online advertisement by offering plot and production information for each film—including interviews, pre-production art, and lots of other behind-the-scenes data. Those insights are what really make this a worthwhile destination, but the link to Leia's Wig Shop is fun as well.
WEB http://www.tcfhe.com/starwars

Star Wars Page Movie scripts, sounds, images, FAQs, and addresses for all *Star Wars* actors, from Mark Hamill to James Earl Jones.
WEB http://www.filmzone.com/~vkoser/vader/starwars/star.html

▶**CHARACTERS**

The Boba Fett Homepage A page dedicated to Luke or Leia or Vader or even those annoyingly adorable Ewoks one might expect, but Boba Fett? It seems only natural to devote a corner of cyberspace to one of the deadliest, most efficient bounty hunters in the galaxy. True, he ended up being eaten by the Sarlacc, but his memory lives on here. There's an FAQ, fan club, and all the facts available on the fictitious villain. Find out what actor played Fett, what his stats are in the RPGs, and what toys and comics feature him.
WEB http://www.frii.com/~joe/bf_home.html

The Wedge Antilles Homepage According to this site, Wedge Antilles is the true ace of the Rebellion. You'll find an FAQ, fan fiction, and merchandise devoted to the unsung hero.
WEB http://www.epix.net/~killando/wedge.html

World o' Chewbacca The Wookie Web page. Download that distinct growl (there are five here to choose from), pictures of Chewie, or even the Chewbacca song from the movie *Clerks*.
WEB http://members.aol.com/andrewm675/chewbacca/chewie.html

Yoda's Corner An area devoted to that judicious Jedi master and his lessons for Luke and the rest of us. Peruse Yoda's sagacious lines from the original scripts.
WEB http://www.cli.di.unipi.it/~marenco/yoda.htm

▶**DIVERSIONS**

Cut Scenes from the Star Wars Trilogy What to do when you've seen all three *Star Wars* movies 300 times? Be the coolest kid on your cyberblock and visit this site for never-before-seen scenes, like the one with Luke and Biggs on Tatooine or the one where Han Solo meets Jabba outside the Falcon in Docking Bay 94.
WEB http://www.evan.org/swcut.html

EAR-chives: Star Wars A collection of sounds amassed, no doubt, by a Vader fan. Most of the .WAV files attempt to

draw us to the Dark Side: "It is pointless to resist, my son," "Give yourself to the Dark Side," "Strike me down with all of your hatred, and your journey toward the Dark Side will be complete!!!" Resistance is futile.
WEB http://www.geocities.com/Hollywood /1158/starwars.html

Irresistible Force The good, the bad, and the funny in the *Star Wars* universe, including Roger Ebert's original review of the movie, *Star Wars* toys that failed, and spoofs galore.
WEB http://paul.spu.edu/~kevnord /starwars

Jordan's Page O' Sounds "I don't know… fly casual." "I'd just as soon kiss a Wookie." "Adventure, heh… excitement, heh… a Jedi craves not these things." Re-experience a few of the more memorable lines from Solo, Leia, Yoda, Threepio, Vader, and Lando.
WEB http://www.wam.umd.edu/~tfish /star.html

Lucas Arts Product information, technical support, and press releases from the wizards behind the official *Star Wars* software. The libraries here contain shareware versions of the games and the hints and tips message board is the place to go when you're in a tight spot and tech support just isn't enough.
AMERICA ONLINE *keyword* lucas arts

Mark Bennet's Star Wars Homepage
What makes Mark's *Star Wars* site different from the rest is the behind-the-scenes information and images he's amassed. You'll also find the usual assortment of scripts and drafts of scripts, fan fiction, FAQs, and sounds.
WEB http://phymat.bham.ac.uk /BennetMN/starwars.html

Purdue Picture Archive Pictures of characters and ships, as well as miscellaneous pictures, with miscellaneous defined as "pictures not of ships or people."
WEB http://crank.biggun.com/~vkoser /vader

Star Wars Fan Forum With the first new *Star Wars* film premiering in 1998 or 99, the *Star Wars* Special Edition already in production, and new merchandise released every day, this AOL forum is riding on the resurgence of the *Star Wars* movement. Message boards, a software library, and a chat room keep the SW fandom busy until they can get their hands on the latest from Lucas.
AMERICA ONLINE *keyword* scifi→Science Fiction→Star Wars Fan Forum

Star Wars Multimedia Archive Before jetting here at sub-light speed, make sure your computer can handle RealAudio and QuickTime—otherwise this archive will only remind you of all the swell *Star Wars* stuff you're missing. Covering the multimedia gamut from movie trailers to film stills to the NPR radio dramas, this is a *Star Wars* smorgasbord for your eyes and ears. But even if you can't listen in or watch things in motion, the General Information text links will feed your curiosity—particularly the hefty Bloopers Guide that tracks every minute gaffe in the *Star Wars* saga.
WEB http://bantha.pc.cc.cmu.edu:1138 /SW_HOME.html

Star Wars Sounds Music to the Imperial citizen's ears. More than 50 sound files from that galaxy far, far away, including words of wisdom and wit from such characters as Jabba the Hutt, the galaxy's most well-known crimelord, to Princess Leia, the head of state with the most interesting head of hair.
WEB http://www.link-net.com/sounds /movies/Star_Wars

Uni-Stuttgart Picture Archive *Star Wars* images from a German site.
URL ftp://ftp.rus.uni-stuttgart.de/pub /graphics/pictures/tv+film/starwars

WPI Picture Archive .JPGs and ASCII art from the trilogy.
URL ftp://wpi.wpi.edu/starwars/Pictures

WPI Sound Library From soundtrack samples to dialogue bites, this sound

library includes a number of audio clips from the *Star Wars* trilogy.
URL ftp://sounds.sdsu.edu/sounds/movies/starwars

GAMES

A Republic Against an Empire Fifteen years after the Battle of Endor, the small Imperial factions left are united under a mysterious leader, Grand Admiral Calion. Calion stages a stunning assault on the New Republic base and drives the Republic presence back, announcing the return of the Empire, renamed the Great Calion Empire (GCE). As you enter the story, the clash between GCE and the New Republic has begun... Choose a side in the current episode of this RPG, read up on its history, and may the Force (or the Admiral) be with you.
WEB http://www.stic.net/users/genesa/page1.htm

Beyond Hyperspace A *Star Wars* RPG Sourcebook provided by David A. Kanger (better known to some of you as Genghis902). This RPG resource contains characters, settings, and events created for a *Star Wars* RPG campaign run during David's high school years.
WEB http://studentweb.tulane.edu/~kanger/sw/hypspace.html

Jedi Academy Interested in bringing back the ancient knowledge of the Jedi Knights and in learning how to use the Force wisely? This Academy fosters your abilities and teaches you to use them to help the New Republic, in the tradition of the Jedi Knights who kept peace and order in the Old Republic for a thousand generations. Those who show aptitude for piloting spacecraft will want to attend the Starfighter Training School.
WEB http://home.ptd.net/~ralph/jedi.html

Rebel Assault I/II When the force just isn't enough, you'll find cheat codes, tricks, and tips to help you on your latest mission, courtesy of Doug "Slug" Merian.
WEB http://acm.cs.umn.edu/~slug/rebel

rec.arts.sf.starwars.games Dark Forces, X-Wing, Tie Fighter, Rebel Assault I & II. There's certainly no lack of software for the would-be Jedi with a computer. And here all the games are discussed in full, right down to the best joystick for each. Veteran pilots help newbies straighten up and fly right while Han Solo wanna-bes (who clearly don't see enough of the outdoors) share their secret starfighter maneuvers. Discussion also includes RPGs and there's always some spillover from the collectors newsgroup.
USENET rec.arts.sf.starwars.games

Sabacc Sabacc is a card game played with a deck of 76 cards. In the *Star Wars* universe, this game is played with an electronic deck in which the cards change value due to electronic impulses. In cyberspace, it's a bit simpler—you just need a mouse and a browser. Make like Han Solo (you'll remember how he won the Falcon from Lando playing Sabacc) and try your hand at any number of the versions of the game available here. You may need a little time to get used to the new suits (staves, sabers, flasks, and coins), ranked cards, and face cards.
WEB http://gamera.syr.edu:3456/sabacc

Star Wars Adventure Database A database of adventures, players, and personalities collected from SWRPG players and GMs.
WEB http://www.mgl.ca/~burnett/sw/sw1.htm

Star Wars Arcade Game There's something sentimental about playing the 1983 arcade game version of *Star Wars*. Relive arcade and *Star Wars* chic all at once and download the software version here. To make the atmosphere complete, download the *Star Wars* Theme and a wish from Obi-Wan.
WEB http://magenta.com/~jess/starw.htm

Star Wars Miniatures Battles Page Players and GMs around the world will appreciate this handy reference on the *Star Wars* Miniature Battles game. The Imperial information here covers troop

lists, weapons, vehicles, skills, and rules—a welcome resource when your game manual isn't readily available.
WEB http://www.webzone.net/bvogle/swmb/swmb.htm

Star Wars RPG Home Page Similar to the West End role-playing game in form, this *Star Wars* RPG enacts events and scenarios that West End mostly uses as background. Rather than running adventures with already written events like the Galactic Civil War or the Battle of Endor as a background, new settings are created here. If that intrigues your Imperial sensibilities, stop here to find out how to join the *Star Wars* RPG Club.
WEB http://www.webcom.com/jperry

Star Wars Sim Forum In an attempt to bring the *SW* simming universe to those on AOL, this forum maintains message boards on the Alliance and the Empire, software libraries, and information on how to join in the fun.
AMERICA ONLINE *keyword* star wars

X-Wing vs. Tie Fighter The ultimate *Star Wars* shoot-out. Lucas Arts is finally embracing multi-player gaming and you and your friends can suit up for the battle between the Empire and the Rebel Alliance. But here you'll only get a preview. For the goods, you'll have to pay a visit to your favorite software or shareware source.
WEB http://www.indirect.com/www/gomez/fgn2/xvstie.html

▶ HUMOR

Everything I've Ever Learned, I Learned From Star Wars A thread from the *Star Wars* newsgroup including 300 Imperial insights. For instance: "Never trust men in dark helmets." Or "Always check the backgrounds of people you want to get intimately involved with—they may be your relatives." And the ever-relevant "When parking your spaceship, make sure you aren't in the stomach of a huge worm-like monster."
WEB http://www.cc.gatech.edu/people/home/ccraig/everything.html

▶ MARKETPLACE

Gus Lopez's Star Wars Collector's Archive Who would have thought your old Han Solo action figure would be worth so much? One of the main online sites for *Star Wars* collectors, the Lopez archive includes price lists, product descriptions, and a brief history of merchandise related to the film. With extraordinary attention to detail, this site concentrates on Kenner action figures, but also lists other toys, and much of the collectors' information is nicely illustrated.
WEB http://www.cs.washington.edu/homes/lopez/collectors.html

rec.arts.sf.starwars.collecting As you might imagine, here adults mourn *Star Wars* action figures lost, destroyed, stolen, or tortured by terrorist siblings during their childhoods while other cyberactive collectors wax nostalgic over their first *SW* toy. More utilitarian threads in this active newsgroup focus on collecting, trading, and selling.
USENET rec.arts.sf.starwars.collecting

Star Wars Collectors' Bible Maybe you have all the Kenner toys and the 20th Century Fox publicity materials. Maybe you have the Princess Leia earmuffs. But have you laid your hands on *Star Wars: A Collection of Ten Prints* by Gene Day, published in Canada only by Aardvark-Vandheim Press? Well, unless you want to be just like every other obsessive collector of all things *Star Wars*, you had better hurry on over to the Collectors' Bible, where you'll find a detailed list of *Star Wars* merchandise organized alphabetically by company.
WEB http://www.cis.ohio-state.edu/~thurn/SWB

GEORGE LUCAS

LONG AGO, IN THE GALAXY YOU INHABIT, GEORGE Lucas expected *Star Wars* to fail miserably. In 1977, he left the country, rather than experience the humiliation he thought would accompany opening weekend. But as every droid knows, the film was a worldwide blockbuster, became an instant classic, spawned two massively successful sequels, and made Lucas a household name. Clearly George's talent far outshines his judgment.

Online, Lucas is a near-deity and, accordingly, his worshippers never tire of telling the story of his life. At the **George Lucas Biography**, find out that there is more to the man than Jedi. Learn that in 1971 Lucas took his first steps in sci-fi with *THX 1138*, a vision of a soulless future; that in 1973 he wrote and directed *American Graffiti*; and that in 1979 he was sucked into *More American Graffiti*.

At the just-plain-votive extreme there is the irresistable, **George Lucas Thank You Page**. "This page is a thank you to the creator of *Star Wars*. The man whom we all want to live forever, so his stories may continue." **Lucas: In Front of the Camera** shows the how he made his epoch-marking movie, and in the 1995 **Interview With George Lucas** the director reflects on his '70s success story.

With the 1980s came successful collaborations with Steven Spielberg (the Indiana Jones series,) and, increasingly, the title of Executive Producer. It also brought an unfortunate association with mondo-flops (remember *Howard the Duck*?) However, in 1992, Lucas was rightfully honored at the Academy Awards with a lifetime achievement award.

An essay about Lucas' film career, **George Lucas: The Creative Impulse**, reveals just how much he and his companies have contributed to cinema, especially in the area of special effects. The most special of these is the billions of dollars of revenue he has earned, cash which may have urged him to give something back. In 1991 he founded **The George Lucas Educational Foundation**, whose excellent Web site contains audio clips of Lucas discussing its mission, to make education more entertaining. If Lucas makes learning a fraction as entertaining as his films, he can be forgiven the godlike status he now commands.

Launch pad

George Lucas Biography
http://www.wilpaterson.edu/home/students/glyn/lucas.htm

George Lucas Thank You Page
http://www.outreach.com/~starwars/lucas.html

Lucas: In Front of the Camera
http://phymat.bham.ac.uk/BennetMN/starwars/glthumb.html

Interview with George Lucas
http://www.cs.wku.edu/~jcherry/lucas.html

George Lucas: The Creative Impulse
http://www.cwrl.utexas.edu/~daniel/309m/project4/christal

The George Lucas Educational Foundation
http://glef.org

THE X-FILES

MORE THAN ANY OTHER RECENT television show, Fox's *X-Files* has captured the imagination of sci-fi fans around the world. With its blend of the paranormal, the classic girl-guy detective story, government conspiracies, and the just-plain-nasty, this show manages to touch all of our deepest fears while maintaining a gloss of sophistication and wit. The two stars, David Duchovny and Gillian Anderson, are possibly the most popular actors among netizens—we know, at least, that Anderson was recently voted the sexiest woman on the Web in a newsgroup poll, beating *Lois and Clark*'s Teri Hatcher by a few thousand votes. Other more minor characters are just as admired, and *X-Files* pictures and sound clips are coveted treasures. X-Phile-dom knows no bounds, and fantastic fan pages number in the hundreds. When it comes to the Web, the truth is really out there.

▶ CLICK PICK

Official X-Files Site The Fox official *X-Files* site is subtle marketing disguised as a fan page, but you knew that already and, if those in control are going to amuse us this well… Also, because it's legal promotion, we know that the copyright hit men won't be stalking it as they do the sites created by dispensable fans. So put on your trench coat, grab some sunflower seeds, and go "undercover" to meet creator Chris Carter, the writers, directors, and special effects crew. This section also provides slick info about Scully, Mulder, Skinner, Cancer Man and the rest of the gang. Classified Tapes offers vid clips from "Pilot," "Deep Throat," "Conduit," "Ice," "Fallen Angel," and "Eve." X-Quest (an interactive simulation) and X-Sightings (fan merchandise and Operation X, an excellent trivia contest) round out this conspiracy to make you watch no other show. Except, of course, *Millenium*, Chris Carter's other pet project.
WEB http://www.foxhome.com/trustno1

▶ MOTHERSHIPS

Ben's X-Files Page Like most *X-Files* fan pages, Ben's is black and green, but few have such an interesting collection of international *X* links as this one does. Sounds, pictures, trivia, the whole works—even links to the CIA, NASA, and Rome Air Force Base, for "rumored UFO research."
WEB http://web2.iadfw.net/~brk/x-files

Bureau of Federal Investigation—X Files Division Do you have a governmental security clearance? Or can't you even get past the metal detectors at the airport? Either way, you'll enjoy this site. Somebody with way too much time on his hands has made an awesome version of a top secret government agency's files. Get past the first password-protected page (don't be intimidated, just enter any old thing) and into the heart of *The X-Files* Division. FAQs, images, newsgroup archives, episode guides, and more are waiting for you.
WEB http://www.ssc.com/~roland/x-files/x-files.html

IDDG X-Files "The truth is here." Yeah, yeah, yeah. After a while, these pages start to look the same. But this one has particularly good links to articles that have appeared in magazines and newspapers. And the links are blue instead of green. Wow! This just mocks convention at every turn.
WEB http://www.rahul.net/ziggyb/www/x-files.html

The Official X-Files Web Site The mysterious agency which has created this other official site is rumored to have something to do with Fox Television. Is it a trap? Will an unsuspecting special agent be kidnapped by aliens from the marketing department? Will they spend, spend, spend in the online merchandise store? No. An anonymous source has told us that the site is safe if you trust no one (and cut up your credit cards).

Listen to Sunset Boulevard's talking *X-Files* billboard (the entire file is 20 minutes long), find out about Chris Carter or the characters, and read an extensive episode guide. Finally, take a test and (possibly) win a T-shirt. There's more here, but we have to have enough plot for next week.

WEB http://www.thex-files.com

Purity Controlled Webpage There's no shortage of creative approaches to *X-Files* fan sites, and this one has incorporated one of the most charming and alarming, a JavaScript warning that looks just like a "real" computer error message. Other than that, this page has more of the typical stuff—all in that *X-Files* mandatory green on black.

WEB http://www.halcyon.com/mulder /xfiles.html

Terminal X By far one of the best (if not the best) multimedia-packaged fan sites available. Terminal X is neither overpowered by animations over content nor does it shortchange animation-lovers. It is colorful and comprehensive—a rarity on the Net. Read an *X-Files* comic book, visit a government agency or two, and get all the usual graven images, clips, and articles. Trust us, this is a must-see.

WEB http://www.neosoft.com/sbanks /xfiles/xfiles.html

To the X This may be the only site on the Web where X-philes can see Scully morph into Mulder right on the screen. It's almost all Shocked, so proceed no further than the home page if you don't have the necessary plug-ins. But do visit, because there's a long series of excerpts from an exclusive January '95 interview with David Duchovny—the author of the page is making it last.

WEB http://www.hmg.com/staff/rick/x

The Truth is Here Just when you think you've seen a list of all *The X-Files* sites in the world, you get that nagging feeling. Australia, Europe, the odd bit of U.S. of A. There must be another enclave of fans somewhere. You suddenly remember Canada. Aliens must have abducted all thoughts of the Great White North from your brain; how else do you explain your egregious oversight? You rush to the computer, eager to analyze the Canadian perspective on the actions of Agents Mulder and Scully. Luckily you find this list of Canadian *X-Files* links, and you will sleep soundly. For now.

WEB http://gpu3.srv.ualberta.ca/~vichan /www/x-files.html

The X-Files This is the place to find details of every episode of The *X-Files*. Plot summaries, cast list, writers— they're all here—with hot-linked names and searchable text. Upcoming shows, both in the U.S. and Australia (which is on a different show cycle) are previewed in detail. This is also your source for images, as these Aussies have loaded over 600 different pics for your perusal. The show may warn viewers to "Trust no one," but make an exception. These folks will deliver the goods.

WEB http://muse.cs.mu.oz.au:8089/xfiles2 .html

X-Files Germany Break out a new manila folder, because it's definitely a global conspiracy! This German page links up (in English, fortunately) to all the best FAQs, pictures, sounds, links, videos, fan fiction, and more.

WEB http://www.unix-ag.uni-kl.de /~kleinhen/xfiles/x-files.html

X-Files Home Page Audio clips of the theme music and second-season promo, along with dozens of links to FAQs, FTP areas, episode guides, cast information, and fan club data. This page (and the X-Philes who created it) has been around a long time, so it can be counted on for a mature and knowledgeable collection.

WEB http://www.rutgers.edu/x-files.html

X-Files: Operation Paperclip Some applause for Toby Cook, the man with the ability to index! Operation Paperclip is in table format (very readable) and sorted into 14 divisions. Soon, it will also be an *X-Files* search engine of sorts, with reviews of fan sites and other pages by visitors to Paperclip. Cook's

site is on its way to being the easiest to use of *X-Files'* sites.
web http://www.powerup.com.au/~tcook/xfiles.html

X-Files: Trust No One! "You know you're an X-Phile when… you won't even go NEAR a porta-potty." That's just some of the wisdom to be gleaned from this fan page's list of clues to your own addiction. Plus, you can download the entire *X-Files* opening sequence in .AVI form, or just copy an odd, wet-look picture of Gillian or one of David as a happy little boy.
web http://www.wam.umd.edu/~kris

X-page What lies beneath that rare and beautiful long-haired Scully photo, or the nasty shot of Mulder squinting in the sun? Why, it's more green links to the X-ification of the Web! Tollef Biggs has made it easy for you to vote for your favorite character, see a humongous list o' links to X-elsewhere, a Scully and/or Mulder FAQ, and pictures galore. There's even an outline for every single episode aired since that fateful day, Sept. 10, 1993.
web http://www.nbn.com/people/eddieb/believe.html

▶ MULDER

The David Duchovny Photo Gallery Hang onto your hats and your libido, ladies, because devoted fan Miri has scanned in our David in every sexy pose you can imagine—even one à la Luke Perry. The best thing, besides those oh-so-ladylike pastel colors, is that the photos are in thumbnails first, so your browser won't die.
web http://www.eden.com/~miri/photos.html

David Duchovny's Home Page No, it's not really. But if he wanted it, he could have it (along with its creator, no doubt). A worshipping fan has placed a sexy picture, an autograph, and links to just about every interview and article about the very special agent from the last few years.

web http://duggy.extern.ucsd.edu/~linny/David.html

DDEB (David Duchovny Estrogen Brigade) First they loved Patrick Stewart, but that all changed in January, 1994, after half-a-season of X-viewing. Now they're the oldest and most exclusive email fan club devoted (almost) whole-heartedly to the man behind Mulder. They swear they're "not nuts," and they even talk about women's issues from time to time. They must be entertaining, because they have spawned two other clubs: DDEB2 and DDEB3. All three are now closed to new members, but provide plenty of David-data, fan fiction (most involving a woman discovering him near death, nursing him back to health, etc.), and other free goodies.
web http://www.exit109.com/~fazia/DDEB.html

The Definitive David Duchovny FAQ Sheet Definitive, possibly. Unbiased? Not on your life! This FAQ is a product of the ever-swooning David Duchovny Estrogen Brigade, and thus contains every minute detail about this "uncommonly gifted actor" as part of the DDEB's mission "to serve David." This FAQ is full of the answers to such burning questions as "Does David believe in UFOs?" (No) and the breed of his dog Blue (mixed Border Collie).
web http://www.webcom.com/munchkyn/ddfaq.html

The Fox Mulder Studio Twenty-four photos of the Duke can be found here. The best part about this collection is the filenames for the photos, like "Blinky" and "1000mStare." Make sure to read them before clicking.
web http://www.t-i-p.com/gapg/media/FMS/FMS.html

▶ SCULLY

Gillian Anderson NeuroTransmitter Association Post-feminism and *Baywatch* notwithstanding, there are many women who dream of being loved for their brains and not their bodies. To them, Gillian Anderson is a beacon in the wilderness, living proof that on TV a woman can be admired for her mind. Sure, she's beautiful, but in her own way. What she has is a brain, or at least, in the part of brainy Dana Scully, she is absolutely credible. GANTA is a group of men and women (mostly men, we suspect) who thought there was too much testosterone flying around the Net. Now, like their heroine, they will find rational explanations for bloopers, and be the rational voice in newsgroups. Oh, yes, and love, love, love Gillian, that sexy babe. Ahem.

WEB http://www.interlog.com/~tigger /ganta.html

The Gillian Anderson Page It's nice to look at and fun to use, too! This annotated set of links and pictures is the closest thing to absolutely reliable that a fan of Ms. Anderson can find. In other words, it emphasizes quality over quantity, a balanced counterpoint to the super-comprehensive Mulder... It's Me site. Subscribe to a mailing list, read an interview or two, and even mourn the loss of a formerly-posted yearbook page of you-know-who.

WEB http://gpu3.srv.ualberta.ca /~mlwalter/GAHP.html

The Gillian Anderson Photo Gallery Here's the source for pictures of Gill, be they video captures or magazine shots. Don't miss the series of Duchovny, Anderson, and David's dog Blue in bed, having a "three-fur-all."

WEB http://www.t-i-p.com/gapg/gallery .html

Gillian Anderson Testosterone Brigade They're the second in a long line of X-philes naming themselves after body secretions, after the original DDEB. But they're absolutely sincere in their love for GA, as this page shows. A photo gallery, a sound page, and links are what this private email club has to offer, as well as a justification that Gillian is "not another bimbo chasing after criminals in high heels." This of course begs the question: Does she ask them to take off

their shoes first?

WEB http://www.bchs.uh.edu/~ecantu /GATB/gatb.html

Mulder, It's Me...The Gillian Anderson Link Pages Gracing this page, along with a lovely photo of Gillian dressed for the opera, are 181 (count 'em!) links to GA sites on the Web. The site's creator has collected (he hopes) not just some, but ALL the sites dealing with our favorite agent and doctor of forensic medicine. Fans will want to leave this site open all the time—easy, since clicking on a link opens a new browser.

WEB http://cygnus.rsabbs.com/~kwitzig /gillian.html

► SKINNER

Mitch Pileggi Estrogen Brigade A must-see for those who eschew the overexposed stars and prefer instead the quiet, often mysterious A.D. Skinner. Fan fiction, an FAQ, a mailing list, chat transcripts and much, much more can be found here.

WEB http://www.pe.net/~mpeb

Office of the Assistant Director He's "quietly intense" and "fence-straddling." He's a "complex and fascinating creation." He's Skinner, he's "Mitchly" and this is his page in which he has played a small, behind-the-scenes role. Read an exclusive interview or the bibliography compiled by M.P. himself, plus reviews, photos, and more.

WEB http://www.tpoint.net/~rmayhall

► THE OTHERS

Deep Throat Talks He's been dead since the first season, but Deep Throat and Jerry Hardin, the actor who plays him, haven't gone away. This interview is from late 1995.

WEB http://www.ecr.mu.oz.au/~simc/xf /articles/TV_Week.Nov4,1995.html

The Lair of the Rat Did Krycek really starve to death in a top secret military facility (silo #1013, of course) after oozing alien all over the place? Was "Apoc-

rypha" Nicholas Lea's last episode? Don't bet on it. The seemingly innocent FBI agent-turned-Ratboy has overcome such obstacles before. Everybody loves a villain, right? (Even if he did kill Melissa.)
web http://weber.u.washington.edu/~kmrobrts/rat.html

Nicholas Lea (Alex Krycek) Hey, copyright violation! Some enterprising X-phile has typed up the recent *Entertainment Weekly* interview with Nicholas Lea, a.k.a. Ratboy. Did you know that he used to date Melissa Scully in real life? Then his character killed her on the show. This must have been a break-up they will talk about for years.
web http://vivanet.com/~ferrellm/nicholas.html

The Stupendous Yappi Homepage He's the world's premier psychic, so the hosts of the Psychic Friends Network had better watch out. But put down that phone, because the Stupendous Yappi is really only the hilarious and possibly charlatan Fox Mulder double who has appeared in two *X-Files* episodes. Why is he so similar in size and shape to Mulder? Because Jaap Broeker, the actor who plays Yappi, is David Duchovny's stand-in.
web http://cyberstation.net/~mariah/yappi.html

William B. Davis (Cigarette Smoking Man, Cancer Man) Fit as a flea, he water-skis and doesn't smoke at all, but his nicotine-wreathed screen persona is generally described as "malevolent." Who is the man behind the Morleys? Find out in this brief interview, taken from *Entertainment Weekly*'s special on *The X-Files*.
web http://vivanet.com/~ferrellm/william.html

> **EPISODE GUIDES**

JYW's Domain—The X-Files For totally subjective, humorous reviews and ratings of episodes, visit JYW. He's an X-phile who actually dares to miss an episode once in a while.

web http://www.naples.net/~nfn04195/x-files.html

The X-Files Episode Guide This is the ultimate amateur episode guide, referenced by everyone and written by superfan Cliff Chen. It's in unattractive ASCII format, but for the detailed dirt (including an FAQ and lots of miscellaneous resources and information) it can't be missed. When you get bored reading the summaries in English, you can finish the rest in Finnish. If you ever find an X-Files trivia contest that requires answers in Finno-Ugric, you know where to go.
web http://bird.taponline.com/~cliff

> **CHAT**

alt.tv.x-files Doubt not that this is a big and active newsgroup; posts by the dozens accumulate here each day. And doubt not that some pathetic little peon at the FBI is monitoring this newsgroup for signs of real government conspiracy activists. (Paranoid? No, not us.) Alt.tv.x-files is a fantastic starting ground for those who love *The X-Files* and those who really love *The X-Files*. Recent threads concern a vicious rumor that the aliens, oops, executives at FOX are conspiring to pull non-Official X-philes sites from their exalted Web thrones. Say it ain't so!
usenet alt.tv.x-files
FAQ: **web** http://bird.taponline.com/~cliff/20q.txt

The X-Files on CIS Not much strangeness here, not much strangeness here, but it's a hot spot for X-fans, nonetheless. Topics include "Why we like Mulder," "Top 10 X-Files Eps Poll," "anti-Philes," and "You converted me!" Mulder's got lots and lots of fans here. If he ever shows up at a CompuServe face-to-face, he'd better wear rip-protected clothing. Opinions? "Gorgeous." "Incredibly cute." Enough already! These fans have a cult-like allegiance to their show, and they want others to share it; they brag about getting their friends hooked. The libraries include an episode guide, a glossary for acronyms often used in posts about the show, and *X-Files* lyrics for Christmas carols like "Silent Night" and "Frosty the Snow-man" (sounds subversive, don't you think?).

COMPUSERVE *go* sfmedtwo→Libraries *or* Messages→The X-Files

X-Files Forum X-philes and AOL-aholics rejoice! The popular *X-Files* Forum is one-stop shopping for any X-topic. Find out where Anderson and Duchovny were last seen in print or in person—did rabid fans rush the stage? How was the latest con? Check out the discussion boards, with their tens of thousands of post-ings—is David Duchovny leaving the show? Why do we love Flukeman so much? Files of photos, live chat, and ever so much more are here.

AMERICA ONLINE *keyword* scifi→X-Files Forum

▶ DIVERSIONS

alt.binaries.x-files Fans never seem to get enough of Dana and Spooky, and this newsgroup provides them in spades. Plus, there seems to be a gen-uine underground trade in dubious pics of Gillian Anderson naked and perform-ing various lewd acts. They don't even look like her! Posters to this newsgroup also provide sounds, screensavers, and off-topic questions. It's a grab bag.

USENET alt.binaries.x-files
FAQ: **WEB** http://www.cris.com/~tof

Songs in the Key of X If a CD containing music "inspired by" a TV show doesn't make you smell exploitation and market-ing conspiracy, then you'll no doubt love *Songs in the Key of X*. The music, how-ever dubiously related to the *Files*, is excellent. Visit the CD's official Web site to listen to samples, and link to informa-tion about the videos.

WEB http://www.wbr.com/x-files

X Files Sound-O-Rama The ultimate source for just about any line spoken by Mulder or Scully at any point, in any episode, in any season. From the sub-lime ("I've seen stranger things, believe me.") to the ridiculous ("Mango-kiwi tropical swirl, now we know we are deal-ing with a madman!"). As Scully says in Piper Maru, "I'm just constantly amazed by you."

WEB http://www.bchs.uh.edu/~ecantu /xfsounds

X-Files Theme There are plenty of places to download the notably creepy theme song to *The X-Files*, but not all are clear and most are only partial. This is the whole thing, in .WAV format.

WEB http://rschp2.anu.edu.au:8080 /XFsounds/xfilesth.wav

▶ FAN FICTION

alt.tv.x-files.creative Since the series has a nasty habit of leaving its plots open-ended, fans are wont to fill in the blanks with creative efforts of their own. While some stick close to formula— madmen, extraterrestrials, and the para-normal—others strike out for parts unknown.

USENET alt.tv.x-files.creative

The X-Files Creative Archive Where do posts from alt.tv.x-files.creative go to die? Nowhere. Instead, they are posted here to live into perpetuity. Topics range from erotic (Mulder and Scully do it a hundred different ways) to comic. If you need more than a dozen episodes per season to get your full X-fix, try reading some of these creative efforts.

WEB http://gossamer.eng.ohio-state .edu/x-files

▶ GAMES

The Basement One of three home pages for the IRC *X-Files* Sim. This page con-tains the weekly newsletter, a typical sim log, and scads of information for new players and those who have taken to the game with a passion. Plus, there's a hot tub!

WEB http://members.gnn.com/abbebeck /basement.htm

Kennedy Ryan's Homepage This third page for *The X-Files* Sim is a comple-

ment to the others. Find out about the characters who participate, past and present cases, and detailed general information.
WEB http://www.inxpress.net/~paisans/Kenedy'sHomePage

X-Files Sim If you have access to IRC and have nothing to do on a Friday night, perhaps you'd like to chase aliens? This simulation game makes you an FBI agent, and unlike the X-Quest you'll actually have some control over the outcome. Read all about the paranormal goings-on at the Sim's home page, and while you're at it, create a character and take the opportunity to become an online blue flame from Quantico.
WEB http://www.ime.net/~pbreshe/Sue'sPage.html

X-Quest "The FBI needs your assistance!" Apparently, Scully and Mulder are too busy being TV stars to handle all *The X-Files*, so the FBI is recruiting you to help. Fill out the application and when you're accepted, begin your first case. You need Netscape 2.0 and Shockwave to play, and each case consists of a case file and Shockwave puzzles to solve.
WEB http://www.tcfhe.com/trustno1/low/quest/qmains.html

▶ TRIVIA

The Conspiracies (i.e. Inside Jokes) A text version of all those inside jokes and nudge-nudge references from *The X-Files*. It seems as if the writers have never named a character without referencing someone's daughter, spouse, or dog. A fascinating look at all the stuff you never knew.
WEB http://www.halcyon.com/mulder/sidenotes.html

Inside Jokes and References Why so many 1013 and 10:13s? What's up with 11:21? Is it ever any other time when Scully and Mulder look at their watches? Did you know that the Piper Maru is named after Gillian Anderson's daugh-

ter? Read this page to be in-the-know about all those inside jokes.
WEB http://www.winternet.com/~dbrekke/xfjokes.html

X-Files Quiz Think you're an X-phile? Take this pretty impossible ten-question quiz and find out.
WEB http://www.guernsey.net/~spaceman/page11.html

SCI-FI SCREEN A-Z

DID YOU STAY HOME FROM WORK the day Brigitte Helm passed away? When you start gushing over *Fantastic Voyage*, do people think you're talking about the Coolio album? Do you have a laminated ID card proving you're an agent of The OSI? Have you ever been drummed out of a sci-fi con for trying to hoist up a pirate *Tomorrow People* booth? Despite what merchandisers believe, fandom isn't exclusively the territory of *Star Wars* and *Star Trek*. Obsession runs just as deep in fans whose taste intrudes into the more obscure corners of the sci-fi universe. You may think that no one else in the virtual world has a small shrine to Sally Knyvette in their linen closet, but you're wrong. The Web is a big place, and while you may not have time to trawl through cyberspace for that blipvert download from *Max Headroom*, you'll find its Nethome here.

TV Century 21 The Gerry Anderson Home Page "Spectrum is Green," "Yus m'lady," "Anything Can Happen in the Next Half Hour!" "Thunderbirds Are Go!" If you know nothing of these mantras then blessed are you for there is a world of "Fanderson" to be explored and myriad videos to rent. If, on the other hand, you are steeped in the lore of master Supermarionator Gerry Anderson, familiar with the voice of his wife Sylvia ("Oh, Paaahka"), and know your favorite Thunderbird, then this is a cyberstep to heaven. Webmeister Wickes demonstrates an obsessive attention to detail you can revel in even as you take comfort in the fact that yours is not so intense.
WEB http://www.netaxs.com/~wickes/tv21 .html

► 12 MONKEYS

12 Monkeys Talk about the power of promotion. This first-class site is truly interactive; it has the feel of a CD-ROM. Register as a volunteer and find out that "Prison Block 675/B accepts no liability for personal injury to volunteers, whether physical or psychological in origin." Then, tour through such areas as a decontamination unit and the streets of Philadelphia. Get close to the bulletin board in the engine room and read news clippings about the disappearance of Dr. Kathryn Railly (Madeleine Stowe). There are interviews and movie clips available, and you can even read excerpts from Jack Lucas's book, *Vanishing Act: The Making of 12 Monkeys*. That is, if you can find it. (Hint: broken window.)
WEB http://www.mca.com/universal _pictures/12/index.html

12 Monkeys Did you know that the story of *12 Monkeys* is just a pumped-up version of the haunting 27-minute classic *La Jetée* by Chris Marker? The writer includes story details such as this in his review and also gives extensive credit to director Terry Gilliam, as well as to the actors for a job well-done. Robert Horton's review is brief and less than positive, but includes Gilliam info.
WEB http://www.film.com/film/reviews /T/twelve.monkeys.horton.html
• http://www.film.com/reviews/t/twelvem .simanton.html

FAQ—12 Monkeys "Who is Ms. Jones, Insurance?" The short FAQ, composed by screenwriters David Peoples and Janet Peoples, addresses such questions as, "Why does Jose give Cole a gun?" and "Is Ricky Neuman, the boy in the pipe, really Cole?" But as they say, "there are no right or wrong answers when it comes to *12 Monkeys*, so your personal interpretation is as valid as any other." This being the case, is there any reason why you should not be writing million-dollar screenplays?
WEB http://www.mca.com/universal _pictures/12/faq.html

Screen Saver Bring the future to your desktop with two different versions of a

12 Monkeys screen saver. PCs only. Shower scene not included.
web http://www.uip.com/twelvemonkeys/index.html

⟩ 1984

1983 Continues—Film Version to Orwell's Atmosphere This page offers the only Web content related to the film version of George Orwell's bleak tale of the future is at this site, so it's probably just as well that it takes a positive view—ironic, isn't it? Taken from MIT's school paper, author Lauren Seely writes, "Unlike many film versions of books, *1984* is true to the Orwellian vision. Every scene, from Winston's comfortless apartment to the crowded dining halls in the Ministry of Truth complete with surveillance screen, reeks of a totalitarian, inhuman society." Seely also comments on the laudable performances by John Hurt, Richard Burton, and Suzanna Hamilton.
web http://the-tech.mit.edu/V105/N3/1984.03a.html

⟩ ALIEN NATION

Alien Nation A guide to all 22 episodes of *Alien Nation*'s first (and only) year. Learn intimate details about the experiences of the alien families who came to Earth—central California to be more exact. The author even included a Tenctonese translation guide (e.g., "jeffers" means "permission" and "vacwasta" is "understand").
url ftp.doc.ic.ac.uk/pub/media/tv/collections/tardis/us/sci-fi/AlienNation

The Alien Nation Home Page For fans of those bald-headed aliens of the West Coast, here's a place to land. In addition to scheduling events and fan talk, the creators of this site have documented the Newcomers' linguistic development to a frighteningly detailed extent. There's a lengthy report from a fan who got to be an extra, original fan fiction, and a couple of links. True believers will want a glass of sour milk while perusing. This home page is based in the UK, so be careful how you read the dates for discussion groups and conventions you find—they're Eurostyle.
web http://www.cms.dmu.ac.uk/~c2kd/tencton.html

Alien Nation Pics Good news *AN* Fans, there are to be three post-cancellation TV movies doing the rounds henceforth. While you wait, download photos of the cast from this handful of stills that seem to be scanned in from *Alien Nation* trading cards. Take your pick of .GIF or .JPG formats.
web http://www.uaep.co.uk/pages/alienph1.html

On Alien Nation "Well, yes, the Tenctonese seemed to be different in subtle ways, rather than gross ways. But that, I suspect, is what we'll find in real aliens," wrote Robert J. Sawyer, Canada's only native-born, full-time science-fiction writer. Here you'll find more of his thoughts on the show.
web http://www.greyware.com/authors/Sawyer/rmalienn.htm

Sci-Fi Channel: Alien Nation Not much more than a two-sentence summary of the show's idea, this page is handy for finding out what episodes will be airing monthly.
web http://www.scifi.com/aliennation

⟩ THE ARRIVAL

The Arrival Charlie Sheen takes a departure from his usual roles in this sci-fi flick. Download stills of the cast while reminiscing about Zane Zminski, the man who records a "shockwave" (an indication of extra-terrestrial life forms) but then falls victim to a government coverup plot. The film's official site has the same text, but also features a downloadable trailer.
web http://www.thearrival.com/b2.htm

⟩ BACK TO THE FUTURE

Back to the Future Sounds Download George McFly's historical battle cry, "Hey you… get your damn hands off her!"

WEB http://www.moviesounds.com/bttf
.html

Back to the Future Sounds Marty
McFly: "Hey Doc, we better back up. We
don't have enough road to get up to 88."
Doc Brown: "Roads? Where we're going
we don't need roads." This clip and
more (such as the Delorean skidding in
the Twin Pines Mall) are available here.
WEB http://www.xis.com/~hansolo/future
.html

Back to the Future...the Web Page The
only site you'll really ever need for *BTTF*
information. There are throrough biographies on all of the cast members, information on joining the worldwide fan club,
and even a time travel chronology of all
three films. *This Week in Hill Valley*, the
fan club's newsletter, includes cast members' upcoming online events. Well-
designed, well-written, and well worth
any fan's time. Its background image is
the famous California "OUTATIME"
license plate, and Deloreans zip around
and disappear. There are also links to
other *BTTF* sites, but you probably won't
need to visit them. Brilliant work.
WEB http://www.hsv.tis.net/~bttf/main
.htm

FAQ—Back to the Future A section of
Back to the Future... the Web page, this
FAQ is rich with information—questions
about all three films are answered by
Bob Gale and Robert Zemeckis, BTTF's
creators. A sample: "Q: When Marty
goes into the 'Blast from the Past'
antique store in 2015 to purchase the
Grays Sports Almanac, there is a man-
nequin in the store window that is wearing Marty's jean jacket from the first
film. What was the significance to this
subtle detail? A: We thought it was
funny, so we put it in—that's all! Just an
inside joke."
WEB http://www.hsv.tis.net/~bttf/bttf_faq
.htm

▶ BARB WIRE

Barb Wire Just don't call her "babe."
The companies behind *Barb Wire* have

assembled a hands-on site for Pamela
"Babewatch" Anderson's sci-fi flick; it's
got loads of goodies. Photos, film clips
(see "Pambo" in action), and a downloadable trailer are presented clearly. For
those who are interested in more than
Anderson's cleavage, there are links to
production notes and Dark Horse, the
company that first created the Barb Wire
comic. An alternate site is housed on a
server in the U.K.
WEB http://spider.media.philips.com/pfe
/barbwire • http://www.foresight.co.uk
/pfi/barb

Barb Wire Check out production notes.
Read about the town of Steel Harbor and
the Hammerhead Bar and Grille, the joint
owned by the tough-as-nails Barb Wire.
Listen to sound clips in Mac, .AU, .WAV,
or RealAudio formats. Download the
movie's trailer, which opens with the
tough gal statement: "In a world gone to
hell, even angels carry guns." Ho-hum.
WEB http://www.hollywood.com
/movies/barbwire/bsbarbwire.html

▶ BARBARELLA

Barbarella Homepage An absolute must
for those obsessed with Jane Fonda's
1968 cult classic. Catch up on the
adventures of the svelte heroine, as she
travels through space in search of
Durand-Durand. Read about her adventures with such characters as Pygar, Dil-
dano, and Professor Ping. Movie stills,
sound clips including the theme song,
cast, crew and production information,
as well as historical tidbits: We are told
that Fonda's "costumes were often more
than uncomfortable; her breasts and
waist were pushed into a transparent
mold." Duh.
WEB http://www.gem.valpo.edu/~cnavta
/Barbarella

**If You Travel Through Intergalactic
Space, Don't Forget Your Go-Go Boots**
This humor piece, written by one Kathy
Valladares, takes a special jab at Bar-
barella—the sexy, sci-fi spectacular. The
major critique, almost obviously, is of
Jane Fonda's rampant costume changes

(eight of them in the film) and what they might possibly symbolize. Good fun, courtesy of the *Chicago Tribune*.
WEB http://www.chicago.tribune.com/fun/badmov/barbar.htm

BATTLESTAR GALACTICA

Battlestar Galactica Episode Guides Do you remember the high-flying adventures of Apollo, Starbuck, Adama, and the rest of the characters that populated the Wings of outer space? This episode guide provides airdates, plot summaries, and full credits for every single *Galactica*, from the premiere (with guest stars Jane Seymour, Rick Springfield, and Lew Ayres) onward. Remember Muffitt the Daggett? How about those special appearances by Britt Ekland, Fred Astaire, and Randolph Mantooth? No? Well, refresh your memory here.
WEB http://mcmfh.acns.carleton.edu/BG/archives/guide.html

Battlestar Galactica Homepage Click here to find that rare thing—a slick site that uses high-concept graphics, yet respects the fact that information can travel the Web only at limited speed. Cleanly organized into archives, images, dialog and sound effects, fan-created stuff, and software, the site also includes the obligatory stuff about the campaign to revive the show.
WEB http://mcmfh.acns.carleton.edu/BG

Galactica 1980 Episode Guide Revived after a season's cancellation, *Battlestar Galactica* changed its face for the eighties, and this episode guide details the new look. Apollo is dead. Starbuck and Tigh are gone. Adama has a beard. But the adventures in space continue.
WEB http://mcmfh.acns.carleton.edu/BG/archives/guide80.html

Galactica Home Page "Leave no survivors." Cylon's quote seems appropriate, since this site aims to someday become the central repository for all things *Battlestar Galactica*. With a complete series FAQ, episode guides, fan registry, fan club information, sounds,

images, software, archives of the *Battlestar Galactica* Collection at TARDIS, and important information from the *Battlestar Galactica* revival campaign, it's well on its way.
WEB http://mcmfh.acns.carleton.edu/BG

BEWITCHED

Bewitched "Bewitched, Bewitched, You've got me in your spell, Bewitched, Bewitched, You know your craft so well, Before I knew what I was doing, I looked in your eyes, That brand of woo you've been brewin', Took me by surprise…" This, lest you are unaware of Nick at Nite or have no comprehension of the era known as "the '60s," is the first verse to the *Bewitched* theme song. It was wisely discarded so that the audience could concentrate on the credits and that hep animation. Other treats here include trivia that answers such questions as Who came up with the nose twitch? There's background info on all the cast and crew, with lots of sound clips coming soon. There's even a section where fans share their *Bewitched* stories: "*Bewitched* affected my life in a number of ways. It showed me that a woman could be powerful even if she was trapped in a sexist, 1960s-style traditional marriage."
WEB http://www.sappho.com/bewitchd

The Bewitched & Elizabeth Montgomery Page This has to be one of the most enthusiastic, comprehensive, and downright lovely fanatic pages on the Net. The memorabilia will make you salivate with envy—paper dolls, dress up dolls, coloring books, Halloween costumes, comics, board games, videos, autographs, even *TV Guide* covers (check out 1970, trippy, man!). Rare images include a group of stills from the famous pie fight episode, and an unbelievable wallpaper slide show of our beloved Sam goofing it up. The site author even owns a set of proof sheets (contact prints showing each frame of a shot, which is then marked for use). Now that's devotion. There's an episode guide with search engine, bios of the cast, and three fantastic articles—a *Cos-*

mopolitan feature on Elizabeth when she was just starting out, a *Time* article on the sitcom when it first aired, and a really strange interview from *Screen Stars* called "20 Mischievous Questions" which includes this kind of risqué repartee: "Q—As a typical American witch, could you tell us what your people generally think of sex? A—Well, we are in favor of it, provided that the proper conditions prevail—no lights and eerieness." But if you come here for one reason only, let it be the sound clip of Serena's "Iffin" song, in its entirety.
WEB http://www.erols.com/bewitchd /index.html

Nick At Night: Bewitched A really nice collection of character profiles, actor biographies, and an episode guide as well as lots of image and sounds. Magically transform your computer's alert sound to the noise of Sam's nose twinkle, pay attention to the very active BB called New Salem, where modern witches and warlocks chat about the show, give potion recipes, and debate various issues of the day. It's a very close knit group that meets for semi-live chat every week in a FAC—a Friday Afternoon Coven—where important questions are breached, such as the real differences between witches and genies. (For one thing, witches don't have to wear diaphanous bloomers, live in a bottle, or call their men "Master." Even in the '60s.)
AMERICA ONLINE *keyword* tv→Shows→ Bewitched

▶ BLAKE'S 7

Blake's 7 Blake, Avon, Vila, Jenna, Gan, Cally, and Zen—not exactly the Mickey Mouse Club. The creators of this site are really trying to establish a Web presence for the 1970s BBC series about the infamous group of interstellar terrorists trying to destroy the evil Terran Federation. A cast list with images and an incomplete (contributions requested) episode guide are available here.
WEB http://www.ee.surrey.ac.uk/contrib /SciFi/Blakes7

Blake's 7 A stateside tribute to the sci-fi series. The usual goodies—scripts, sound bites, an episode guide, and pictures are here, but so are a costume index and an investigative look into the origins of the character's names. ("Travis's is from the Old French and means 'from the crossroads.' Well, he certainly 'crossed the roads' of our heroes often enough, didn't he!") Bloopers, blunders, and fan club information can be found here as well.
WEB http://hawks.ha.md.us/blake7

Blake's 7 Main Page Did you happen to notice that in "Cygnus Alpha," Vargas appears to materialize somewhere to the left of the teleport bay? Bloopers are only a part of this well-designed page that's got tons of *Blake's 7* information. Photo galleries, an FAQ, and even a drinking game round out this writer's Web tribute to the show. This is the ultimate *Blake's 7* resource.
WEB http://ernie.bgsu.edu/~sclerc/Blakes7 .html
FAQ: **WEB** http://ernie.bgsu.edu/ ~sclerc /Faqs.html

▶ BRAZIL

Consuming Film Student Matthew Levy wrote a number of papers to help his understanding of a number of popular theorists. His works, which include "Foucault's *Brazil*," are gathered on this Web site. Stay away if you've wary of intellectual lingo; "Freudian analysis stands beside Marxism as an important tool of the Frankfurt school, and indeed psychoanalytic criticism is especially relevant in the case of *Brazil*, whose dream sequences represent a large part of the film," Levy writes.
WEB http://www.uta.edu/english/mal/con- sume/film.html

Hypermedia Brazil What does the singing telegram girl sing? What do all the signs say? This FAQ should help answer the most elusive questions, as well as the more obvious ones, such as "I didn't understand the film at all. What's it all about?" That's a tough one,

but the answer is thorough and includes informative quotes from director Terry Gilliam.
WEB http://www.minet.uni-jena.de/~erik/brazil

▶ BUCK ROGERS

Buck Rogers Remember those halcyon days of Buck Rogers? Handsome, wry Gil Gerard? Bewitching, seductive Erin Grey? And how about that little computer that sounded like the *Knight Rider* car and hung around the old guy's neck? Less serious than *Battlestar Galactica* and less sophisticated than *The Six Million Dollar Man*, Buck Rogers managed to become a huge hit, and has embedded itself in the consciousness of all twentysomethings—or at least most of us.
URL ftp://ftp.doc.ic.ac.uk/pub/media/tv/collections/tardis/us/sci-fi/BuckRogers

Buck Rogers in the 25th Century Did you know that the same actor, Buster Crabbe, played both Buck Rogers and Flash Gordon in their respective 1930s film serials? Crabbe's bio and other fascinating facts are all part of this history of Buck Rogers—from his inception in a 1928 serialized Armageddon novel, through his reincarnation (in the guise of actor Gil Gerard) in the 1979 movie and subsequent short-lived TV series, and to the character's current popularity as a role-playing game model. The site wilbl link you to a few of the games starring the twenty-fifth century's most famous hero.
WEB http://www.attistel.co.uk:8000/jnp/br25c.html

Buck Rogers in the 25th Century Follow Buck from his creation in the 1928 serial novel *Armageddon 2419 AD* through 1995's book *Buck Rogers: My Life in the Future*. Extra attention is paid (obviously) to the 1980s television series. Read or download synopses of every episode.
WEB http://www.kfs.org/~jpetry/br25c.html

Ektek, Inc. Presents Buck Rogers If you're willing to part with lots of bucks for collectibles from this sci-fi fave, this

company has the goods. If you've worn out your 1935 XZ-38 Disintegrator, this is where you can can buy a new one.
WEB http://www.starsystem.com/buckrogers

▶ BUCKAROO BANZAI

The Banzai Institute Blue Blaze Irregulars, whenever you need inspiration to carry on with your mission, take a tour around the Institute and surrounding areas. Yoyodyne offers extensive information, including images and sound files, on the Lectroid/Adder War and the two sanctions behind it. The Conference room offers info on other BB sites on the net, as well as one part of the press packet sent out by 20th Century Fox announcing the Banzai Intitute's cooperation with the studio in dramatizing one of Bukaroos adventures, this document gives the background info on Buckaroo and Professer Hikita. In the Lab, you'll find Dr. Caryl Sneider's paper on the movie's particle physics theories, the formula for the antidote to the Lectroid Electronic Brainwashing, quizzes and puzzles, and the offical answer to the Watermelon Question. The Bunker houses an interview with Peter Weller, the part of the press release giving background on the Cavaliers, Penny Priddy (and Peggy Priddy). The Garage offers sketches of the evolution of the jet car, and specs on the World Watch One bus. And World Watch one credits the original Team Banzai Fan Club, and offers links to other Banzai sites on the Net. One trip through the facilities will buck up your courage for anthing that comes your way. And remember everybody, wherever you go… there you are.
WEB http://bbs.annex.com/relayer/bbanzai.htm

Rafterman's Buckaroo Banzai Page "Treat me good, I'll treat you better; treat me bad, I'll treat you worse." So goes the motto of the Hong Kong Caveliers and the Blue Blaze Irregulars, warriors at Buckaroo's side in the fight to save us from ourselves, protect the planet, and thwart undue cruelty doled to crying, suicidal women in smoky nightclubs. Rafterman lives by this motto, and has taken it upon himself to provide this page full of links to information, articles, multimedia, mailing lists, and other Blue Blazer pages on the Net. Rafterman: helping him to help us.

WEB http://ourworld.compuserve.com /homepages/ecline/banzai.htm

Buckaroo Banzai BB The BBBB will tell you where to get a bootleg copy of the soundtrack, offers news on the occasional New York lounge act of Peter Weller and Jeff Goldblum (on jazz trumpet and piano), and speculates on who would play Buckaroo if there's ever a sequel. One fan endorses Adrian Paul of TV's *Highlander*, who, God knows, bears a striking resemblance, in appearence, voice, and mannerisms, to Peter Weller.

AMERICA ONLINE *keyword* fictional realms→ Message Boards →Science Fiction→ Films List Topics→Buckaroo Banzai

FAQ-Buckaroo Banzai While the FAQ doesn't ask or answer any narrative questions about the movie, it nevertheless offers background on Buckaroo, the Cavaliers, and the Blue Blazers, as well as the people who played them in the movie. It also tells you where to get the videos, LD, book, script; addresses the possibility of a sequel; and answers the infamous and ever popular Watermelon Question. No, I'm afraid this isn't shortcut. I'm not going to tell you the answer, monkeyboy; you're going to have to go and read the FAQ.

WEB http://www.slip.net/~figment/bb /bbindex.shtml

Buckaroo Banzai Script "You like Jerry Lewis, you give me hope to carry on, then you leave me in the lurch while you strap on your six guns." The one and only.

WEB http://kumo.swcp.com/synth/text /buckaroo_banzai_script

▶ CLOSE ENCOUNTERS / 3RD KIND

EARchive: Close Encounters "Do-do-do-do-doooo. Do-do-do-do-do." Oh,

come on. You know how it goes. This site offers just a handful of sound clips from the film, documenting our interaction with the pre-*E.T.* extra-terrestrials. That *Close Encounters* sound effect is there, of course. Visitors will still be required to create their own mysterious mountains out of plates of mashed potato, however.

WEB http://www.geocities.com/Hollywood /1158/closenc.html

Voyager: Close Encounters of the Third Kind It's 1977, and Teri Garr and Richard Dreyfuss act as our ambassadors to the alien visitors. The impact this film has had on most of us is probably immeasurable. If you want to check just how much, the Criterion Collection's advertisement for the movie features a few clips, along with an essay about the history and making of Steven Spielberg's ground-breaking sci-fi blockbuster. It's definitely an amazing story.

WEB http://www.voyagerco.com/CC/ph/p .closeencounters.html

▶ THE DAY THE EARTH STOOD STILL

The Day the Earth Stood Still Homepage This is one of the only Web sites for this influential 1950s sci-fi flick starring Michael Rennie as the alien Klaatu whose request for a government audience is denied. Not surprisingly, he gets pretty upset, although he doesn't allow that to affect his impeccable manners. Strangely, the site has nothing more than an overview of why the site was created and an incomplete cast list. Perhaps fans of the movie will put their knowledge of page design together and create a site that's out of this world. "Klaatu Barada Nikto." (Or: Shape up or ship out.)

WEB http://admin.inetport.com/~rgylford /klaatu.html

The Day the Earth Stood Still Sounds "Your choice is simple. Join us, and live in peace, or pursue your present course and face obliteration," Klaatu says as he threatens the complete annihilation of Planet Earth. His forceful ultimatum and a few other audio tidbits from the film are available, too.

WEB http://www.moviesounds.com /daystill.html

DEATH RACE 2000

Death Race 2000 "Did you ever drive down the road, see someone walking along the side, and say to a passenger, 'how many points do I get if I hit him/her?' Did you ever wonder where that particular sentiment came from?" For the uninitiated: a thorough review and synopsis of the film, starring David Carradine and Sylvester Stallone, which gave rise to the appreciation of pedestrian pummeling for prizes.

WEB http://www.midwest.net/scribers /willie/dr2000.htm

Death Race 2000 A humorous interpretation of the 1970s "classic." Read about Nero The Hero, Mathilda the Hun, Calamity Jane, Machinegun Joe Viturbo, and Frankenstein as The Trans-Continental Road Race is re-told in the present tense. Favorites such as the scoring system are presented, as well as the odds on each navigator and his car. Pretty scary stuff.

WEB http://www.mcn.net/~netrencher /dr2k.html

DR. STRANGELOVE

Dr. Strangelove "I can no longer sit back and allow Communist infiltration and indoctrination, Communist subversion, and the international Communist conspiracy to sap and impurify all of our precious bodily fluids…" General Jack D. Ripper loses his mind, succumbing to his theories of Communist conspiracy, and the world's fate lies in his hands. For years, fans have celebrated this film, another one of Stanley Kubrick's influential masterpieces. This black-and-white page, created by a fan, features audio clips and image files from the 1964 movie also known as *How I Learned to Stop Worrying and Love the Bomb*.

WEB http://www.lehigh.edu/~pjl2/films /strangelove.html

Monte's Dr. Strangelove Sound Page "If, on the other hand, we were to immediately launch an all-out and coordinated attack on all of their airfields and missile bases, we'd stand a good chance of catchin' 'em with their pants down." A nice-sized collection of audio samples from Kubrick's black (and white) comedy.

WEB http://xis.com/~dainjeur/ds.html

Voyager's Dr. Strangelove Released just two years after the Cuban Missile Crisis, Kubrick's film offered a shocking, yet brilliant way to look at what then seemed the imminent destruction of the planet as a direct result of human irrationality. Movie clips, images, and a great essay about the film are provided here for fans and those unfamiliar with the classic, no matter how different the world may now seem.

WEB http://www.voyagerco.com/CC/ph /p.strangelove.html • http://www .voyagerco.com/CC/sfh/strangelove.html

DUNE

alt.fan.dune "I was just thinking about this the other day, how Luke's [Skywalker] home planet, and Arrakis are very much the same. Both have fringe cultures, large dangerous animals, no surface water, and are deserts. I'm not sure what I'm trying to say, maybe George Lucas based his planet on Dune?" wrote a fan in a recent post to this active and interesting newsgroup. Discussion erupts about topics such as Arabic and Islamic themes in the movie, the director's cut, favorite characters, and even the latent homophobia.

USENET alt.fan.dune
FAQ: URL ftp://nctuccca.edu.tw/USENET /FAQ/alt/fan/dune

Dune Page The ultimate *Dune* site. Behind-the-scenes details, cast information, and even the entire script. Find cut scenes, mistakes, laser disc and soundtrack information, as well as links to other *Dune* sites on the Web.

WEB http://phymat.bham.ac.uk/BennetMN /dune/dune.html

Dune Sounds "I must not fear, fear is the mind killer." Two sets of sounds from the desert drama starring Sting, Kyle MacLachlan, Sean Young, and Jose Ferrer are available online. At the U. of Idaho site, you have the option of downloading many of them with the press of one button. (But be warned. That file is a not insignificant 1.76Mb, so make sure you really do want to press that button.)
WEB http://www.iig.com.au/~cns01019 /movies/dune/dune.htm • http://kuoi .asui.uidaho.edu:8000/~darkmark /dunewav.html

▶ E.T.

E.T.: The Extraterrestrial It doesn't get simpler (and, sadly, doesn't get more comprehensive) than these two sound clips. "E.T. phone home!" and "I'll be right here…" Where were you when red geraniums, flying bicycles, a closet full of stuffed animals, and Reese's Pieces first had something in common? For that matter, where were the Web heads? Too young to care?
WEB http://www.geocities.com/Hollywood /1158/et.html

▶ EARTH2

Earth2: A Gaian Hypothesis If you're not an *Earth2* fan—after all, there was almost no time to become one—but are thinking about it, read this guide to the show. You will then be an expert on all that is Terrian and human on Planet G889.
WEB http://www.arcade.uiowa.edu/proj /earth2/index.html

Earth2: A Journey of Second Chances There are some character backgrounds here, but they're mostly along the lines of "Alonzo was not to even set foot on the planet of G-889. But when he did, something extraordinary happened to him." Otherwise, there are some pictures, info about a related role-playing game, some links, and little else. Maybe this page will get a second chance.
WEB http://pages.prodigy.com/earth2 /earth2.htm

New Pacifica Reruns! We have reruns! *Earth2* fans are cheered by the news that the Sci-Fi Channel will be rerunning episodes—soon! Also cheering is this page, which contains an episode guide, actor bios, pictures, sounds, fan fiction, and fan club info. Also offered here are links to other *Earth2* sites and a how-to guide to help get the show back on the air. The show may be out of production, probably forever, but not out of its fans' hearts.
WEB http://www.serve.com/e2cheer /earth2.html

Save Earth2 Home Page Old habits die hard, and old fans never die at all. All the latest news about *Earth2* past, present, and future can be found at this framed and Shocked site. Subscribe to mailing lists—they'll keep you posted about the non-events leading up to the non-resurrection of the show. *E2* fans can find plenty of nostalgia in the form of sounds and synopses.
WEB http://ppsa.com/ppsa/e2/e2form .html

The Sci-Fi Site: Earth2 Devon Adair would never have left Earth1 if she knew that this stuff was available on the Net! Anything an *E2* fan might desire is here, from very recent news to photos and detailed descriptions of villains from Terrians to Gaal. (Funny, he looks an awful lot like Tim Curry.) A must-see.
WEB http://www.abacus.ghj.com/sci_fi /earth2/e2_main.htm

TV's Earth Mother Entertainment Weekly's December, 1994 profile of the actress Debrah Farentino, who plays the commander of the *E2* expedition to a new, alternate world.
WEB http://pathfinder.com/ew/941202 /scifi/251scifiE2bar.html

▶ ESCAPE FROM L.A.

Escape From LA This time, la la land has the PR problem. It's 2013, the Big One has hit, and LA Island is a playground for New Moral America's deviants. Snake fits right in. The official site has summer

blockbuster written all over it. The interactive game is a blast—you're sent into L.A. as a spy, and for each encounter with the natives you can "run," "negotiate," or "draw gun." Fortunately, you don't have to listen to Kurt Russell's tracheotomy impession for more than a few seconds.
WEB http://www.escape-la.com

ESCAPE FROM NEW YORK

Escape Fans everywhere still enjoy their memories of that classic futuristic thriller, "Escape from St. Louis," right? Ummmm… no. But, as Escape will inform you, the entire 1981 movie *Escape from New York* was filmed in the great state of Missouri. Weird. More factoids, pictures, and ecstatic plot summary here.
WEB http://vlsi2.elsy.cf.ac.uk/bright /escape.html

FANTASTIC VOYAGE

Internet Movie Database: Fantastic Voyage Why did the book come out before the movie? What was the name of that character who died? Were there goofs in the movie (besides those huge blood cells that look a lot like Lifesavers?). There's not a lot of information here, but those questions and a few others are answered.
WEB http://us.imdb.com/cache/title-exact /25692

FLASH GORDON

The Unofficial Flash Gordon Movie Page News "Flash": This site will answer all your pressing questions about everybody's favorite 1980 movie. Who played the Arborian initiate? What are the words to the song "Flash," by Queen? How can a poor, desperate fan get his or her mitts on a picture of Max von Sydow in full imperial regalia? Where are other fan pages on the Web? It's all here on the unofficial site. By the way, there is no official *Flash Gordon* site.
WEB http://www.geocities.com/Hollywood /4262/index.html

THE FLY

The Fly Movie Poster (original) "The FLY with the head of a man…! And the man with the head of a FLY!" Not a picture of Jeff Goldblum with a detatched jawbone, this is the poster that drew in the crowds to a movie that will always be a sci-fi favorite.
WEB http://www.cat.pdx.edu/%7ecaseyh /horror/poster/fly-01.jpg

The Fly/Return of the Fly Poster Who said sequels are a recent trend? The Fly came back as much more than a maggot, and a scary double-feature was born at drive-ins across the country. "See them together but don't see them alone!" is the classically-charged advice you'll find here.
WEB http://www.cat.pdx.edu/%7ecaseyh /horror/poster/fly-post.jpg

FORBIDDEN PLANET

Forbidden Planet The home page for the film that science forgot is jam-packed with pictures of Robby the Robot and pals, a guide to the Krells, movie credits, an analytic essay, .JPGs of the beautiful, original posters, and, of course, sounds. This site should be the first step in a *Forbidden Planet* Web tour.
WEB http://www.tizeta.it/home/duo /fbhome.htm

Forbidden Planet Sounds "My evil self is at that door, and I have no power to stop it!!!" If you've ever felt that way, or if you just happen to be a *Forbidden Planet* fan, don't miss these eight great sound clips from the classic (and downright charming) movie.
WEB http://www.geocities.com/Hollywood /1158/forbid.html

GHOST IN THE SHELL

Ghost in the Shell When bandwidth gets wide enough to download your relatives, and can be considered an actual as opposed to virtual form of travel, the world will inevitably be plagued by evil creations like the Puppet Master. This

was the conclusion of popular manga artist Masamune Shirow, creator of the *Ghost in the Shell* series. Manga and anime fans turned cartwheels when they found out that the exciting series was going to be released as a feature-length animated movie. This, the official site, collects video clips, a synopsis, a Shockwave (or forms) quiz challenge, pictures of the characters, and links to other sites in *The Shell*.
WEB http://www.manga.com/manga /ghost/ghost.html

The Ghost in the Shell A truly amazing interactive multimedia kit, despite annoying and repetitive music and overly enthusiastic prose. No, really, it's fun! There is a game, movie credits, character information and more, all combined in a fascinating interface that bodes well for otaku. But return to this Web site for the rest of the goodies, including video, pictures, sounds, notes, and the complete movie trailer.
WEB http://www.hollywood.com/movies /ghost/bsghost.html

▶ GHOSTBUSTERS

The Ghostbusters Homepage In 1984, *Ghostbusters* was one of the highest grossing movies of all time. Maybe part of that has to do with the fact that Bill Emkow has seen the movie more than 56 times. Emkow obviously knows the movie inside and out and shares his knowledge at this site. Not only do you find the usual sites and sounds from the flick, there's also a *Ghostbusters* Manual. If you ain't afraid of no ghosts and have what it takes to hunt the spooky specters, play the role playing game.
WEB http://www.msu.edu/user/emkowbil /ghostbus.htm

▶ HACKERS

Hackers Another excellent little multimedia kit, more pictures, sounds, videos, tons of actors' info, and lots more make up this pseudo-official site. Now there's no need to break into the computer network at MGM when all you need is right here. A considerable improvement on the movie from *Backbeat* director Iain Softley.
WEB http://www.hollywood.com/movies /hackers/bshackers.html

Official Hackers Site Do all computer geeks have such expertly uncoiffed hair? Pull a "hairy hack" with the *Hackers* game, and suck up more non-lingo in the other areas of this dark and gloomy site. Visit the part of the site which may or may not have been hacked and destroyed by "real" hackers, possibly employees at MGM/UA's marketing department. Then check out information about the movie, its characters, and all its fast-paced cyberpunkness.
WEB http://www.mgmua.com/hackers

▶ THE INCREDIBLE HULK

Incredible Hulk Television Series Homepage An FAQ with the basics on the big green TV star, covering the cast and crew, the origins of the show, and questions about old green biceps: "Why is McGee obsessed with capturing the Hulk?", "Does anyone find out about David's true identity?", and "Does the Hulk ever fight any animals?" (does he ever—try a bear, a group of Doberman Pinchers, a gorilla, a bull, and a pack of wolves).
WEB http://www.uoguelph.ca/~mrathwel /Hulk.html

Incredible Hulk Web Site As a TV personality, the Incredible Hulk first appeared on the small screen in a television show called *Marvel Super Heroes* which aired in the 1960s. The whole history and storylines of the comic-book Hulk were later reworked for the television series that aired on CBS from 1977 until 1982. This Hulk hub offers insight into the history of the *Hulk* series (such as the fact that the producer changed Dr. Bruce Banner's name to David because he thought the name Bruce sounded gay); bios for Bill Bixby, Lou Ferrigno, and Jack Colvin; an episode guide and list of famous faces that made appearances on the show; and a compilation of

the 20 most memorable episodes.
WEB http://ezinfo.ucs.indiana.edu
/~abloomga/hulk.html

The Sci-Fi Channel: Incredible Hulk
Don't make him angry. You won't like him when he's angry. The Sci-Fi Channel is devoting a page to Dr. David Banner and his alter-ego now that the series is running in reruns on their cable channel.
WEB http://www.scifi.com/hulk

INDEPENDENCE DAY

Independence Day (Official Site) Those who were first in line to get tickets for summer '96's most hotly anticipated blockbuster will find plenty to see and do at this official site. Not only does it provide the typical sound-and-video promotion (including two surprisingly challenging text-based adventure games) but also enough background on alien lore and the real Area 51 to satisfy anybody's desire for a close encounter. Unlike most movies' official sites, this one may warrant a second visit.
WEB http://www.id4.com

INVASION / THE BODY SNATCHERS

IOTBS Poster "Send your men of science" with a color printer straight to this site, to get a copy of this gorgeous original poster. The scan job is excellent (no crinkles or wrinkles) and besides, who could resist the high camp of Dana Wynter running away in a ball gown?
WEB http://www.avalon.net/~cope/IOTBS
.html

Voyager: Invasion of the Body Snatchers When a typical '50s drive-in date movie turns into a cult feature to outlast any other, even "serious" sci-fi fans pay attention. Such is the case with Body Snatchers, offered here in a new laserdisc edition. Helpful and fascinating background information, credits, and—bonus!—film clips. Now anybody's computer can say, "They're like huge seed pods!"
WEB http://www.voyagerco.com/CC/ph/p
.invasion.html

JOHNNY MNEMONIC

Hollywood Online: Johnny Mnemonic
Hollywood Online is always home to the coolest of Web toys: interactive multimedia kits. Here's one for *Johnny Mnemonic*, plus the usual complement of videos etc.
WEB http://www.hollywood.com/movies
/johnny/bsjohnny.html

Movieweb: Johnny Mnemonic Here's the place to download the entire *Johnny Mnemonic* trailer, view about a dozen movie stills, and read plenty of background information.
WEB http://movieweb.com/movie
/johnnym/index.html

Official Johnny Mnemonic Site If you blinked once, you may have missed the rapid-fire opening and closing of *Johnny Mnemonic*, starring Keanu Reeves. But it was a banner event in the lives of William Gibson's cyberpunk fans, who anxiously awaited Gibson's script. This official site is now largely abandoned, but still contains audio, video, and stills, as well as a "virtual reality experience in William Gibson's Cyberspace."
WEB http://www.spe.sony.com/Pictures
/SonyMovies/06jonmnu.html

JUDGE DREDD

Judge Dredd: Out Now on Video More than just an excuse for Stallone to flop hard and perhaps a little unfairly while wearing plastic armor, *Judge Dredd* was the culmination of an artist's efforts 17 years ago, when the comic book character Judge Dredd was first created in England. The movie spent 12 months in pre-production alone, and its entire history is traced at this site, along with other goodies such as movie stills. Worth a visit to see how easy it can be to go wrong.
WEB http://www.foresight.co.uk/dredd

JURASSIC PARK

Jurassic Park Sounds Quite simply a better collection of *Jurassic Park* sound

files than at any other Web location, this page contains plenty of ways to make the most high-tech computer growl, scream, and roar like a Commodore 64.
WEB http://www.moviesounds.com /jurassic.html

NBC: Jurassic Park Thanks to their recent network broadcast of *Jurassic Park*, the peacock gang has found it in their hearts to post this excellent homage site. It's blessed with original content, such as a feature on the combinations of animal sounds it took to produce each dinosaur species' roar. When a velociraptor attacks, it's a combination of goose, dolphin, and walrus, for example. Profiles of Crichton and Spielberg round out the page.
WEB http://www.nbc.com/entertainment /jurassic/jurassichome.html

Unofficial Jurassic Park Home Page A fan's love for *Jurassic Park* can be as hard to contain as a hungry T-Rex, and this site is a testament to that kind of fierce ardor. It is constantly updated, and full of dinosaur roars and actor screams in sound and video. Don't forget to follow that teeny-tiny link at the bottom of the home page to the first draft of the screenplay by Michael Crichton.
WEB http://uslink.net/~warrior

Welcome to Jurassic Park Besides the array of clips, pictures, sounds, and links that discerning *JP* fans expect from the many Web sites devoted to the dino pic, this site contains one particularly unique feature. It's a set of bulletin boards, where puzzled friends of raptors ask when the sequel is coming or where collector's memorabilia is available. The answers aren't always posted here, but are answered by direct email.
WEB http://www.azstarnet.com /~newmann/jp

KOLCHAK: THE NIGHT STALKER

Kolchak: The Night Stalker "Next question: Do you think the combination of Kolchak's realistic fear of the situations he finds himself in is consistent with the fact that he ends up doing 'heroic' things to resolve them?" Be prepared for equally refreshing, intellectual, philosophical discussion of the influential 1970s program.
AMERICA ONLINE *keyword* fictional→ Science Fiction→Message Boards→ Vintage Television Shows→List Topic→ Kolchak: The Night Stalker

Kolchak: The Night Stalker Featuring a hilarious, unsurpassable self-promo, this entry describes the object of its affections as "An *X-Files* for the seventies." A channel on the Sci-Fi Feed's virtual dial, the Kolchak page offers the basic background on the various vampires and spirits tracked by the intrepid, straw hat-sporting Chicago newsman Carl Kolchak, plus airtimes and episode info.
WEB http://www.scifi.com/kolchak

Kolchak: The Night Stalker An episode guide and list of characters for the supposed inspiration for *The X-Files*.
WEB http://www.abacus.ghj.com/sci_fi /kolchak/kolchak.htm

LA JETÉE

La Jetée So when Terry Gilliam's told us it was the influence for his movie *12 Monkeys*, we all nodded and pretended we had already seen it. This guy is a fan of the post-apocalyptic vision of what passes for life after world destruction even if he can't spell it. Still, click under the picture to find more than 30 images from Chris Marker's film. Follow them by clicking on the airplanes; they're supposed to be arrows.
WEB http://www.favela.org/frenzy/lajette /lajette2.html

LAND OF THE LOST

Krofft Goodies Among the H.R. Pufnstuf and Sigmund the Sea Monster themes and clips littered about at this site are a large quantity of *Land of the Lost* goodies. Fans can find Mac desktop textures, sound files, and all kinds of pictures.
WEB http://www.west.net/~popomatic /goodies.html

Land of the Lost Those cheesy dinosaurs, those ultra-cheap floods, and those unconvincing time-vortex effects. Yes, it's none other than Sid and Marty Krofft's *Land of the Lost*. The page is about as basic as the show, but that helps to capture the feel; a high-tech Java-powered site just wouldn't be right for one of the lowest budget sci-fi shows ever made. This presentation will bring back memories if you were one of those who woke up early on Saturdays to see the misadventures of Marshall, Will, and Holly. Learn to speak Pakuni, read an extensive episode guide, and even get pictures of Sleestaks and Marshalls alike. **WEB** http://www.execpc.com/~nolsen/lotl /lotl.html

LOTL Program Guide Which episode debuted the spooky Sleestak? Why does Cha-ka have to steal Big Alice's egg? Find out here, in this guide to every *LOTL* episode. The descriptions, unfortunately, are exceptionally brief. **WEB** http://yakko.cs.wmich.edu/%7Eochs /guides/landofthelost.html

LOTL Theme Song Sing along to the entire "Laaaaand of the Lost" theme song, downloadable here. **WEB** http://members.aol.com/mclainserv /lotl.wav

> ### LAWNMOWER MAN

Cyber Jobe: The Lawnmower Man Gallery Computer animation played a large part in the *Lawnmower Man* movies, and a fan has placed some of the best images here for your viewing enjoyment, proving once again that we've come a long way since Max Headroom. **WEB** http://www.cyberramp.net/~sydney2 /jobe.html

Lawnmower Man 2: Beyond Cyberspace What's here besides a few pictures, a pre-release hype essay, and a pointer to Movielink? Why, it's the entire eight-mega movie trailer. This is a true treasure for those who loved *Lawnmower*

and have lots of time and scratch disk space. **WEB** http://movieweb.com/movie/lawn mower/index.html

Lawnmower Man 2: Beyond Cyberspace-Official We thought he was dead, sucked into the phone system of the world and then blown to bits. But Jobe came back, this time without a body. He's a virtual reality threat now, and this official site should be full of marketing with a VR twist. There is a nifty interactive multimedia kit but mainly, this is just a large collection of photos, sound files, and quite a few clips. **WEB** http://www.extratv.com/encore/96 _01_03/doc2.htm

> ### LOST IN SPACE

Alpha Control: Lost in Space Every space chariot should stop here, for a cute and colorful look at one of 1965's contributions to pop culture. See pictures of the major players, read a detailed episode guide including inside dirt on each episode's scrapped plot twists or "firsts," and download photos, movies, and sounds. Click on Virtual Dr. Smith for a silly Shockwave goodie in which Dr. Smith spontaneously generates insults for Robot. Return to the intro to find out when the Sci-Fi Channel will be airing reruns. **WEB** http://www.scifi.com/lostnspace

LIS Sounds Page All the witticisms Robot and Will ever spoke, with some miscellaneous sound effects thrown in to boot. Like the *Lost in Space* Pictures site, there are no explanations accompanying the downloads, so each sound file can be regarded as an intriguing mystery. (Less charitable surfers may regard this absence of information as a Zachary Smith-size pain in the neck.) **WEB** http://vader.mgmt.purdue.edu/vader /lost_in_space/sounds

Lost in Space Episode Guide Marvel as the show degenerates from a legitimate sci-fi offering to the *Gilligan's Island* of outer space. Another guide to the show's

episodes, from the black-and-white first season to later, sillier episodes such as "The Thief From Outer Space," "Princess of Space," and even "The Vegetable Rebellion," in which the Robinsons are turned into giant plants.
WEB http://www.ozemail.com.au/~groakes /episode.html
URL ftp://www.snowcrest.net/fox/Space .html

Lost in Space Fannish Alliance It's the oldest and largest *LIS* fan club, and it's free! Send email from here to join up, and you'll get a newsletter, a photo from the show, and other freebies. Plus, find out how you can build a robot replica for just $12.45. That doesn't include the scrap metal.
WEB http://www.as-inc.com/lisfan /lisfan.html

Lost in Space Page The poor Robinson family, lost in space in 1997. That's right, 1997, which must have seemed like a distant future when the show first aired, during the same years as the original *Star Trek*. A superfan has put up this extensive site, including the most current information about the rumored movie, magazine articles, and more. Plenty of sounds, movie clips, and pictures, of course, plus a hugely long, alphabetized list of robotic insults. Leadlined Lothario! Silver-plated Sellout!
WEB http://www.filmzone.com/~vkoser /vader/lost_in_space/lost_in_space .html

Lost In Space Pictures What's your pleasure, earthling? If it's *Lost in Space* pictures, this site is destined to be your favorite. There are more than a hundred stills of the show, its fans, their memorabilia, and more. It ain't pretty and there are no explanations or captions, but comprehensive? You bet your planet it is.
URL ftp://vader.mgmt.purdue.edu/pub /lis/pics

Lost in Space Trivia Challenge "Danger, Will Robinson!" This page will suck you into the *Lost in Space* void with a few

trivia questions (it's an ongoing contest,) a guide to the actors who made *Lost in Space* great and where they are now, and links to other sites that are lost in (cyber) space.
WEB http://www.lookup.com/Home pages/47451/space/trivia.html?

Opening Credits QuickTime and .MPEG movies of the show's opening credits, including the haunting and beautiful theme music.
WEB http://www.mgmt.purdue.edu /~vkoser/lost_in_space/movies.html

▶ MAX HEADROOM

alt.tv.max-headroom Talk about *Max Headroom* and other sci-fi sites on the World Wide Web, chat about the new episode guides, and ask for whatever it is you want. A recent request was for .WAV files of the *Max Headroom* opening theme music. A great place for Max-mania.
USENET alt.tv.max-headroom

Max Headroom Data Data files, that is, a collection of Max-related documents, including a summary of an unproduced *Max Headroom* episode called "Theora's Tale," are up for grabs at this Web site with a smart, user-friendly layout. The extensive library of images should be a treat for any Max fan.
WEB http://river.tay.ac.uk/~ccdmlh /max/index.htmlx

The Max Headroom Home Page This colorful site features lots of information on Max and his mid-'80s television show. The author has his own version of the episode guide with subjective commentary, as well as a glossary of terms and characters' backgrounds. There's a small collection of "sights and sounds" from the program, as well as the obligatory links to other Max sites on the Web.
WEB http://jean-luc.ncsa.uiuc.edu /People/Andy/max/max.html

Max Headroom Shrine Josh races mountain bikes, dislikes rednecks, and loves science fiction. His one page trib-

ute to the 1980s show includes a description of the series' pilot episode and the *Max Headroom* theme songs in .AU format. Also, download the insidious Blipvert commercial (the one that made people's brains explode).
WEB http://ssl.cs.wvu.edu/~flaf/max .html

The Max Headroom Squares The Sci-Fi Channel is rerunning the ill-fated pioneering cyberspace drama *Max Headroom*. To celebrate, the channel's staff created a fun online game that actually works. The game is based on *The Hollywood Squares*, and even has audio-clip commentary from Max. The questions are easy and the prize is only a link to an episode guide, but the game itself is an impressive piece of Web writing.
WEB http://www.scifi.com/headroom

Max Headroom's Wav Page Here's a great big collection of sounds taken from the original shows. Re-experience Max's technological stutter when you listen to clips such as, "Well I don't know about you p-p-p-people, but, I'm going for a walk."
WEB http://www.stoutman.qbd.com /wavs/max/headroom.html

Network 23: The Max Headroom Section *Max Headroom* went off the air after a few episodes; ABC just didn't know how to market the show, and it probably didn't help that *Headroom* was about devious, cutthroat TV executives. Maybe the weasels in suits took it personally. Of course the short run means that there is very little to work with and this tiny Max Headquarters sorely needs more attractions to be worthwhile. Dig through your old files and help them out if you can.
WEB http://www.net23.com/0/max /main.html

▶ **METROPOLIS**

Blackangel's Academic Papers Throughout her years of liberal arts studies at the University of Texas, Rebecca, a.k.a. Blackangel, has acquired a fair share of academic papers. In order to make her Web site a reflector of her personality and studies, she's put some of her works online. They include "Gender and Utopia: The Roles of the Dual Woman in Metropolis," "The False Woman in Metropolis and Blade Runner," and "The Implications of the Dual Woman in *Metropolis*." Truly interesting, insightful stuff.
WEB http://piglet.cc.utexas.edu /~blkangel/academic/acadmndx.html

Discussions and Comments about Metropolis A collection of posts to various newsgroups and mailing lists about the movie, including opinions of the soundtrack and other things related to recent versions. Some talk about movies that try to portray the effects of technology on society, as well as debates regarding different translations and formats of the original story.
WEB http://poppy.kaist.ac.kr/cinema /metropolis/usenet.txt

Fritz Lang's Metropolis From Brazil, a small, but useful, Web site devoted to *Metropolis*. There's a full list of the different versions of the film (there are five!), as well as a collection of images of the city, some of which are in color.
WEB http://www.persocom.com.br /brasilia/metropo.htm

The Metropolis Home Page Reviews, commentaries, and excerpts from books on Lang and his work are included here, along with great, high-quality images from the film. It's an insightful resource, reflecting the genuine interest the site's creator has in the film and sharing it with the rest of the world. He's even put a very touching obituary on the site in honor of Brigitte Helm, the actress who played Maria and the evil robot, who passed away half-way through 1996. Links to other worldwide *Metropolis* sites are included, up near the top of the page.
WEB http://members.aol.com/PolisHome /metropolis.html

Movie Reviews Home Page: Metropolis (1926) Written by one Damien Cannon, this is a thorough and thoughtful critique

of the film, notable mainly for a powerful justification for the melodramatic acting style that carries the silent classic.
WEB http://www.sr.bham.ac.uk/~dbc /Movies/Reviews/Metropolis.html

► MIGHTY MORPHIN POWERRANGERS

alt.fan.power-rangers Discuss the rainbow-colored heroes, their enemies, plot twists, and more. Fan fiction pieces, such as "Travels in Time," are frequent topics.
USENET alt.fan.power-rangers

Mighty Morphin Power Documents Grab your Power Coins and get morphin'! An FAQ, an episode guide, and biographical information on nearly everyone involved with the *Power Ranger* phenomenon.
WEB http://www.geocities.com/Hollywood /3875/mmpr.html

Mighty Weenie Pathetic Rangers The staff of Artist Bros.', whoever they may be, have written lenghty parodies of every single episode of the show.
WEB http://www.cyberverse.com/~piero /mwpr.html

► NOWHERE MAN

alt.tv.nowhere-man Saving the series is a priority for the show's fans. Topics range from Emmy prospects and the soundtrack to planning live, online discussion groups for aficionados.
USENET alt.tv.nowhere-man

FAQ—Nowhere Man Conspiracy at its finest. Read all about the series and the characters in this document. Find out who Thomas Veil really is.
WEB http://www.aquila.com/sandra.jones /faq.htm

Nowhere Man Episode Guide "Unknown forces conspire to erase Thomas Veil's identity and without warning, every aspect of his life is turned upside down—his wife acts as if he's a stranger, his credit cards are suddenly invalid, his keys no longer fit the door to

his home and in one way or another, his family and friends are silenced." This is an episode-by-episode look at the short-lived series, right down to the production code and original air date.
WEB http://www.nts.mh.se/~blajo /nowhere.htm

The Sci-Fi Site: Nowhere Man Main Page Did you think that Bruce Greenwood, *Nowhere Man's* star, happened to look familiar? That's because he played Dr. Seth Griffin in the television series, *St. Elsewhere*. Lots of information and resources are gathered here, including facts about the series, biographical information on the cast and creators, synopses of the episodes, and links to other *Nowhere Man* home pages.
WEB http://www.abacus.ghj.com/sci_fi /nowhere/nowhere.htm

► OUTER LIMITS

Episode Guide From 1963 to 1965, *The Outer Limits* terrified television viewers with its *Twilight Zone*-like plots and chilling ironies. This guide offers a complete list of all episodes, along with ratings, air dates, and special guests; William Shatner, Adam West, and Robert Duvall all made appearances in '64.
URL ftp://sflovers.rutgers.edu/pub /sflovers/TV/EpisodeGuides/outerlimits .guide

The Outer Limits The great TV series *The Outer Limits* began airing in 1963, and was recently resurrected on Showtime when MGM remade the original shows. Unlikely as it sounds, some of the remakes were really rather good, if not in the league of the originals. This page highlights the remakes, and that's the only drawback of an otherwise truly creepy, state-of-the-art Web site. Check out the unsettling animated eye in the episode guide, but not right before bedtime.
WEB http://www.mgmua.com/outerlimits

The Outer Limits: The Original Series Neat-looking Java that mimics the famous sine-wave opening sequence of the groundbreaking sci-fi show from the '50s greets you upon arrival. Download the "control voice" to complete the effect: "There is nothing wrong with your television set…" Historical facts, an episode guide, and images make this a must-see for those even remotely intrigued by not only this show, but any science fiction TV.

WEB http://www.webzone1.co.uk/www /brendan/outer.htm

PHENOMENON

Phenomenon Notes, credits, clips, stills, and music from the movie about how a small town's life turned upside down when one of its ordinary citizens is struck by light on his 37th birthday. Feeling especially enlightened yourself? Play the intelligence game here, too.

WEB http://www.movies.com/ph/index.html

The Rendezvous Phenomenon Style What's more phenomenal—a man who can learn the Portuguese language in 20 minutes or the fact that John Travolta was able to make such a complete career comeback? Or that the tenets of Scientology would be so transparently crow-barred into a mainstream movie? Pictures, sounds, and links pertaining to the film and Travolta's first non-thug role since the turnaround.

WEB http://www.li.net/~kirkg/phenomenon /enter.htm

PLAN 9 FROM OUTER SPACE

Plan 9 from Outer Space Vampira, the pale, buxom beauty who was Elvira's inspiration, not only performed in Ed Wood's "classic"; she also starred in *Sex Kittens Go To College*, *The Beat Generation*, and *Night Of The Ghouls*. Here's a brief, but informative review of *Plan 9* with background info on the cast of the movie voted "The Worst Film of All Time" in a 1980 poll.

WEB http://www.iguide.com/movies /mopic/pictures/10/10755.htm

Plan 9 from Outer Space There is a lack of working Web pages for this cult

movie, also known as "Grave Robbers from Outer Space." That's sadly demonstrated by this home page. It's just a scan of the poster from the film, but makes for a great desktop image.

WEB http://www.avalon.net/~cope/Plan9 .html

PLANET OF THE APES

The Forbidden Zone This site is a useful resource for any and all Ape fans. There are articles and excerpts and trivia, as well as an episode guide to the *Return to the Planet of the Apes* animated television series. Images, sound bites, and movie clips can be found within the great music hall.

WEB http://members.aol.com/rogerapple /forbiddenzone.html

The Sci-Fi Site: Planet of the Apes Main Page Burke, Urko, Galen, and Virdon: only a few of the many characters of the film and television series. This dedicated home page features everything from an episode guide to a collection of articles related to *Planet of the Apes* and its cast. Be sure to catch the highly enlightening Chronological History of *Planet of the Apes*.

WEB http://www.abacus.ghj.com/sci_fi /apes/apes.htm

POWDER

Powder—The Movie The basics from the movie about a chalk-white boy with luminous powers who is rejected by his father and eventually his peers after his mother is struck by lightning and killed. Often overlooked due to the fact that the director was a convicted criminal, this is nevertheless a touching tale. Images and info on the actors are also available.

WEB http://www.angelfire.com/pages0 /powder/index.html

PREDATOR

Crow's Predator Homepage "Silent. Invisible. Invincible. He's in town with a few days to kill." After the Arnie movie, the Danny movie, the comic books, and the franchise comes the Web site. Hunt for what you need and find it here. Pictures from the movies and comics, as well as sounds and scripts. Check out the translations of the deeply philosophical Predator language: "Dtai'k-dte sa-de nav'g-kon dtain'aun bpide—The fight begun would not end until the end." **WEB** http://pages.prodigy.com/Crow /predpage.htm

QUATERMASS

The Quatermass Home Page You know, Quatermass. Or maybe you've never heard of Nigel Kneale's character, Dr. Bernard Quatermass—a button-down, Brit rocket physicist who spent his time in the limelight repelling alien invaders. Featured in various TV and film incarnations from 1953 to 1979, Quatermass was a plum role for Andre Morell, Brian Donlevy, Andrew Keir, and John Mills, and this page discusses various issues from the entire lifespan of the character. **WEB** http://pine.shu.ac.uk/~lfmarm /quaterma/qhome.htm

ROBOCOP

The Criterion Collection: RoboCop "This future is a technological nightmare that all workers fear: star Peter Weller, as the murdered officer who gets recycled into the half-machine, half-man of the film's title, plays a supporting role to his character's robotic armature. And the Detroit of the future, its mirror-and-steel skyscrapers reflecting crumbling, crime-ridden slums, is less metropolis than war zone," writes Carrie Rickey of the influential Reagan-era film. Look into the heart of the film with this in-depth essay. **WEB** http://www.voyagerco.com/CC /sfh/robocop.html

RoboCop Episode Guide In "Prime Suspect," "RoboCop becomes a fugitive after a corrupt TV evangelist, who called the cyborg a 'tool of Satan,' is murdered." The adventures of RoboCop continued on the boob tube with short-lived television series, starring Richard Eden as Alex Murphy, RoboCop. Detailed

information, including a link to the actual, original broadcast schedule, is a treat from a fan in the U.K. **WEB** http://www.tardis.ed.ac.uk/~dave /guides/RoboCop

RoboCop Sounds "Excuse me. I have to go. Somewhere there is a crime happening." Gotta love that RoboCop—he's so dedicated. A handful of samples from the film. The MovieSounds library is much more extensive. **WEB** http://www.geocities.com/Hollywood /1158/robocop.html • http://www .moviesounds.com/robocop.html

SEAQUEST

alt.tv.seaquest David wants the writers of *seaQuest, DSV* to have enough creativity not to steal characters and episodes from *Star Trek: The Next Generation.* "If you're going to steal stories," he wrote, "at least don't make them WORSE than the original!" Another viewer—not a fan, exactly—dubbed this show "Fish Trek, 90H2O" for its combination of hardbodied hunks and salvaged *Trek* plots. You'll find ample comparisons of Captains Kirk and Picard to *SQ*'s Captain Bridger. "Let's face facts," one person wrote, "Bridger doesn't and can't compare to either of those captains." Aside from the *Trek* references, this group is heavy on science, with plenty of arguments about proper air pressure and vertebrates with gills. **USENET** alt.tv.seaquest

Mike's seaQuest Page Self-promotion is, after all, a large part of what the Web is about, so it's hardly surprising to see a site where the main raison d'etre seems to be the posting of the names of (and brief anecdotes about) the people who did the animation playback and live video for *seaQuest.* Other than those much-in-demand credits and a few images, there isn't much here at all. **WEB** http://users.aol.com/mnoles8889 /seaquest.html

seaQuest DSV—2032 The serviceable graphics and standard-issue links to

crew bios and show merchandise are fine as far as they go, but the real highlight is the wacky Quotable Quotes section. The text introduction makes grabbing the sound files impossible until you stop laughing. Bridger's "Look at me, Charlie Tuna, chauffeur of the sea," deserves to be on anyone's all-time list of post-modern punchlines.
WEB http://www.stgenesis.org/~leigh /seaQuest

SLAUGHTERHOUSE FIVE

Slaughterhouse Five "*Slaughterhouse Five* has two narrators, an impersonal one and a personal one, resulting in a novel not only about Dresden but also about the actual act of writing a novel—in this case a novel about an event that has shaped the author profoundly. The novel's themes of cruelty, innocence, free will, regeneration, survival, time, and war recur throughout Vonnegut's novels, as do some of his characters, which are typically caricatures of ideas with little depth." This essay is a comparison between Vonnegut's novel and the film adaptation. The author discusses such issues as narration, transitions, and the "bugs in amber" theme. The book fares much higher than the film in the author's eyes.
WEB http://sunsite.unc.edu/brian/slaughter .html

SLIDERS

alt.tv.sliders This newsgroup, for lovers of the series, contains typical sci-fi fan fare: debates and questions about minutiae. Is that the real Professor Arturo sliding with our heroes? Did the Sliders actually make it back home and not know it? And will the show be renewed? Sign on only if you're a real fan.
USENET alt.tv.sliders

Sliders Web meister Tim Lucas has done a great job of cataloging all of the alternate Earths and personas that have appeared on *Sliders*, the Fox sci-fi show about a group of people who "slide" from

one parallel earth to another. The show is always under the threat of cancellation (perhaps on a parallel world the show is highly rated), but it has a group of devoted fans, who can check out this address to see a photo gallery, actor and character bios, and an interview with series star and NYU grad Jerry O'Connell.
WEB http://washington.xtn.net/~lucast /sliders/sliders.html

Sliders Creative Archive Fans' adventures for Quinn are just as interesting as the original series itself; maybe the show's producers should have come here for some story ideas. Tales such as "Quantum Slide" and "Silent Lucidity" make for some adventurous reading. Some of these stories, as well as discussion about them, can be found on the alt.tv.sliders
.creative Usenet newsgroup.
USENET alt.tv.sliders.creative
***Archive:* WEB** http://gossamer.eng.ohio -state.edu/sliders

Sliders FAQ Web Page Everything you ever wanted to know about those dimensionally-challenged funsters from Fox's *Quantum Leap*-wannabe show. What TV-reference page would be complete without the ubiquitous episode guide? You'll also find a list of every alternate earth our intrepid travelers have frequented; it's quite an interesting assortment of realities.
WEB http://www.best.com/~edhall /sliders

Universal Channel: Sliders Shameless commercialism reigns in this self-promoting coverage of Universal's sci-fi show. All the standard series info is there, but you can also play the Sliders WWW game—which is fun—even if you don't know anything about the show. Feel compelled to express yourself on the burning issues of *Sliders*'s quality, the stories and characters? Or do you just have the hots for one of the main actors? You can send email to the cast, writers, or producers.
WEB http://www.univstudios.com/tv /sliders

► **SPACE: ABOVE AND BEYOND**

alt.tv.space-a-n-b What to do while the fate of your favorite sci-fi show is in the hands of the network gods? Indulge in cyberconsolation and communication in its newsgroup with fellow fans. Here, followers of *Space: Above and Beyond* relive every detail of the first season of shows devoted to the adventures of a few good space marines, while they await a reprieve.
USENET alt.tv.space-a-n-b

McQueenisms OK, listen up. It's another "Can You Imaging McQueen As…" list. And it's OK to be scared. Here we imagine the lieutenant colonel as an Internet tech supporter, and even an opera singer.
WEB http://www.quicklink.net/bham /draddog/mcqueen.html

Mission Status: Space: Above and Beyond Whether you've only seen half an episode or follow the series religiously, Mission Status is the ideal Web resource to Fox's *Space: Above and Beyond*. With this encyclopedia of info, you can decipher the show's many acronyms, translate the characters' military lingo ("Zoomie" means pilot), and learn more about their technology. The timeline and episode guide helps put the plot in perspective, while the episode reviews remind you that this is only a TV program. Most intriguing is the Wild Card MOO area, which allows you to not only interact with other visitors but also with the rooms themselves on board the Saratoga space carrier.
WEB http://www.microserve.net/space:aab

The RoundHammer Times A mock-up of a front page news story from October, 2063, covering the confrontation between the 58th Squadron and an alien ship. Lt. Col. T.C. McQueen is quoted as saying, "It was a real knife fight out there. The enemy attacked in coordinated groups that were almost impossible to defeat." When asked if he had any advice for the pilots going out to face the alien attackers, he said, "I would tell

them that the only thing that matters is life. Their lives. The lives of their comrades. And one more thing… I would tell them 'It is okay to be scared!'"
WEB http://www.mint.net/~jmurph/SAAB /NEWS/index.html

SAABFIC-L Mailing List The *Space: Above and Beyond* fan fiction list.
EMAIL listserv@server.microserve.net
✍ *Type in message body:* subscribe saabfic-l

The Set of Official Space: AAB Lists If your *SAAB* obsession is getting out of hand, stop here, where you'll find such lists as You Know You've Been Watching Too Much *SAAB* When…, Everything I Need to Know, I Learned from *SAAB*, and Can You Imagine McQueen As… lists. There are even some *SAAB* carols for holiday time.
WEB http://www.teleport.com/~honcho /lists.html

Space A&B Sunday The AOL *SAAB* Forum was formed even before the premiere of the FOX series in anticipation of a show with an *X-Files*-esque following, and it continues on even though the show has been cancelled. Now it's the AOL fans of the show who are going above and beyond. Message boards and chat rooms focus on the last two episodes of the show—"If They Lay Us Down To Rest…" and "Tell Our Moms We Done Our Best" as well as efforts to bring the sci-fi show back from the network dead.
AMERICA ONLINE *keyword* space a&b

Space: Above and Beyond Fans FAQ The hyper FAQ here answers all the hard-hitting questions, such as why *Space: Above and Beyond* episodes were always being pre-empted (apparently it wasn't a Chig conspiracy) it was usually because the football ran on. Also included are character profiles, plot summaries for each episode of the first (and perhaps only) season, and technical information about the spaceships and weapons.
FAQ: **WEB** http://www.paranoia .com/~phoenix/saabfaq.html

The Space: Above and Beyond Internet Yellow Pages & Directory They're young, gorgeous, foul tempered, and they take their frustrations out on evil aliens. They're the heroes of *Space: Above and Beyond*, and if you can't get enough on TV, point your rockets here for a large number of official and unofficial servers that will give you everything from technical info to *SAAB* Love Tips. **WEB** http://mvhs.fuhsd.org/~vpeng/space /space.html

Space: Above and Beyond Multimedia Web Site In addition to an extensive list of links, this site (the first devoted to the show) holds the multimedia mother-lode—sounds, pictures, animations, director's cuts, the theme song, interviews, magazine articles, the intro, and even jigsaw puzzles from the one-season sensation. **WEB** http://rampages.onramp.net /~brummett/space.html

Space: Above and Beyond Quiz Site Do you know who is second in command of the 58th Squadron Wild Cards? Is that person an IV (In Vitro)? If you followed *Space: Above and Beyond*, here are a series of multiple-choice quizzes that are more taxing on the bandwidth than your attention span. Even if you don't watch the show, the plot synopses tell you enough to get a nearly perfect score. Only an utterly obsessed fan will be satisfied. **WEB** http://www.geocities.com/Hollywood /3476/index.html

Space-L Mailing List The official forum for the *Space: Above and Beyond* faithful to discuss the show. List members are referred to as the 59th Ready Reserve Squadron. **EMAIL** listserv@server.microserve.net ✍ *Type in message body:* subscribe space-l <your full name> *Archives:* **WEB** http://www.microserve .net/space%3aaab/mail

Studio Tours: Space: Above and Beyond A day in the life of the crew of the 58th United States Space Aviator Cavalry sta-

tioned on the U.S.S. Saratoga. Tour the flight deck, the air lock, the Armored Personnel Carrier cockpit, the bunk room, and Tun Tavern—the only place to unwind after a full day of fighting Chigs and A.I.'s. Never mind that the short-lived show's been canceled. Suspend disbelief for a bit—this is science fiction, after all. **WEB** http://www.fox.com/st2spce.htm

▶ SPACE: 1999

Space: 1999 One fan says that he holds out hope that with time, *Space: 1999* will begin to shine like a newly found gem. Then, slightly wiser, he sighs and admits that it's "still horse excrement." For a group of supporters, the *Space 1999* camp is pretty negative, but in an affectionate way. Remember the episode where the crew "passed through some weird gas and devolved into cavemen?" They do. Does anyone know where to get diecast models of the series? They do. How about pictures, videocassettes, novelizations, and laserdiscs? Yep. If you're one of the lucky few with a jones for collecting horse excrement, this is the place for you. **AMERICA ONLINE** *keyword* scifi→Star Trek /Comics/TV/Star Wars Boards→ Television→Space 1999

Space: 1999 Opening screen shots and sounds from the first two (and only) seasons of the show. **WEB** http://www.kfu.com/~nsayer/space -1999

Space: 1999 Mailing List *Space: 1999* wasn't on the air for long, so naturally its online fans are rabid. And if you're one of them, get on this list. Topics include announcements of upcoming fan events, talk of *Space: 1999* models and merchandise, and mentions of film and TV appearances by the show's stars. Where else can you find such great offers as a complete set of Year 1 video-tapes for $55, or a bunch of 1999 books, ranging in price from $2.50 to $4. Talk of other sci-fi works is generally tolerated, especially if Gerry Anderson had any involvement. Disputes center around technical issues, such as why Alpha couldn't send an all-is-well message in the first episode, "Breakaway" ("systems on Alpha had been badly damaged by the explosion," one person guessed).

EMAIL space-1999-request@quack.kfu.com ✍ Write a request

Space: 1999 Page Was *Space: 1999* the sequel to *UFO*? What happened to Paul Morrow and David Kano? What other shows have cast members appeared in? This FAQ's got the answers. Also available are episode guides for 1999's two seasons and the film compilations that were made.

WEB http://www.brookes.ac.uk /~p0054463/space1999/1999.html

SPACEBALLS

EARchives—Spaceballs: The Movie "May the Schwartz be with you," an overabundant use of the word "suck," and other Mel Brooksisms from his space spoof.

WEB http://www.geocities.com /Hollywood/1158/spcballs.html

SPECIES

Movieweb: Species It's certainly no *Ghandi*, but *Species* was graced by Academy Award winner Ben Kingsley. The movie is about the dangerous consequences of mixing alien DNA with our own, and Movieweb offers production info, stills, a trailer, and stats on the cast and crew.

WEB http://movieweb.com/movie/species

Species In 1993, the U.S. government decides to accept the invitation from another world to combine human DNA with that of another life form. A new life—a token of the union of two species across the void of space—is created. So begins the movie *Species*. At this official MGM site, you can take on the role of the new species in their Web Adventure—your instincts and survival skills are put to the test as alien and human

psychology go to war inside your mind. If that's a little too intense for you, simply visit the Species Inventory of exclusive information on the making of the movie.

WEB http://www.mgmua.com/species /index.html

Species Sounds A few sound files from the movie starring Ben Kingsley, Michael Madsen, Alfred Molina, Forrest Whitaker, Marg Helgenberger, and Natasha Henstridge.

WEB http://www.geocities.com/Hollywood /1158/species.html

STARGATE

Stargate *Indiana Jones* meets *Close Encounters* in this story of a mysterious artifact unearthed at the pyramids at Giza, which turns out to be a stargate—a portal to another world. This site is a multimedia melange of info about the movie, clips from the films and the soundtrack, the behind-the-scenes cast and production scoop, and all about the CD-ROM, Secrets of Stargate, and the video game.

WEB http://www.foresight.co.uk/stargate

Stargate Sounds Five .WAV files from the pyramids-meet-space saga starring Kurt Russell and James Spader.

WEB http://www.geocities.com/Hollywood /1158/stargate.html

STARMAN

Starman *Starman* began as a 1984 movie (directed by John Carpenter) about an extraterrestrial (Jeff Bridges) who comes to earth after encountering the Voyager II probe, aided by and eventually fathering a child with Jenny Hayden (Karen Allen). In 1986, a television series based on the movie, in which the Starman (now Robert Hayes) returned to heed a call for help, ran for one season. The TV version still airs on the Sci-Fi Channel while the movie pops up on cable every now and then. This site focuses on the former with an episode guide for the series as well as details on

Spotlight *Starman* International (*Starman* fandom).
WEB http://www.calweb.com/~smccrory/starman.html

STRANGE DAYS

Hollywood Online: Strange Days Hollywood Online's usual array of multimedia kits and video clips, sights and sounds, notes and trailers, this time for a film that at least purports to be concerned with complementary subject matter. Check out the buff Angela Bassett and the always psychotic Juliette Lewis. Listen to a digitized Ralph Fiennes. Or find out how the production designer created the dark and edgy atmosphere of the approaching millennium.
WEB http://www.hollywood.com/movies/strange/bsstrange.html

Movieweb: Strange Days View stills and info from the movie that explores the last midnight of this century, in which pandemonium reigns and human experience are bought and sold in the digital underground as the latest form of illicit titillation.
WEB http://movieweb.com/movie/strangedays

Strange Days Strange days, indeed. "Jack in" here and explore earth on the eve of the year 2000. "This is like TV, only better. This is life. It's a piece of somebody's life. Pure and uncut, straight from the cerebral cortex. You're there. You're doing it, seeing it, hearing it… feeling it." The economy sucks, gas is three bucks a gallon, and fifth graders are shooting each other at recess. Meet the inhabitants of the world on the brink of Armageddon, explore the environment, and stop by the bar.
WEB http://www.strangedays.com

STRANGE LUCK

Strange Luck Main Page Everything you need to know about the show in which D.B. Sweeney plays a photographer whose—you guessed it—luck leads him into strange circumstances. Saving the

life of a suicide jumper, witnessing the shooting of a cop, rescuing a woman from a blazing inferno, tracking down a killer—it's all just part of a typical day in the life of Chance Harper. You'll find the latest news, an episode guide, and an index of other *Strange Luck* sites. But don't get too attached. *Strange Luck* Wasn't lucky enough to get a new series commissioned.
WEB http://www.abacus.ghj.com/sci_fi/luck/luck.htm

The Unofficial Strange Luck Homepage Did you know that episodes of *Strange Luck* featured music from such artists as Lorenna McKennit, Jan Arden, Sinead O'Connor, Sarah McLachlan, Live, and Mary Black? That's one of the topics covered in this FAQ about the one-season wonder. Die-hard Chancers will already know the details, but it's a great source of information for those who have never seen (and as it stands now, may never see) the show. Much of the rest of this site reads like a personal fan page for D.B. Sweeney—D.B.'s real-life strange luck,what it's like to work with D.B. Sweeney, an interview with Sweeney in *The News Times*, etc.
WEB http://www.swcp.com/~jamii/sl.html

Strange Luck List Discussion of the now-defunct series.
EMAIL email listserver@wildbear.on.ca
Type in message body: subscribe strangeluck-l <your full name>

TANK GIRL

Hollywood Online: Tank Girl Downloadable multimedia kits, movie clips, still shots, sound bites, and trailers from the movie version of the comic book *Tank Girl*, starring Lori Petty. The Hollywood Online pages also include notes on the movie and some of its stars, including Petty, Malcolm McDowell, and Ice-T.
WEB http://www.hollywood.com/movies/tank/bstank.html

Tank Girl Enter the world of *Tank Girl*, a wasteland of bleak desert and relentless sun baking in the aftermath of a cosmic

cataclysm that has robbed the earth it of its water. Get acquainted with the fearless lass herself, play the game, find out about the making of the movie, or write the spunky heroine a letter.
WEB http://www.mgmua.com/tankgirl

Tank Girl Soundtrack Courtney Love served as executive music coordinator of the film and soundtrack, which featured Love, Belly, Veruca Salt, L7, Portishead, Ice-T, and Devo, among others. Download clips from the lead single, "Army of Me" by Bjork.
WEB http://www.elektra.com/artists /tankgirl/tankgirl.html

Tank Girl—The Movie A fair amount of film was cut in the making of *Tank Girl* (the studio was worried about such issues as drug use and sex with kangaroos), and what remained may have seemed like a sell-out to the cult that followed the character's adventures on paper. This site recounts all the behind-the-scenes happenings which led to the end result.
WEB http://www.cs.ucl.ac.uk/staff/b .rosenberg/tg/movie.html

THE TERMINATOR

EAR-chives: The Terminator All of Ahnold's one liners and clever rejoinders from "Hasta la vista, baby" to "I'll be back" via "Come with me if you vant to live" and "Fok yew ersehurl."
WEB http://www.geocities.com/Hollywood /1158/termnatr.html

Terminator 2 Sounds Who says Schwarzenegger gets all the good lines? It was Sarah who said, "Anybody not wearing two million sunblock is gonna have a real bad day, get it!" Plus more of the same.
WEB http://www.moviesounds.com/t2.html

Terminator Home Page You'll say "hasta la vista" to other *Terminator* pages once you've visited this all-inclusive site. Its *T2* FAQ presented in hypertext form includes explanations of different movie versions, detailed listings of available

soundtracks, and speculation on whether or not there will be a third movie. Also, a scripts page, featuring both *The Terminator* and *T2*.
WEB http://www.contrib.andrew.cmu.edu /~atreides/Terminator/welcome.html

The Terminator Movies "Listen. Understand. That Terminator is out there..." We've found him right here: FAQs, sights, sounds, and scripts from the indomitable duo of movies.
WEB http://www.ifi.uio.no/~haakonhj /Terminator

THE TOMORROW PEOPLE

Galactic Federation Communications Hub This page of all things *Tomorrow People* is mostly links. You'll find links to a F.U.D.G.E. template for *TP*, book reviews, fan fiction, photo pages, and the new series drinking game. Among the original content here are sounds from the shows, *TV Guide* articles on the series ("*The Tomorrow People* isn't exactly a buried treasure...")
WEB http://www.xmission.com/~ladyslvr /gftch.htm

Teleporter Take-Out The twice-canceled sci-fi show featuring teenagers born with the powers of teleportation, telepathy, and telekinesis. Whether you're a fan of the independent British sci-fi series produced by Thames Television from 1973 to 1979 or the recent remake which ran on Nickelodeon from 1992 to 1995, you'll get your fix of those freaky kids with a *TP* character page, episode synopses, a periodic poll of your faves, and links to other *TP* lovers on the Web.
WEB http://www.cyhaus.com/tp

THX: 1138

Plot Summary This sci-fi film about a bleak futuristic society where life is highly regulated, sex is illegal, and daily ingestion of sedatives is required by law, may be one of the least far-fetched in the genre. It's definitely one of the most overlooked. You'll find a hypertext plot summary of the Lucas film starring

Robert Duvall as THX 1138 and discussion of the film on many levels.
web http://info.latech.edu/~mike/thx.html

TREMORS 2

Tremors 2: Aftershocks As if the first one weren't enough. In *Tremors 2*, worm hunter extraordinaire Earl Bassett is back for a second battle with the hungry graboids. Meet the actors who play the unlikely heroes, play the graboid hunting game, or scroll through the AOL chat with the director, S.S. Wilson.
web http://www.mca.com/home/tremors2/index.html

The Tremors 2: Aftershocks Official Fan Page Dedicated to the video-release sequel to *Tremors*, in which pre-Cambrian, post-Kevin Bacon predator worms resurface in Mexico. Two faithful fans have filled this site with information on the cast, the production team, behind-the-scenes happenings, news, and trivia. The original *Tremors* only became a box office success following fan word of mouth, and it looks like Allan and Linda are hoping to use the same tactics to support the sequel.
web http://www.keytech.com/~wrmkllr/index.html

TRON

The TRON Home Page Relive '80s arcade chic in all its computer-blipping splendor. For those who believe that *TRON* was the defining movie of that era (and there are plenty of them here), this page is paradise. *TRON* images and sounds, chat rooms and links to fellow *TRON* fans around the world, and even a list of arcades around the country that still have the *TRON* game.
web http://www.3gcs.com/tron

TRON Sounds "On the other side of the screen, it all looks so easy." Doesn't it though? Listen to this and other insights from that movie that explored the inner workings of a super computer.
web http://www.geocities.com/hollywood/1158/tron.html

The Unofficial TRON Home Page The Total Player Killing MUD based on the Disney film. In this game you take on the role of a Program taking part in wars on the games grid. Select from eight war types, choose your weapon, and battle for your own honor and that of your circuit.
web http://www.geocities.com/motorcity/1156/tron.html

TWILIGHT ZONE

T-Zone A mailing list devoted to the spooky side of life, the dark side of human nature, and plots that go bump in the night.
email tzone-request@hustle.rahul.net ✍ Write a request

Twilight Zone Welcome to the fifth dimesion. A dimension of sight and sound. Welcome to AOL's *Twilight Zone* message board.
america online *keyword* scifi→Message Boards→Vintage TV Shows→List Topics→Twilight Zone

Twilight Zone Episode Guides Remember the first *Twilight Zone*, from 1959? That would have been "Where Is Everybody?" with Earl Holliman, which told the story of a man stranded in a deserted city. Or maybe you'd rather spend your time reviewing such classics as "Stopover in a Quiet Town," or hit-and-miss efforts such as "Caesar and Me." This document lists all the episodes from the original run of the show, along with full credits and capsule reviews.
url ftp://sflovers.rutgers.edu/pub/sflovers/TV/EpisodeGuides/twilight-zone.guide

UNFORGETTABLE

Unforgettable A forensic examiner's wife is murdered, he gets the rap, then discovers how to isolate memories from spinal fluid and starts to inject himself with his wife's memories in order to learn about her real killer. "It's sci-fi!" say the studio execs, "let's plug it in cyberspace!" And so one of the biggest flops of 1996 has one of the most elabo-

rate, media-rich home pages online. As an "insider" of some sort, you're taken through the movie and the characters' lives with forensic reports, diary entries, police records, and of course, memories. The page deserves two awards—the first for design and the second for the most unsuccessful Net promo ever.
WEB http://www.mgmua.com /unforgettable

► V

"V" Home Page An index of links, and so much more. Even if you know a lot about the series, check out the "history" of *V* feature, which offers long synopses of lost scripts, articles about the show's creator and its later creative problems, and background on all the various versions, formats, and spin-offs that the series produced.
WEB http://www.prairienet.org/~drthiel /v.htm

► VIRTUOSITY

Virtuosity Denzel Washington is an ex-cop in prison for killing the man who murdered everyone in his family. For years he's been a lab rat in a virtual reality experiment where he battles supervillain Sid 6.7—a computer compilation of hundreds of mass murderers. Somehow Sid escapes the game and starts killing real people—and it's Denzel to the rescue. Hey, it could happen! So of course there's an interactive game, but guess what? It doesn't work right now. It's a relatively low-tech Web site for a film whose entire premise comes from the online medium. Nothing special. But Denzel looks damn fine.
WEB http://www.paramount.com /virtuosity/index.html

► VOYAGE / BOTTOM OF THE SEA

Voyage to the Bottom of the Sea All the information available in cyberspace on the Irwin Allen creation, including episode and cast lists, when and where you can see the show, plus infromation about conventions, and how to get on the Irwin Allen Mailing List.
WEB http://www.portup.com/~hjbe /voyage.html

Voyage to the Bottom of the Sea "You know, the show was done before sci-fi became so obsessed with social commentary. I think I enjoy it now because the themes, if any, are so simple and basic. And most of the time, everything is presented for entertainment only," writes one fan in this active forum for the 1960s television series. Similarly deep thought, queries about videos, memorabilia, and greetings from fans abound.
AMERICA ONLINE *keyword* science fiction→ Message Boards→vintage television shows→list topics→voyage to the bottom of the sea

Voyage to the Bottom of the Sea [IANN] Information on *Voyage* airings across the county, conventions devoted to the 1960s series starring Richard Basehart and David Hedison, clubs, video releases, and links.
WEB http://ourworld.compuserve.com /homepages/tvnfilm/voyage.htm

► VR .5

alt.tv.vr5 This newsgroup enjoys inexplicably heavy business, and groupies' posts range from the slightly off-topic— serious debate concerning a crossover between *VR.5* and *Gargoyles* ("I think the human neurochemistry will work when I have Syd call [Demona] during the day but when Demona's a gargoyle what would happen? Because I doubt Gargoyle neurochemistry is anything similar to human neurochemistry") to nowhere near the ballpark (a collection of samples from *Solitude in Stone*, and a 'zine that features unique and offbeat tombstone inscriptions, such as "Sacred to the memory of Jerod Bates; His widow, aged 24, lives at 7 Elm St. Has every qualification for a good wife and yearns to be comforted.").
USENET alt.tv.vr5

VR.5 Just goes to show ya, make a show about cyberspace and netheads will do

anything to keep it alive. Ages after its quick and painless death, *VR.5*'s fans are fighting the good fight to bring it back to the other side. Enjoy endless elevator music (or is that the theme song?) as you move through this enormous site, which explores the cast and characters, offers background on virtual reality, and updates *VR.5*ers about what's going on at the frontlines of the resurrection battle.
WEB http://www.abacus.ghj.com/Sci_Fi/vr5/vr5.htm

▶ THE WAR OF THE WORLDS

War of the Worlds, The (original movie) Sounds "…and now, fought with the terrible weapons of super-science, menacing all mankind and every creature on earth, comes…" Yup, Martians with death rays. Get all the cool sound effects and the best quotes from the original movie.
WEB http://www.geocities.com/Hollywood/1158/warworld.html

▶ WATERWORLD

Waterworld Polar ice-caps melt. World under water. Fish men. Search for dry land. Bad guys on dirty Kawasakis. You know the deal. Relive the adventure on the *Waterworld* home page. You didn't see it? Then live the adventure for the first time! This is actually quite a neat little interactive adventure with sound clips and some animation. And there's also links to the live action show at Universal Studios, as if you hadn't already caught that seven times…
WEB http://www.mca.com/unicity/waterworld

▶ WONDER WOMAN

Lynda Carter A rather large collection of photos of Wonder Woman. Some titles include "Sultry Linda," "Dressed to Kill," and "My Vacation With Wonder Woman."
WEB http://users.aol.com/newxan/lynpic.htm

Wonder Woman "All the world is waiting for you / and the power you possess / In your satin tights…" isn't something you hear every day. Unless, that is, you log in to the *Wonder Woman* site of sites every day. A masterpiece of restrained design and decorated by a fully gorgeous Joe DeVito *WW* illustration, this is a genuine fan site. Under the headings you would expect to see (Collectibles, the Television Series, Comics Reviews, and so on) are critiques that show just how involved this particular Wonder Woman nut is. Check out his take on action figures. Pick of the site is the Bullets and Bracelets Shockwave game, perhaps the very reason Shockwave was invented. "Wonder Woman! / Get us out from under, Wonder Woman."
WEB http://www.io.org/~arhythm/phpl.cgi?ww/ww.htm

The New Original Wonder Woman Admit it. You've always wanted a magic lasso. Discussion of William Moulton Marston's superhero for girls, from the comics to the big screen, includes a hypothetical casting call for a new Wonder Woman (Julie Strain is a favorite), inquiries into the episode guide, and debates on whether shows such as *Xena* are based on the classic character.
AMERICA ONLINE *keyword* fictional→ Science Fiction/Message Boards→ Vintage Television Shows→List Topics→The New Original Wonder Woman

Wonder Woman This site is Amazonazing! It takes you through the entire history of the scantily clad, well-endowed superheroine, with features on her comic book incarnation to start with, and then sends you diving head first into Lynda, Lynda, Lynda!—Dozens of Lynda images, a Lynda filmography, Lynda fan art, and a *WW*-spin-off fan comic modeled on Lynda (the fan can't put her in *WW* attire or he'll get sued). Everything's coming up Lynda! Now that's a healthy looking woman.
WEB http://users.aol.com/newxan/toenter.htm

FAN FICTION

CI-FI MOVIES ARE OCCASIONAL EVENTS. Fewer than 20 new episodes of most sci-fi TV shows are broadcast each year. And when a network realizes a sci-fi show has a passionate, devoted, but microscopic fan base, the show's days are numbered. Many sci-fi fans don't believe they get enough, so to satisfy their endless hunger they have learned to write their own. The results, both fine and diabolical are all over the Web.

Apparently the hacks who write sci-fi for a living have it easy—fan fiction auteurs seem to have no trouble churning out stories starring their favorite characters. Some merely expand upon a show's premise: New *X-Files* for Mulder and Scully, new creatures to fight for the *Earth2* gang, and even new pre-commercial sketches for *Mystery Science Theater 3000* are typical examples. Then there are the crossovers, which offer appetizing conjunctions, such as "What if Spock and Captain Sheridan met and conquered a new planet?" Parodies of every show from *Doctor Who* to *Strange Luck* abound, but to get the true flavor, to see exactly why every fan fictioner is not a full-time employee of a network, you have to see some of the work for yourself. Peruse this selection and prepare to be amazed.

Launch pad

INDEXES

Fan Fiction on the Net
http://members.aol.com/ksnicholas/fanfic/index.html

The Ultimate Fan-Fiction Archive
ftp://ftp.magic.ca/users/fan-fic

The Grey Archive
http://www.mulberry.com/~dabrooks/index.htm

BABYLON 5

Archive of Creative Works: Babylon 5
http://www.dal.net/b5

Earth Alliance: Fan Fiction: Stories from B5 Creative
http://www.anxst.com/b5/story

BATTLESTAR GALACTICA

Battlestar Galactica Creativity
http://mcmfh.acns.carleton.edu/BG/creativity

DOCTOR WHO

alt.drwho.creative

Doctor Who: The Other Adventures
http://www.zoom.com/personal/nocturne/dwoa.html

EARTH2

Earth2 Fan Fiction
http://www2.best.com/%7Eftmexpat/e2/fan/e2-ff.html

HIGHLANDER

Highlander: The Anthology
http://krakowka.cit.cornell.edu/hl

HITCHHIKER'S GUIDE

Hitch Hiker's Guide to the Galaxy Fan Fiction
http://www.comp.lancs.ac.uk/computing/users/sean/HHGTTG

KINDRED: THE EMBRACED

Kindred Fan Fic Webpage
http://home.imsweb.net/~kamala/kind/fanfic.htm

MST3K

MST3K Fan MiSTings
http://www.coredcs.com/~cbeattie/bj/mst3k/mst_hi.htm

QUANTUM LEAP

alt.tv.quantum-leap.creative Archive
ftp://ftp.cisco.com/ql-archive/alt.tv.quantum-leap.creative

alt.ql.creative Archive
ftp://ftp.cisco.com/ql-archive/alt.ql.creative

SPACE: ABOVE AND BEYOND

SAaB Fan Fiction Archives
http://www.microserve.net/space%3aaab/fanfic

The Space: Above and Beyond Fan Fiction Site
http://www.wazoo.com/~nitehawk/fanfic.html

STAR TREK

Star Trek Fan Fiction
http://www.pitt.edu/~djtst18/st_ff.html

STAR WARS

Star Wars Fan Fiction
http://www.ftech.net/~monark/starwars/sw.htm

STRANGE LUCK

Strange Luck Fanfic
http://www.abacus.ghj.com/sci_fi/luck/fanfic.htm

THE TOMORROW PEOPLE

The Tomorrow People Creative List Archive
http://expert.cc.purdue.edu/~ladyslvr/tpfict.html

TWIN PEAKS

Directory of Fan Fiction
ftp://lutetia.uoregon.edu/pub/twin-peaks/Creative

V

The "V" Fan Fiction Page
http://members.aol.com/babseyd/vfanfic.htm

THE X-FILES

alt.tv.x-files.creative

The X-Files Creative Archive
http://gossamer.eng.ohio-state.edu/x-files

DDEB Creative Archive
http://www.exit109.com/~fazia/DDEBCreative.html

Funny Fanfic
http://www.alphalink.com.au/~vlen

PART 3

Star Trek

STARFLEET ACADEMY

WHEN WE FINALLY REACH THE twenty-fourth century, the Internet will no doubt be remembered as that quaint computer system which enabled humans on Earth to discuss a late twentieth-century entertainment phenomenon known as *Star Trek*. Let's put it this way—even if you were a Trill, you still wouldn't have time to get through all the *Star Trek* sites online. If you're beginning as a green Cadet, just spend a few days online and you'll know enough to get a field promotion to Ensign. And even if you're an old crusty Admiral, there are still a few things the Net can teach you about *Star Trek*. Study everything from episode guides to Treknology, Federation policy to *Trek* sexuality, and you'll graduate at the top of your class.

▶ CLICK PICK

Vidiot Home Page Wouldn't you like to own a house next to Rick Berman or have a friend who worked on the set of *Voyager*? Ahh, for the inside scoop on storylines. Here's the next best thing. Mike Brown's *Trek* pages have a somewhat official air about them, and since they often reveal news about upcoming episodes and Paramount decisions, they may be the closest you get to an inside source. Each *Trek* series has its own page, with casting news, air dates, images, and episode summaries. If you have a graphical Web browser, be sure to check out the image pages—especially those for the premier episode of *Voyager* and the movie *Generations*. The images take a while to load, but they're well worth the wait.
WEB http://www.cdsnet.net/vidiot

▶ MOTHERSHIPS

Captain's Gig Captain's Gig is a good-looking piece of Web writing, but sorely fails to live up to its promise. After stepping up with a fair recreation of a *Star Trek* computer screen, all that's offered

are links to a small handful of other *Trek* sites, one for each major series, and some other random links, such as job opportunities in Minnesota. Ready for Deep Space Woebegone?
WEB http://Prairie.Lakes.com/~captain /captain.html

Curt Danhauser's Guide to the Animated Star Trek For some reason the Great Bird of the Galaxy decided to disregard the 22 high-quality animated *Trek* episodes produced by Filmation in the early '70s. So they were wiped from the official canon by Paramount—but not by fans. Now with this delightful and cel-heavy page, Danhauser restores respect to the forgotten *Trek*. You'll learn about the show's innovations (Kirk's middle name, Tiberius; Captain Robert April) and how many of its episodes sequeled classic TOS shows. Culled from many sources, the info Danhauser has compiled is truly impressive. Check out episode guides and live-action and animated pics of characters.
WEB http://www1.ridgecrest.ca.us /~curtdan/TREK/Main.html

Eva's Star Trek Warp Engine Eva's Engine functions primarily as a link to other *Trek* sites, involving all five series and the movies. Click to newsgroups, Telnets, picture archives, fan clubs, and *Trek* sites in Austria, the U.K., and Sweden. Character sites, including those for Major Kira and Chief O'Brien of *DS9*, are fun to browse through. Gamesters may want to download info on the *Star Trek* Role Playing Game.
WEB http://www.mds.mdh.se/~elt93epn /trek.htm

Holodeck 3 Top-notch, gee-whiz Web programming makes this collection of stills and clips seem like a lot more. The sense of moving from room to room on the deck of the Enterprise couldn't be more perfectly realized. But for some odd reason, the News icon links you to CNN and *The New York Times*, not *Star Trek*

news. Be careful not to miss the *Trek* stuff hidden among these strangely misplaced time portals back to what Earthlings used to call the twentieth century.
WEB http://www.starbase21.com/holodeck3

Jellinek's Star Trek Page With a Shatner for every Stewart and more than enough Nimoy to go around, this site includes links to sounds, pictures, episode guides, quotes, stories, parodies, comics, and quotes.
WEB http://www.netshop/Startrek/web

List of Star Trek Web sites Divided into major and minor sites, this page lists *Trek* resources across the Net, including the official *Star Trek: Generations* home page and the Terry Farrell Internet Fan Club.
WEB http://gagme.wwa.com/~boba/trek.html

Loskene's Tholian Web Those ruby-quartz Tholians are at it again. They've taken over the will of one weak-minded Earthling and have forced him to feature their kind at an excellent Internet site. The terrific graphics welcome you to a motherload of Tholian data and other uniquely stellar *Star Trek* info. Sample some cocktails from Quark's bar, using Terran ingredients. Review *Voyager* ship schematics in the Utopia Planitia. Jump through the Gateway for a listing of select SF links. You can even download the submission guidelines for aspiring *Trek* teleplay writers, particularly if you want to bring back those pesky Tholians.
WEB http://www.loskene.com

PC's Guide to Star Trek No, the guide isn't for your PC, nor is it a politically correct guide; the Web master's initials just happen to be PC. Donning his or her *Star Trek* uniform, PC takes you on a guided tour of the shows' and films' different ships, using detailed stills and blueprints, and introduces you to each crew. Hop aboard; the next tour is leaving soon.
WEB http://www.afn.org/~afn32406/startrek/main.html

The Round Man's Star Page The Round Man is apparently the paper-bag-wearing Web master for Wichita-based Feist Systems, Inc., which hosts numerous similar comprehensive listing sites. The result is a list of links to some basic sites devoted to the brainchildren of George Lucas and Gene Roddenberry. (There are easily more *Trek* sites here.) It may not be the most comprehensive list available, but it should be an adequate starting point for newbies.
WEB http://www.fn.net/~roundman/jwz/st.html

Sector 001 Want to boldly go where all other Internet Trekkers have gone before? Then engage at warp nine to Sector 001 and discover a wealth of *Star Trek* resources that cover every aspect of the *Trek* universe. Keen graphics and a great interface lead you through the Bridge to various portions of the starship: the Holodeck will connect you to episode and movie information; the Library offers acres of literature links that range from interviews with actors to treatises on Federation philosophy; and a visit to Sickbay will allow you to access disturbingly detailed data on Starfleet medicine.
WEB http://www.powernet.net/users/jcrafton

The Spider Web's Star Trek Page Another of the endless stream of linking sites for *Star Trek*, this particular attempt distinguishes itself by throwing in a few minor games (such as *Star Trek: The Next Generation*—The Daily Trivia Test) and some not-so-funny lists (including the Top Ten Phrases You Never Heard on the Enterprise). Still, it may amuse some younger and more hard-core fans of the enduring saga.
WEB http://miso.wwa.com/~boba/trek.html

Star Trek Yet another in the seemingly endless listings of *Trek* links, this page also includes information on each *Trek* series, with episode guides, cast information and FAQs for TOS, *TNG*, *DS9* and *Voyager*.

WEB http://web.city.ac.uk/~cc103/startrek.html

Star Trek and BizWork Remember the episode where the aliens reduce the whole crew to 12-sided blocks of salt? These pages remind one of that. There's some appealing stuff here, but it's all been reduced to something really dry. Even the almost-forgotten *Star Trek* animated series is represented, but in charts that remind one of calculus class. It's a good jumping-off point for exploring *Trek* on the Web, especially if you want FAQs.
WEB http://www.netshop.net/Startrek/web

Star Trek Archives Here you'll find the following lists: other roles held by *Trek* characters, books on tape, *Trek* worlds and locations, ships, TOS and *TNG* novels and comic books.
WEB http://gopher.univ-lyon1.fr
USENET rec.arts.startrek

Star Trek Gopher A group of several excellent *Star Trek* gopher links, including some to *Trek* reviews, parodies, fan fiction, TOS sounds, and FAQs.
URL gopher://gopher.ocf.berkeley.edu
:70/11/Library/Star_Trek

The Star Trek Page Links to other Net sites for each of the series, including the less-frequently linked TOS. In addition to series sites, there are links to alien information, ship pictures and descriptions, and large sound and picture archives.
WEB http://nirvana.bioc.cam.ac.uk
/~owde100/startrek.html

Star Trek: Points of Interest The Web master of this list has found that others have pretty much exhausted the topic of *Star Trek*. Rather than compete, many new sites simply choose to compile, and this one is no exception. Set this as a no-nonsense, no-graphics bookmark and then browse the extensive links for what you want, from official Paramount corporate sites to homespun pages written in Klingon. If you can't find something of interest among these links, you're not really a *Star Trek* fan.

WEB http://www.crc.ricoh.com/~marcush
/startrek.html

Star Trek Services Pack your home page with choice selections from this *Trek*-happy spot, where you're greeted by a Spock sound byte. In fact, it's the extensive sound bytes, which lean toward TOS, that are some of the coolest things at this page. There are episode guides and pictures from every movie and series, TrekMUSE game info, rules for 3D Chess, and a TOS drinking game. The nicest surprise is an extensive listing of romances on *Star Trek*; just how many woman did Kirk show his phaser to?
WEB http://tos-www.tos.net/services

Star Trek The Federation Database OnLine Somebody put a lot of work into creating an online database that captures the feel of the show. The clever design makes your screen look like one of the *Next Generation* computer displays. After you click on a topic, half your screen fills with text and pictures. The amount of info seems endless. A must-see stop for *TNG* fans seeking Data *data*.
WEB http://www.noord.bart.nl/~svdheide

Star Trek: WWW Luca Sambucci delivers on a promise "to boldly go where no Web browser has gone before." Besides extensive links (to official Paramount sites, fan pages, merchandise offerings, newsgroups, and mailing lists), Sambucci provides a wide variety of *Trek*-related articles and reviews. The best feature is the USS Internet, where a new *Trek* site is reviewed each week—a helpful guide for the beleaguered fan. Sambucci encourages feedback and advises Trekkers to "live long, prosper… and have fun."
WEB http://www.vol.it/luca/startrek/index
.html

The Star Trek Zone Ranking *Trek* sites on the ol' starship scale, the *Star Trek* Zone is no *U.S.S. Defiant*, but it's not a shuttle craft either. Think of it like the *U.S.S. Grissom*—visually appealing without packing all that much firepower. Full of graphics, there are scads of pretty pictures, yet nothing that any *Trek* fan hasn't been exposed to many times before. The listing of actors' birthdays is rather unique, but the trivia questions are fairly unchallenging and most of the links are unremarkable. One notable exception: a connection to the "music" of the *Star Trek* actors, including Brent Spiner's unforgivable "Ol' Yellow Eyes is Back." As Spock would say, "Argh— pain! Pain!"

WEB http://wane-arc.scri.fsu.edu/~janecek /trekkie.html

The Terran Web Node of Andrew C. Eppstein If you can tolerate his interminable boasting about attending Yale, the Terran Web Node of interstellar blowhard Andrew C. Eppstein is an above-average nexus of *Star Trek* bric-a-brac. Andy does have a springy sense of humor with which he peppers his page, as well as the good taste to present only the finest (but least widespread) graphics. His offering of links is rewarding, particularly since he offers a synopsis of each one so you won't be clicking away blindly. No visit would be complete without a stop to the hilarious "Captain Kirk Sing-A-Long" and the ludicrous "Particles of *Star Trek*." Finally, as proof that he has friends, he offers links to his cronies' non-*Trek* pages.

WEB http://pantheon.cis.yale.edu/~acepps /acepps.html

To Boldly Go …where every Netter wants to go—a site full of *Star Trek* pictures, parodies (several of Commander Riker), and resources. Choose the wormhole option to link to other great *Trek* Web sites.

WEB http://ws207.iso.ksu.edu/startrek.htm

The Ultimate Star Trek Page The Ultimate *Star Trek* Page? Not even close. Nazeer Ali puts a bit too much of himself into his *Star Trek* shrine—it's like *Where's Waldo?* at times, as the Web master has inserted his mug into one episode still after another. In his defense, Ali offers a bevy of *Trek* images, with extra emphasis on his favorite *TNG* episodes. His listing of "Whatever Happened to…" dangling plot participles is equally interesting. But since Ali himself admits that the page is a work in progress, couldn't he have held back on the superlatives?

WEB http://www.cen.uiuc.edu/~sn-ali /StarTrek.html

The Wormhole As a nexus of *Star Trek* sites, this is more of a black hole than an intergalactic short cut. The category divisions operate on some non-Vulcan logic that makes little sense. For example, the humor links list is the longest feature, but it's lumped under the Misc. heading, while the much shorter list of tech sites gets its own section. Once you manage to find what you're looking for, it usually proves to be fairly interesting, such as the 72 reasons Janeway is better than Picard, some of which include the fact that Janeway has more hair, and that her ship doesn't split in half when the going gets tough.

WEB http://www.branson.org/students /James/WormHole.html

WWW Star Trek Page Web master Adam Staines claims that his is "the only *Star Trek* site that lists all *Star Trek* sites." And he may be right. His massive undertaking is neatly divided into such categories as shows and movies, character pages, clubs, fan home pages, archives, articles, simulations, conventions, and FAQs. Sites are reviewed and cleverly rated on a scale of one ("like stale ga'kh" [sic]) to five ("like a holiday on Risa") com badges. Staines also uses symbols to note if a site has text, pictures, movies, sounds, is new, or is under construction. Fans can also participate in Staines' Final Unity games, which take place in the *Trek* universe.

WEB http://www.chem.ed.ac.uk./adamstar .html

▶ **FEDERATION**

List of Member Planets When you're agreeing to pursue common goals of peace and harmony, it's nice to know who you're harmonizing with, and this page lists the member planets of the

United Federation.

WEB http://lal.cs.byu.edu/people/black/StarTrek/memplanets.html

Starfleet Academy Tour One can only hope that this site is still under construction. It claims to be based on the Final Frontiers MOO, and promises a tour of the Academy grounds in *TNG*-era San Francisco. But all it delivers is a picture of the gardener and a description of a corridor. Why in the world would anyone want to go to this Academy if all you can do is look at flowers from a hallway? Stay tuned for further developments.

WEB http://www.geocities.com/CapitolHill/1025/fedsfa.html

Starfleet Intelligence Cardassian agent Lt. Durham has infiltrated Starfleet data banks through a security feed at Deep Space Nine. As a result, information on everything from Vulcan philosophy to Ferengi slang to Klingon chocolate has been forwarded to Cardassian leaders. That same information was also inadvertently posted on Earth's World Wide Web. Which is fortunate for us, as this is a great selection of *Star Trek* links that pays particular attention to the various races in the *Trek* universe. Jump from here to language generators, characters' home pages and even a wide variety of newsgroups and newsletters. And be sure to take a look at the Borg Institute of Technology, where "Graduation is Futile."

WEB http://www.wctc.net/~durham

United Federation of Planets Like most enormous bureaucracies, the United Federation of Planets does things the hard way and does it poorly. Swearing to "Promote all that is good and remove all that is evil" (funny, we don't remember that slogan from any episode), the UFP offers a ponderous search engine coupled with shreds of text-only information on the Starship *Enterprise*. In fact, most of the links here take you to non-*Trek* shareware and FTP programming campaigns. You come away with the feeling that this Federation is actually a cartel of alien computer geeks posing as intergalactic politicians.

WEB http://www.ufp.org

▶ STARFLEET 101

FAQs by Category The staff at Oxford University has done what they do best; namely, list things. In this case, they've undertaken the task of compiling a list of all available *Star Trek* FAQs. But read the page carefully and you'll discover that no person actually performed this chore: the stuff is churned out automatically. Oxford has a staff of robots that spends all day (weekends too—what a bunch of slave drivers), finding categories to make lists. Their robots have won awards for being hyper-efficient little list makers. It's rather spooky, the idea of robots compiling *Star Trek* information that you can access from your home computer.

WEB http://www.lib.ox.ac.uk/internet/news/faq/by_category.star-trek.html

List of Periodic Postings to rec.arts.startrek A hypertext version of a list of *Trek*-related FAQs often appear on the newsgroup. Several of the list names are linked to sites where the document can be read or retrieved.

WEB http://www.cosy.sbg.ac.at/ftp/pub/trek/lists/listolis.html

To Boldly Go: The Star Trek Research Home Page Ever ask yourself why *Star Trek* is so popular, and what that popularity says about our today's society? Here's an overview of books by various authors, all with their own theories on how *Star Trek* affects our individual lives and collective popular culture. Many different views are expressed, such as the serious philosophical discussions of the Federation's possessive capitalism, colonialism, and social Darwinistic attitudes, and the more positive, Utopian ideals of the show. As interesting a social critique as this may be, for the *Trek*-oriented crowd—happier recreating the sound of photon torpedoes in the bath—it's a little dry.

WEB http://www.clo.com/~rvk

SHOW BY SHOW

The Complete Star Trek Book, TV, and Film Guides A collection of *Trek* guides, including the guide to the Pocket Book series, episode guides to the three principal TV series (*TOS*, *TNG*, and *DS9*), and a checklist of all TV and book titles. The files are self-extracting. For Macintosh users.
COMPUSERVE *go* sfmedia→Libraries→ *Search by file name:* TREKGU.SEA

Deutsche Voyager Folgenliste und Spoilers *Star Trek: Voyager* has become popular around the world. *Voyager* episodes are shown (with their original English titles) in Germany; one fan in Deutschland has translated those titles and rounded up all the German show dates in this nice little folgenliste (episode directory). He's even gotten hold of plot summaries of unaired shows, and are willing to share them in advance (that would be the und Spoilers part). Brush up on your German before trying to read the summaries.
WEB http://olis.north.de/~hart

Star Trek Air Schedule Schedule of past *Trek* shows with episode name, episode number, and air date. Some episodes are linked to press releases.
WEB http://www.mit.edu:8001/people /shabby/startrek.html

Star Trek Episode & Book Checklist A straightforward list of *Trek* television episodes and novels.
COMPUSERVE *go* sfmedia→Libraries→ *Search by file name:* STLIST.TXT or STLIST.ZIP

Star Trek Episodes Guide Three-part episode guide covering TOS, *TNG*, and *DS9*. *Voyager* should soon be included.
WEB http://www.cis.ohio-state.edu /hypertext/faq/usenet/star-trek/CS-guide /tv/top.html

Upcoming Episodes Science fiction fan David Henderson keeps a list of recent sci-fi episodes for *DS9*, *Voyager*, and *Babylon 5*, among others. Each listing includes the episode's air date and a very brief plot synopsis. Henderson also collects rumors and interesting tidbits about the series.
WEB http://squirrel.bradley.edu/~davidh /scifi.html

WHO'S WHO

Captains of the Enterprise Captain Pike, sure, and Captains Kirk, Picard and Janeway. But did you know about Captain Robert T. April and Captain Kangaroo (sorry! couldn't resist)? This is a complete list of all the brave men (and the one brave woman) who have taken the helm on a *Trek* show.
COMPUSERVE *go* sfmedia→Libraries→ *Search by file name:* CAPTAI.TXT

List of Names, Ranks, and Serial Numbers Lists of the ranks in each *Trek* series are available here. The rank status of several main characters is clarified— "Wes was made an acting ensign by Picard in 'Where No One Has Gone Before,' then made full ensign in 'Menage a Troi' and given a uniform"— and brief character biographies are included.
WEB http://www.cosy.sbg.ac.at/ftp/pub /trek/lists/namerank.faq

SPELLING

The Star Trek Movies Spelling List Do you remember Chancellor Gorkhan (or was it Gorkon? or Goarkan?) from *Star Trek VI: The Undiscovered Country*? If it's spelling that's keeping your *Trek* star from rising, here's a list of characters, races, and locations encountered during the first six *Trek* movies.
WEB http://www.cosy.sbg.ac.at/ftp/pub /trek/lists/spelling.movies.faq

Star Trek Names Consider Morn, the plump alien who can always be found sucking down brews in Quark's bar. A slight anagrammatic exercise and Morn becomes Norm, the plump human who could always be found sucking down brews on *Cheers*. Here's a nifty listing of more than a dozen names from the *Star*

Trek multiverse and their terrestrial origins. Even names from the animated series are included and, fortunately, each one's listed with the episode title and a character description. After all, if you don't remember who Eneg was, it doesn't do you much good to know that it's Gene spelled backward.

WEB http://www.infocom.com/~franklin/startrek/names/welcome.htm

Star Trek Spelling List The next time you're planning to invite the crew of the *Enterprise* to a social function, download this document, which lists the correct names and spellings for hundreds of characters from the *Star Trek* universe. Does the Transit Aid Bajoran in *Deep Space Nine* spell his name Zaira or Zayra? Are the warriors in "Elaan of Troyius" Elasians or Illyrians?

WEB http://www.cosy.sbg.ac.at/ftp/pub/trek/lists/spelling.txt

▶ PROGRESSIVE TREK

Gay Trek on AOL Equal rights for gays? Sure. Gays in the military? No problem. Gays adopting children? Right on. But gays on *Star Trek*? You gotta be kidding. Boldly going where Starfleet refuses to tread, the various boards dealing with the conspicuous absence of gay characters on *Star Trek* are among the most active and enduring. The debate is in the realm of unenlightened science fantasy as forum members speculate that homosexuality is "cured" by the twenty-fourth century or the Q Continuum mercifully wipes out homosexuality. Many gay fans blame Planet Paramount for the lack of developed gay characters. Much discussion centers around the *TNG* gender-bending homily on sexual conformity, "The Outcast," and whether or not Paramount has indeed done its duty. The problem, say the gay fans, is not the lack of a storyline, but that they are not represented in Starfleet at all. When multi-culturalism is the writer's Prime Directive, why not? The answer, sad to say, can be found in the postings of many adolescent males who swear they'd stop watching if *Star Trek* intro-

duced a gay crew member.

AMERICA ONLINE *keyword* trek→Message Boards→StarTrek Voyager→LesGay Characters on Voyager

▶ TREK SEX

alt.sex.fetish.startrek Are you curious about which of the ST women have done photo spreads, ah-hem, "out of uniform"? (Denise Crosby, Marina Sirtis, but never Gates McFadden.) Do you wonder which of the male officers on deck has the biggest Ten-Forward? (Apparently, at least as far as *TNG* is concerned, the Captain's Log is most impressive, with No. One a close No. Two.) Ever wished that phasers had a setting marked "stimulate"? Well, then, post haste to alt.sex.fetish.startrek. One of the few sex.fetish groups dominated by female posters, it is a remarkably close-knit community, bound by an intense and absolutely serious lust for the men and women of *Trek*'s past, present, and future. The occasional bin-hex-encoded naughty picture does show up here, but the true draw for most alt.sex.fetish.startrek readers is the conversation, which is equally divided between speculation (what would a sexual interface with Lt. Commander Data be like?) and starry-eyed report (I touched Patrick Stewart's hand!). The undisputed queen of alt.sex.fetish.startrek is New York's Christina Faltz, whose abiding passion for the bald eagle of the spaceways, Jean-Luc Picard—and the actor who plays him—have led her to write a remarkable multi-part epic erotic fantasy entitled "Oh Captain, My Captain." Faltz's exploits have made her something of a star in the Net *Trek* community, and even beyond—the Los Angeles Times and other mainstream 'zines have written about her—but fame hasn't diminished her ardor. A recent trip with members of the self-styled Patrick Stewart Estrogen Brigade (made up of female Net admirers from across the country) to Stewart's play *A Christmas Carol* led to an actual face-to-face meeting between luster and lustee, with dreamy, weak-in-the-knees results... all of which was then documented in hilarious and heart-felt detail on the group. Impulse thrusters on full, Captain… oh, Captain! **USENET** alt.sex.fetish.startrek

Sexy Trek Sometimes raunchy and often slightly twisted, regulars here alternately spin tales about their personal (read, sexual) involvement with *Trek* characters and attack others for doing the same. Lt. Illyria, an active contributor in the Neutral Zone and a constant target of attack, describes her relationship with the *DS9* Doctor Bashir: "We fell in love almost immediately after that strangely magical night, and now he's the only guy I'll ever need or want. :) Julian's a really special person. I hope you know that, Pooh. He really is." The 14-year-olds are here in force as well: "Have you seen the size of Kira's chest WOW! And that Vulcan's boobs in 'Maquis,' way to go Para-MOUNT!!" Then, there are those who dream of a love scene between Dax and Kira, a menage a trois with Riker, Troi, and Dr. Crusher, and a date with a Betazoid woman. Occasionally, someone will engage in serious soul-searching: "I can't explain it. I'm not usually attracted to short-haired masculine women (Dax would be more my personal style) but when she [Kira] gets angry or indignant about something (sometimes surprise will bring it out), RRRRRrrrrrrr!" **AMERICA ONLINE** *keyword* Trek→Message Boards→The Neutral Zone→Sexy Trek II

Star Trek Erotica What with Kirk going around having sex with every female alien in the known universe, it was bound to happen: sex meets *Star Trek*. Check out the crew's racy interaction with the Q continuum. Of course, we've had hints of characters lusting after their fellow twenty-fourth-century denizens, as when LaForge wanted to get down with the holodeck simulation of the *Enterprise*'s designer, but that stuff's nothing compared to the antics described at STE. Find out, in explicit detail, what happens when Janeway and Chakotay get trapped together. Get a load of Kes explaining to the captain how a crew member's needs aren't being met. It's disgusting—they take a perfectly wholesome show and smut it up. Alas, there are no pictures, just strong sexual content. **WEB** http://www2.rpa.net/~storybox /eroticindex.html

> **TREKNOLOGY**

The 14 Enterprises A list of 14 ships christened the *Enterprise*. **WEB** http://www.cosy.sbg.ac.at/ftp/pub /trek/lists/enterprises.txt

Deck Layout of Federation Vessels Which way to the holodeck? This document details floor plans and layouts for five classes of Federation starships— *Constitution, Enterprise, Excelsior, Constellation,* and *Galaxy*—with deck and hull locations for the main areas on the starships. **AMERICA ONLINE** *keyword* trek→Record Banks→Deck Layout and Breakdown

Discussion of Star Trek Cloaking Devices Ever wonder how *Trek* ships cloak? Well, here's one explanation: "The ship generates a gravitational distortion that causes electromagnetic radiation to curve halfway around the ship before escaping." If high-density tech-talk like this makes you want to curve halfway around the ship before escaping, you might want to be careful approaching this document, in which "all ideas were bounced around within a dedicated panel of Treknicians, including two physicists, a chemist and a mathematician, with the aid of three *ST: TNG* Tech Manuals, two VCRs, a large collection of video footage, and a particle in a pear tree." **WEB** http://wiretap.spies.com/Gopher /Library/Media/Trek/cloaking.dev

History of Ships Named Enterprise An annotated timeline written in 1989 that chronicles both the history of the *Enterprise* and *Trek* history in general. The plots of each of the episodes and movies covered in the timeline are described. **COMPUSERVE** *go* sfmedia→Libraries→ *Search by file name:* STHIS-.TXT

The Particles of Star Trek "Wait a minute, wait a minute… if the food replicators are connected to the warp core and then the ship performs a baryon sweep, there might be enough reserve energy for a single plasma discharge that will vacate all of the onboard lavatories." Find out if this is at all possible in the world of *Star Trek* at this page, which references all particles on every show, including the original series (remember quadrotriticale with the Tribbles?), *TNG* (on which we were introduced to psilocynine, which pulled Deanna out of hallucinations), the movies (trilithium, natch), and *Voyager* (tricobalt). And you can use the Particle Generation Form to submit the names of new discoveries.
WEB http://www.hyperion.com/~koreth /particles

Quantum Singularity Download pictures of the *Enterprise* zooming at warp speed or approaching at impulse. Get motion pix of all of the show logos, including the one picturing *Voyager* coming through the letters of that show's title. Addicts can preview upcoming projects, including the latest on the feature-film franchise, whether it's *First Contact* or beyond. Of course, there are plenty of links to *Voyager* and *DS9* home pages, tours of the Enterprise (with Jeffriestube travelling and sickbay access on the way), and interactive tours of the good ship *Voyager* as well.
WEB http://www.harborside.com/home/k /korey/startrek

rec.arts.sf.science If you want to discuss hyperspace, intelligence enhancement, or the possibility of receiving phone calls from the future, you've found the right place. The regulars of this newsgroup don't limit their conversations to the pseudo-science of sci-fi. You're as likely to read about relativity as the mechanics of transporter travel. One thread concerned the writing of a "future history." Some of the predictions for the next couple of centuries: genetic tailoring of bacteria, education by virtual reality, the arrival of alien missionaries. This is a friendly and intelligent group of sci-

fi-addicted science types, including some youngsters; Damian, an eighth-grader into astronomy, posted a question about chaos theory.
USENET rec.arts.sf.science

rec.arts.startrek.tech The heart of *Star Trek* may well be its human (and alien) relationships, but its soul, surely, is its new machines. Where would *Trek* be without the flash of phasers, the zoom of silver ships, the mix of whimsy and hard science in the Cochrane Drive? Well, it wouldn't be in eternal syndication and box-office nirvana, anyway. Rec.arts .startrek.tech is perhaps the most curious of the rec.arts.startrek* groups, requiring its participants to find semi-rational explanations for implausible, and often inconsistent, Treknology. How does a deflector shield work? A warp drive? A phaser? A transporter? (This last one, at least, is easy—it has something to do with Heisenberg Compensators and Annular Confinement Beams.) This is the most male-dominated of the rec.arts .startrek* groups, since it caters expressly to boys-and-their-toys conversation. Still, always an interesting read—not least when RAST'ers gather together to pound *Trek* for tripping itself up with YATIs (Yet Another Technical Inconsistency). Back to the drawing boards…
USENET rec.arts.startrek.tech

The Star Trek Archive Navigate through a plethora of *Trek* technobabble at D. Joseph Creighton's site, which contains a ton of technical and factual data in easy-to-digest form. Laymen's explanations of subspace physics and FTL travel are prime examples of complex-sounding topics that are rendered somewhat accessible to the average schmo. And nautical Trekkers can scope out the history of ships named *Enterprise*, which spans back to 1700-era sloops. Perhaps one of them was the inspiration for the sailing ship in *Generations*.
WEB http://www.ee.umanitoba.ca/~djc /startrek

Starbase 907 Map Visit Starbase 907 to check out the Star of Alderaan campaign

or visit the prayer room. This site fuses all sorts of *Star Trek* and *Star Wars* miscellany (and other weird stuff that doesn't really belong here) with sound bites (hear Data recite his first poem or listen to the *Knight Rider* theme—if you ask us, it's no contest). Use software to create a custom 3-D *Star Wars* galaxy or see what a newly designed TIE-fighter might look like. Peek into the Art Gallery to find images of race-cars and spaceships. Enter the commander's quarters (better knock first) and many other concourses on the Starbase. View the ships registry to learn all kinds of neat facts about the spaceships that might dock here in this fusion of fictional galaxies.
WEB http://hpserv.keh.utulsa.edu/~rlr

Starfleet's Fleet A list of ships that have appeared on The Original Series, *The Next Generation, Deep Space Nine*, and in the movies. Registry number, ship name, ship class, and the ship's status are included, and the document is easy to import into a database.
COMPUSERVE *go* sfmedia→Libraries→ *Search by file name:* FLEET.TXT

▶ TREK TIME

A Star Trek Chronology and The Star Trek Future History A timeline cataloging *Trek* history through the first five seasons of *TNG*. It also contains some fascinating annotation, including speculation on some confusing temporal matters. Where was the *Enterprise* between 2263 and 2264? What happened during the command of the first captain of the *Enterprise*, Robert T. April?
AMERICA ONLINE *keyword* trek→Record Banks→ST Timeline

How the Star Date Came To Be In 1968, smack in the middle of the first run of the first series, Gene Roddenberry took time out of his busy schedule to help author Stephen Whitfield with his book *The Making of Star Trek*. This document is a reprint of Roddenberry's explanation of the Stardate.
COMPUSERVE *go* sfmedia→Libraries→ *Search by file name:* SDATE.TXT

Mac Star Date 1.0.1 Launch the application and today's stardate appears. For Macs.
AMERICA ONLINE *keyword* trek→ Record Banks→MacStardate 1.0.1

NetTrekker's Complete Stardate Index A comprehensive chronology noting the stardates of hundreds of *Trek* adventures, including all events portrayed on television and in movies, books, and comics. Adventures are cross-listed if the story used flashbacks, time travel, or visions of the future. Each listing is also tagged with the type of story (e.g., Pocket Books *Deep Space Nine* novel; Animated Series episode). Compiled by Dayton Ward, an active member of AOL's *Star Trek* club, the list also includes a detailed set of footnotes that often preempt arguments over an event's occurrence.
WEB http://users.aol.com/nettrekker/its -net.htm

The Star Trek Timeline One more *Trek* timeline. Chronicles events in the universe beginning with 597,630 BC, when a Supernova destroyed the The Tkon Empire, through the fifth season of *TNG*. Not incredibly detailed.
WEB http://www.cosy.sbg.ac.at/ftp/pub /trek/lists/timeline.txt

Stardates On what exactly is a stardate based? This document calculates stardate units (at 1,000 per year, they clock in at approximately 8.76 hours for a non leap-year) and then illustrates how to convert Stardates into actual years. Jan. 21, 2363? Well, that's 40057.5, of course. Learn the system and amaze your friends as you render their birthdays in stardates.
WEB http://wiretap.spies.com/Gopher /Library/Media/Trek/stardate.st

▶ THE GREAT BIRD

Gene Roddenberry (August 19, 1921–October 24, 1991) Brief biography from Paramount of Roddenberry's life and his involvement with *Star Trek*.
WEB http://cruciform.cid.com/~werdna /sttng/gene.html

ALL THOSE ALIENS

IN THE OLD DAYS OF THE ORIGINAL series, if it didn't resemble something serving on the *Enterprise*, Kirk would blast the living hell out of it. Nowadays, all captains try the diplomatic approach with every alien race, whether friend or foe. From humanoids with cabbage-heads to Yar-eating oil slicks, the Net is swarming with alien life. And if it seems there is a little species-ism online, it's just that the some races have had more time to build up a following. TOS spawned Vulcans, Romulans and Klingons, and they all have enormous cultures on the Net. *TNG* brought forth Ferengis and the Borg, and they have tons of disciples. *DS9* is in transition—Bajorans and Cardassians are building nice little colonies, but the Dominion has yet to cross the wormhole. And *Voyager* aliens are lost in cyberspace, nary a Vidian, Ocampa, or Kazon has made an appearance on the Web.

▶ CLICK PICK

The Wonderful World of Borg You will come to this page. Resistance is futile. Wallpaper your screen with images of Locutus or the whole wacky collective. Check out the cheesy puns—Why wasn't Jean-Luc naturally a Borg? Because he wasn't Bjorn Borg—who knew they were such fun-lovin cut-ups? Study Cubism (the architecture for Borg ships) at the Borg Institute of Technology. Sing along with the dowloadable Borg Theme Song, or hear the Borg recite such memorable zingers as "Surrender or we will destroy your ship" or "Death is irrelevant." You might as well bulk up on your Borg lore now, because they will assimilate you. **WEB** http://www4.ncsu.edu/eos/users/d/dsaraned/WWW/borg.html

ANDORIAN

Andorian Home Page Andrea Izzoti has done a favor for classic *Trek* fans. Many of the aliens encountered by the *Enterprise* have been given a home page by

Izzoti. Surf from here to find Horta, Kohms, Yangs, Melkotians, and Gorn. At this page, the Andorians (you'll remember their blue skin and two antennae) are the subjects of a detailed history and analysis. You can also check out great pictures of a sweaty Kirk battling the Andorian spy from "Journey to Babel." **WEB** http://www.geocities.com/Hollywood/4272/andorian.htm

▶ BAJORAN

alt.startrek.bajoran Clear away the deep drifts of spam and you'll find some Bajoran-related discussions here, but the forum, at the moment, tends to slip into various marginally related topics. Your best bet for finding a thread of interest is to start one—the area is visited often, and you never know who might show up. **USENET** alt.startrek.bajoran

▶ BORG

A Borg Home Page The collective has collected the most complete set of Borg files on the Net, including fantastic images and unforgettable sound clips like "Freedom is irrelevant, self-determination is irrelevant, you must comply." **WEB** http://www.cs.indiana.edu/hyplan/awooldri/borg/borg.html

alt.startrek.borg Those followers of the Borg are not among the world's friendliest folks, judging by a particularly vituperative recent exchange in this chat spot, but this gathering place does attract a reasonable amount of traffic, and it remains a good spot for asking personal questions about cybernetic prostheses, improvements, amplifications, and the like. **USENET** alt.startrek.borg

Borg Borg sounds, Borg images, and excellent plot summaries capturing the drama and existential anguish of a Borg separated from his co-beings, all in a nicely laid out, conveniently organized

site. As a bonus, they've thrown in that rarest of rarities: *Star Trek* links.
web http://www.rpi.edu/~destem

The Borg HomeWorld As vast and huge as intergalactic space itself, this is a compilation of everything Borg related, from a RealAudio clip entitled Theme Music for Borg Episode to pictures galore and an intelligent FAQ discussing, among other things, Borg being and nothingness.
web http://www.tamnet.interbusiness .it/htmlpages/adds/borgpage/index.htm

Borg Jokes Q: How many Borgs does it take to change a light bulb? A: All of them!
compuserve *go* sfmedia→Libraries→ *Search by file name:* BORG.TXT

Borgisms Off-beat list of hundreds of Borgisms posted on Usenet: "Cause I'm a Borg, yea, yea, yea," "Even the Borg won't assimilate a Macintosh," "Frankly my dear, you will be assimilated—Butler of Borg," "McBorgs, over a half-billion assimilated," "Me and you and a Borg named Hugh," "My other computer is a Borg," etc. Get the picture?
web http://ftp.cis.ksu.edu/pub/alt.startrek .creative/misc/Borgisms.zip

The Collective Watch the Borg cube explode as the humans triumph. Download a picture of a standing Borg. Trekkers who "wish to improve themselves" or find their "defensive capabilities useless" may want to lose all sense of individuality, join the collective, and even email the Borg. There are the requisite episode summaries, but The Collective's webmaster goes one step further, presenting a few "lost" episodes. For fun, find out just how screwed Bill Gates would be if he took on the Borg, and discover secret connections with *The Simpsons*. A top ten list informs you of ways in which you can surmise whether or not your roommate is a Borg ("Your entertainment center disappears, and two days later he's wearing it").
web http://webpages.marshall.edu /~swann1/borg.htmlx

▶ **CARDASSIAN**

alt.startrek.cardassian Not much strictly of Cardassian interest at this frequency except posts from a pair of hardcore specialists, but there is a lively gathering of SF fans talking alternatively about *Dr. Who* and about getting the *Dr. Who* discussions out of a what's-supposed-to-be a Cardassian site.
usenet alt.startrek.cardassian

The Cardassian Page Every aspect of *Star Trek* has its own group of fans. Cardassians are the none-too-handsome tyrants of *Star Trek: Deep Space Nine*. The fans of the ugly despots have set up an Internet home, albeit a tiny one, and joining their club gets you a T-shirt. Free online features include Cardassian wallpaper, image and sound files, plus a lot of gossip on the actors who seem to be genuinely nice people under all that gruesome makeup. How they remain pleasant after enduring those torturous makeup sessions, we'll never know.
web http://members.gnn.com/cardassia /prime.html

Cardassians Archive Covering Cardassian sex appeal, biology, spirituality, and general villainy, this is an archive of a discussion about the baddest of the bad guys in the *Trek* universe.
america online *keyword* trek→Record Banks→Cardassians

▶ **DARMOK**

The Darmok Dictionary "Shaka, when the walls fell." Come again? "Zinda, his face blank, his eyes red." What?!? If you haven't seen the *TNG* episode "Darmok," those quotes are going to make even less sense than they did to Captain Picard. But in the interests of furthering intergalactic communication, The Darmok Dictionary is available online for the research and celebration of the metaphor-laden Talarian language. Every quote from the episode is offered (some in RealAudio), complete with their approximate translations. The Darmok Dictionary also cheerfully considers

some of logical "peculiarities" from the episode and links to sites that examine other weird science-fiction languages.
WEB http://www.wavefront.com/~raphael /darmok/darmok.html

▶ FERENGI

The Grand Nagus Zek's Ferengi Home Page A great all-around *Trek* page with special emphasis on the master merchants. The Grand Nagus offers audio files ("new customers are like razor-toothed Greeworms: they can be succulent, but sometimes they bite back!"), reviews of CD-ROMs, an image gallery, fan fiction, and of course, the Ferengi Rules Of Acquisition—all at no cost to you! You'd think there had to be a catch, but there isn't. There's also a feature on the Grand Nagus's newly commissioned ship the *USS Vancouver*, with ship statistics and crew information—they're still looking for a few good humanoids to fill key positions, so apply today!
WEB http://www.geocities.com/Hollywood /8110/index.html

The Ferengi Rules of Acquisition Dozens of RoA lists are floating around cyberspace, but this is the best by far. It updates immediately after a new rule pops up on *DS9*. Each rule is linked to detailed info on the episode it originated from, and it even fills in the unaired rules with Trekker submitted Netquisitions—Rule 13: Wounds heal, but debt is forever.; Rule 42: What's mine is mine, and what's yours is mine too; Rule 112: Celebrate when you are paid, not when you are promised; Rule 71: There's a customer born every minute.
WEB http://www.bradley.edu/campusorg /psiphi/DS9/rules.html

Ferengi Alliance A basic A-Z of everything Ferengi, from Oo-mox to Argine. The entries are sometimes perfunctory, even out-of-date—e.g. the entry for Ferengi death rituals does not mention the recently profiled tradition of selling off the remains of the deceased. But a number of them are priceless (well, everything has a price): Upon entering a Fer-

engi home—Host: "Welcome to our home. Please leave your imprint on the legal waivers, and deposit your admission fee in the box by the door." He then places his hands together at the wrist (hands apart) and says "Remember, my house is my house." The guests respond, "As are its contents."
WEB http://www.amaranth.com/~jlock /ferengi.html

▶ GORN

Gorn Home Page The Gorn are cheesy but fondly remembered aliens from the original Star *Trek* series that were never seen again (except in an animated-series episode). Now the seven-foot-tall, iridescent-eyed, warrior lizards finally get some respect with their own home page, mastered by *Trek* lost-race champion Andrea Izzoti; this gallery even links to other Izzoti sites featuring Tellarites, Horta, the Talosians, and more. Learn about Gorn history and politics and download pics of cowboy diplomat Captain Kirk battling a Gorn in "Arena."
WEB http://www.geocities.com/Hollywood /4271/gorn.htm

▶ KLINGON

A Page Written in Klingonese To get some level of consistency in the *Star Trek* projects, linguist Marc Okrand invented a Klingon language, both words and grammar, from the ground up. We're not talking about a few grunts and utterances that sound vaguely alien; we're talking an entire language. At this point, Klingon has pretty much eclipsed Esperanto in popularity and is now inching its way onto the Web with various language resources. You can even get "Hamlet" and "The Gospel According to St. Mark" in Klingon. If you are a *val yoq*, you can use the English equivalent page.
WEB http://galaxy.neca.com/~soruk /tlhIngan

alt.shared-reality.startrek.klingon The Klingon role-playing newsgroup is similar to long-established newsgroups such as alt.dragons-inn and alt.callahans: users post role-playing style messages for others and collectively create stories in which all play a part. Please be aware that a.s-r.s.k is not for people to come in, post a one-liner, and then wait for someone to respond. Messages are expected to be fairly lengthy, with a description of your character's participation in the story as well as the surroundings and character development such as inner thoughts, life history, plans, and dreams. New characters can join—for example, if after reading a series of messages, you could create the role of a Klingon crewman in for a drink at the bar, walk into the bar and "note the fist fight between the two drunken officers, pay it no heed, and step over the comatose form of Captain Krang on the floor next to the Terran jukebox…" and go on from there. Warning: do not develop other people's characters. If a character has been created with certain motivations and character attributes, like history or rank, it is not for you to reveal that someone else's character is a Cardassian spy or accidentally reveal some lacy pink underwear underneath someone else's battle armor. Nor should you turn an opponent into a cringing coward just because it's your turn to write part of the story. The group is not here for discussions of the current week's *Star Trek* episodes or making plans to attend a *Trek* convention. There are more than enough newsgroups for that. Buyer beware: some of the more dedicated posters to alt.shared-reality.startrek.klingon like to use the actual Klingon language in their postings. The simplest way to get around them is to take part in one of the other discussion threads; posters for whom a.s-r.s.k is a language contest are best left to their own joys. Some days, traffic is light but gets going again with a good new jumping-off point for the storytelling. The group is only carried on about one out of every four Internet sites worldwide; if your site does not carry it, simply ask the people who run your site to add it to their newsfeed.

USENET alt.shared-reality.startrek.klingon

alt.startrek.klingon The newsgroup for those who find mainstream *Star Trek* fandom too milquetoast and sissified—you might call them the Weathermen of the Trekkers. This is a group of irritable idealists who seem to have an insane amount of free time on their hands—enough to have learned Klingon, the velar- and glottal-laden tongue spoken by the warlike aliens. Want to know the Klingon for "meter maid?" Someone did, because the readers of this newsgroup had a whole thread about it. Alt.startrek.klingon also takes time out to discuss Klingon customs and technology: one discussion centered on the question of how a hostile race could survive to the point where they developed spaceflight. The highlight of this group is the translations of Klingon dialog in the movies and TV shows. If the readers here are telling the truth, the Klingons we see onscreen have a very, er, spicy vocabulary.

USENET alt.startrek.klingon

The Emrys Bloodline Jeez, we've never seen a more human-looking bunch of Klingons. Does that mean they're pretty ugly for Klingons or rather handsome for humans? Check out the red, green, and blue Klingon Banner, trace the Emrys Bloodline all the way back to those rascals Q'Dulv and Heghghop, and learn which members joined the foreboding Black Fleet. See full color photos of G'Broch battling Chadnibal (or are they dancing?). *Trek* aficionados will want to check out the posted bios and family-tree illustrations.

WEB http://www.fiu.edu/~awenze01/emrys.html

General Chang's Cloaked Domain With its offer of pricey *Star Trek* memorabilia, this page looks more like it belongs to trader Harry Mudd than to Chang, the Klingon leader. For those who are somewhat tightfisted with their hard-earned credits, go ahead, swipe the .WAV file of Shatner singing "Lucy in the Sky with Diamonds." That is just one of several sonic embarrassments wrought by the original crew that Chang has posted here. Check out his gallery for some more laughs. The general has an odd sense of humor. And we love him for it.

WEB http://www.biochem.abdn.ac.uk /~frazer

HolQeD: Journal of Klingon Language

You'll find it in your libraries alongside *Representations and Critical Inquiry*. *HolQeD*, the quarterly journal of Klingon language. And you'll also find it online, sort of: the editors of the publication reprint their table of contents and highlight selected articles for online display.

WEB http://www.kli.org/kli/HolQeD.html

The KAG Domain

The acronym stands for Klingon Assault Group, a club that collects no dues—after all, they're Klingons, not Ferengi capitalists. They party where and when they choose—that is to say, meetings are not on a scheduled basis. Frequently, these impromptu meetings break out when two or more properly attired Klingons meet up at the nearest Creation convention and get suckered into providing free security for the show. These setbacks aside, The KAG Domain promises to grow from the basic info pamphlet that it is now into a larger Klingon resource, as soon as the Klingon takeover of the galaxy gets past the planning stages.

WEB http://www.kag.org

Klingon Assault Group I.K.V. Purple Haze Newsletter

From Minnesota to Ohio, marauding squadrons of Klingons are laying waste to the American Midwest. Actually, it's just an organization of human Klingon fanatics who enjoy charity fund-raising and attending conventions while fully costumed. *The Purple Haze* online newsletter features such Assault Group-activity coverage as the location of new-crew-member recruiting and the latest promotions of crew members. Oddly, the last edition of the newsletter came out in November 1995; perhaps their Warbirds got blown out of the sky by New England-based *Deep Space Nine* crews during their holiday maneuvers.

WEB http://www.ecc.cc.mo.us/~randy /kag.html

The Klingon Languages

Languages? Well, in addition to tlhIngan-Hol, there's Klingonaase—a dialect created by fans of John Ford's *The Final Reflection*—and both tongues are untied at this site. Includes a translation of Shakespeare's "Sonnet 97," and a link to the Klingon Language Institute.

WEB http://www.netship.net/Startrek /web/Klingon.html

Klingon World Home Page

At long last, the Klingons have a site that rivals what those gee-whiz, high-tech goody-goody Federation folks offer. Klingon World Home Page has an interface like the computers on the Klingon ships, an online encyclopedia, and all the other goodies you'd expect in a top-notch resource for a sci-fi show. You've got info on fan clubs and soon-to-be-released CD-ROMs, plus the answer to that all-important question: Just where do they get those impressive leather uniforms?

WEB http://www.itw.com/~zer0

Kronos (the Klingons)

The Klingon discussion "We are Klingons!" became so large, they gave the Klingons a permanent folder on AOL's *Star Trek* Club. If you've longed to try Boiling Worm Wine and Slimy Tongue Balls, but just can't find the recipes, stop by. A great resource for Klingon warriors-in-training, you can talk about anything here as long as it's Klingon. Are Klingons alien Samurai? Well, did you know, for instance, that the Klingon martial art, Mok'bara, is based on Tai Chi? Or that the bat'telh, the Klingon "Sword of Honor," is based on an ancient Chinese battle sword? You can also get information on Klingon ships, the Klingon Assault Groups, the Klingon Language Institute, and the myriad other Klingon organizations.

AMERICA ONLINE *keyword* trek→Message Boards→Kronos (the Klingons)

Teach Klingon

How many eighth-graders have the time and gray matter to write a computer program that will teach the numbers, greetings, and standard phrases of a fictional language? Well, this kid has, and his HyperCard program is available for downloading if you want to tutor yourself in the galaxy's most guttural language. To start your Klingon education, you will need, in addition to an unhealthy amount of phlegm, a Macintosh with at least a 12-inch monitor, HyperCard 2.0, and Microsoft Word 5.1. **WEB** http://www.duke.edu/~nbuckley /klingon.html

tlhIngan-Hol Immerse yourself in Klingon language and culture. Messages will pour into your mailbox all day and night from members conversing in Klingon and list grammarians, pabpo'mey, who are intent on correcting mistakes. (List grammarians are chosen by the list owner.) High Klingon rather than Clipped Klingon is preferred. You may want to introduce yourself to the Klingons on this list when you first subscribe (try and post the message in Klingon). They're a friendly bunch—for Klingons. **EMAIL** listserv@kli.org ✍ *Type in message body:* subscribe tlhIngan-Hol <your full name>

Writing Klingon A brief description of the Klingon writing system followed by a picture of the character set. **WEB** http://www.kli.org/kli/pIqaD.html

▶ Q

alt.fan.q Dedicated to Fans of Q, this chat forum leaves no question unanswered in its relentless pursuit of information, speculation, and plot and script continuity issues. The group seems to be of above-average literacy, and the flaming and spamming are, at the moment, minimal. We think his Eminence might even approve of this pathetic Terran attempt at reaching out in a vain and shallow gesture of friendship and brotherhood. After all, it's all done in his name. **USENET** alt.fan.q

The Q Continuum Presented in a straightforward manner, but stuffed with delicious and numerous Q-ish links, The Q Continuum explores various aspects of Q-ness, from inquiries into the nature

of their being to news about *Trek* stars' (particularly John De Lancie's) personal appearances and conventions. **WEB** http://www.europa.com/~mercutio /Q.html

▶ ROMULAN

alt.startrek.romulan After a thorough application of Spam-B-Gone, this area will yield some pretty decent Romulan news and information, including the name and address of an international club sponsoring everything from War College classes and fanzines to a bimonthly newsletter for beings whose blood runs green. **USENET** alt.startrek.romulan

Romulan Language Generator Science-fiction writer Diane Duane was scheduled to write a book about Romulans, but she had neither the time nor the energy to create an entire language for the pointy-eared warmongers. So she whipped up a bare-bones BASIC program that could do the work for her by converting English to Romulan with the twist of few algorithms. That program, and its C incarnation, can be downloaded for free, so now everybody can sing Romulan drinking songs in the original tongue. Of course, the language turns out to be mostly vowels. Good luck saying "Aa'iotekii-eo!" when you're inebriated. **WEB** http://www.ibmpcug.co.uk/~owls /romlang.htm

The Romulan Star Enterprise You may come for Romulan Ale, but you'll probably stay for the camaraderie. The BBS is home to The Romulan Star Empire, an international fan club, and members dial in to exchange news and thoughts on the state of the Empire. **WEB** http://www.homeworld.com **EMAIL** info@Homeworld.com ✍ *write a request* <your full name>

Romulan Starship Scandia The latest meeting of the high order of the Romulan Empire is in session aboard the Starship *Scandia*, which orbits high above Dayton, Ohio. For a nominal fee, you can

agree to uphold the principles and traditions of those wacky, honor-bound Romulans. The low level of activity seems to indicate that Romulans-as-nice-guys is a tough sell. If you want, you can send subspace messages to the seven-person crew via email.
WEB http://www.ts.umu.se/~ltcinge /Scandia/index2.html

Star Trek: The Cyber Generation
Trekkers desiring to defect to Romulus can click to this page, which serves primarily as a link to the Web master's *Star Trek*: Romulan Spy Network—which in turn features neat graphics and some fun about a spy named Spanky, the man-eating cow, but which is really just a link to The Romulan Spy Network Home Page. It's all very mysterious. When you've finally found your target, you can learn Romulan history, locate a Romulan dictionary and role-playing game, and get a hearty "Aefvadh!" when you get there. Gesundheit!
WEB http://www1.usa1.com/~mayhews /startrek/startrek.html

▶ VULCAN

alt.fan.surak The teachings of the Vulcan Surak are debated here. No, not Spock's father Sarek. Surak is a person from ancient Vulcan who, according to the group's FAQ, "created and popularized the philosophies of peace, logic, mastery over one's emotions, and IDIC." (That's infinite diversity and infinite combinations.) Step into a forum where members theorize about whether a Vulcan's ability to negotiate with other cultures (and a Romulan's ability to dominate others) are related to a Vulcan's long lifespans. Messages to the mailing list Vulcan-l are often echoed in this Vulcan philosophy newsgroup.
USENET alt.fan.surak

alt.startrek.vulcan Unfortunately knee-deep in spam, this chat location somehow manages to get around to offering some specialized Vulcan information, but a post asking a key interplanetary etiquette question (What is the proper

response to the Vulcan phrase "Live long and prosper"?) has gone unanswered for a disturbingly long time.
USENET alt.startrek.vulcan

Intro to Vulcan Philosophy This site offers a very short article originally posted to the newsgroup alt.startrek.creative. Written in character as a Vulcan Ambassador, the author of the piece argues against claims that Vulcan behavior is often illogical and questions whether Vulcans have any sense of individuality.
URL ftp://ftp.cis.ksu.edu/pub/alt.startrek .creative/misc/VulcanPhilosophy.zip

Location of Vulcan: The Final Word
Copy of a 1991 article from the magazine *Sky & Telescope* in which Gene Roddenberry and three scientists from the Harvard-Smithsonian Center for Astrophysics determined that the star 40 Eridani was the Vulcan sun.
WEB http://wiretap.spies.com/Gopher /Library/Media/Trek/vulcan.loc

Vulcan-L Do you fancy yourself a sort of Surak, a man who will lead his society out of violent turmoil into a New Eden of logical precision? Or are you just hungry for a little *Pon farr*? If you've answered yes to any of these questions, you may want to subscribe to the Vulcan mailing list, which discusses issues of Vulcan culture, philosophy, physiology, and technology. Discussants here are at work on a nascent Vulcan language project which builds on a sizable body of Vulcan-oriented *Star Trek* literature (Spock's World and the Vulcan Academy Murders are the list's favorites). Regular contributors include several students of extraplanetary studies at the Science Academy in the Eridani system (on the planet "which you call Vulcan") who claim to patch into the Internet through subspace frequencies. As is the case in most *Star Trek* forums, members just can't resist speaking in character. Those whose earpoints have been worn dull through misuse or neglect need not apply.
EMAIL majordomo@netcom.com ✍ *Type in message body:* subscribe vulcan-l <your email address>

COMMUNICATIONS

TRUE *TREK* FANS CAN'T KEEP THEIR mouths shut about their favorite topic for long, to the ongoing regret of their non-Trekker friends, families, and loved ones. And when they've driven everyone away and there's nobody around to help them soothe that jones, the Internet is a perfect place to turn for a little relief. Chat rooms, newsgroups, message boards, and mailing lists abound for those gallant explorers of the twenty-third and twenty-fourth centuries. Don't think Paramount's licensed enough *Trek* merchandise yet? Send out a call for a letter-writing campaign to rectify the situation! Curious about the running time for the latest flick? Compare your stopwatch results with other obsessed fans in the appropriate newsgroup. Want to shake things up? Post a rumor that Wesley's going to be the captain in the ninth movie! Then sit back and watch the sparks fly.

▶ CLICK PICK

Star Trek Newsgroups (rec.arts .startrek*) The heart of Net Trekdom is the rec.arts.startrek.* news hierarchy, which consists of two primary groups: rec.arts.startrek.current (discussion of first-run and forthcoming *Trek* shows, books, movies, and paraphernalia) and rec.arts.startrek.misc (discussion of *Trek* in general). For more advanced Trekkers, the hierarchy also includes rec.arts .startrek.fandom (fan conventions and politics), rec.arts.startrek.tech (brain-bending physics and fancy), rec.arts .startrek.info (FAQs and announcements) and rec.arts.startrek.reviews (critical analyses). Quirkier, non-rec.arts .startrek* fixes are in the alt hierarchy— alt.sex.fetish.startrek and alt.wesley .crusher.die.die.die among them. Engage! **USENET** rec.arts.startrek*

▶ TREK TALK

IRC information and IRC #startrek users list This site includes addresses for various IRC servers, including EFnet, DALnet, and Undernet, as well as lists of *Star Trek* ops and ordinary users. **WEB** http://www.maths.tcd.ie/~sj/www-irc .htm

The Neutral Zone Gene Roddenberry's vision of mankind's future may have been one of peace, but the real *Trek* universe is filled with hatred, injustice, and passionate differences of opinion. The same is true of the inaptly named Neutral Zone. Same here. This message board hosts a folder for those who want to crush Wesley Crusher, another for the anti-Ferengi contingent, and still another for those fascinated with homosexual and homosocial undercurrents on *Star Trek*. Some of the more bizarre instances of hostility erupt in the People Who Think They're On *DS9* folder. It seems Lt. Illyria (a friend of Bashir's) and some friends have time-traveled back to the twentieth century, where they have decided to inhabit the online universe. Unfortunately, people neither believe them nor want them around. **AMERICA ONLINE** *keyword* trek→Message Boards→The Neutral Zone

The Promenade Welcome to the Promenade. The Klingon and Starfleet fan clubs each have a discussion folder on this board where members talk *Trek*. But Starfleet officers and Klingons are not the only ones frequenting the Promenade. Discussion folders opened here often address broad *Trek* themes that are not limited to a single series, cover Paramount news and gossip, or serve as hubs for trading merchandise, collecting lists, or discussing games (especially the *Star Trek* Club's popular trivia games). If you're a fan of all things *Trek* and not just a TOS or *TNG* fan, check out the comings and goings on this board. **AMERICA ONLINE** *keyword* trek→Message Boards→The Promenade

rec.arts.startrek.info A moderated collection of information about *Star Trek*, including press releases, new episode synopses, and reliable rumors.

USENET rec.arts.startrek.info

Star Trek And Guinan thought the Nexus was hard to leave… With more than 100 active topics, this is the hub of *Trek* talk on CompuServe. Suggest that Picard is an atheist and someone will cite episodes and scenes where Picard appeared to reject the idea of a supreme being. Someone else will mention that Picard came from a traditional French family and was probably Catholic. Soon, another forum member will pipe in, "perhaps by the twenty-fourth century, *traditional** French families may not be Catholic." Then, of course, someone will wonder about Spock's religious beliefs. And, that's only one topic! In others, people are begging for information about where and when shows are airing, searching for role-playing games, asking technical questions, reviewing the last episode of *DS9*, and debating about whether or not they would, if possible, forgo cooking entirely and just use a replicator. The *Star Trek* library is a huge collection of *Trek* images, sound clips, episode guides, FAQs, timelines, interviews and trivia questions. Paradise!

COMPUSERVE *go* sfmedia→Libraries *or* Messages→Star Trek

STAR TREK Conference With a slogan more inclusive than America itself ("Classic *Trek*, *Next Generation*, *Deep Space Nine* and *Voyager*, all views and opinions are welcome!") this conference allows fans plenty of space to roam across the universe of rhetoric—comparing Tuvok and Spock, celebrating the beauty of Jadzia Dax, expressing grudging admiration for the Ferengi. Though there's plenty of talk about Deanna Troi, not everyone here is an empath, and sometimes tempers get hotter than a Klingon's blood. But with scheduled *Trek* talk every Monday at 9:30 p.m. EST and a second conference room called Ten-Forward, this is one of the friendlier quadrants in *Trek* space.

COMPUSERVE *go* sfmedia→Conference→ Ten-Forward

#startrek The netizens of #startrek know their *Trek* lore, but they're just as likely to talk about occupations and end-of-semester anthro papers as their feelings about the latest flick or series. Occasionally, a devoted fan will try to bring the conversation back to *Star Trek* with a question like, "Anyone glad Kirk kicked it in *Generations*?" Pvall admits he wept. Shocker says, "Picard is better," Pvall agrees ("Kirk is SOO cheesy"), and then it's back to talk of life offline ("where ya from pilgrim," "where do you work pvall," and so forth). If you want the conversation to stay on *Trek*, ask a provocative question, like "Don't you totally think Crusher should've married Picard?" Now that'll get things started.

IRC #startrek

TREK MAIL

Dateline: Starfleet Monthly electronic publication with double handfuls of Paramount news, *Trek* TV ratings, lists of new books and comics, convention updates and reports, and *Trek* storyline analysis. In case you missed one, all back issues are archived in AOL's Dateline library.

EMAIL datelined@aol.com ✍ *Write a request*

AMERICA ONLINE *keyword* trek→Record Banks→Text/Other Files →Dateline: Starfleet

Voyages: The Star Trek Newsletter A mix of speculation, news, reviews, and features about all the *Trek* series and products. Who's thinking of leaving *Deep Space Nine*? What are the best new *Trek* books? Where can you download the best online *Trek* demos? America Online *Trek* events are also announced. The editors of this newsletter can be reached through a folder on AOL's Promenade bulletin board, should you have any pressing concerns.

EMAIL voyages1@aol.com ✍ *Write a request*

AMERICA ONLINE *keyword* trek→Record Banks→Text/Other Files →TEXT: Voyages: The ST Newsletter #

TREK CRIT

TREKKERS ARE NOTORIOUSLY PROtective of their shows—that is, when they're defending them from clueless outsiders. But inside the circle, fans pick *Trek* apart: Episode by episode, scene by scene. So what are you, undoubtedly the only true Trexpert in cyberspace, waiting for? Share your ultimate wisdom on one of the many sites devoted to discovering just what you think. Whether you are out to prove that "Tapestry" is the best *TNG* episode ever made, or you feel the need to point out that Dax's bat'telh was in her right hand in the 750th frame of "The Sons of Mogh" and in her left hand in the 751st, you'll find a place to set people straight. Then, just for laughs, check out other fan's reviews (did they even watch that episode, how could anyone be so wrong?), and try to find even a single glitch, goof, or inconsistency you didn't pick up the second it was broadcast.

▶ CLICK PICK

Nitpickers Central Phil Farrand watches way too much *Star Trek*. He has written five books "of minute and usually unjustified criticism" that nip away at every little plot oversight, equipment oddity, and production problem in the *Trek* universe. At his Web page he has assembled a legion of fellow nitpickers—more than 4,500 fans who love to tear apart their favorite shows. Warp here to apply for membership and peruse the weekly persnickety newsletter for the latest nits. The best online feature is the Glossary, pointing out hilarious stuff like the "He's Dead, Jim" and AOTW (Alien of the Week) Syndromes.
WEB http://members.gnn.com/nitcentral /thisweek/thisweek.htm

▶ CHEERS 'N' JEERS

The Australian Star Trek Ratings Analysis (ASTRA) Web Site How does *Trek* fare Down Under? Surveying only Australian residents, the Web master has compiled impressive-looking charts and numbers on TOS, *TNG*, *DS9*, and *Voyager*.
WEB http://www.iinet.net.au/~sentient /ASTRA

Prime Directive Not to be confused with the Federation's hands-off doctrine (which is elsewhere on the Net), *Prime Directive* is a cheery little weekly *Trek* newsletter that's been plugging away since Sept. 1995. Offering reviews of the latest episodes, TV schedules for upcoming shows, regular trivia contests, and a joke of the week, *Prime Directive* is fairly small, but that makes it easy to squeeze into your emailbox. From this server you can review all the past issues and request a free subscription for future installments.
WEB http://freenet.buffalo.edu/~bp309 /prime.html

rec.arts.startrek.reviews Reviews of *Star Trek* books, episodes, films, and comics.
USENET rec.arts.startrek.reviews
FAQ: WEB http://www.cosy.sbg.ac.at /ftp/pub/trek/lists/rec.arts.startrek .reviews.faq

Ships of Star Trek Survey *Constitution, Miranda, Intrepid,* and *Defiant.* What are "ships of the U.S. Navy," Alex? Wrong! These are *Star Trek* ships. The people have spoken. Well, a handful of them: Voted coolest ship design were the Galaxy-class starships, winning with a whopping 11 votes. The site's new survey includes such zingers as best captain (Janeway all the way, or is Picard the likely candidate?), the best *Enterprise* (the original, A, B, C, D, or E?), the best movie, and—of course—the best TV show.
WEB http://www.geocities.com/Hollywood /1461/ships.html

Star Trek Poll Would you pick "The Best of Both Worlds, Part 1" or "City on the Edge of Forever" as your favorite *Trek* episode? Web master Philip Gaines is taking a poll to determine which *Trek* adventures are most popular with Internet residents. He asks participants to list the top five episodes of each of the four live-action shows, and then the top 15 episodes of all time—any series, any season. Gaines compiles lists of the voters and the ongoing results. No real surprises so far in the results, but they're always changing, so perhaps "Spock's Brain" has a fighting chance. It would be nice if Gaines added some commentary. **WEB** http://weber.u.washington.edu /~pryrates/trek.poll.html

Star Trek Poll Results This poll bravely attempts to assess *Trek* fans' favorite movie, TV show, protagonist, and villain. The results are clearly shown in colorful, easy-to-follow charts. Best news: Wesley Crusher and Lwaxana Troi scored high on the villains poll! Some fans will be upset that they can't add their two bars of latinum—but there are plenty of other polls in the universe. **WEB** http://www.bluefin.net/~paykroyd /results.html

Star Trek Polls With all the different incarnations of *Star Trek*, there's bound to be a friendly difference of opinion about which one is superior. You can check in to see how many people have the foresight to agree with you, and mentally laugh at those who are just dead wrong. Can nine percent of *Trek* fans really believe that Christopher Pike was the best captain? Time to check the counter function. **WEB** http://www.itsnet.com/home/dnielson /startrekpoll.html

Star Trek Reviews Electronic Forum If you like Siskel and Ebert, check out the Trekker version—a mailing list of reviews posted to the rec.arts.startrek .reviews newsgroup. The whole range of *Star Trek* material, from the original series to the latest parody, is fair game for this list's no-holds-barred brand of criticism. Don't expect puff pieces at this end of the galaxy. Writing about the L.A. Graf novel *Firestorm*, one reviewer said

he was "pleasantly surprised" the book ended up being "less than average," having found Graf's two previous novels "at best abysmal." If you disagree, write a review of your own—you'll get the guidelines after you subscribe. **EMAIL** listserv@cornell.edu ✍ *Type in message body:* subscribe trek-review-l <your full name>

Subspace News Network You can link to a lot of *Star Trek* news groups from here, but only if your service already carries them. Some groups are pretty obscure, as in alt.wesley.crusher.die .die.die, so good luck. Otherwise, you'll have to be satisfied with the standard update on the latest movie, and some fan-generated fiction. The one good feature buried in here is the international list of upcoming conventions. **WEB** http://www.wctc.net/~durham /news.html

Trek Reviews Archive Transport yourself to this site and indulge in volume after volume of reviews. The busy fingers of this group have touched upon every episode past and present, plus all the movies and most of the books. The index is easier to read than an Academy star map, so finding some opinions on the latest *Deep Space Nine* episode is no problem. Those who post here are also very spoiler-conscious, and will give you plenty of fair warning before ruining any episode for you with their review. **WEB** http://www.mcs.net/~forbes/trek -reviews

The Trekker Reviews Some people actually dislike *Star Trek*. "It's very easy to hate the Federation—they stand for everything that is boring and overused in a soap opera. They finally have a chance to back up the moral high ground with a bit of action, and once again they hang themselves in a Treaty of Impotence. Now where are my *Babylon 5* tapes… " One question: If he hates the programs so much, why does he watch? **WEB** http://ringo.psy.flinders.edu.au /trekker

TREKKERS

IN CASE YOU DIDN'T ALREADY KNOW, the Internet is just one big *Star Trek* con. But when you enter those sites For Trekkers Only, you can almost smell the spirit gum and dry-cleaned uniforms. *Trek* merchandise is everywhere. Long ago, manufacturers realized that if something has the *Star Trek* logo on it, someone will buy it, regardless of quality. Trekware pages will help you determine what's worth spending your Latinum on, and which items should be shipped off to Ceti Alpha V. And while you're shopping, you can stand around and argue with other authentic Trekkers about issues only authentic Trekkers care about—what is and what is not canon, ridiculous details like actor's birthdays, and of course, the size of your collection. If you still feel the urge to schlep to an offline meet 'n greet, you can get all the details on upcoming cons, and highlights of cons past, online.

CLICK PICK

Star Trek Club One of America Online's most active areas, the *Star Trek* Club is host to several live *Trek* trivia games each week (quick, what's the name of Jean-Luc Picard's sister-in-law? And name the three actors that have played Picard), a monthly club newsletter, new stories submitted every day by aspiring *Trek* writers, and suitably passionate discussions about *Trek* aliens, spaceships, *Deep Space Nine*, and the Prime Directive. The club menu features a schedule for the current series, a list of upcoming conventions, a schedule of Club activities, a message board, file libraries, and The Bridge (live chat).
AMERICA ONLINE *keyword* trek

MINUTIAE

Canon vs. Non-Canon If there's one topic more passionately debated than Picard vs. Kirk, it's canon vs. non-canon. This FAQ lists the *Trek* sources that can be considered canon, from *The Star Trek Chronology* to each of the series.
WEB http://www.cosy.sbg.ac.at/ftp/pub /trek/lists/canon.faq

List of Actors' Birthdays for TOS, TNG & DS9 Though most of the *Star Trek* characters were born in the future, the earthling actors and actresses who play them were born in the past. Find out exactly when with this document, which lists the birthdays of many of the actors from TOS, *TNG*, and *DS9*.
COMPUSERVE *go* sfmedia→Libraries→ *Search by file name:* B-DAYS.TXT

CON-TACT

The Icelandic Star Trek Page You'd need a good reason to make your server go all the way to Iceland to see a generally well-designed (but not spectacular) collection of series guides and stills. But just because it's in Iceland doesn't mean that the pics and latest movie rumors aren't just as hot.
WEB http://www.rhi.hi.is/~arnthors

Jetcom: Your Trekker Group in Rio Not all *Star Trek* news comes from Hollywood; some of it comes from sunny Brazil. You can find out what they think about the future space travelers in both English and Portuguese and read such exclusive features as a Brazilian interview with Brent Spiner. If you've been looking for a perfect excuse for that longed-for South American excursion, check out the Latin American *Star Trek* convention schedule, and then call your travel agent.
WEB http://aquarius.ime.eb.br/~cursino /JETCOM-engl.html

Neutral Zone Bar and Grill Apparently, the nearest restaurant to the Neutral Zone is located in Jackson, Miss. This intergalactic bistro's online incarnation offers a membership packet, its newsletter, *The Replicator*, and links to other *Star Trek* pages, including the European 'zine *Engage*. Too bad they don't offer a menu—where else on earth could humans possibly score some Romulan ale?

WEB http://www.gtlug.org/~chris/startrek.html

Novacon *Star Trek* conventions come in all shapes and sizes. Novacon is one of the big ones, boasting appearances by top-of-the-line *Trek* stars. Trivia contests promise to be a big part of the goings-on. Don't beam down unprepared; download the trivia modules and study up. You'll also find other useful features such as the convention, ticket, and Washington, D.C. hotel information.

WEB http://members.gnn.com/novacon/index.htm

Scottish Star Trek Conventions' Home Page Britain's largest *Trek* group is the Away Team. They bring episodes of the new series to their big projection screen long before the snail-paced release patterns of the European video distributors that are the main source of *Trek* for folks in Europe. They also run two alternating conventions, Contagion and Conundrum. There's one simple way to find out the difference between the two: visit the Away Team's Web site. A lot of the original cast members beam in to these conventions, and fans take the shuttle craft from all over Europe just to be a part of it all.

WEB http://www.cityscape.co.uk/users/fn45/startek.html

Star Knight As organizers, developers, and producers of *Star Trek* conventions, Star Knight really should try harder to promote their conventions on the Web. Some of us probably need more than a couple of weeks just to assemble a costume for a big con, but Star Knight's online convention calendar nevertheless covers only the next month. If nothing else, you can connect to more information about Star Knight itself and a smattering of other *Trek* convention links. Those cheesy commercials for *Trek* cons during late-night reruns are more rewarding than this.

WEB http://www.spyder.net/star

Star Trek Conventions This is the only place you need to aim your mouse for online information on *Star Trek* conventions. A far-ranging listing of national and international cons, the only drawback being that they're listed by date, so it takes a measure of browsing to find one in your area. Postings are free, so gatherings both large and small are available. The site also sponsors a convention of sorts every night with live chat from 9 p.m. to 9 a.m. EST. Since this site is a subsidiary of World Wide Collectors Digest, you can also link to info about all kinds of collectibles, from pogs to telephone cards.

WEB http://www.wwcd.com/shows/strekconv.html

Star Trek Homepage in Graz, Austria! Austrian *Star Trek* fans meet for dinner once a month; any *Trek* fan is welcome, and the location of the restaurant is available online. If you're beaming in from far away, a helpful map can be accessed. For people who'd rather limit their visit to the virtual kind, over 400 megs of data is available, including where to write for autographs.

WEB http://fvkma.tu-graz.ac.at/star-trek

Starfleet Command Page Starfleet Command is a global *Star Trek* fan club that divides the planet into three Quadrants: North America, Europe, and (oddly enough) Singapore. Members of the nonprofit Starfleet Command join the crew of a local ship and advance through Starfleet rankings with club activities. This page leads you to the European Quadrant, which features information about available crews, how to apply for membership, and their upcoming events. You can also link to the Singapore Quadrant's page. While Quadrant 1 in North America doesn't yet have a central site, you can connect to an assortment of Quadrant 1 units.

WEB http://whirligig.ecs.soton.ac.uk/~shd94/sfc/index.html

Trek Productions Besides congratulating itself for its recent *Voyager* Celebration, *Trek* Productions isn't doing much of

anything on its Web site. A link to Tick-etmaster implies that one can acquire tickets for its conventions, but no upcoming dates are listed. When it does get underway, its cons attract the biggest stars (for example, the entire cast appeared at the *Voyager* shindig), so if you're a die-hard fan it couldn't hurt to drop by occasionally.
WEB http://www.shamag.com/trekprod /index.htm

U.B.S. Casual The humor of this page could be considered off-color at best, and utterly tasteless the rest of the time. Posing as a Federation starship that decommissioned itself into a galaxy-roving party mobile, the crew of the United Bar Ship Casual promises to "boldly sin sins no one has sinned before." From the unpleasant Polaroids of the ship's officers to the dirty jokes and shameless illustrations of their "tactical systems," the UBS Casual shows what happens when you mix *Porky's Revenge* with *Star Trek*. You'll want to wash your hands after visiting this page.
WEB http://www.en.com/users/abiron /index.html

▶ TREKWARE

Playmates Star Trek Collectibles List For collectors, a list of over 100 *Star Trek* figurines, and 15 playsets.
COMPUSERVE *go* collect→Libraries→*Search by file name:* STARTO.TXT

Playmates Buy/Sell/Trade Few people understand the unadulterated joy of finding an unopened Playmates figure that you've despaired of getting because you live in the only town in America that doesn't have its *Trek*-collectibles-act together. Sigh. But here, the success stories just roll in. From Utah: "I just got back from my local toy store with Data in dress uniform and ENSIGN RO!" From Knoxville, Tenn.: "You can find everything at Wal-Mart." And, in Southwest Virginia, there's both success and failure: "Just found the Klingon Generations Bird of Prey! It is absolutely BEAUTIFUL. The lights and stand and everything

makes it, what I believe, to be the best ship produced yet! Definitely better than the battle-damaged *Enterprise*." But… "Hugh Borg is not that abundant."
AMERICA ONLINE *keyword* trek→Message Boards→The Promenade→PLAYMATES Buy/Sell/Trade

Star Trek Fine Art Net shoppers at STFA are continuously advised that the computer "does not do justice" to the five detailed *Trek* paintings by English artist G. W. Hutchins for sale through this address. So how can you tell what you're getting? Each 400 x 610-mm portrait is individually signed; the subjects include a couple of *Enterprises*, a Klingon attack squad, and a Romulan encounter. Snail and email addresses are provided for ordering info.
WEB http://www.mag-net.co.uk/Starship

Star Trek MasterCard To boldly take advantage of fans' consumerist tendencies… Decorated with the *Enterprise D*, the *Trek* MasterCard comes with no annual fee and other enticing features. But to snare Trekkers, the Masters have thrown in a free six-month membership to the *Trek* fan club; a free limited-edition SkyBox *Trek* trading card (after you buy something); a 10 percent discount on merchandise ordered through *Star Trek Communicator* (the fan club magazine); and five bucks off entry fees to Paramount theme parks. If you simply must have a *Trek* credit card, this is where you can get it.
WEB http://www.webapply.com/startrek

Star Trek Next Generation—Collectibles & Gifts Features *Star Trek* key rings, clocks, and a lighted halodome (with Klingon warriors shouting orders in their native tongue). Email for more information, or to order, complete a Web form.
WEB http://diamond.sierra.net/trek

LITREKTURE

WHETHER YOU'RE INTERESTED in an official *Trek* novel that reveals Spock has a son by Zarabeth, or a fan fic story that divulges what really happened between Chakotay and Janeway in "Resolutions," you'll find plenty of *Trek* fiction to tide you over in between shows, reruns, rentals, and cons. In fact, between oversized trade paperbacks, hardcover books, novelizations, ongoing TOS, *TNG*, *DS9*, and *Voyager* paperback series, reprints of the old '70s novels, and thousands of fan fic stories, novels, and screenplays, you may have to clone yourself to have time for it all. And if you feel like further jeopardizing your job and all meaningful relationships, you can try writing the stuff instead of just reading it. Always wanted to kill off Paris in a horrible pool cue accident? Figured out a way for the original crew to defeat the Borg? Think the world needs a ten-volume definitive biography of Dax? Get to it, and get it online.

▶ CLICK PICK

alt.startrek.creative There's a lot of general *Trek* discussion here, but this is also the best place to discuss the hundreds of *Trek* books in circulation, and discover the freshest fan fiction. Anything goes here—including slash fiction, interspecies sex, and just plain strange couplings (Janeaway and Riker? Unlikely.) If your tastes don't run to erotica, you have two choices: go elsewhere, or post your own story. In fact the nonerotic fan fic tend to be some of the best around—after all, what is *Trek* without dialogue like this: Kes sits back, and sighs. Tuvok is about to say something, but she's too quick for him… "Mister Tuvok! You said that with a positive twinkle in your eye! It looks to me like you've discovered the comic potential of hyperbole." "That would be impossible. You know as well as I, Kes, that my eyes do not twinkle."
USENET alt.startrek.creative

▶ BOOKS

Davin Murry's Star Trek Book Reviews Tired of weeding through the slew of *Star Trek*-related titles at the local bookshop as you look for that unlikely winner? Stop in and have the grunt work done for you. Murry's in-depth reviews of many entries in the never-ending onslaught of *Trek* books are plot-specific and leave out virtually no details, so if you don't want to be tipped off to plot twists and even the ending, you might want to steer clear. Otherwise, the man is most definitely providing a service.
WEB http://phrantic.com/space/c5.html

Star Trek Book Guide A two-part summary of *Star Trek* books. Each description includes title, author, publication date, and plot synopsis. Several series by various publishers are covered.
WEB http://www.cis.ohio-state.edu /hypertext/faq/usenet/star-trek/CS-guide /books/top.html

Star Trek Guides: Books/Books on Tape/Comics A collection of the popular Net lists devoted to cataloging *Trek* books, comics, and books on tape.
WEB http://www.http://www.netshop .net/Startrekweb/Novels.html

TNG Books/Mags Everybody here has a favorite *Trek* book to recommend, although—you'll be warned—they're not part of the *Trek* canon. But, given that *TNG* episodes are now only in syndication and movies only happen every couple of years, *TNG* books will be the only steady source for new adventures with Picard and crew. When a high school English teacher asked for help picking her first *Trek* novel (she loved the episodes "Offspring" and "Inner Light"), a fellow teacher responded: "Being an ex-high school/university English instructor, I, too, prefer books with strong character development over those with a lot of special effects and 'battle scenes.'"

AMERICA ONLINE *keyword* message boards→ The Next Generation→TNG Books/Mags

▶ FAN FICTION

The Hitchhiker's Guide to the Borg

Find out what happens when Arthur, Eddy, and Ford encounter the Borg as they roam the universe in the *Enterprise*. "The Hitchhiker's Guide to the Galaxy suggests the following course of action: The best thing to do at this point is to place this copy of the Guide in a safe place, so that it will be of use to whoever may find it in the future, because your hitchhiking days are now over."

COMPUSERVE *go* sfmedia→*Search by file name:* HITBRG.TXT

Star Trek Fiction

Jason Tardiff wants to write four sequels to the *TNG* episode "Lower Decks," the one featuring four whiny junior officers. Two have been posted, and they feature those same obnoxious brats. In the second sequel, they venture to *DS9*. The stories are slow, the characters are unlikable—not very engaging. Keep trying, Tardiff.

WEB http://www.mcm.acu.edu/~tardiffj /story.htm

Star Trek Parodies

A series of parodies and jokes—*Trek* crossed with classic Warner Bros. cartoons, *Trek* surrealism, Borg jokes ("What do you call a Borg with a long nose? Cyrano De BORGerac"), and other interstellar giggles.

URL ftp://ftp.std.com/obi/Star.Trek .Parodies

Star Trek Stories

Stories and parodies, from the taut suspense of "Purely Alien" (in which Ripley and crew meet up with the TOS *Enterprise*) to the low, low comedy of James "Kibo" Parry's "They Saved Biff's Brane!" ("OW OW !!!!111 OW !!!! I GOT A BLISTER!" shouted BIFF. He tried to pop it only to discover it was his eyeball").

URL ftp://ftp.std.com/obi/Star.Trek.Stories

Trek Fan Fiction

In the story "Star Trek: Destinies," the author writes "Time is about to meet its end…" In "Nightmares from a Distant Time," the story is one "of loyalty tested, of friendship held, of faith's tenaciousness. It's the story of the heart of a Bajoran…" And, in "Kirk's Other Enterprise," the story suggests an alternative to the movie *Generations* in which Kirk doesn't buy the farm. Written by AOLers, these are just a few of the *Trek* stories, parodies, and filks archived in the *Star Trek* Club.

AMERICA ONLINE *keyword* trek→Record Banks→Fiction

Trek Writers

Discussion for aspiring *Trek* writers. Flesh out story ideas, strategize about how to get Rick Berman or S&S Pocketbooks to read your stuff, and ask about general writing tips.

AMERICA ONLINE *keyword* trek→Message Boards→The Promenade→Trek Writers II

USS Astound

Red alert! It's proselytizing disguising itself as *Trek*! What begins as typically benign fan fiction (two stories about the *U.S.S. Astound*) turns suddenly into Judeo-Christian hubbub. Hey, didn't Picard say religion went out of fashion on Earth in "Who Watches the Watchers?" Still, if you don't mind religion (not of the Vulcan or Bajoran sort) mixed in with your Roddenberry, you might make a pilgrimage here.

WEB http://users.aol.com/theastound /main.html

Writers' Forum

Every week on Thursday evenings at 10 o'clock, *Trek* fan fiction writers gather on The Bridge to exchange feedback and critique each other's writing. The sessions are open to everyone, but if you want to be able to participate fully you need to get on the *Star Trek* writers mailing list. Send an email to Elftrek, and ask to be added; each week someone's *Trek* story (or chapter from the story) will appear in your email box. Although the critique sessions are only scheduled for an hour, general *Trek* talkers and new friends often linger long after the writing workshops have ended.

AMERICA ONLINE *keyword* trek→The Bridge

GAMES & DIVERSIONS

YOU SPENT HOURS IN A FLAME war arguing the schematic differences between phasers and destructors. You posted your thesis paper on neo-feminism in the Klingon culture—in Klingon—to the appropriate seven mailing lists. You finished updating your Bently's Holosuite Addiction Clinic site. Now you just want to relax. You deserve it. Why not play a nice game of tri-dimensional chess or Netrek with a friend? Listen to a few sound clips, wallpaper your screen with images, and watch a few QuickTime videos. Perhaps you could have a laugh over a spoof page, or learn some great rebuttals for those "get-a-life" flames. But the highlight of your downtime must be to throw yourself into the all-encompassing fray of *Trek* role-playing. There, every bit of *Trek* knowledge will be put to the test as you are hurled head-first into battle and interstellar intrigue. Just remember—it's only a game.

▶ CLICK PICK

Starfleet Online (SFOL) So you want to explore the universe? Interested in making friends from distant M-class planets? So Wesley and Nog are your role models? Consider joining Starfleet. You'll have to attend the Academy, where you'll learn how to role-play *Trek* adventures: an attack by the Borg, a plot contrived by the Romulans, a Klingon trial of honor, a warp drive failure, etc. Even if in an alternate universe (or different Net site) you had risen to the position of captain or admiral, you still have to begin as a cadet here. Drop by the Starfleet Resource Center and the Starfleet Misc Articles archive in Starfleet Online for some background on what SFOL is and what you need to know to get through the Academy. Here in the bowels of the libraries, you'll be able to read the cadet manuals on *Star Trek* ships, ranks, races, locations, and technology.
AMERICA ONLINE *keyword* academy

▶ MOTHERSHIPS

An Amateur's Guide to Playing Netrek
ST has inspired a number of computer games. Netrek, one of these, is a popular multiplayer online game. The Web master, who has risen to the rank of Captain, has posted some prey-stalking and phaser-aiming hints to increase your chances of a kill. Even though this is an amateur level guide, it assumes a basic knowledge of the game. If words like plasma, torp, and tractoring are Romulan to you, pointers lead to even more basic games.
WEB http://www.atkinson.yorku.ca/~ayee /online/netrek.html

BattleTrek Defeat deadly opponents in this *Trek*-like game. For Macs with a HyperCard player.
AMERICA ONLINE *keyword* mac software→ Search The Libraries→Games Forum→ BattleTrek v2.0.sit

BattleTrek: The Metron Encounter
You're Captain of the *Enterprise* and you've been captured by the Metrons and forced into a winner-takes-all battle with a Klingon battlecruiser. Plot taken from the TOS episode, "The Arena." For IBM compatibles.
COMPUSERVE *go* sfmedia→Libraries→ *Search by file name:* TREK.ARC

CCG Web site A great space station for customizable card game players. Study the rules, rule variants, and checklists, then transport to other CCG ports in cyberspace.
WEB http://www.cs.indiana.edu/hyplan /awooldri/st-game.html

DoomTrek Change your *Doom* game from a battle against monsters in dungeons to one against aliens on the *Starship Enterprise*. Includes a text file with instructions and a .WAD file to patch your version of *Doom*.
COMPUSERVE *go* sfmedia→Libraries→ *Search by file name:* DOOMTR.ZIP

European Netrek League The European Netrek League plays the game by their own rules. According to the postings on what resembles the *Enterprise*'s computer screen, they take those rules seriously. To join the league, you have to be committed to playing on a regular basis at times convenient to Europe. If you can't make the commitment, tune in and follow the tournament progress of the Chainsaw Hamsters, DEAD (Dutch Extra Aggressive Dudes), and other Network teams.
WEB http://pmwww.cs.vu.nl/service/Netrek/enl

Klin Zha Includes .GIF images of the pieces required to play Klingon Chess and a Windows Write file with the rules of the game.
COMPUSERVE *go* sfmedia→Libraries→ *Search by file name:* KLNZHA.ZIP

The Netrek Game Board Seasoned Netrek players are too dignified to leave messages on a simple message board, and too scruffy to care. According to BloodEagle, they should lift their leg and leave a sign on the old oak tree. Netrekkers from Oslo to Ohio leave their game commentary on this board, making it a prime location for meeting fellow Netrekkers or finding out just what this Netrek thing is all about.
WEB http://www.cwi.nl/~frankt/game_board/game_board.html

Netrek Information Archive So many questions and answers about the online *Star Trek* computer game Netrek have accumulated over the years that they now require their own archive. Various players offer hints for and help with different aspects of the game. The archive is currently in dire need of updating; the old archivist has hung up his phaser and keeps the archive open as a service to the gaming community while he looks for someone to take on the challenge.
WEB http://www.cs.cmu.edu/afs/cs/user/jch/netrek/README.html

rec.games.netrek For people not familiar with Netrek, most of the messages posted to this specialized *Star Trek* game user group will be fairly incomprehensible jargon (had trouble "ogging" lately?). Beginner-level questions seem to be met with rude answers and self-serving braggadocio; typical comments run along the lines of "if you can't figure it out, you don't deserve to play." Some say that help for the frustrated is out there, just a bit quieter than the public rudeness. Others say that Bolo players are more polite to newcomers.
USENET rec.games.netrek

Rules for 3-D Chess Rules for playing 3-D chess are available here. Relies heavily on diagrams.
COMPUSERVE *go* sfmedia→Libraries→ *Search by file name:* 3DCHES.TXT

SFB Tactics If you're not seriously into the board game *Star Fleet Battles*, the messages sent to this list will look like a combination of Klingon and theoretical physics. Here's an example: "1 hex/turn == c (Speed of light) == 3e8 m/s." Uh, you lost me. It's not all like that, but there's an awful lot of talk of "positional stabilizers," "relativistic effects," "drone-users vs. direct-fire weapons," and other tactical issues related to the game. "I think the complexity of the rules is what makes SFB," wrote one player. "You have to study, practice, and fight—a lot. It makes SFB a little exclusive." Yet even some SFB fans get fed up with the endless techno-talk: "It's a GAME, for goodness sake." If you're into SFB, or you think you might be, this is a great destination. If not, steer clear—or risk being "photonned" by a techno-weenie with a stash of big weapons.
EMAIL hcobb@fly2.berkeley.edu

Star Trek Bolo Maps Maps of different quadrants of the *Trek* universe that may be used with the shoot-em-up tank game Bolo. For Macs.
AMERICA ONLINE *keyword* macsoftware→ Search the Libraries→Star Trek Bolo.sit

Star Trek Card Game List Do you have the Cloaked Mission card? How about the Yridian Shuttle or the Romulan Outpost? Check this very simple list to see what you're missing. Cards are grouped in categories such as Artifact, Dilemma, Equipment, Mission, and Romulan.

AMERICA ONLINE *keyword* trek→Record Banks→Star Trek Card Game List

Star Trek Quiz Machine None of that "What is Kirk's middle name?" crap here; these are tough questions in such categories as image recognition and sound recognition. The quiz covers all of the series except the animated one. If you're not up to taking another SAT-style test, the downloads include several well-chosen video clips. There's also a news section which, in trying to be all-inclusive, had postings of two separate outlines for *First Contact*.

WEB http://www.geocities.com/Hollywood /1461/quiz.html

Star Trek Simulation Select your ship and your computer opponent's ship and engage in star battles. For IBM compatibles with a CGA.

COMPUSERVE *go* sfmedia→Libraries→ *Search by file name:* STARIB.ARC

Star Trek Tridimensional Chess Another set of rules for the multi-level chess game made popular by Kirk and Spock which continues to be played by members on *DS9*. No set of rules for the game were revealed on the show, but *Trek* fans have come up with their own.

AMERICA ONLINE *keyword* trek→Record Banks→Text/Other Files→Tri-Dimensional Chess Rules

> ## RPG

alt.starfleet.rpg Ensign Fred(dy) Krueger of the *USS Excalibur* detects an energy build-up on Mockra IX. "I have never seen such immense energy concentrated in one place," he reports to his superiors. "Perhaps this is a new type of power generator the Borg are after." Meanwhile, Lieutenant Cameron Raeghar of the *USS Caesar Augustus* tests the distortion field and works on modifications to the third warp nacelle. It's a tough job, but somebody's got to do it.

In this active role-playing club loosely based on *Star Trek: The Next Generation*, members create characters and weave an action-oriented interactive fiction. To get started, look for the Starfleet Command document SF.RPG FAQ, frequently posted to the group and available at the newsgroup's Web site. Before you join, be sure to read the FAQ, the Starfleet Manual, and the etiquette document. You'll start off as a lowly ensign, but you can move up the ranks quickly; your progress is gauged by the skill and frequency of your posts. Become a regular, and you'll be at the front lines staving off the Borg, in no time.

USENET alt.starfleet.rpg

Archives: **WEB** http://rzstud1.rz.uni -karlsruhe.de/~ukea

Stargame Will Alison, Selara, and Phantom be able to disengage the control umbilical from the Starbase? That's their task, and to learn the results—or to get a piece of the action yourself—subscribe to this *Trek* role-playing game, a mailing list in which each member assumes a character and participates in the creation of a complex, multi-threaded virtual world of sci-fi adventure. You never know what's going to happen on a list like this one. You could be asked to review a set of computer logs, ordered to repair the Warp core, or told to work on a "level five diagnostic," whatever that is. If you want to test your ability to write with Kirk-like bravado, this is the place for you.

EMAIL listserv@listserv.net ✍ *Type in message body:* subscribe stargame <your full name>

Trek Sim Manual For Dummies A manual with advice about *Trek* role-playing.

COMPUSERVE *go* sfmedia→Libraries→ *Search by file name:* TREKDU.TXT

> ## DIVERSIONS

The Athena Star Trek Archive You're no Goddess to us, Mister! Still, the lady Athena has provided a comely selection of images (some original art and screenshots from the show), all culled for

Trekkers' delight. You say you want sounds and video? This baby's got it all; in general, it's an eclectic, if not slightly eccentric collection. The compilation images includes a few non-standard selections, *Trek* trading cards, cast members' album covers, and a vast sound archive.
WEB http://www.cen.uiuc.edu/~paron/athena/trek

The Definitive Trek Collection You're not considered a real Trekker until you hear William Shatner's distinctive version of "Mr. Tambourine Man." Fortunately, at TDTC you can hear this and other dubious musical selections from *Star Trek* cast members Leonard Nimoy, Nichelle Nichols, and Brent Spiner. The best audio clip, however, is the hilarious battle of Barney versus the original *Enterprise*. The perspective here seems to be from the lighter side of the franchise, as the jokes in the *Star Trek* Humour League should prove. There's also an impressive list of links to *Trek*-related sites, newsgroups, FTPs, and Telnet sites.
WEB http://www.execpc.com/~lam/startrek.html

Federation Frontiers Some *Star Trek* sites look great but don't have much else to offer. Other plain-Jane sites have tons of info and downloads but come in a generic wrapping. Federation Frontiers takes the middle road, looking fairly spiffy, and offering a good amount of downloads. It's not the most gee-whiz site, but it does offer that notorious audio file of Captain Kirk versus Barney the dinosaur.
WEB http://ccc-shop.wpi.edu/rogue/trek/default.htm

Ken's Trek Page You'll find plenty of neat attractions at this pseudo-Captain's log entry. Two trivia quizzes (the second is easier) are not just your run-of-the-starship Q&A sessions; look for image and sound recognition and fill-in-the-blanks segments to make it both a little more taxing and a little more fun! Music (in .AVI and .WAV formats) and Quick-

Time videos are ready to be downloaded, but the cool *Trek* stills are look-but-don't-touch, which is downright frustrating. But the otherwise attractive graphics, sleek style, and a multitude of features make for a fun ride.
WEB http://www.geocities.com/Hollywood/1461

Star Trek Images This collection of the work of a *Star Trek* artist houses images created on various graphics applications and posted online for all to see. Some of them you can download, others you can't; there's no rhyme or reason why, and no telling why you'd want them in the first place. These, plus some movies and sounds the artist has picked up along the way, are pretty much the whole deal here; further proof that free time can be dangerous in the wrong hands.
WEB http://members.aol.com/cblim1/private/startrek/trekpage.htm

The Transporter Slick-looking graphics help make this an attractive place to spend a little time, perhaps downloading some of the 80 available *Trek* images, sounds, music, and fonts. Having a hard time keeping all those alien species straight in your head? Take a look at some pictures and major race characteristics of your planet's neighbors. Visit the Federation section to learn what makes it such a revered and lasting space government. Everything's pretty much regulation here; strictly middle-of-the-road *Trek* stuff.
WEB http://lausd.k12.ca.us/~png1/www/2nd.html

Trekdom For the serious Trekker with some time on his or her hands, Trekdom seems as vast as space itself. With the countless pages devoted to each *Trek* spin-off, images, sounds, and links, you may look up hours after first stumbling into the site and think you've fallen off the space-time continuum without noticing. There's inside info on *First Contact*, such as a look at the revamping of the Borg by creepy sci-fi artist H. R. Giger. Take your butt out of impulse and warp

over; you won't be disappointed.
WEB http://users.colloquium.co.uk
/~white/trekdom/trekdom.htm

▶ TREK HUMOR

Are Tribbles Kosher? Hold the mayo!
Excerpts from a message thread where
eating Tribbles is considered.
COMPUSERVE *go* sfmedia→Libraries→
Search by file name: KOSHER.THD

Filking Although a message board and
library are dedicated to the joys of sci-fi
and fantasy filking, the place is often
deserted. For newbie filkers, the library
holds a few introductions to creating and
submitting filks.
COMPUSERVE *go* sflit→Libraries *or*
Messages→Filking

Get a Life—and How to Respond Dos
and don'ts for responding to "get a life"
messages on the newsgroup.
WEB http://www.cosy.sbg.ac.at/ftp/pub
/trek/lists/getalife.txt

Good Ol' Geeky Star Trek Stuff In its
early stages, the site includes *Trek* skits
(e.g, Microsoft—The Next Generation)
and a few sound clips.
WEB http://kelp.honors.indiana.edu
/%7echrome/trek/index.html

Humorous Episode Synopsis Remember
the TOS episode "Flipside of Paradise"?
Well, "Spock gets the girl, so Kirk gets
jealous and starts a fight. Spock beats
him up, but by then he's no longer in the
mood, so they leave the planet." According to Warren Siegel, who compiled synopses for all TOS episodes and the first
three seasons of *TNG*, that's exactly
what happened. Not exactly, but close…
WEB http://www.cosy.sbg.ac.at/ftp/pub
/trek/fun/trek-synopsis-humor.html

LCARS: Alexi Kosut's Star Trek Page
While this page links to some of the
more serious *Trek* sites, its focus is on
Trek fun. Drop by to read the Silly Top
Ten lists, *Trek* filks, or Alexi Kosut's own
fan fiction—*Star Trek: Affliction of Paradise* and *Star Trek: Return to Hellgate*.

WEB http://www.nueva.pvt.k12.ca.us
/~akosut/startrek

Mock Plot Summaries Twisted (but recognizable) descriptions of all the original
series episodes and the first three seasons of *The Next Generation*. So, what
was the "Miri, Miri" episode about?
According to this summary, "The *Enterprise* discovers an Earth-like planet with
no adults where everybody gets a certain
fatal disease as soon as they reach
puberty, so Kirk risks violating the Prime
Directive by giving them condoms."
WEB http://www.cosy.sbg.ac.at/ftp/pub
/trek/fun/trek-synopsis-humor.html

Star Trek Humor League Book passage
on the USS Radish (the fictional ship all
list members ride) for nonstop parodies,
jokes, and *Trek* silliness.
EMAIL listserv@nic.surfnet.nl ✍ *Type in
message body:* subscribe sthl-l <your
full name>

**To Boldly Go Where No Man Has Ever
Gone Before…** A humorous list of 20
unlikely *Trek* plot lines. To wit: "Counsel-
lor Troi states something other than the
blindingly obvious."
URL ftp://ftp.vslib.cz/pub/mirrors2/OBI
/Nerd.Humor/Star.Trek

Trek Plots Fan Warren Siege takes on
TOS and *TNG* with parodic plot summaries. "The Galileo Seven-Eleven," in
which "Spock takes the shuttlecraft to
make a quick stop at a local planet to get
a Slurpee, but the natives refuse to
accept his Vulcan Express card" and
"Skin of Evil," in which "the *Enterprise* is
attacked by a being of pure acne."
WEB http://www.cosy.sbg.ac.at/ftp/pub
/trek/fun/trek-synopsis-humor.html

The Uselessness of Star Trek Well,
some people just don't know a good
show when they see it. A non-fan has
rounded up many of the odder *Trek* Web
pages on a plain gray links list. He then
claims that this proves his point that
Star Trek fans need to get a life.
WEB http://www.chaco.com/useless
/useless/trek.html

Yet Another Star Trek Page If you like your *Star Trek* with a healthy dollop of humor, this destination is sure to turn your dilithium crystals pink. The author of this page has a wicked wit and an apparent abundance of time—or at least enough to plaster a bunch of *Trek* jokes across this home page. Laugh out loud to such knee-slappers as the hilarious lyrics of "Riker Croons All" or the satirical script outtakes of the Spoiler Zone. There's even a growing episode guide that features not only production credits and plot summaries, but also listings of memorable quotes that are painfully funny when taken out of context, or even in context.
WEB http://ws207.iso.ksu.edu/startrek .htm

> **TRIVIA**

All Time Great Lines From Star Trek The unique interplanetary situations in which the *Enterprise* crew routinely finds itself are fertile ground for outrageous dialog. Here, you can nominate the absolute best line-spewing and vote on fellow Trekkers' choices. All of the movies and each series are represented, but it looks like Captain Kirk… wins… the cornball… dialog prize… hands… down! (Grimace.)
WEB http://www.localnet.com/~rseiden /startrek/lines.html

Fri/Sat Trivia games info More than three years old, this *Trek* folder contains a collection of the scoring results of trivia game matches held on the *Star Trek* Club's Bridge, along with the questions and answers asked during the matches.
AMERICA ONLINE *keyword* trek→The Bridge→ The Trivia Center→Trivia Game Library

Star Trek 101—Midterm Exam A 20-question exam for diehard Trekkers. True or False: Commander William Riker has slept with more alien robots than Captain James T. Kirk (ret.). Essay question: Citing Freud and Mill, discuss the odd pleasure of retrieving pointless facts.
COMPUSERVE *go* sfmedia→Libraries→ *Search by file name:* ST101.TXT

Star Trek Dialog Generator Pick 5, 10, or 15 lines, then click "Cook 'em up." The Dialog Generator spits out talk you might expect to hear on any *Trek* bridge (or Ops center). Many standards are included ("He's dead, Jim," "Go to red alert," and "Make it so"), but it all gets repetitious—a commentary on the franchise, perhaps? "Initiate evasive pattern Janeway Four." "Initiate evasive pattern Picard Nine." "We have encountered a problem on the holodeck."
WEB http://www.planetary.net/robots /trek.html

Star Trek Quote Game Match a quote with the character who said it. Questions are in the first file and answers in the second.
COMPUSERVE *go* sfmedia→Libraries→ *Search by file name:* TREKMA.TXT *and* MACANR.TXT

Star Trek Trivia Chats Do you consider yourself a *Star Trek* trivia expert? Well, "RED ALERT!! Classic Stumper Questions Coming!!" The 48 room members quiet down briefly to watch for the upcoming question: "Who did the voice for Alice in Wonderland in 'Once Upon a Planet?'" (Oh no! It's the *Trek* Animated Series!) Hope you've got the answer because "HAILING FREQUENCIES CLOSED!!" Time's up—did you guess Majel Barrett? Or perhaps Abe Vigoda, as some chose to answer? The correct answer is "Nichelle Nichols." BirdOfPrey and DocObee, two AOL *Trek* Club forum staffers host a real-time trivia game every Saturday night at 11 p.m. ET. Another real-time trivia game, based on *The Next Generation* and hosted by Net-Trekker and Data1701D, is held every Friday night at 11 p.m. ET on The Bridge, the *Star Trek* Club forum's live chat room. Both of these games are extremely popular, and The Bridge is always filled to capacity with trivia-meisters, so get there early to get a place on board.
AMERICA ONLINE *keyword* trek→The Bridge

THE ORIGINAL SERIES

NOW THAT THE ORIGINAL CREW OF the *Enterprise* has retired and is resting comfortably at the Actors' Nursing Home (which they leave only to pop up in the new shows as wise old codgers), one of the few places to keep up with the world of the twenty-third century is the Net. You can reminisce about the good times and the bad hair pieces with fellow fans, buy and sell *Trek* memorabilia from breakfast trays to tribbles, and read fan fiction by the more creative elements of the *Trek* brethren. Furthermore, you can get updates on the latest novels featuring the gang, catch up on the conventions, debate the defensibility of Kirk's flagrant violation of the Prime Directive, post a query asking why alien women always wore outfits that matched their skin color, and still have time to catch tonight's repeat. *Trek* has lived long, and is prospering in cyberspace.

▶ CLICK PICK

The Capt. James T. Kirk Sing-a-long Page No matter what his other accomplishments may be, fans will never forget, or let William Shatner live down, his 1968 album *The Transformed Man*. It's in such demand that collectors will gladly part with an arm or an antenna for the original pressing. Exactly why is one of the great mysteries of the universe. If you want to hear bits of the songs at a bargain price, download them for use with the Netscape audio player. Then you'll see why Shatner never hit the top of the charts.
WEB http://www.ama.caltech.edu/users/mrm/kirk.html

▶ MOTHERSHIPS

Largent's No New Trek Guide Web master Largent waxes nostaligic about a time when Trek depended more on imagination than special FX. To that end, he dedicates this guide to the original series' crew and villains, with episode guides that contain a little bit of trivia and a lot of memories and opinions about each show. The site may not have much new information, if any, but Largent's enthusiasm and point of view will invigorate many TOS fans.
WEB http://www.msms.doe.k12.ms.us/~mlargent/Trek.html

Star Trek: The Original Series Central Do you want a picture of Captain Sulu aboard the *Excelsior* signed by George Takei? Or pictures of many of the members of the TOS crew, autographed by the actors? Of course you do. Surf to yet another of Jeff "Koganuts" Koga's picture galleries for nice (but static) publicity photo shots from the later *Trek* movies. Aside from being a great source for pics, Koga's pages (there are similar offerings for the other shows) are also fantastic starting points for linking to sites about *Trek* and other SF entities.
WEB http://underground.net/~koganuts/Galleries/sttos.html

▶ CAST & CREW

The Classic Star Trek Game For IBM compatibles.
COMPUSERVE *go* sfmedia→Libraries→Search by file name: TRKEGA.ARC

In Search of Middle C: The Music of Leonard Nimoy A cabal of evil aliens, seeking to discredit the Federation, persuaded Leonard Nimoy to follow in the steps of William Shatner by recording an album of pop tunes. Two of the songs were later put on a Rhino CD called *Golden Throats*. All of the .AIFF sound clips come from that CD, as the Web master does not have Spock's original album.
WEB http://www.calweb.com/~ejr/spock_sings.html

Kirk & Spock Relationship? For years fanzines have speculated about a sexual relationship between Spock and Kirk— bisexual buddies, if you will. Who knows

if Spock had accessed the Captain's Log after hours? Their camaraderie has always inspired a tremendous response in Trekkers, with fans even now hoping that Kirk will be brought back somehow to help Spock with his mission to influence the Romulan Empire. But, lovers? Most fans don't think so, although, says one, "part of the fun of *Star Trek* is to speculate on all possibilities." And, taking his advice, Todd writes, "I doubt it [that Spock and Kirk are lovers]... but that doesn't mean I've never fantasized myself into a three-way with them both!"
AMERICA ONLINE *keyword* trek→Message Boards→Classic Trek→Kirk & Spock Relationship

Match McCoy's Quotes Match "Dammit, Jim. I'm a doctor" quotes with the right episodes. Fun for kids. Fun for doctors. Fun for kids of doctors.
COMPUSERVE *go* sfmedia→Libraries→ Search by file name: MCCOY.TXT

Star Trek TOS Episode by Episode Quiz Quiz with a question for every episode.
COMPUSERVE *go* sfmedia→Libraries→ Search by file name: EPQUIZ.TXT

▶ MARKETPLACE

TOS Buy/Sell/Trade For serious fans only, this site is devoted to the granddaddy of all *Trek* series, which has the longest history and also the most precious merchandise. If you want to unload a lobby card from *Star Trek: The Motion Picture*, or you have a movie poster that confirms William Shatner's appearance in *The Brothers Karamazov*, this is the place for you.
AMERICA ONLINE *keyword* trek→Message Boards→Classic Trek→TOS→Buy/Sell /Trade

▶ DIVERSIONS

Star Trek (original TV series) Sounds "It's worse than that he's dead, Jim, dead Jim, dead Jim, it's worse than that he's dead Jim, dead Jim dead." OK, so they don't have the song, but they do have "Don't love her! Don't love her!!

She'll kill you if you love her!!!"
WEB http://www.geocities.com/Hollywood /1158/sttos.html

TOS Sounds "You're too beautiful to ignore. Too much woman." Sex, sex, sex. That's all Kirk ever though about. If an alien had lips, they were in big trouble. Get the come-on lines and more at this archive. Requires a Mac and a HyperCard player.
AMERICA ONLINE *keyword* mac software→ Search the Libraries→Trek1.sit

Trek Button Sounds Button sounds created a lot of the atmosphere on TOS. Now you can recreate some of the best on your computer, if you have a Mac and a HyperCard player. Relive the *all* the magic here.
AMERICA ONLINE *keyword* mac software→ Search the Libraries→Trek buttons 3.0.sit

THE NEXT GENERATION

WITH AN ENSEMBLE OF ACCOM-plished actors portraying some of the most memorable characters in TV history, hundreds of engaging, innovative scripts—not to mention a million-dollar-per-episode budget—*TNG* is considered by many to be the best *Star Trek* show of them all. *The Next Generation* was a ratings winner for all of its seven seasons—until it was ignominiously pulled from the air so that its crew could occupy the bridge of a big-screen *Enterprise*. Patrick Stewart, Jonathan Frakes, Brent Spiner, et al. are paid tribute for their work both past and present at a group of sites devoted exclusively to *TNG*. As the series is still fresh in people's minds, and still in reruns, there's a large demand for online *TNG* material. And with the film series progressing, there's more to come, from movie rumors and previews to online plot synopses, scripts, and stills. Set course for these sites and engage.

▶ CLICK PICK

Star Trek: The Next Generation The well-designed but slightly overwhelming graphics were obviously created with frame-capable browsers in mind. But if you have the equipment, you can access Starfleet personnel profiles and keep up to stardate on your favorite crew members' stats. *ST: TNG* fonts and screensavers, as well as Jerry Goldsmith's wonderful theme music are available in the file library, but they're Windows-compatible only. Is your warp theory a little rusty? Brush up in the document library. Before you leave, check out the Letterman-esque top ten lists.
WEB http://home.sprynet.com/sprynet /laforge

▶ MOTHERSHIPS

20 Questions Star Trek TNG Quick Quiz Twenty-question quiz based on *TNG*. Question one: "What warp speed, since 'Force of Nature,' are all starships forbid-den to exceed unless in emergencies?"
COMPUSERVE *go* sfmedia→Libraries→ *Search by file name:* QKQUIZ.TXT

alt.ensign.wesley.die.die.die Have you ever been inspired to kill *TNG*'s annoying child prodigy? Members of this group have—repeatedly and creatively. David wants to unearth the story in which Wesley "wired up some console to watch some porno, and he was walking behind Counselor Troi and looking at her butt and she turns around and smacks him." Richard sends it to him. When posts to the group suggest that members are secretly attracted to Wil Wheaton and jealous of him, Frederick responds: "We hate the character, not the actor. In fact, if you had read this group for more than 5 minutes, you would know that Wil Wheaton knows about this group and thinks it is hilarious. So go away. Log out. This is the information superhighway, and you are about to get run over."
USENET alt.ensign.wesley.die.die.die

The Newt Generation Image of Newt Gingrich as a Borg. If only we were so lucky to have the *Enterprise* on his tail.
COMPUSERVE *go* sfmedia→Libraries→ *Search by file name:* NEWTGE.JPG

Star Trek: The New College Generation This site offers a *Next Generation* spoof in the form of a several plays written over the course of three college semesters. The crew of the *Enterprise* reside in a college dormitory: Picard has Beatles posters on his wall and Worf watches "Gorgeous Ladies Of Wrestling" on television. Stay tuned.
WEB http://www.virginia.edu/~newcoll /ST:TNCG.html

Star Trek: The Next Generation Prevent the Romulans from taking over a vital sector of the universe armed only with a Hypercard-playing Macintosh
AMERICA ONLINE *keyword* mac software→ Search the Libraries→ST-TNG.sit

Star Trek: The X Generation The *USS AMC Pacer* treks through space with Captain Jean-Luc Slackard in command, to boldly go… in style. Much of the crew spends most of their time thinking up cool band names, playing air guitar, and getting tattoos. Most inspired casting is Lt. Waif, a painfully thin Klinger (the codependent version of Klingons) with stringy hair who enjoys walking about the starship in designer jeans and no top. It's a cool mix of social and *Trek* commentary, with no real fiction yet, but the Web master welcomes more ideas to expand this slacker universe.
WEB http://www.netaxs.com/~tgi/stxgen/xgen.html

Warped Trek: The Next Generation A site that was initially developed at Paramount, Warped Trek soon went independent for various reasons, and it puts most other fantasy-team matchup pages to shame. Hear compelling sound clips as different TOS and *TNG* characters square off against one another. Will Spock outlogic Riker? Does Crusher's feminine perspective give her an edge over Bones? With such forceful questions nicely illustrated with color pics, you may not need to follow the links to other *Trek* sites.
WEB http://www.gj.net/~pcconfig/warp1.html

▶ CAST & CREW

alt.sexy.bald.captains Dominated by a group calling itself the Patrick Stewart Estrogen Brigade ("that's PSEB, with a silent P, as in psychotic," notes one member). Devotees post their desire to "grope him like a piece of meat." Three members visited New York to see Stewart in "A Christmas Carol," and after the show, they got to touch him! ("Yes, my shaking little hand reached out and gently stroked the captain's l-l-l-leather jacket. It was lovely.") Of course, Picard's not the only bald captain to lust after… there's always *The Love Boat*'s Captain Stubing. One of the strangest spots on the Net; an amusing frontier for lurkers.
USENET alt.sexy.bald.captains

Brent Spiner Page Do androids dream of escaping the makeup chair? That's about the only unanswered question here. Keep track of his skyrocketing post-*Trek* career. Find out which upcoming *Star Trek* conventions will be graced by Spiner and what anecdotes he's likely to share. Download your favorite Brent Spiner photo, pale-droid or human style. With his album, *Ol' Yellow Eyes is Back*, Brent follows the song-steps of some formidable fore-Trekkers; sample in the OYE section. It's not as good as Shatner's or Nimoy's recordings, but not every scribble can be a Picasso. For those who can't leave well enough alone, link to one of the other Spiner sites at the bottom of the page.
WEB http://www.millennianet.com/lee/brentpage.html

Patrick Stewart Appreciation Society The PSAS is a group of fans obsessed with the beauteous bald one's many alter-*Trek* activities. See Mr. Stewart in a Tux (Stewart… Patrick Stewart) looking pretty darn sharp. Peruse Patrick's bio, from his humble beginnings through his distinguished career. Wondering wistfully what dreamy Patrick's doing right now? Check it out in What's New with Patrick. This site features credits from his various film, TV, and theater ventures and, of course, photos galore. They'll even post your personal message here—perhaps someday he'll come across it as he treks through cyberspace.
WEB http://ourworld.compuserve.com/homepages/psas

Patrick Stewart Estrogen Brigade Society This predominantly female group sings the praises and considers the qualities of the much-admired Stewart. FAQs on PSEB and the divine Mr. S are available to all peons, although it seems like much of the "inside" information is reserved for members only-sections. Download pictures of the man himself both in and out of uniform (no, not naked, just not in Starfleet uniform) and the impressive array of his roles past, present, and near future. There's also

info on how to become a PSEB member if you wish to make it so. It's pretty simple, and doesn't cost anything.
WEB http://www.ecst.csuchico.edu /~jennifer/OTHER_PAGES/PSEB/pseb.ht ml

The Patrick Stewart Page It's Pat! Hear the man read a Vivaldi poem in that sexy voice, which (aside from that famously shiny pate) may just be his best feature. Lots of pictures at the outset make this look like it's going to be chock-full-o'-Stewart, but the substance is not as good as its first impression might imply. There's primarily a group of basic Stewart stats, such as his marital status (was he ever "Engage"d?) and the age at which his hair began to disappear. The image gallery is fairly full but isn't downloadable. There are a few links to other sites.
WEB http://www.tu-berlin.de/~gruhlke /forum/stewart.html

Riker's Place Dedicated to ST: TNG's stiff-backed second in command, Riker's Place links to four home pages, each centering on a different live-action series. "What the hell is going on?" you bellow, in a striking imitation of Picard's Number One. Well, we'll tell you: there are cast pics (including one of the Webmaster on the Enterprise bridge at a Paramount theme park) and series info, but the most appealing features are the Trek screensavers, icons, and fonts.
WEB http://www.itek.net/~riker

Star Trek: The Next Generation Central You want cast photos? Well, here they are. Every conceivable type of cast photo, from group shots to individual head shots. Download your favorite: be it the bald but hunky Captain Jean-Luc Picard or sexy space shrink Deanna Troi. Wait! Don't order yet, there's still more... you also get supporting-cast shots, from the obnoxiously omniscient Q (John de Lancie) to Miss Astro-Thing herself, Guinan (Whoopi Goldberg). Now how much would you pay?
WEB http://underground.net/~koganuts /Galleries/sttng.main.html

► CHAT

Star Trek: The Next Generation Rather boring, text-driven descriptions of what the show is all about, for those of you who've been under a rock for the past decade. Think of it as a Star Trek primer. There's a little introduction to the show and cast, some fun trivia questions and episode guides, a description of everyone's favorite Galaxy Class Cruiser, and brief views of the alien species one is likely to run into whilst gallivanting through the galaxy.
WEB http://www.ee.surrey.ac.uk/Contrib /SciFi/StarTrek/STTNG

Star Trek: The Next Generation—The Daily Test How many episodes can you name just by looking at stills from the show? This challenging and informative quiz changes daily to test your Trek acumen, but be forewarned—the surgeon general has yet to rule on whether getting a high number of right answers is a sign of mental deterioration.
WEB http://www.sci.kun.nl/thalia/funpage /startrek

Starbase 211 The well-executed main information kiosk lets you interface with a Starfleet computer and access the Federation database. Starfleet vessel specs, with each ship's complement of crew members and maximum speed and ordnance capabilities, are the type of stats you'll be able to access. Visit the Klingon, Romulan, or Ferengi home worlds. Take the Starfleet Academy entrance exam (this is pretty serious stuff—if you get more than 15 out of 30 right you might want to seek professional help), and see if you've got what it takes to fly around the Milky Way in a brightly colored, crotch-grabbing jumpsuit.
WEB http://www.efn.org/~d_mills/top.html

TNG Anonymous "Hi! My name is Ensign Rand and I'm a Trekaholic. Join me and we'll such share TNG highlights as Data's beautiful poem to his pet cat, Spot, which you can either read or hear Data recite. You'll also find, for your downloading pleasure, the rousing main

theme and various sounds from the series. Plus the inevitable episode guide and some A-OK *ST: TNG* FAQs." A cheerful welcome to a lovely site.
WEB http://netnet.net/~tnglover/tnga

Worf's Star Trek Page Desperate for a study guide to help you compare quotes from one *Star Trek* series to another, or even the first seven movies? They're available to download. You can even pick up Data's "Ode to Spot," as lovely a poem as ever written by an artificial life form for its pet. Bone up on the Ferengi Rules of Acquisition or read some original *Trek* humor by people with entirely too much free time on their hands. Still not satisfied? Look through the small sampling of miscellaneous links, FAQs, and newsgroups before you leave.
WEB http://www.maths.tcd.ie/~sj/trek

> **DIVERSIONS**

Darmok & Jalad's ST Next Generation Sound Site Boldly go into a world of great sounds, from the Trek of old to its latter day incarnation. These guys boast some prime Shatner sound-bites, although you'll primarily find links to FTP and HTTP sound archives. If you're a purist, stick to the early stuff or go for the old standards (phasers, sliding doors, "Beam me up, Scotty," and the like), but for the Postmodernist Trekker in you, there are some marvelous Picardisms to be had. If you prefer, download some sound F/X and make your computer sound like it's from the twenty-fourth century.
WEB http://copper.ucs.indiana.edu /~mchaifet/tng.html

Star Trek Communications This trio of Trek sounds includes Worf saying "link established... Receiving" and "transfer of information complete," in addition to the sound of a very familiar *Enterprise* computer beep.
WEB http://sumex-aim.stanford.edu /info-mac/snd

Star Trek: Next Generation Icons "Trek-orate" your computer with icons based on 13 *TNG* characters and 4 members of the Borg. For Macs running System 7 or greater.
AMERICA ONLINE *keyword* mac software→ Search the Libraries→Star Trek-TNG icons.sit

Star Trek: The Next Generation Sounds Booting up your computer? Install a sound bite of Captain Picard saying, "Energize!" Opening up files? The honorable captain will accompany that act with his trademark saying—"Engage!" These and about 25 other sound samplings from *TNG* can be downloaded from this page. From the chilling Locutus of Borg to the warm intonations of Majel Barrett as the Enterprise's computer voice, you'll have your work station sounding like the hallways of the Federation flagship in no time.
WEB http://www.geocities.com/Hollywood /1158/sttng.html

Star Trek: The Next Generation Sounds If "Encounter at Farpoint" is but a distant memory, download sound clips from the first *TNG* season here. Requires a Macintosh and a HyperCard player.
AMERICA ONLINE *kevword* mac software→ Search the Libraries→StarTrek_TNG.sit

Tong's TNG Sounds This enormous collection of *TNG* sound clips will make your ears ring. The ship noises and the character dialogue downloaded from this site will keep your computerchirping and humming. See the "STTNG _SOUND-INDEX" for a brief description of each clip and its size.
WEB http://cruciform.cid.com/~werdna /sttng/sounds

TrueType TNG Fonts Fonts based on those used in *TNG*, including the Crillee font used in the credits, a dingbat typeface of Klingon-like symbols, and a font similar to the sans serif typeface used on the Enterprise control monitors can be found here for you to download. For Windows 3.1.
AMERICA ONLINE *keyword* winforum→ Search the Software Libraries→ TREKFONT.ZIP

DEEP SPACE NINE

SINCE THE INTRODUCTION OF WORF and the *Defiant* to *Deep Space Nine*, fan support for the show has increased exponentially. No matter how much Trekkies insist that they are for peace and equality among all races and species, they still like to see things get blown up. *DS9* is now the elder show on the air, a fact that undoubtedly helped win cast members hard-earned respect. This is reflected by the Web sites fans have created in the show's honor. You can easily get the latest scoop on cast dalliances, convention appearances, air dates, episode summaries, and sounds and images online. Obviously, the keepers of these sites are ignoring Ferengi/Paramount Rule of Acquisition number 209: "Don't put on the Web for free what people will pay to see."

▶ CLICK PICK

Deep Web Nine With a title that someone, sooner or later would have to have used, the good news is that this is a site that delivers everything you need to know about the shows, and probably more. What about the season-ending cliffhanger on *Star Trek: Voyager*? What's this about *Star Trek* TOS helmsman Sulu, a.k.a. George Takei, guest-starring on *DS9*? The Web master quotes the Ferengi Rules of Acquisition ("Keep your ears open") and certainly lives up to it by providing a tremendous, almost intimidating amount of data. Not only can you read about aspects of all the *Trek* series and movies, you can also catch up on the current doings of cast members (guess who's starring in the latest *Trek* CD-ROM interactive game?).
WEB http://www.tut.fi/~pekka

▶ MOTHERSHIPS

The Astounding Deep Space Nine Plot-o-matic A famous European director once said he could tell the end of a Hollywood movie based on the first scene. Later, somebody woke him up to tell him about an unusual movie. After hearing what the opening titles looked like, the director predicted the ending and went back to bed. In the same vein, modern technology can do the same, but even simpler fashion. You can use the amazing Plot-o-matic's pull-down menus to generate predictable *Deep Space Nine* plots in minutes, and still get a good night's sleep.
WEB http://metro.turnpike.net/anomaly/dstale.htm

Oops Homepage Welcome to Operations control, the center for *DS9* humor. While some bits are inevitably silly (e.g., the long lost Shakespeare play "Deep Space IX"), most of what's here is fairly intelligent and funny. The Plot-o-matic plays on the series' predictability. Bright spots (Why is Sisko better than Picard? He punched Q instead of hiding in his ready room) will leave you asking for more. Check out the list of famous last words for the series, including this zinger: "I let Nog and Jake take the Defiant out for a spin."
WEB http://metro.turnpike.net/anomaly/oops.htm

The Deep Space Nine Archive *DS9* fans can come up with their own Rules of Netquisition—patterned after the Ferengi's Rules of Acquisition—for a contest sponsored at this spot. Many of the submitted rules are silly and sound as if Quark himself thought them up. This information-packed page also boasts episode synopses and production data from the first four seasons of Paramount's *TNG* follow-up. Find out what episode of *DS9* is currently airing in Finland, Japan, New Zealand, and a host of other countries.
WEB http://www.bradley.edu/campusorg/psiphi/DS9

Deep Space Nine Around the World Are you planning a vacation anytime soon? If so, you wouldn't want to miss an episode of *DS9*. Forget about passport information and vaccinations, look up the *DS9* TV schedule in 19 countries around the world, then make sure your hotel room has a TV. A table of countries links you to their *DS9* schedules, related news, and an episode guide. Amazingly enough, some so-called civilized countries aren't even showing the series yet. **WEB** http://www.bradley.edu/campusorg /psiphi/DS9/countries.html

The Habitat Ring: Unofficial Outpost for Deep Space Nine The birthday list is probably the most inventive page on this *DS9* shrine; the remaining pages contain your standard actor pics and bios, episode guide, and links. To be fair, the site is still obviously in its infancy, and the clean, though unspectacular graphics make things easy to read and simple to navigate. If the Web master's stated desire—to make this spot an interactive discussion area for the current week's episode—ever comes to pass, the site could be a fun mecca for chat-hungry *Deep Space Nine* fans. **WEB** http://home.earthlink.net/~hilarie /habitat.html

▶ CAST & CREW

The Doctor's Exchange (Bashir) Two photos of Siddig El Fadil, the actor who plays Dr. Julian Bashir on *DS9*, catching women's underwear while speaking at a convention—what more could you want from the unofficial home page of Siddig El Fadil's Official Fan Club? Site master Laura Cooksey includes some background on the Sudan-born, British-bred actor, but not much more. And certainly nothing current; there's nothing about his name change to Alexander Siddig or the baby he's about to have with costar Nana Visitor, things they must know by now—even in the Delta Quadrant! **URL** ftp://ftp.clark.net/pub/lcooksey /sid.html

DS9 Rocks and Quark Rules Quark's Latinum Lady is the Web master of this page and although the site is undergoing heavy construction, it promises to be alluring for those who'd like to know more about Quark and Armin Shimerman, the actor who plays him on *DS9*. Quark's Latinum Lady thinks Shimerman is the sexiest man on earth and promises a page to prove that. Also featured are a *DS9* image gallery, links, and fan fiction (erotic and otherwise). **WEB** http://www.walrus.com/~quark /ds9rocks.html

"In Exile": The Elim Garak Homepage Garak is the mysterious tailor who used to be, and probably still is, a Cardassian spy on *DS9*. This is the man who said the moral of "The Boy Who Cried Wolf" is "Never tell the same lie twice." Pete Mokros thinks Garak is the series' most interesting character, and so dedicates this page to both the character and the actor who plays him—Andrew Robinson. Read various Garak quotes and synopses of related episodes, and check out Robinson's bio, as well as his movie and theater credits. Would you believe his repertoire included playing Liberace? **WEB** http://www.math.macalstr.edu /~pmokros/garak.html

▶ DIVERSIONS

Deep Space Nine Central Beam yourself all the way over here to download images of *Deep Space Nine* characters. View the lovely Major Kira (Nana Visitor) and Lt. Dax (Terry Farrell) in uniform. Call up shots of Avery Brooks's Captain Sisko (in his first hair phase only), and even get images of nonregulars, including John de Lancie's omnipotent Q. **WEB** http://underground.net/~koganuts /index. html

MULTIMEDIA

Star Trek Deep Space Nine Icons Care to show your appreciation of your favorite characters? Decorate your computer with a collection of *DS9* icons— one for each of the seven major characters (Quark, Dax, Kira, Odo, Sisko, Julian, and O'Brien), one Cardassian, and the space station. For Macs only. **AMERICA ONLINE** *keyword* mac software→ Search the Libraries→DS9 icons.sit

VOYAGER

THE LONE, BRIGHT STARSHIP ON UPN's schedule, *Star Trek: Voyager* is attempting to keep the television franchise alive in the face of greater competition and an increasingly apathetic audience. Still, it's been widely acknowledged that *TNG* and *DS9* didn't hit their stride until their third seasons, so let's give the new kids a chance, shall we? If the tension on the show, sexual tension, Starfleet/Maquis tension, Voyager/any-alien-race-they-ever-encounter tension, continues to rise, the future of *Voyager* could be promising indeed. Its online presence has greatly increased over the years. New pages are popping up all the time in honor of the youngest sibling of the *Trek* clan, and so are fan-generated shrines to some of the show's most popular characters. Check out these sites to see what's cooking in the Delta Quadrant.

▶ CLICK PICKS

Star Trek Voyager Paramount's official *Star Trek* page is accessible only to Microsoft Network members and has many of the attractions you'd expect at an official, corporate site: terrific graphics, plenty of audio and video. The site has show and film synopses, news updates, pictures and clips, reprints from *Star Trek Communicator* magazine, a directory of stations airing *Trek*, and a guide to the Klingon language and culture. This page replaces the older, charming Paramount Voyager page. As a part of their unholy alliance with Bill Gates, Paramount is doing its best to control all use of *Trek* images, text, and even related fonts on the Web. Talk about a Dominion.
WEB http://startrek.msn.com

▶ MOTHERSHIPS

Adventure: Voyager Khal Shariff from Winnipeg really loves his Trek. This beautiful page features an animated *Starship Voyager*, Yahoo Trek links, and

Shariff's Trek fiction (he's come up with an alternate ending to *Star Trek Generations* that may finally satisfy fans). But Shariff isn't just a Trekkie; he's also got sports info here and links to the official sites of the University of Manitoba and *Late Show with David Letterman* (good for keeping up with Brent Spiner interviews.)
WEB http://home.cc.umanitoba.ca /~umsharif

alt.tv.star-trek.voyager The more than 1,000 messages here tell you a hell of a lot about *Trek* fans—chiefly their barely masked misogynist attitude toward Captain Janeway. Besides the expected plot nitpicking, it seems every other message deals with how she screwed up, how her character is badly written, or how she sounds like Katharine Hepburn on helium. You'll also find the usual rumors (Will the show be canceled? Will Wil Wheaton be added to the cast? Did Robert Picardo actually storm the shores of Normandy on D-Day?) and, of course, discussions about the latest cliffhanger (Should Chakotay have gone after the kid? Why didn't the Kazon kill them all? Anyone remember corbomite?).
USENET alt.tv.star-trek.voyager

The Delta Quadrant The quote from Neelix at the start of this page—"You need a guide. I'm your guide…"—gives you some idea of what Web master B & L Consulting is planning. Certainly some heavy duty *Star Trek: Voyager* info will be found here—in the future. Currently under construction, The Delta Quadrant features only general *Trek* links, but promises a *Voyager* shrine akin to the Taj Majal is on the way. In the meantime, it's fun to surf to the series-and-films rumor pages.
WEB http://www.htp.com/bill/delta.htm

Psi Phi's Star Trek: Voyager Archive Tim Lynch's intelligently written reviews give this page an edge over similar *Voyager* sites. A tough critic, Lynch sums up

an episode and then critiques every aspect of its writing, directing, and acting. Trekkers who resent his pickiness can email the man to get their frustrations off their chests. Fans with empty emailboxes can also sign up for email lists to receive *Trek* rumors, press releases, and general info.
WEB http://www.bradley.edu/campusorg/psiphi/voy

Riker's Voyager Homepage Devoted exclusively to Captain Janeway and her crew, this comprehensive page features an updated episode list with corresponding stardates, a healthy selection of *Voyager* images—including some pics that you probably haven't seen a hundred times over—and a generous helping of *Star Trek* links. The original content offered on this page is prefaced with a link to a picture of the Web master sitting, in full Starfleet regalia, in the captain's chair at the Star Trek Adventure—a theme-park experience that allow you to be a crew member on the *Enterprise*. Is that haircut regulation, Captain?
WEB http://www.itek.net/~riker

Star Trek: Voyager Joshua Allen's site, which is devoted to the latest incarnation of the *Trek* franchise, may be skimpy when it comes to graphics and episode synopses, but has one rather unique draw for *Voyager* fans: a great map of the *Trek* version of the Milky Way galaxy. Now you can get a clear look at exactly what Federation space encompasses, and where *Voyager* is located in relation to it. He also advises fans as to when the best time to FTP about *Trek* is: during a *Trek* show, of course!
WEB http://studentweb.tulane.edu/~jallen/voyager

Star Trek: Voyager Central Known for his excellent online photo archives, Jeff "Koganuts" Koga scores again with this brief collection of autographed *Voyager* cast pics. They're all in color and in character—except for one black-and-white shot of Garrett Wang in a sweater (doesn't he look cute?) Both .JPG and .GIF formats are available. Click here to

transport to Koga's other impressive sites.
WEB http://underground.net/~koganuts/Galleries/stvoy.html

Star Trek Voyager Reviews Jim Wright is a guy with a lot to say. If you want a complete synopsis of and commentary on every *Voyager* episode, along with an in-depth analysis the series as a whole, Jim's site is the place for you. His Short Attention Span reviews, working on a rating system from "Perfect 10 Transwarp Instant Classic" down to "Moored in Spacedock," are both funny and thoughtful. Wright warns you if there are spoilers in the review. And he makes a number of good points—if the crew of *Voyager* is in such a hurry to go home, why haven't they put the Kazon and the Vidiians far behind them?
WEB http://www.xmission.com/~jlwright/voyindex.html

The U.S.S. Star Trek Voyager Who will keep count of the ship's dwindling crew? Seth Dilday has announced that he will not be updating this extensive site, which currently includes some choice *Voyager* material: a compendium of great quotes, a chart of the show's Nielsen ratings, the ship's technical stats, and some fairly funny *Trek* humor (don't miss the short but hilarious list of reasons Neelix should be killed). Dilday is still publishing his email newsletter, *The Star Trek: Voyager Update*, which is available through this page and contains much of the same material.
WEB http://www.aplus.co/seth/trek/voyager.htm

Vidiot's Star Trek: Voyager Home Pages Vidiot's *Trek* pages are probably the best place to catch up on mainstream *Trek* press. Did you miss those *TV Guide* cover stories? You'll find them at this site, along with many other articles featuring *Voyager* cast members. The press releases will help you wade through those rumors you'll find elsewhere on the Web. And you'll also be able to access the UPN Q&A segments (transcribed or on audio), character and

episode info, and, if you're brave enough to look, the series' ratings.
WEB http://www.csdsnet.net/vidiot

Voyaging Web master Peter Sneddon warns Trekkers who take *Voyager* too seriously to steer clear. A devoted *Voyager* fan ("the only reason anyone watches that UPN anyway"), Sneddon uses his site to have a little fun with the franchise. The spotlight here is on the Deep Space Adder episode guide, created for a fictional series combining *Trek* with *Black Adder*. Peter offers a new species, a teaser victim, and a moral ("As Neelix says, keep away from the nebulae"), for each episode.
WEB http://metro.turnpike.net/voyager

▶ BOOKS

Star Trek Voyager Novels Watching too much TV and it's all *Star Trek*? Can't you make some time to read a few books? OK, what if they're *Trek* books? See, all you needed was proper motivation. Before you make the plunge and slap some cash down for the lastest *Trek* tome, come to this Web site and scrutinize a full list of *Voyager* books, including novelizations of show storylines and original works. Just don't come looking for artwork or reviews, as you'll find only titles, authors, and the text blurbs from the back covers—end of story.
WEB http://www.bradley.edu/campusorg/psiphi/voy/books.html

▶ CAST & CREW

Hair Trek Update Gene Cowan works at uncovering the frightening truth about Captain Janeway's ever-changing 'do. Is it a Starfleet experiment in phaser-absorbing materials? Is it a classified weapon? Cowan provides quick, goofy fun with pics of Janeway's face superimposed under famous coiffures—including the resultant Whoopi Janeway, Farrah Janeway, and Cleopatra Janeway. The Kate Ricardo is truly frightening, and the Patsy Janeway is the most imaginative ("Sweetie, who cares about Talaxi-

ans, do we have any champagne and nibbly things?").
WEB http://www2.ari.net/home/gene/janeway/janeway.html

Now Voyager: Kate Mulgrew's Official Fan Club Still under construction, this fan page for the actress who captains *Star Trek: Voyager* has promise. At the time of our visit, it was primarily a place to subscribe to or read back issues of the bimonthly *Now Voyager*, the fanzine of the Kate Mulgrew Appreciation Society, which is fun enough in and of itself. You get a lot of writing about the show, brief pieces about Mulgrew's other films (remember *Remo Williams*?), and some humor: "What would Captain Janeway have on her powerpad? Nude pics of Captain Picard, of course!"
WEB http://www.gl.umbc.edu/~mpanti1/kate/kate.html

The Roxann Biggs-Dawson Online Fan Club Brains! Brawn! Beauty! With the cooperation of Maria Russell's RBD Fan Club, Albert Chiu curates this dynamic fan site, significantly distinguished by the fact that it's approved by and contains writings from its object of appreciation. Biggs-Dawson can be seen with and without the makeup she wears when playing the half-Klingon, half-human B'Elanna Torres. Read about fans' experiences with her, updates about her con appearances, a filmography, and a her immersion in the *Trek* franchise. T-shirts, autographed pics, and other goodies are available, and proceeds go to Biggs-Dawson's favorite charity.
WEB http://www.ualberta.ca/~tgee/rbdfc

BRIDGE BATTLE

KIRK WAS ALWAYS READY FOR action. Women or wombat-people, it made no difference. But some complain he was too arrogant and his speech pattern could drive even a Vulcan to murder. Picard is a brilliant diplomat with the heart of an explorer and a voice that could melt polar ice caps. But many consider him too cerebral (read gutless). Sisko seems to have it all—a kick-ass warship, a warm family, love interests, spirituality—but some viewers say the one thing he lacks is a discernible personality. Janeway helms the most trouble-fraught show in *Trek* history—a crew of Maqui, Starfleet, and spies at each others throats, a ship alone and lost in a hostile territory, and there's no holodeck downtime—yet she's flamed for getting teary-eyed and speaking in that annoying whisper. Take your side and throw your punches at these war-torn sites.

▶ CLICK PICK

Kirk v. Picard Over the last couple of years, countless threads have debated the relative merits of the two captains. This is a collection of some of those lists, including the top 100 reasons why Kirk is better than Picard and a point-by-point response by Picard fans. Just listen: "Kirk has sex more than once a season." Rejoinder: "Sex with Picard is worth waiting for a whole season." "Kirk never once stood up and had to straighten his shirt." Rejoinder: "Picard never once stood up and had to suck in his gut." "Kirk never asks his bartender for advice." Rejoinder: "Picard never asks his Chief Medical Officer to be bartender." And, that's only three.
WEB http://ftp.cis.ksu.edu/pub/alt.startrek.creative/misc/Kirk.v.Picard.zip

▶ KIRK VS. PICARD

Picard v. Kirk An animation program in which Captain Kirk turns into Captain Picard. Requires a program that runs FLI animations.

COMPUSERVE *go* sfmedia→Libraries→
Search by file name: TREKMO.ZIP

Tiberius of Borg Captain Kirk's been Borgified!
COMPUSERVE *go* sfmedia→Libraries→
Search by file name: TIBERI.GIF

The Top 100 Reasons Kirk Is Better Than Picard Kirk and Picard face off. The list in various manifestations is often posted to the rec.arts.startrek* groups.
COMPUSERVE *go* sfmedia→Libraries→
Search by file name: 100.TXT

The Top 100 Reasons Picard Is Better Than Kirk The debate continues.
COMPUSERVE *go* sfmedia→Libraries→
Search by file name: REBUTT.TXT

Who's better: Kirk or Picard The rules of the ring are simple: no kicking, no biting, and may the best captain win. That's "captain," not "actor." Picard and Kirk may not have swapped punches in outer space, but in Cyberspace, and paticularly in the *Generations* folder of AOL's *Star Trek* Club, fans constantly fight over the relative merits of the *Enterprise* captains. Kirk's more clever. Picard's a better diplomat. Kirk makes split-second decisions and is comfortable in command. Picard has more control. Quickly, very quickly, the positions get passionate: "Space is a FRONTIER, not a TEA PARTY. It demands a gambling and arrogant nature to get anywhere. Kirk wins the Captain contest hands down." Or, "Picard kicks ass!!"
AMERICA ONLINE *keyword* trek→Message Boards→Star Trek Movies→Who's better: Kirk or Picard

▶ PICARD VS. SISKO

The All-Crew Heavyweight Trek Championship See Sisko kick Picard's butt. See Dax kick Data's butt. See O'Brien kick LaForge's butt. See Kira kick Riker right between the legs! Ouch!

WEB http://207.67.198.21/anomaly/dsfight.htm

Top 16 List Why Sisko is Better Than Picard All right, we admit it: We're kinda partial to ol' Jean-Luc. And half of the reasons on this list are due to lazy writing, not true character defects. Plus, Picard had seven years and one feature film to screw things up. Let's compare stats when Sisko's got that much command time under his belt, shall we? WEB http://www.nueva.pvt.k12.ca.us/~akosut/st/l/list/sbtp

▶ JANEWAY VS. ALL

Comparing Star Trek A side-by-side analysis of Janeway and Sisko comes up with the definitive conclusion that the former is a "wimpy, no-good captain." Now that's telling 'em. WEB http://www.contrib.andrew.cmu.edu/~haney/trek.html

Reasons Why Captain Janeway is Better Than Captain Picard The top 73 list, because you demanded it. And it goes beyond the expected hair jokes by entry number three—hey, now that's an accomplishment by itself. WEB http://hou.lbl.gov/~gmonsen/janeway.html

Reasons Why Kirk and Janeway Would Make a Great Couple The first reason pretty much sums it up: "She's a woman. He's Captain James T. Kirk!" WEB http://hou.lbl.gov/~gmonsen/janewaykirk.html

▶ FREE-FOR-ALL

Pick Your Favorite Starfleet Captain Vote for one of the big four, or nominate another possibility—perhaps the frighteningly green captain of the *Enterprise B* in *Generations*? Kirk fans, take note—Picard was slightly ahead as of our visit. WEB http://www.vis-con.com/singles/starfleet1.html

Starbase 400 Survey Let your voice be heard. Choose your favorite captain, class of starship, series, or film. WEB http://staff.feldberg.brandeis.edu/~davidn/sb400_7.htm

Who Is the Best Captain? Email the crew of Trekker Talk with your opinion. Kindly keep justifications for that opinion under 35 pages. WEB http://www.ogi.edu/~jeffs/ttalk/best.html

PART 4

Sci-Fi Literature

SCI-FI LIBRARY

WHAT IS SCIENCE FICTION? FIND out from the literary giants who create it at Definitions of Science Fiction. Or spend a little time with those on the receiving end of speculative literature at rec.arts.sf.written or the SF/Fantasy Forum on CompuServe, and formulate your own definition of the literary genre. Before you buy another book to add to your sci-fi library, check out the online reservoirs of reviews. Everyone's a critic at rec.arts.sf.reviews, the Internet Top 100 SF/Fantasy List, Bjorn and Sven's Sci-Fi and Fantasy Book Reviews, and the Good Reading Guide. For the latest insider info straight from the publishers, try the Del Rey Internet Newsletter or Tor SF & Fantasy. And for a taste of both new and established sci-fi authors, scroll through the latest issue of Quanta, an established 'zine that has served the cyber sci-fi community since 1989.

▶ CLICK PICK

SFF-NET This is a bustling space station for serious cyberactive fans of sci-fi literature. The Science Fiction/Fantasy Network site links to author- and fan-maintained Web pages from Orson Scott Card to S.M. Stirling. Ezines and publishers, literary agents and agencies, and all of the appropriate book honors from the Bram Stoker award to the Nebula are also listed. SFF-NET also serves as a sort of Internet White Pages of cybersavvy sci-fi fans with a list of home pages of people with a penchant for the genre. You can easily set up a home base here, but it's just as useful for picking up directions to other book nooks in cyberspace.
web http://www.sff.net
picture: **web** http://biotech.chem.indiana .edu/~lusnyde/cover.html

▶ MOTHERSHIPS

Books Of All Kinds Daniel Moore has taken it upon himself to classify speculative fiction into three categories: that

which you should own in hardcover, that which you should own in paperback, and that which you should just check out at the library. Need a frame of reference? The Ender Saga by Orson Scott Card and *The Lord of the Rings*—shell out for the hardcover. Larry Niven's books—get out your library card. It's a pretty subjective site, but Daniel also provides objective links, where possible.
web http://www.whitman.edu/~mooreds /books/books.html

Corwin's Favorite Authors Corwin's favorite sci-fi authors don't stray too far from the norm, including everyone from Adams and Asimov to Vonnegut and Wells. His author index, complete with links to Web pages, etexts, and FAQs, is a handy reference for any sci-fi follower trying to find his way around the Web.
web http://malkuth.sephiroth.org /~corwin/authors/index.html

Definitions of Science Fiction Sci-fi literary greats have not only wrestled with the limits of the universe, but also the outer limits of their genre. Trying to pin down an exact definition, staking a recognizable territory in the vast world of fantasy, this is not an easy task (trust us, we know). This is an archive of the attempts made by some of sci-fi's most accomplished authors—including Isaac Asimov and Frank Herbert.
url gopher://gopher.lysator.liu.se:70 /11/sf_lsff

Feminist Science Fiction, Fantasy, & Utopia Need an antidote to the mostly pale, male world of science fiction in cyberspace? A good dose of feminist sci-fi may be in order. This sub-genre of SF/fantasy isn't clearly defined and can be used to refer to everything from eutopias (utopias and dystopias) to hard science fiction, from fantasy to magical realism, from fiction with a definite political agenda to any fiction which includes a female character. This site covers the spectrum and includes bibliographies and synopses by author, a non-fiction bibliography on feminist sci-fi, a women science fiction writers index, an FAQ, Internet resources, and information on anthologies.

WEB http://www.uic.edu/~lauramd/sf /femsf.html

rec.arts.sf.written Fan fiction and professional sci-fi writing meet without colliding. Many of the newsgroup's contributors struggle with the fact that sci-fi has expanded so much that it's no longer possible for fans to keep up with everything that's published. A large number of semi-regular participants therefore rely on reader reviews—both brief and not-so-brief—posted here for advice on which new fantasy, cyberpunk, horror, political, or foreign books to check out. At its best, this newsgroup is a terrific sci-fi book club. A senior editor at Tor Books, one of the most important sci-fi publishers today, occasionally throws in his two cents.

USENET rec.arts.sf.written

Science Fiction and Fantasy Writers of America You don't have to be a published sci-fi writer to make a stop at the SFWA. Unpublished writers and fans alike will find writing tips, info on the business side of sci-fi publishing, award announcements, and the SFWA Bulletin, just as their favorite fantasy and SF authors would.

WEB http://www.sfwa.org/sfwa

Transformation Stories List What do Douglas Adams's *The Long Dark Tea-Time of the Soul*, Piers Anthony's *Apprentice Adept* series, and Isaac Asimov's *The Bicentennial Man* have in common? In each book, the author takes transformation as a theme. In Adams's book, certain Norse gods deal with perceived pests by transformation, and a lurking refrigerator changes itself into a new horror. All seven books in Anthony's series involve shape changers—primarily werewolves and shape-changing unicorns. And Asimov's robot transforms himself into a human over the course of two centuries. This online resource

includes hundreds of other references to abrupt and unnatural change as a device in literature, both in and out of science fiction. Don't be surprised if you find, say, some Shakespeare here (in *A Midsummer Night's Dream*, Bottom is turned into a donkey).

WEB http://www.halcyon.com /phaedrus/translist/translist.html

▶ **REVIEWS**

Bjorn and Sven's Sci-Fi and Fantasy Book Reviews Everyone's a critic, and Bjorn and Sven (the Scandinavian pseudonyms of Derek and Christian) are no exceptions. The two Northwestern University students rate (on a scale of one to ten) the best of the best in the subsets of High Fantasy, General Fantasy, Comic Fantasy, Science Fantasy, Hard Science Fiction, General Science Fiction, Comic Science Fiction, Cyberpunk, and Comic Books. The wanna-be Swedes tend to agree, except when it comes to Robert Heinlein.

WEB http://pubweb.acns.nwu.edu /~bjorn/sfflist.html

The Good Reading Guide The entries in this encyclopedia of reviews of science fiction authors and their works are actually compilations of posts collected from the readers of Aus.SF, the Australian fantasy and science fiction newsgroup, rec.arts.sf-lovers, and rec.arts.sf.written.

WEB http://julmara.ce.chalmers.se /SF_archive/SFguide

Internet Top 100 SF/Fantasy List Tristrom Cooke has compiled and organized a list of the top 100 science fiction and fantasy books, as voted by the science fiction cybercommunity. Published each Monday, the weekly ratings serve as sort of a reader's choice chart of sci-fi/fantasy books, as well as a guide for sci-fi fans looking for a good read. *Lord of the Rings*, *Ender's Game*, and *Dune* were holding steady at the top of the chart when we visited. Read the FAQ here to find out how to cast your vote.

WEB http://www.clark.net/pub/iz /Books/Top100/top100.html

Search SF & Fantasy Reviews Thinking of adding to your sci-fi library? Before you buy your next book, you may want to check and see if it's reviewed online. This search site makes that a little easier. It scans Usenet posts, back issues of *Eric Raymond's Reviews*, and 'zines for the author or book you enter.
WEB http://julmara.ce.chalmers.se/stefan/WWW/saifai_search.html

SF-RIYL Pages The Science Fiction Recommend-If-You-Like Pages, as in "If you like… then you'll like…" Submitted by cybersavvy sci-fi fans, the reviews read something like: "If you liked *Rendezvous with Rama* by Arthur C. Clarke, you might like *Red Mars* by Kim Stanley Robinson. Set in same time frame, same type of technology, a story about the colonization of Mars, very well written, characters are very human. The technology is very realistic (no warp drives, or the like). You might not like it because the story jumps around a bit. Starts out a decade after the colonization has begun, then jumps back to when the 'first hundred' left earth."
WEB http://metro.turnpike.net/C/chriss

PUBLISHERS

Aspect Warner's imprint committed to sci-fi and fantasy. The Aspect page links to Warner writers on the Web, serves up advice for sci-fi writers, and offers excerpts from its latest releases. Major authors published by Aspect include Kevin J. Anderson, Marion Zimmer Bradley, Octavia Butler, and C.J. Cherryh.
WEB http://pathfinder.com/twep/Aspect

Bantum Spectra Science Fiction Forum Each month, Bantam Doubleday Dell's *Spectra Wavelength* newsletter features its latest titles, complete with excerpts from the books and interviews with the authors. Receive free advance copies each month by signing up for the mailing list here or browse through past issues. Out of bedside reading material? You may want to refer to Spectra's guide to science fiction and fantasy with its "If You Like…You Should Try" list, but be aware that by happenstance all the You

Should Trys are published by BDD.
WEB http://www.bdd.com/forum/bddforum.cgi/scifi

The Del Rey Internet Newsletter A monthly newsletter about Del Rey science fiction and fantasy novels, including book descriptions, news about upcoming releases, author bibliographies, and features. The archive includes back issues as well as order information, manuscript submission requirements, and sample chapters of Del Rey Books.
EMAIL ekh@panix.com ✍ *Write a request*
Archives: **URL** gopher://gopher.panix.com:70/11/DRB

ZINES

Tor SF & Fantasy The page of the publisher devoted to science fiction and fantasy works features Tor's publishing schedule, sample chapters, upcoming author appearances, and (gasp) links to the competition. One of its more popular and prolific authors, Robert Jordan, is featured prominently.
WEB http://www.tor.com

E-Scape Isn't that what it's all about? This bi-monthly digital journal of speculative fiction publishes science fiction, fantasy, and horror, along with game reviews, convention schedules and announcements, and other articles of interest to fandom.
WEB http://www.interink.com/escape.html

Infinity Online The baby of the speculative fiction Web 'zines, *Infinity Online* includes sci-fi short stories, reviews, real news from NASA, and related links.
WEB http://infinity.america.net

Quanta This award-winning online fiction magazine, specializing in science fiction and fantasy, has been around longer than most of us have been on the Web—since 1989. Check out the latest issue of this Internet institution, browse *Quanta* stories by issue or author (you'll find both new and established authors here), or search the archives.
WEB http://www.etext.org/Zines/Quanta

DOUGLAS ADAMS

DON'T PANIC. ALTHOUGH THERE hasn't been much new from Douglas Adams of late, the author himself refuses to say that *The Hitchhiker* series is through. So what if he killed off the entire cast? Some devotees think it's for a good reason—when Adams finally writes a follow-up, all the characters will be in the same place, so he won't have to waste half the book reuniting them. There are plenty of ways for cyberhitchers to get their fix during the long, dark teatime in between books. Whether it's a guide to the Guide, a directory of quotes or a myriad of explanations why the number 42 is the answer to the question about *Life, the Universe, and Everything*, you'll find the answers here. And once you have them, join the club at the Deep Thought site, or help to create an electronic encyclopedia of the universe. Alternatively, find out what else the old boy's been up to.

▶ CLICK PICKS

alt.fan.douglas-adams If consciousness is a dense, blurry fog, then the humor of Douglas Adams is an out-of-control lorry that emerges from that fog and rebounds off street signs and the occasional pedestrian before crashing through the window of a corner off license. This is the place for PanGalactic Gargleblasters, Vogon poetry, and the answer to the question of Life, the Universe, and Everything. Alt.fan .douglas-adams showers readers with incredibly unenlightening points of philosophy and anecdotes of how the number 42 has influenced/changed/ended their lives. While old reports suggested that Adams himself was a no-show at the group, new surveillance has revealed that the the head honcho occasionally drops by for a laugh. When he's not in the bath. **USENET** alt.fan.douglas-adams

▶ THE AUTHOR

Dirk Gently's Detective Agency Help determine if Zaphod Beeblebrox is in fact

popular enough to win the next universal election. Cast your vote in the Galactic Ruler Poll—the two-headed, three-armed alien candidate with a criminal record may actually have a fighting chance. Look at the alternatives—Bill Clinton, Newt Gingrich, and the Brain. **WEB** http://carbon.cudenver.edu /~mstilman/zaphod/index.cgi

Douglas Adams "'He believed in a door. He must find that door. The door was the way to… to… The Door was The Way. Good. Capital letters were always the best way of dealing with things you didn't have a good answer to.'—The Electric Monk discovering the reason why there are so many acronyms in computing." This Douglas Adams cybercult maintains a quote directory covering: *The Hitchhiker's Guide*; *The Restaurant at the End of the Universe*; the original radio scripts; *Life, The Universe, and Everything*; *So Long, and Thanks for All the Fish*; *Mostly Harmless*; *Dirk Gently's Holistic Detective Agency*; *The Long Dark Tea-Time of the Soul*, and some choice quotes from DNA (Douglas Noel Adams) himself. You'll also find a bibliography, an index to *The Hitchhiker's Guide*, and Douglas Adams's Guide to the Macintosh. **WEB** http://anubis.science.unitn.it /services/sf/DA/adams.html

Douglas Adams This message board touts itself as the place to talk about things ranging from the question of Trillian's sex life to precise nutritional value of towels stains. Recent message topics include discussions of the latest book, *Mostly Harmless*, the upcoming book, *Salmon of Doubt*, and everyone's favorite Adams character. **AMERICA ONLINE** *keyword* scifi→message boards→SF Authors A-L→List Topics→ Douglas Adams

Douglas Adams Worship Page A galaxy of FAQs—including the attractive, not-so current alt.fan.douglas-adams FAQ, the not-so-attractive, oh-so-recent version of the bibliographical FAQ, and the differences between the U.S. and U.K. versions of *Life, the Universe, and Everything*. Dedicated DNA devotees will also find searchable indexes for *The Hitchhiker's Guide* and *Dirk Gently*, links to online parodies, copies, and spoofs like *The Coffee Machine at the End of the User Area* and *How to Build Your Own Asylum*, and information on joining ZZ9 Plural Z Alpha, the official DNA fan club. **WEB** http://www.umd.umich.edu /~nhughes/dna

FAQ—alt.fan.douglas-adams This FAQ features everything you ever wanted to know about DNA: from his favorite computer (The Mac PowerBook), to the theme music fatured on the radio show ("Journey of the Sorcerer" by the Eagles), to an improvised recipe for the Terran Pan Galactic Gargle Blaster (Ever-Clear, Bombay Sapphire gin, Wild Turkey, Herredura tequila, rum, and the worm from a bottle of Mezcal). But be careful, you'll need two heads to down the whole thing. You'll also find explanations to some of the less lucid moments in Adams's writing, like the ending to *Dirk Gently's Holistic Detective Agency* and "Young Zaphod Plays It Safe." **WEB** http://www.umd.umich.edu /~nhughes/dna/faqs/dnafaq.html

Oxford University Douglas Adams Society "We at Dougsoc do recognise that there is life outside of *The Hitchhiker's Guide to the Galaxy*. We propose that it should be explored with caution and not inconsiderable amount of alcohol." This oft-soused society at Oxford lets aliens (those outside of Oxford) in on their role-playing pub crawls, based on DNA books and other cult phenomena, like *Rocky Horror* and *The Prisoner*, and provides access to their highly-amusing magazine, *Zarking Fardwarks*. **WEB** http://users.ox.ac.uk/~dougsoc

The Web Page at the End of the Universe Just can't get enough of the Cosmic Cutie? The green guy greets you (yet again) at this page, where you can read the *HHGTTG* quote of the week, learn

about the latest Douglas Adams news, or subscribe to the newsletter, *DNA News*. **WEB** http://www.angelfire.com/pg0 /dontpanic/index.html

▶ **HITCHHIKER'S GUIDE**

Deep Thought Elvis Presley died at the age of 42. A Playtex Wonderbra consists of exactly 42 parts. The city of Jerusalem covers 42 square miles. Coincidence? Hundreds of DNA fans think not, though Adams himself has tried to dispel any myths about the number by posting to Usenet, "The answer to this is very simple. It was a joke. It had to be a number, an ordinary, smallish number, and I chose that one. Binary representations, base thirteen, Tibetan monks are all complete nonsense. I sat at my desk, stared into the garden and thought '42 will do' I typed it out. End of story." Nonetheless, the legend of 42 lives on. **WEB** http://www.empirenet.com /personal/dljones/index.html

The Guide Homepage Talk to other hitchhikers in the cybergalaxy through the magic of Telnet. This hitcher, based at Louisiana Tech, welcomes you into The Spaceport: "The shortstop in the left field of our beloved galaxy. Here one may enjoy the peaceful hum of fluorescent lighting, eat a good barbecue dinner, and venture into the plane of experience as a refreshed traveler. No, not merely a traveler; rather a hitchhiker in the carpool of adventure trying to pass the toll gate without paying. So please, enjoy your stay, contribute to our knowledge, and please, please don't forget your towel." **WEB** http://www.latech.edu/~jfond /panic.jpg

Hitchhiker's Guide to the Galaxy "*The Hitchhiker's Guide to the Galaxy* is the first book in a five-book, increasingly inaccurately-named trilogy written by Douglas Adams, based on an original radio series which aired in 1978. There are, of course, forty-two words in this paragraph." So begins this simple page which includes links to sites and sounds, as well as memorable Adams quotes.

Don't be alarmed if the visitor counter reads "42" every time you stop by.
WEB http://www.cs.cmu.edu/afs/andrew/usr18/mset/www/42.html

Hitchhiker's Guide to the Galaxy—The Infocom Game Just what you're looking for: a guide to the guide. *The Hitchhiker's Guide to the Galaxy* game, that is. Infocom informs new players that familiarity with the original story may make a few of the early puzzles easier, but over-reliance on previous knowledge may be misleading.
WEB http://www.csd.uwo.ca/~pete/Infocom/hitchhikers.html

Milliways: The Restaurant at the End of the Universe Milliways isn't an inter-galactic restaurant at all, but a Net Bulletin Board System serving up DNA discussion. On the menu you'll find *The Electric Thumb* (*The Hitchhiker's Guide* newsletter) and a transcript of Douglas Adams's appearance on Prodigy. But if you're looking for meatier fare, you're better off trying one of the newsgroups.
WEB http://pages.prodigy.com/M/I/S/Milliways

Vogon's Hitch-Hiker's Guide to the Galaxy Page This Web version of the fictional electronic encyclopedia of the universe allows you to look up original entries on everything from the Annual Ursa Minor Alpha Recreational Illusions Institute Awards Ceremony—"Nick-named 'The Rories,' the Annual Ursa Minor Alpha Recreational Illusions Institute Awards Ceremony recognizes extra-ordinary accomplishments in Galactic cinema. However, due to the length of the acceptance speeches after receiving a 'Rory' and the number of people thanked in such speeches, the Annual Ursa Minor Alpha Recreational Illusions Institute Awards Ceremony now ends only a fortnight before the next one begins"—to Zaphod Beeblebrox—"Adventurer, ex-hippy, good timer, (crook? quite possibly) manic self-publi-cist, terribly bad at personal relation-ships, often thought to be completely out to lunch. Also elected President of the Imperial Galactic Government."
WEB http://www.vogon.com/megadodo
• http://www.vogon.com/guide

GALACTIC GUIDE

alt.galactic-guide An online forum for editors and contributors to Project Galactic Guide where they can communi-cate with one another as they master the fine art of writing like DNA without pla-giarizing him.
WEB http://megadodo.com/pggfaq.html • http://www.realtime.net/~lthumper/pgg/pggfaq.html

Project Galactic Guide Homepage The dedicated server for the project, the Megadodo Publishing PGG site provides a complete archive of all 536 articles, plus a full table of contents, index, search engine, random article selector, and complete cross-referencing hyper-link capabilities. If you're worried about sensory overload, just check out the most popular articles page, which includes topics such as Tourists, Death and the After Life, and Häagen-Dazs Day.
WEB http://megadodo.com/index.html

INDEXES

The Consummate Hitchhiker's Guide All sorts of DNA links (the man, not the strand), from Not Douglas Adams But Close to full texts to The Wonderful World of Forty-Two.
WEB http://www.vu.union.edu/~ellinj/42

Hitchhiker's Guide to the Galaxy *HHGTTG* links galore, including a cult whose members consider the book its bible, and a fan page in French. Bon appetit.
WEB http://asylum.cid.com/hhgttg/hhgttg.html

The New Hitchhiker's Guidebook Links to nearly 100 hotbeds of Douglas Adams activity. In true Adams form, this page allows you to view the links 42 at a time, if you so desire.
WEB http://www.en.com/users/xvr27/otherguide2.html

PIERS ANTHONY

MANY TEENAGERS WHO ARE exploring science fiction for the first time begin with Piers Anthony and his magical, imaginative otherworlds. This has led to criticism by older sci-fi fans who claim that Anthony actively caters to his adolescent audience by offering plenty of big-breasted heroines and sexually compromising situations—and little else. Those critics are obviously just Mundanians, since no one can diminish the enthusiasm for Piers that infects fantasy-loving fans of all ages. The Xanth books have spun off into fantasy and role-playing games across cyberspace, and his newsgroup is always crammed with admiring posters. Join other devotees in attesting that Anthony is a master at his many fan pages, and spend hours off-planet on the Xanth pages sprinkled across the online universe.

▶ CLICK PICK

Unofficial Xanth Page Think you've seen everything Xanth-related under the sun? Not if you haven't seen Andrew's encyclopedia of links. For one thing, you might have missed the "Proof that Xanth Exists" and the many pictures, including one of Piers and his dog, a mid-sized mutt. There's a fairly recent listing of Xanth news, all kinds of hint lists for Companions of Xanth players, and even an actual letter from Piers Anthony. All of Piers's book covers are viewable here, by permission of the publishers, as well as ASCII art by Andrew. Because every word is taken literally in Xanth, don't skip a trip to the many pun-related sites. You'll also get your chance to submit puns you've created to Piers himself. Maybe they'll show up in a book.
WEB http://www.best.com/~wooldri /awooldri/Xanth.html

▶ **THE AUTHOR**

alt.fan.piers-anthony Fans of Piers Anthony books and games come here to lament the untimely end of the Modes series, review the latest hypertext version of the Net release of *Volk*, or get cheat hints for *Companions of Xanth*. They also flame spammers with sophisticated retorts like "Bite… Suck, suck, suck… Slurp… BURP!! What's left of NetGuy's withered husk slithers to the ground." Somebody's been reading too much SF.
USENET alt.fan.piers-anthony

Piers Anthony Here's a photo of the old Xanth master himself. He's not, as fans might expect, "On A Pale Horse" or contemplating "The Color Of Her Panties." Instead, he's wearing a silly sweatshirt and typing. Scroll down further, and see that the Big Fan who put up this page has provided a very brief biography and a complete alphabetical list of Anthony's works.
WEB http://www.catch22.com/~espana /SFAuthors/SFA/Anthony,Piers.html

Piers Anthony Another fan of Piers Anthony is responsible for this page, which contains a slightly more complete biography (even revealing the names of Anthony's daughters—Penny and Cheryl). Plus, there's a list of his books organized by series, with links to the blurbs on the back covers. Although we all know that these blurbs rarely bear any resemblance to the actual plot, they make for an excellent shopping guide.
WEB http://malkuth.sephiroth.org /~corwin/authors/panthony/index .html

Piers Anthony: High Lord of Hack Writers "Anyway, as I implied, I did indeed read his crap when I was a teenager," says Scott, the writer of this rant. Scott is not a fan. His criticisms, though, are exactly those that are consistently trumped out whenever the topic of Anthony's books arises—namely, that they are aimed at teenagers who are mostly fascinated by "the continuous stream of sexual innuendo and heaving

breasts which constitute what might be taken for a plot." Diehard Anthony fans will definitely want to avoid this site, unless they have a forgiving sense of humor.
WEB http://rampages.onramp.net/~scottgl/piers.htm

SF Archives Reviews: Piers Anthony
What's more fun than reading a Piers Anthony book? Discussing it, of course. This collection archives various commentaries and reviews. Many are quite old, but the criticism stands.
WEB http://sf.www.lysator.liu.se/sf_archive/sf-texts/books/A/Anthony,Piers.mbox

---

► THE WORKS

Chas's Xanth Page Xanth, the setting of Piers Anthony's most popular series of books, is "a land of magic, full of dragons, elves, & flying carpets." It's also a place where puns are taken literally, and everyone has a magical talent like the spontaneous conjuring of overripe fruit. This site delivers a complete guide to Xanthian characters, including their status as magician or sorceress, and even a Xanth Family Tree.
WEB http://www.angelfire.com/free/xanth.html

Neysa's Piers Anthony Apprentice Adept Page Not all Piers Anthony fans think that Xanth is the end and the beginning. In fact, Neysa likes the Apprentice Adept series so much that she has not only named herself after one of the characters (a shapechanging unicorn), but has placed much of the lovely, colorful illustration from the books on this page. There are also links to the artist, Rowena Merrill, and the series' publisher.
WEB http://www.servtech.com/public/neysa/adept.html

Nitpicker's Guide to Piers Anthony's "Incarnations of Immortality" Series
Ah, yes, the Nitpicker strikes again. Piers Anthony's *On a Pale Horse* is the target this time, and the seeming inconsisten-

cies in the text are many. For example, on page 41, while the arrow points northwest, Zane goes north and then east. Hmmmmm… Other nitpicks deal more with literary criticism than outright bloopers. True fans will love it.
WEB http://www.rt66.com/~proveit/incarnpickf.html

Xanth Talent Generator "Age large fruit." "Banish large dragons." "Speak to small centaurs." They're not exactly the kind of talents that make Juilliard come calling, but to Xanth fans they're everything. If you're one, randomly generate a talent for your persona here. But don't be surprised if the adjectives get stuck and you find the word "large" or some such word repeating over and over.
WEB http://www.best.com/~wooldri/awooldri/Xanth-dir/talentgen.html

Xanth Thread "Greetings Mundanians and Magical Xanthians alike!" StormWing Centaur (do you think that's his real name?), is the creator of this mailing list for people who share an interest in the Xanthian works of "wonderful creator, master fantasy author" Piers. Current activity in the thread is geared to a collaborative Xanth story based at this site. About 50 fans of Piers Anthony make up the group, most with their own Xanth names and personas. The members' biographies are also available here.
WEB http://www.dialnet.net/mikoes/xanth.html

ISAAC ASIMOV

PERHAPS THE MOST PROLIFIC science fiction writer of all time, Isaac Asimov published 477 titles before his death in 1992. He began writing science fiction at age 11, applied and was accepted to Columbia University at 15, and worked as a biochemist at Boston University for nearly 50 years. Yet Asimov, a card-carrying MENSA member, appears to have been the most humble of his breed. He once said, "I have been fortunate to be born with a restless and efficient brain, with a capacity of clear thought and an ability to put that thought into words… I am the lucky beneficiary of a lucky break in the genetic sweepstakes." Those "gentle readers" who consider themselves the lucky beneficiaries of Asimov's big break in the gene lotto will want to explore the sizeable amount of Asimov material available online.

▶ CLICK PICK

Isaac Asimov Home Page A collection of Asimov resources almost as comprehensive as the works themselves. An FAQ, a list of his works, the best places to go to get your hands on the books, Asimov's publishers on the Web, links to reviews, and a list of worlds mentioned in the Foundation series from Anacreon to Zoranel. A guide to Asimov's short fiction lists every story Ike ever wrote, by genre, in order of publication, and sites where each is published. A guide to his essays chronicles the publication of each of Asimov's 1,600 articles. This site even provides a graph of the number of books Asimov published each year throughout his career. Apparently, it took 19 years for Ike to publish his first 100 books, 10 years to publish the next 100, and only 5 more years to bring the total up to 300. **WEB** http://www.clark.net/pub/edseiler /WWW/asimov_home_page.html

▶ THE AUTHOR

A Visit With Isaac Asimov Bantam Doubleday Dell provides an online visit with

its most prolific author. The "Good Doctor" published more than 470 books on every conceivable subject in his lifetime. He was quite the correspondent as well, receiving more than 100,000 letters in his career, over 90,000 of which he answered. Here you can take a peek at *Yours, Isaac Asimov: A Lifetime of Letters*, edited by his brother Stanley. BDD also provides a profile of the prodigious man along with reviews of his most well-known works. They will even forward fan email to the Asimov family or to Isaac's editor at Doubleday. **WEB** http://www.bdd.com/athwk /bddathwk.cgi/10-27-95/menu

Asimov Interview Polish science fiction fan Slawek Wojtowicz interviews the man. Apparently, the interview made Wojtowicz the envy of sci-fi followers in Poland, where Asimov is enormously popular—despite the fact that only a small fraction of his works has been translated into the native language, and the majority of the people can't read English. **WEB** http://home.interstat.net/~slawcio /asimov.html

FAQ—Isaac Asimov Along with the typical what-books-did-he-write, what-awards-did-he-win questions, this hyperFAQ answers more probing questions about Asimov, the man. Did Asimov do anything other than write all day and night?—"Famous for writing over eight hours a day, seven days a week, Asimov found time to do a few other things beside writing." Is it true that Asimov had a fear of flying?— "Yes, the same author who described space flights to other worlds and who argued valiantly for the cause of rationality suffered from an irrational fear of heights and flying." What religious beliefs did he have?— "Asimov had no religious beliefs; he never believed in either God or an afterlife." Apparently, the extraordinary author also was a claustrophobic, never learned how to swim or ride a bike, and

hated having his named misspelled—thus, the short story "Spell My Name With an 'S'". The FAQ also explores questions about both the Foundation and the Robot series.
web http://www.clark.net/pub/edseiler/WWW/asimov_FAQ.html

Isaac Asimov Biography A one-paragraph biography of the Russian-born writer of hundreds of books, including the classics *I, Robot* (1950), *The Foundation Trilogy* (1951-53), and *The Gods Themselves* (1972), which won both the Hugo and Nebula awards. Brevity is an art form, but when it comes to Asimov, one paragraph is far too cursory.
web http://www.lsi.usp.br/usp/rod/text/isaac_asimov.html

▶ THE WORKS

alt.books.isaac-asimov There's a lot of debate over the lineage of Asimov story lines now that they're being farmed out to other science fiction writers (à la the post-Fleming 007). The most soulful participants are making repeat pilgrimages through the Foundation series and wondering out loud about character motivations with the kind of active curiosity that would make a high school English teacher think she had been transported to a parallel universe. Perhaps because so many of the group members have shared experiences treading through Asimov's work, the conversation tends to be extremely polite and reasoned, even when debating the data storage potential of black holes.
usenet alt.books.isaac-asimov

I, Robot: The Illustrated Screenplay For more than 25 years, attempts were made to adapt Asimov's *I, Robot* to the motion picture medium. All efforts failed until Harlan Ellison took a crack at it, producing a screenplay from the memorable tales of mechanized servitude. Asimov claimed this film would be, "the first really adult, complex, worthwhile science fiction movie ever made." Although the movie was never made, selections from the screenplay in illustrated book format are available here, complete with full-color paintings by Mark Zug in .GIF or .JPG format.
web http://pathfinder.com/twep/Aspect/I_Robot/Robot.html

Isaac Asimov With nearly 500 works in print, there's certainly plenty of fodder for this AOL Asimov folder. Mostly, posters discuss the inconsistencies in and chronology of the Foundation series.
america online keyword scifi→Message Boards→SF Authors A-L→List Topics→Isaac Asimov

Jenkins' Spoiler-Laden Guide to Isaac Asimov John Jenkins has taken on the seemingly insurmountable task of reviewing every one of Isaac Asimov's works, from his science-fiction series to his short stories and children's books. Jenkins warns that his reviews are highly personal and that he has no training in literary criticism. However, his hundreds of entries, each accompanied by a rating, are certainly worth a look and provide an interesting glimpse into the psyche of the Asimov addict. Most importantly, Jenkins doesn't let his pro-Asimov bias influence his reviews. You'll find rave reviews such as the one for *I, Robot*—"…my memory of reading it for the first time is unusually vivid. It is one of the books which built his reputation, in the form of its original publication as a series of stories in the *Golden Age*. Astounding (and, for that matter, one of the books that made the *Golden Age* golden)." But there are also a number of less-than-complimentary, harsher critiques, like the one for "True Love"—"…Pointless, but thankfully short."
web http://www.sj-coop.net/~tseng/Asimov/Asimov.html

ORSON SCOTT CARD

MOST FOLKS WOULDN'T THINK that sentimental stories with heavily Mormon overtones could be enormously popular in the sci-fi/fantasy genre. If you think like most folks, then you haven't discovered Orson Scott Card. Card, or OSC to his fans, is an extremely religious Latter-Day Saint who has written several best-selling series including the Ender Wiggin books and the *Tales of Alvin Maker*. His presence on the Net is stronger than most of his contemporaries—in fact, from his official sites on AOL and the Web, anxious readers can download portions of his novels as he works on them. Role-playing enthusiasts and *Ender's Game* lovers will want to enroll in The Virtual Battle School, and those shopping for a good book to read will love Orson Scott Card Reviews. Finally, read Quietus, a wickedly eerie fantasy about a hardworking Mormon man.

/cardlist.html

EMAIL majordomo@hundred.acre.wood .net ✍ *Type in message body:* subscribe orsoncard

▶ THE AUTHOR

Hatrack River: The Official Web Site of Orson Scott Card Despite the construction signs scattered across the landscape, this official site is still the best place to find what you need to know about Card's books. Detailed descriptions and a cover shot are provided for 20 of OSC's most popular books, and there's an extended section devoted to the latest release. A blinking sign informs visitors that soon, the first chapter of each of these books will be available at Hatrack River. That'll whet your appetite! Meanwhile, visit the Download section to retrieve zipped files of OSC's Works in Progress. Poetry, articles, essays, and other works will soon be available, too, so check back often. **WEB** http://www.hatrack.com

Hatrack River Town Meeting Fantasy and reality blend in this official Orson Scott Card forum on AOL. The forum operates in both the present and in 1830s Hatrack River Town. Create a persona and grab yourself a homestead. Don't forget to pick a "knack," which is a minor magical talent most Hatrack residents possess. Homesteaders participate in the daily goings-on of the town, including the weekly town meeting, which alternates between 1830s virtual reality and 1990s topical discussion. If you're the rare science fiction fan who doesn't get into role-playing, you can download the absolute latest of Card's works-in-progress, read and critique others' writing, and join discussion groups. There's something for any kind of OSC fan in this comprehensive forum. **AMERICA ONLINE** *keyword* hatrack

Orson Scott Card The best thing about this fan page is its willingness to link to

▶ CLICK PICK

Orson Scott Card Discussion Mailing List A very busy discussion group devoted to Card, but not in thrall to him. Many of OSC's most fervent Web fans, including Barbara and Khyron, are frequent posters here. A recent lurk on the list revealed thought-provoking examinations of the more controversial themes in Card's work, which supposedly include anti-Semitism and racism. In fact, plenty of posters want to know about OSC's Mormonism, and how it affects his literary take on the world. The discussions sometimes become religiously heavy-handed: "I don't think OSC will bring the messiah (back because I'm Christian) but maybe he will help us prepare for the day," writes one fan. But the give-and-take is enormously polite—in fact, truly exceptional for the faceless Internet world. Any suggestions, however offensive to diehard fans, are discussed, rather than flamed to death. That makes for a refreshing change. **WEB** http://haw.usfca.edu/~khyron/card

tangentially-related pages, which enhance an OSC fan's appreciation of the material. (Too many OSC pages bookmark the same five sites, so visitors just travel in a big circle.) Find book reviews, news, related pages, and lots more.
WEB http://hubcap.clemson.edu/~cadkins /osc.html

Unofficial Orson Scott Card Web Page

Khyron is one of OSC's biggest fans, and he runs not one, but two mailing lists about him. At Khyron's site, you'll find publishing information about each of OSC's books, forms to subscribe to the lists, and links to other relevant places on the Web. You'll also be treated to the story of how Khyron discovered Card in 1986, when his grandmother took him to the bookstore.
WEB http://haw.usfca.edu/~khyron/card

▶ THE WORKS

alt.books.orson-s-card This newsgroup is sparsely populated, but those who hang around are big SF fans and never run out of topics to discuss. Unlike some of the other spam-a-thon newsgroups, the garbage here is kept firmly in the bin. Perhaps that's why the place seems so lonely?
USENET alt.books.orson-s-card

An Open Letter from OSC So, just how dependent is Orson Scott Card on *The Book of Mormon* for plot ideas and thematic devices? Here, in an open letter to his readers, Card responds to criticism that he's nothing more than a Latter-Day Saints plagiarist in his novel *The Memory of Earth*. His major defense is that *The Book of Mormon* represents true history, and one can't plagiarize history.
WEB http://hubcap.clemson.edu/~cadkins /plag.html

Maps in a Mirror, The Worthing Saga Reviews Gareth Rees provides unbiased and fairly intelligent insight into OSC's books. "There is, perhaps, evidence of an ascetic dislike of bodies, perhaps most obvious in *Fat Farm*, which Card describes as 'physical autobiography' in his afterword," Rees declares at one point. Perhaps Rees takes this stuff just a little too seriously, but in any case these essays are certainly worth a read.
WEB http://www.cl.cam.ac.uk/users /gdr11/book/card3.html

Orson Scott Card Bibliography Here's a complete guide to all that the master has written, along with gratuitous commentary and reviews for several of the most popular novels. It's all presented in a very attractive format that would be perfect for printing, on a really long piece of paper.
WEB http://www.nyx.net/~kreme /cardbiblio.html

Orson Scott Card Page Need to know what to read? See reviews by regular folks of almost everything Card has written. Also, peruse all of his 1994-95 "Windows Made Me This Way" columns.
WEB http://www.srv.net/people/daveb /card.html

Orson Scott Card Reviews Barbara E. Walton, who wrote these reviews, is definitely one of OSC's most fervent fans. She's the co-moderator of his mailing lists. Describing her "first time," she says, "I chain-read *Ender's Game* and *Speaker for the Dead* that night, and it felt like coming home." Just a fan? Or someone who really needs to get out more? Either way, she attempts to be objective in her reviews of eight of OSC's books, including the Ender and Alvin series. This is a great place for OSC newbies.
WEB http://freenet.buffalo.edu/~ah 329/card.html

Quietus It should be called *Blindus*, because this story is typed in the teeny-tiniest font you've ever seen. Get out the magnifying glass and enjoy this haunting tale about a man who may or may not be dead! It's not every day you get a free story to read from your favorite author.
WEB http://www.wam.umd.edu /~scarlson/Mosaic/quietus.html

MICHAEL CRICHTON

BEFORE *JURASSIC PARK* BROKE box-office records, before Michael Douglas and Demi Moore got down and dirty on a desk in *Disclosure*, before he wrote the pilot for the mega-successful medical drama, *E.R.*, and even before *The Andromeda Strain* was adapted for the big screen, Michael Crichton was doing his thing in the dead-tree medium—and winning over a massive audience. Although his script-like novels range from *Rising Sun* to *The Great Train Robbery*, Crichton has gained much of his popularity in the sci-fi genre with novels like *Sphere*, *The Andromeda Strain*, *Congo*, *Jurassic Park*, and his latest, *The Lost World*. On the Net, the homage given to his literary works pales in comparison to that given to their screen adaptations, but a handful of sites can be found on the controversial creator.

▶ CLICK PICK

Michael Crichton—Map No matter how trite or reactionary some may think Crichton's sci-fi, there's no denying the fact that his fiction is suffused with the kind of scientific detail that has clearly been lifted from the latest research journals. However, as a novelist unrestrained by the rules of science or academia, Crichton takes the most speculative of theories and runs with them as if they were already as ensconced as the theory of relativity. But apparently that's what keeps his fans coming back for more. This elaborate site takes a look at Crichton the writer, the man, and the moviemaking machine. It is also home to a list of Crichton's lesser known works written under the pseudonyms of John Lange and Jeffrey Hudson in the 1960s.
WEB http://http.tamu.edu:8000/~cmc0112 /crichton.html

▶ THE AUTHOR

alt.books.crichton All washed up or better than ever? That seems to be the recurring question in this rather sparsely populated Crichton newsgroup. Exhibits A and B in the case for or against the illustrious Mike—*Twister* and *The Lost World*.
USENET alt.books.crichton

Michael Crichton A microscopic biography of Michael Crichton and back cover blurbs from *Eaters of the Dead*, *Sphere*, *The Terminal Man*, *The Andromeda Strain*, *Congo*, and *Jurassic Park*. If you're too busy to do your browsing at the bookstore, this site might be worth a visit.
WEB http://www.cei.net/~cthomaso /mc/mc.htm

The Michael Crichton Home Page Brief reviews of Crichton's works from *The Andromeda Strain* in 1969 to his latest, *The Lost World*.
WEB http://malkuth.sephiroth.org/~corwin /authors/mcrichton/index.html

▶ THE LOST WORLD

The Lost World "Behavior is screaming forward, and it might be nonadaptive. Nobody knows. Although personally, I think cyberspace means the end of our species," says Ian Malcolm in *The Lost World*, but it could just as well be Crichton himself speaking. This sequel to *Jurassic Park* picks up the story six years later, adding some computer issues to the plot to keep things current. At this Random House site, you can examine excerpts from the newest novel, explore the island, and download clips from the much-hyped original movie.
WEB http://www.randomhouse.com /site/lostworld

HARLAN ELLISON

I HAVE NO MOUTH, BUT I MUST scream until the real Harlan Ellison stands up, for this is the writer whose fake biographies on the dust jackets of his books are famously unrealistic. If Ellison's life resembled anything written on those book covers, he must have run away from home at 13 to join the carnival, and over the next half-dozen years worked as a logger, a tuna fisherman, an actor, a magazine publisher, and a dynamite-truck driver. But in fact, it's clear that as the author of 45 books, more than 1,300 short stories, several comic book scripts, two dozen teleplays, a dozen motion pictures, and countless essays, articles, and newspaper columns, Ellison could never have found the time for any of his fictitious exploits. For those fans interested in the escapades of the real Ellison, the Web is littered with homages to and information on both the man and the myths.

▶ CLICK PICK

Ellison Webderland The Web site with the seal of approval of HE himself, Ellison Webderland explores Harlan the persona and phenomenon as well as the (never very) serious author. This official site features frequent updates about publishing events and Harlan's health (since quadruple-bypass surgery), a one-of-a-kind photo gallery, biographies (real and surreal) and reviews. There's even an online store stocked with Ellison books and recordings, and a page of HE quotes entitled "Everything I Needed to Know I Learned from Harlan."
WEB http://www.menagerie.net/ellison/INDEX.HTM

▶ THE AUTHOR

alt.fan.harlan-ellison Hardly as active as one would expect considering Ellison's army of adherents—not to mention his enemies. Although his arch rival Charles Platt is an occasional contributor, rumors that Ellison occasionally visits, using a pseudonym, are groundless.
USENET alt.fan.harlan-ellison

Audio Verite: Harlan Ellison QuickTime movies of Ellison elaborating on such topics as computers, Nazis, and the correlation between bad books and Garth Brooks. In text-only (but twice as interesting) are Harlan's views on journalists, cyber-hype, sequels, censorship, religion, and Mark Fuhrman. The quotes were gleaned from HE public appearances by a fan, who also provides us with a Handy Guide To Attending Harlan Ellison Appearances for The Complete Idiot.
WEB http://www.darkcarnival.com/feb96/hellis.html

FAQ-alt.fan.harlan-ellison Much of this page is devoted to clearing up some misconceptions about Ellison and his more notorious exploits. For example—did Harlan really punch Irwin Allen, head censor at ABC (and sometime disaster movie supremo)? Not exactly. After Allen asked Ellison to make more than a few "stupid changes" in his script, Harlan became angry, leapt upon the long conference table, and ran down the length of it intent on kicking Allen in the face. Harlan slipped and slid the rest of the way down the table, hit the guy in the mouth, knocking him backwards out of his chair, knocking a model of the "Seaview" off the wall, and breaking the man's pelvis. Did Harlan really mail a dead gopher to an editor? No, it was the comptroller of a certain publishing house that broke their contract and bound a cigarette ad into one of Harlan's paperbacks. Ellison mailed 213 bricks postage due to the man, had a Lithuanian hit man friend of his have a talk with him, and then mailed the dead gopher, along with Ted Cogswell's recipe for braised gopher stew, fourth class mail, stinking up the mailroom for quite a while. Truth really is stranger than fiction! The rest of the FAQ covers the usual biographical and bibliographical info as well as tidbits of

trivia such as what kind of pipe and tobacco Ellison most enjoyed before he quit (Black Cavendish), how tall he actually is (five foot five, but he says he's much taller when he stands on his charisma), and how many times he's been married (five).
WEB http://www.menagerie.net/ellison/text/faq.txt

Harlan Ellison A brief biography, a lengthy bibliography, and links to more extensive Ellison sites.
WEB http://WWW.Catch22.COM/~espana/SFAuthors/SFE/Ellison,Harlan.html

Harlan Ellison Everyone here is talking about the new *I Have No Mouth and I Must Scream* CD-ROM. Friends of Ellison on America Online also help each other find the often hard-to-locate Harlan works and also delve into discussions of his TV, movie, and comic book work.
AMERICA ONLINE *keyword* scifi→ Message Boards→SF Authors A-L→ List Topics→Harlan Ellison

▶ THE WORKS

Ellison Links to everything from the *I, Robot* screenplay to the Terminator site, cover art to a comic book bibliography, reviews to interviews. Ellison aficionados will also find the latest news, from the release of the *I Have No Mouth and I Must Scream* computer game to the latest issue of the *Dream Corridor* comic.
WEB http://www.phlab.missouri.edu/~c642678/harlan.html

From the ABA Convention "Harlan Ellison has selected the question: 'Sir, what is the future of *The Last Dangerous Visions*?' From Harlan Ellison, to ABA: 'Sir: in reference to *The Last Dangerous Visions*, my response is the same one that Michelangelo gave to the Pope when he bugged him about the completion of the Sistine Chapel Ceiling fresco: It'll be done, when it's done. Get a life.'" Oh that Harlan, what a charmer. For more of Harlan Ellison's gentle wit, you can check out this transcript from the American Booksellers' Association Conference Chat.
WEB http://ambook.org/cgi-bin/www.ail.pl/bookweb/events/transcript/ellison.txt

I Have No Mouth and I Must Scream Although he was not a fan of computer games, or computers in general, for that matter, Ellison nonetheless was intrigued when approached by Cyberdreams about making a work of interactive literature. The result? A double CD-ROM based on his nightmarish tale of technology gone awry, *I Have No Mouth and I Must Scream*. This site contains info on the original short story, the new software, and the sci-fi author behind them both.
WEB http://www.mgmua.com/interactive/nomouth/selection.html

Islets of Langerhans "I undertook this survey of Harlan Ellison's literary output having forgotten just how bloody many books the guy has actually written," moans this site's creator. Yes, Islets of Langerhans are those clusters of endocrine glands located in your pancreas. To the sci-fi fan, it's a reference to a Harlan Ellison short story. To the hardcore Harlan-head, it's an anagram of "The Ellison Fan's Rags." And to the wired segment of his fandom, it's one of the more lucid (albeit less-expansive) sites devoted to the sci-fi king, including a biography and extensive bibliography covering novels, short stories, essays, non-fiction, screenplays, and other Ellisonia.
WEB http://www.teleport.com/~mzuzel

FRANK HERBERT

VISUALLY STUNNING, PERHAPS. Incomprehensible, undoubtedly. Really long—you know it. The 1984 film adaptation of Frank Herbert's series might have killed the following of lesser books, but *Dune's* fans survived. Perhaps less adept at self-promotion than many authors, Frank Herbert remains surprisingly little-known, considering the popularity of the *Dune* saga. Even among fans, few have read his other books, which number nearly 30. Most Internet resources are the creations of *Dune* devotees, but a true fan will be interested in the Eulogy for Frank Herbert, will welcome the Frank Herbert Bibliography, and will definitely enjoy listening to Frank Herbert Reading Excerpts from *Dune*. Afterwards, await the coming of Muad'Dib at the Museum Arrakeen or Welcome to Arrakis. Finally, join a game of Dune or even Dune MUSH II.

▶ CLICK PICK

Museum Arrakeen "Welcome to Arrakis, also known as Dune," says the Princess Irulan Corrino. "Here you will find many treasures from the time of the Padishah Emperor Shaddam IV, my father, through post-Scattering times over 25,000 years from the time of ascension of Muad'Dib." This Web page offers a tour through the world of *Dune* in the guise of a role-playing, choose-your-own-adventure game. The Music Chamber offers sound clips. The Holo-Photo Wing houses movie pics. The Information Desk hosts an FAQ. Other rooms include Document Archives, Gaming Chamber, the Grand Portrait Wing, and the News Room. A must-see for anyone even marginally interested in Herbert or *Dune*.
WEB http://www.princeton.edu/~cgilmore/dune

▶ THE AUTHOR

Eulogy for Frank Herbert (1920-1986) After his death from pancreatic cancer in 1986, Frank Herbert's friend Willis E. McNelly wrote this affectionate, stirring tribute to the man he calls "a bearded bear." Everyone should be remembered so fondly with such beautifully phrased thoughts. It's also rich in details and biographical info and makes an excellent introduction to a very special writer.
WEB http://mr.insa-tlse.fr/~guibouret/herbert.html

Frank Herbert While there's nothing stellar going on here, this is a nice index to most of the best Frank Herbert and *Dune* sites around the Web, along with a small photo and a couple of quotes.
WEB http://www.empirenet.com/~rdaeley/authors/herbert.html

Frank Herbert Bibliography The man is more than the sum of *Dune's* six parts. In fact, he wrote 23 completely non-*Dune*-related books, a fact which *Dune*-obsessed fans often fail to mention. So what's to read over a publishing career that stretched from 1956 to 1985, if one has already done the D-word? Stop by and find out.
WEB http://www.eerie.fr/~tassin/Dune/herbert.html

Vertex Interviews Frank Herbert Although this interview took place in 1973, it's hardly dated. After all, *Dune* and most of its relatives had been around for almost ten years even then. The last installment and the ubiquitous movie were, of course, in the future. So what does the good Mr. Herbert talk about with *Vertex*? Everything from his love of carpentry to the high-speed evolution of the world. Oh yes, and science fiction, much science fiction.
WEB http://www.princeton.edu/~cgilmore/dune/docs/vertex.html

▶ THE WORKS

Dune "Since the release of the *Dune* Chronicles, a six book series, the world of science fiction has never been the same," claims this page. There are bun-

dles of *Dune* sites on the Net, and legions of fans MUSHing and FAQing all over the place. Alex Dunkel has collected links to some of the best, but he has already created some of the most impressive *Dune*-related Web resources himself. Fans can find sounds from *Dune*, a complete guide to each of the Chronicles, a great JPEG of the Arrakis Map, Terminology of the Imperium, and sound files from each of the songs on the *Dune* soundtrack.
WEB http://www.ECNet.Net/users/murjd5/Dune

Frank Herbert Reading Excerpts from Dune Journey to "an imaginary world with a desert climate and a feudal society" by downloading these large sound files of the author reading excerpts from his most popular book, *Dune*, which was published in 1965. The dates of the readings are unclear on this page and the source page.
WEB http://town.hall.org/Archives/radio/IMS/HarperAudio/052494_harp_ITH.launch.html

Place Beyond Your Dreams This page aspires to the excellence of Museum Arrakeen, but doesn't quite make it. That matters very little, because it's a comprehensive index containing a few links that even the museum doesn't have.
WEB http://www.eerie.fr/~tassin/Dune/dune.html

Welcome to Arrakis Just as the subtitle of this page states, this is "no ordinary FAQ." Instead, it's an interactive tour. Stops include that wacky spice Melange, the nasty Little Makers (phallic, no?), and the story of Muad'Dib. Lots of fun for those who live and breathe *Dune*, and even for those who have never had the privilege.
WEB http://bluejay.creighton.edu/~muaddib

▶ **THE GAMES**

Dune II FAQ and Strategy Guide This guide is for the PC *Dune* game called *DUNE II: The Building of a Dynasty*. It contains FAQs, mostly dealing with little

bugs in the game, and also lists cheats and suggested strategies.
WEB http://www.gamesdomain.co.uk/dune2/dunefaq1.html

Dune II: The Battle for Arrakis Put on that stillsuit and help the forces of good triumph over evil, or something like that, as you rescue the desert planet Arrakis. This document introduces the SEGA game, outlines rules, and offers tips for better play and an FAQ.
WEB http://star.pst.qub.ac.uk/~dcjk/dune/main_dune.html

▶ **THE MUSHES**

DuneMUSH II It's 10,181, a full decade before the ascension of Paul Muad'Dib Atreides, and you're standing by as Head of House Major Moritani, Broncalo, presents a gift to His Majesty, the Sublime Padishah Emperor Shaddam IV. How? Through the magic of in-character role-playing, of course. With *Dune*MUSH II you can relive the events of Frank Herbert's novels, and even change them, although you should try to respect local customs and regulations. This page includes information on every faction participating in this role-playing game— the Moritani, the Turenne, and the Wikkheiser—as well as hosts seminars designed to improve *Dune*MUSH play. In addition, it links to the MUSH archive, rules, news, and events.
WEB http://www.princeton.edu/~cgilmore/dune/mush

Revenant After the August 1994 demise of *Dune*MUSH, a virtual world based on Frank Herbert's novels, Revenant rose from the ashes. Set one millenium after the close of Herbert's final novel, *Chapterhouse: Dune*, the MUSH uses the characters, settings, and traditions of Herbert's fiction to create a speculative and interactive computer world. You'll have to be a Wizard or a builder to enter Revenant, but this page gives the necessary background information and status updates for the MUSH.
WEB http://www.artsci.wustl.edu/~revenant

STEPHEN KING

STEPHEN KING HAS EVERYONE fooled. He's supposed to be the most popular, prolific horror writer in the known universe. He's not. He's the most popular, prolific horror and sci-fi writer in the known universe. Once marketers find a place on B. Dalton bookshelves for an author, that's usually where the author stays. But if you take a close look at King's enormous bibliography, you'll see a number of certainly frightening, but fundamentally sci-fi works where the central plot revolves around aliens, mutants, chemical-induced apocalypse, or paranormal phenomena—*TommyKnockers*, *Thinner*, *The Dead Zone*, *Carrie*, *Firestarter*, *Christine*, *The Dark Tower Series*, *The Shining*, and *The Stand*, for starters, not to mention many of his short stories. So next time you're in a bookstore, do a little creative rearranging. Stephen will thank you for it.

▶ CLICK PICK

Stephen King Page Michael from Russia is one of the king of horror's most active Web fans. His online shrine contains some broken English, but is full of unique features King fans will love. Particularly clever is the clickable map of Maine "according to Stephen King." Click on Penobscot and find out about Derry, the imaginary town where *IT* takes place. A nice place to visit, but you wouldn't want to die there! Other features include a scanned book jacket and blurb for every book, an FAQ, news, and information about SKEMERS, a mailing list.
WEB http://mcalcin.ips.ras.ru/sk

▶ THE AUTHOR

alt.fan.authors.stephen-king One poster wants to know what kind of dog Stephen King has. Somebody spreads a rumor that King will be writing an *X-Files* episode. Another complains that this newsgroup is too quiet. She's informed that the action takes place on alt.books.stephen-king. True enough.
USENET alt.fan.authors.stephen-king

Houston Bytes! Stephen King Page Warning to King-o-philes: "Try not to get lost in his imagination" while visiting this site! We'll keep that in mind. Saturated with color, this site's main material is cover shots and photos of the King. But it's not just a pretty face. The page also offers an extensive set of links to related sites, a bibliography and filmography linking to book jacket blurbs, and a guide to what's coming soon from the head-banger from Bangor.
WEB http://www.netropolis.net/slayer/sking.htm

The Many Faces of Stephen King And you thought of him as having only one occasionally-scruffy and always-creepy visage? This page goes far to prove that the master of macabre has morphed over the years from mountain man to geeky professor to leather-jacketed hipster. No wonder he's so hard to pin down.
WEB http://www.iap.net.au/~jules/faces.html

Phantasmagoria Diehard King-worshippers will want to order this "infrequently published, unofficial newszine" devoted to Stephen King's activities. It includes information for collectors and reprints from Bangor-area newspapers. You can also find information about ordering *The Stephen King Companion* and *The Stephen King Story*.
WEB http://www.widomaker.com/~gbpub/8.html

SKEMERS It's an e-mail mailing list and club for Stephen King discussion and chat, sponsored by an unofficial bunch of enthusiasts. To find out if you simply must be a member, read the Rules and FAQ ,which also contains more general King trivia, like his mailing address.
WEB http://mcalcin.ips.ras.ru/sk/SKEMERs

Stephen King Those who go absolutely batty when they're out of the loop will welcome Ed Nomura and his Stephen King home page. He's a compulsive fan who makes *Misery*'s Annie Wilkes look like a casual admirer. Ed collects news on Maine's resident freak show. Included in the two main sections, "Books" and "Movies," are synopses, publishing dates, and all manner of related links. Can any question be answered here somewhere? Faster than you can say *IT*.
WEB http://phrtayl0.ucsd.edu/~ed/sk

Stephen King at the National Press Club A speech King gave at a luncheon on the 13th floor (coincidence? We don't think so!) of the Press Club recently is available for a listen here. The files could prove to be your worst nightmare, though, as they take a long time to download, and you're just sitting there, alone, nothing to do, the minutes tick… tick… ticking by… it's the kind of thing that could drive someone NUTS. All wait and no playback…
WEB http://town.hall.org/Archives/radio /IMS/Club/102993_club_ITH.html

The Stephen King Fan Page Without a doubt, this should be the first stop on any King-themed Web tour. The creator of this page has written extended reviews of each of King's major novels, and provides not one, but two exceptional FAQs. A reference guide to all relevant places, objects, and characters in the books is under construction, but is sure to be a super resource when it's ready. Read favorite King quotes and peruse the long list of freaky films based on his novels from *Cujo* to *The Stand*, sites.
WEB http://elara.chu.cam.ac.uk/~jls20 /sk.html

Stephen King on the Web This site is a utilitarian index of just about everything on the Web that has to do with the twisted tale-spinner. Don't miss the Arnold House Christmas Ornament link… it's worth a chuckle, or for true zealots, a scream of horrific delight.
WEB http://www.acs.appstate.edu /~pl7714/sking_html

Stephen King Survey Everybody has a favorite King book, and James E. Pace wants to know yours. Did you slip into a coma while reading *The Dead Zone*? Are you still afraid of big red cars? Do you remain unconvinced that St. Bernards are anything but cuddly? Register your voice here, and then see what other sick picks were made before you.
WEB http://wwwcsif.cs.ucdavis.edu /~pace/king/sk-survey.html

Stephen King Web Site Want a thrill? Go to the bottom of this page, check out "A brief look at his works," and have a friend read you the descriptions while you try to guess which book they refer to. Just how big a fan are you? Other than impressing friends, this site is a heaping good index and news source. Don't miss out on a King release or a chapter of *The Green Mile*.
WEB http://wwwcsif.cs.ucdavis.edu /~pace/king.html

▶ THE WORKS

The Dark Tower FAQ So what is the Dark Tower, anyway? "The Dark Tower appears to be a lynch pin of time and space, it may connect alternate time lines or realities but its true nature (at this time) remains unclear. What is clear is that Roland's world may not be our own. There are similarities such as the song "Hey Jude" and other snippets of pop culture, but Roland never heard of a place like New York City and remains of lost technology are thousands of years old and yet hundreds of years ahead of our current technology." Read all about the books fans are mad for, as well as how King's non-*I* books fit into the series at this enlightening site.
WEB http://www.d.umn.edu/~chouse /extras/darktowerfaq.html

Grant Books Stephen King Page Stephen King is more than just a good beach read to some really adamant collectors of limited editions of his works. Grant Books is the company that publishes gorgeous, color-plated hardback versions of all the most frightening clas-

sics. Recently, they were even privileged enough to publish a version of *Desperation* six months before it officially came out. Needless to say, there was a lottery to be able to buy it. Visitors to this site can find out about all the latest limited edition releases as well as how to find out-of-print books.
WEB http://www.bluefin.net/~dmgrant /Stephen-King.html

The Green Mile He's been watching you. He knows what you've been doing. He's seen you flip to the last page of the book to find out who's alive and who has died a horrible, bloody death. So Stephen King has borrowed a page from Charles Dickens and written *The Green Mile*, a serialized novel in six parts. You can't flip ahead. You have to wait. Oh, the torture, the pain, the endless torment! Read all about the product of one man's sadistic genius at this site.
WEB http://www.greenmile.com

Penguin USA's Rose Madder Although it was released a while ago, Viking Books still wants to sell you a copy. Read all about why Rose is madder here, and download an oh-so-creepy audio promo. "Sometimes, a woman's got to take matters into her own hands."
WEB http://www.penguin.com/usa /catalogs/titles/king/index.html

alt.books.stephen-king This is where the fanatics hang out. Nearly every one of King's books has an active discussion thread going on at any one time. Fans fantasize about the movies they'd like to see made, and criticize the ones they hated. There is an honest-to-goodness subculture here, and the regulars know each other well. Newbies who aren't too clueless are welcomed heartily—the truly ignorant, the spammers, and those who don't warn about spoilers are fed to Pennywise.
USENET alt.books.stephen-king *FAQ:* **WEB** http://www.acs.appstate.edu/~pl7714 /sking_html/skeetfaq.html

The Jaunt Shhh… don't tell anybody that this story is on the Web. Something tells us that there's some kind of copyright violation goin' on. It's an excellent little sci-fi ditty from *The Skeleton Crew* about a hyperspace trip to Mars.
WEB http://www.daimi.aau.dk/~klang /king/thejaunt.txt

The Lost Haiku of Stephen King For Stephen King, 1970 was a bad year. He hadn't yet published a novel, and was just about broke. In that year, he submitted several macabre haiku to a literary magazine in Connecticut. They were accepted for publication, but ironically the magazine went out of business almost immediately. The haiku were recently rediscovered, and although King has stated emphatically that he will never publish his prodigious production of poesy, curious minds can sneak a peak here at what such a book might be like. These haiku ain't about cherry blossoms in the spring, that's for sure.
WEB http://www.trincoll.edu/othervoi /issue02/king.html

Umney's Last Case "It was one of those spring mornings so L.A.-perfect you keep expecting to see that little trademark symbol—(R)—stamped on it somewhere. The exhaust of the vehicles passing on Sunset smelled faintly of oleander, the oleander was lightly perfumed with exhaust, and the sky overhead was as clear as a hardshell Baptist's conscience. Peoria Smith, the blind paperboy, was standing in his accustomed place on the corner of Sunset and Laurel, and if that didn't mean God was in His heaven and all was jake with the world, I didn't know what did." So begins this fascinating, and rather long short story from *Nightmares and Dreamscapes*. It was electronically published as a teaser before the book was released, and fortunately it's still floating in cyberspace.
WEB http://www.eu.net/king/kingtoc.htm

DEAN KOONTZ

TALK ABOUT A LONG, SLOW buildup. Dean Koontz, now one of the most popular horror writers in the world, published dozens of books in the '70s under almost as many pseudonyms. With all those identities, it's no wonder fans were slow to gather. He now writes almost exclusively under his own name, and why not—he sells millions of books a year. His fans are legion on the Web, and although the actual number of sites devoted to him is surprisingly few, they are bustling with enthusiasts. Check out the action at The Unofficial Dean Koontz Web Site. Shop for an all-night page turner at DITHOTS Koontz Book Registry. And don't forget to look at *The Book of Counted Sorrows*, even though it doesn't exist... yet.

CLICK PICK

The Unofficial Dean Koontz Web Site
Dean Koontz fans, and even those who may not be familiar with Koontz, need look no further for the latest news about upcoming releases or film productions. In the Koontz News topics, fans can find news on the latest books (*Ticktock* was a recent feature, and included excerpts and links to purchase the book) and potential movies or TV miniseries, such as the rumored production of *Intensity*. Those who crave even more Koontzian information can see an enviably thorough FAQ about Koontz and his work. Many visitors weigh in at The Readers' Poll, where *Watchers* is the current fave. From the home page are more links to book reviews, a bibliography, articles, and interviews. In the near future look for a trading post where, presumably, Koontz lovers will be able to barter and buy related merchandise.
WEB http://www.hway.com/zebster/koontz

THE AUTHOR

The Bad Place—Another Unoffical Dean Koontz Home Page The creator of this site is being too modest, even if he is quoting the name of a book. It's actually a very good place, especially if you happen to have read your daily dose of Koontz. Find out the latest news, like transcripts of a recent chat session. View cover shots and read brief plot summaries of all of Koontz's novels. There's a mailing list, related links, an FAQ, and even a list of other authors Koontz-lovers might enjoy.
WEB http://www.webcom.com/~alvear /koontz.html

Dean Koontz Time Warner Books loves its bestselling scaremeister so much that it's put up an entire Web page in his honor. Fans will find a cover shot from *Strange Highways*, and, much more interestingly, a selection from *Highways* called "Snatcher." Notes to the Reader, a biography, bibliography, and an FAQ written by Koontz are here, too.
WEB http://pathfinder.com/twep /Warner_Books/Koontz/Koontz.html

THE WORKS

alt.books.dean-koontz In this busy group, posters quibble over the best and worst Koontz books, anxiously await the arrival of a new novel, and kvetch about the quality of the film incarnations (or rather mutilations) of Koontz's books. In between, they duck spam.
USENET alt.books.dean-koontz

Dean R. Koontz Bibliography Undoubtedly, it's hard to keep track of a guy who has written more than 70 novels under half a dozen pseudonyms. But this site manages to index all of them, including annotations indicating whether they have been printed under different titles or author names.
WEB http://www.cat.pdx.edu/~caseyh /horror/author/koontz.html

Dean R. Koontz Mailing List It's always amazing how many seemingly soft-souled and super-nice people really enjoy horror novels. On this list, members review works they've read recently and recommend novels to others looking for the next step in Koontz fulfillment. They also politely discuss imagery and themes, and debate whether a book sucks or rocks.

EMAIL majordomo@dithots.dithots.org ✍ *Type in message body:* subscribe koontz
FAQ: **WEB** http://www.dithots.org/koontz /dithots.koontz.faq.shtml

DITHOTS Koontz Book Registry Nothing motivates a person to speak up more than a strong opinion, and Koontz fans are no exception to the rule. Besides, with the price of hardcover books rising apace, even diehards are considering waiting for the paperback edition. Here, Koontz readers can complain about the rising costs of Koontz books, submit mini-reviews of the ones they've read, and view the collected reviews of others. Comments range from "I was sweatin' when I finished this one," to "I'm a huge Koontz fan but this book was horrible."
WEB http://www.dithots.org/cgi-bin /dithots.book.koontz.pl

Melinda's Favorite Quotes: Dean R. Koontz Melinda has some favorite quotes / of creepy things that Dean Koontz wrote. / His poems are especially quotable / Too bad his rhymes aren't very notable. / Far better is the Koontzian prose / (A fact Melinda, no doubt, knows).
WEB http://www.uwm.edu/~melindam /koontz.html

Welcome to Intensity Although this is an official promotional page for the novel *Intensity*, it is jam-packed with other stuff. There's a contest—closed now, but containing a challenging quiz. You'll also find excerpts from the novel and other books, plus an extended set of verses from the imaginary (but soon to be real) *Book of Counted Sorrows*.
WEB http://www.randomhouse.com /site/intensity

The Book of Counted Sorrows Probably the most frequently asked question to booksellers and librarians by Koontz

fans is "Where can I get *The Book of Counted Sorrows*?" The truth is that even Koontz doesn't own a copy—he made the whole thing up. The supposed quotes from the book he uses for his epigraphs can be found in the same library as Frank Herbert's *Orange Catholic Bible*. Once enough pithy sayings and little poetic ditties germinate, his publishers will surely publish a real *Counted Sorrows*. Meanwhile, this site has accumulated most of Koontz's lamentations to date.
WEB http://www.cs.virginia.edu/~mam3p /sorrows.html

TERRY PRATCHETT

AS IT MOVED TOWARDS A seemingly inevitable collision with a malevolent red star, a magical world riding through space on the back of four giant elephants, which in turn were riding on the back of a giant turtle (sex unknown) had only one possible savior. Unfortunately, it happened to be the singularly inept and cowardly wizard called Rincewind, who was last seen falling off the edge of the world…" So began the Discworld series, Terry Pratchett's funny and unorthodox mongrel series mixing science fiction and fantasy, now well into the double digits. As Pratchett himself explained, "Sci- Fi and Fantasy gave me the best possible education, 'cause it was one I didn't know about." Pratchett has been passing on what he's learned for more than ten years with his own eccentric style of sci-fi-fantasy. Now his wackiness has spread to the Web.

▶ CLICK PICK

L-Space Web "Knowledge = Power = Energy = Matter = Mass; a good bookshop is just a genteel Black Hole that knows how to read. Mass distorts space into polyfractal L-space, in which Everywhere is also Everywhere Else." L-Space is kind of like the Web, with its links from here to there and elsewhere. Practically speaking, L-Space Web is the permanent home of the random quote generator, a Terry Pratchett Who's Who covering everyone from Angua to Esmerelda Weatherwax, the Clarecraft catalog of figurines, and fandom facts on fan clubs, fanzines, and forthcoming events, as well as the Annotated Pratchett File, the Pratchett Quote File, and the FAQs. There's even a Recipe Exchange.
WEB http://www.lspace.org

▶ THE AUTHOR

alt.books.pratchett The baby brother to the alt.fan.pratchett newsgroup, alt.books .pratchett is less populated but a bit more focused. Discussing annotations (*A*) is a favorite pastime here. But if you're looking for full Pratchett peculiarity and participation, this is your best bet.
USENET alt.books.pratchett

alt.fan.pratchett "Alt.fan.pratchett… is a little like written CB, and something like being at a party. Or several parties. All in one go. Blindfolded…" So say Terry Pratchett and Stephen Briggs in *The Discworld Companion*. To keep things as sane as possible, any relevant messages (comments about Terry Pratchett, his books, his characters, the computer games, and other items Pratchettesque) are marked with *R*, while irrelevant posts (e.g., the suggested casting of Macaulay Culkin as The Antichrist in the film version of the Pratchett/Gaiman collaboration *Good Omens*) are marked with *I*. Pratchett himself seems to enjoy the organized chaos, as he posts to the group quite often.
USENET alt.fan.pratchett

Great A'Tuin Named for, but not devoted to, that great turtle in the sky. Along with the usual games, songs, and biographical info, this site from Sweden offers a unique guide to the gods of Discworld (from Chefet, Dog-Headed God of Metalwork, to Grune, God of Unseasonal Fruits, to Zephyrus, God of Slight Breezes), brief descriptions of each of the Discworld books, and a page of the favorite characters and places of Tobias, the site's owner.
WEB http://www-pp.hogia.net/tati.ryberg /contents.html

Pratchett Quote File This corner of L-Space Web is devoted to indexing quotes, quirky and otherwise, from Pratchett, gleaned from Usenet posts, publicity tours, the Discworld series, and other works, such as *Good Omens* and *Only You Can Save Mankind*.
WEB http://www.lspace.org/pqf/index.html

Some Terry Pratchett Stuff Those not yet acquainted with Granny Esme

Weatherwax, Magrat Garlick, Nanny Ogg, and the rest of the delightfully dysfunctional inhabitants of Discworld will want to visit Colm Buckley's Pratchett pages for an introduction to the Discworld series, and the basics on the Brit who created the books.
WEB http://vangogh.cs.tcd.ie/cbuckley /books/terry.html

The Terry Pratchett FAQs FAQs of all shapes and sizes. A mini-FAQ exists for those just picking up a Pratchett book or posting to the newsgroup for the first time. Those fully immersed in the Discworld series and Pratchett culture will want to skip straight to the full alt.fan.pratchett FAQ. Find out why the U.S. lags so far behind in publishing Terry's books and how to get around that. Read explanations of all the Pratchett-inspired computer games. Check out a list of all of the works of Pterry which have aired on the ptelly. The merchandise FAQ, also resting here, provides info on Pratchett paraphernalia.
WEB http://www.Lspace.org/faqs /index.html

> **DISCWORLD**

Discworld MUD Lacking some of the seriousness of most MUDs, the Discworld MUD can be pretty goofy. But beware—in some places it can be deadly (and still goofy). Your adventure will take place in the city of Ankh-Morpork where you can visit the Patrician's Office, the Post Office, the Drum, and the T-Shop. Among the guilds you can join are fighters, thieves, priests, wizards, and assassins—each having its strengths and weaknesses. If you've read the series, it will make some of the quests a little easier, but you'll need more than an understanding of the books to succeed here.
WEB http://discworld.imaginary.com:5678

Discworld Review This sporadically produced newsletter for Pratchett followers provides a review in each issue as well as a reader poll. Best species? Wizards, with witches a close second. Sexiest character? Magrat, by a long shot. Sex of

the Great A'Tuin? Still up in the air.
WEB http://www.i-way.co.uk/~janthony /discworld.html

Discworld Trivia Mailing List What began as a competition for those who thought they knew more about the Discworld books than CMOT, Briggs has evolved into a trivia mailing list. Some tidbits included in past mailings: What is the Discworld's Premier College of Magic? (Unseen University), Who became Death's apprentice? (Mort), and Why was the Duck looking particularly belligerent? (It had probably heard about orange sauce.)
EMAIL orin@connexus.apana.org.au
Type in subject line: Discworld Trivia <your full name>

Gaspode's Guide to the Discworld A kind of Fodor's for Terry Pratchett's fantasy world. Too bad poor Twoflower didn't get his hands on something like this before he set off for his destination. Gaspode provides a list of Discworld's constellations (like Deformed Rabbit, Ignominus, and Baashwyc, the Condiment Set), the Coat of Arms of Ankh-Morpork and the various guilds, local songs, and games from and inspired by Discworld.
WEB http://cent1.lancs.ac.uk/~ashcrofb /discworld.html

The Terry Pratchett Archive Site Terry Pratchett's work is chock-full of references, allusions, parodies, and insider jokes. The Pratchett faithful have collected 1,300 such annotations in a huge document called the Annotated Pratchett File (or APF) here. Regulars on a.f.p. (not to be confused with APF) respectfully request that newbies check here before posting "to make sure you are not wasting bandwidth on something we already know." Besides the AFP, this anonymous FTP site also contains an FAQ, bibliography, and many other items of Pratchettian interest.
URL ftp://ftp-us.lspace.org/pub/people /pratchett

MARY SHELLEY

FRANKENSTEIN, OR THE MODERN Prometheus is one of the greatest Gothic novels of all time. The product of a story-writing competition suggested by her boyfriend P.B. Shelley, it is also generally thought of as the first science fiction book. Mary Shelley made her mark with the masterpiece at the tender age of 19. Others have borrowed the plot in an attempt to make their own mark—from the Boris Karloff classic to the modern Kenneth Branagh vanity project, to Andy Warhol's Frankenstein. Yet no cinematic rendition has quite captured the spirit of Shelley's novel. Fans of the first and foremost Frankenstein can find several etexts and hypertexts on the Net.

▶ CLICK PICK

Mary Shelley's Private Frankenstein Musical The most comprehensive Mary Shelley site on the Net. Besides the typical biography and bibliography, these pages recount the story of the fateful summer of 1816: storms inspired Lord Byron to challenge a group of authors staying in Switzerland, including Mary Shelley, to write a ghost story. Mary remained unable to write, until one night, she had a "waking" nightmare: "I saw the pale student of unhallowed arts kneeling beside the thing he had put together… " The next morning, she penned the famous phrase that opens Chapter IV, "It was on a dreary night in November…" Mary Shelley's Private Frankenstein Musical also includes information on Shelley's inspirations (Byron, Spenser, Blake, and Milton) and her family history. So why the musical title? If you have the Crescendo plug-in, you'll find out.
WEB http://www.netaxs.com/~kwbridge /index.html

▶ THE AUTHOR

The Mary Shelley Home Page These pages present a rather blunt biography of Mary Shelley, the Dead Babies List (self-explanatory), a timeline of all Mary's milestones, from her birth in 1797 to her death in 1851, and a bibliography. The site also offers insight into the coterie of friends and lovers who influenced on her work. Take some time while you're there to vote for the best and worst movie versions of Frankenstein.
WEB http://www.primenet.com/~huxleyan /mws_web.htm

MWS Letters and Journal "I had a dream tonight of the dead being alive which has affected my spirits," wrote Mary Shelley to Leight Hunt on March 5, 1817. These excerpts provide an interesting perspective of her often miserable marriage to Percy Bysshe Shelley, the devastating death of her children, and her literary inspiration.
WEB http://virtual.park.uga.edu/~232/mws .letandjour.html

▶ FRANKENSTEIN

A Frankenstein FAQ Under what circumstances did Mary Shelley write Frankenstein, or The Modern Prometheus? What is the central theme of the novel? And how the heck did such a literary classic become a much-rehashed horror flick? Whatever the question, you'll find the answers in detail here. The Frankenstein FAQ also features comments from the Mythic Movies group on Kenneth Branagh's Mary Shelley's Frankenstein.
WEB http://www.watershed.winnipeg .mb.ca/Frankenstein.html

Frankenstein: A Real Audio Presentation A full-length audio version of the story of Dr. Victor Frankenstein and his doomed effort to bring the dead back to life for the good of humanity.
WEB http://www.4iq.com/iqa1.html

Frankenstein by Mary Shelley Hypertext version of the original novel.
WEB http://www.literature.org/Works /Mary-Shelley/frankenstein

JULES VERNE

WHEN JULES VERNE WROTE *From the Earth to the Moon*, humans had not yet flown in airplanes or driven a gas-powered car. When *20,000 Leagues Under the Sea* was published in 1870, submarines that could submerge—and resurface—had only been in use for five or six years, and then only in very shallow waters. (Compressed oxygen was unheard of, of course.) Yet, Verne's scientific and technological predictions are so accurate that scientists and mathematicians hold him accountable for the mathematical errors he did very occasionally made. Sci-fi fans can safely acknowledge Verne as the grandfather of the genre. And happily, Verne's greatest works, *Journey to the Center of the Earth*, *Around the World in Eighty Days*, and *The Mysterious Island* are entirely online.

▶ CLICK PICK

Zvi Har'El's Jules Verne Collection If you don't have even a passing acquaintance with Phileas Fogg or his 80-day journey—never mind any trips to the moon—but have heard heard that Verne was a technological visionary who makes Nostradamus pale in comparison, this is the site for you. Zvi Har'El has gathered links to all related sites, particularly an excellent collection of all the places where Verne's works are online. This site is also host to the Jules Verne Forum's email list, which exchanges all kinds of information among Jules Verne enthusiasts. The archive is here, too. Potpourri lists every Jules Verne fan page, and visitors should not miss the related link to Early Science Fiction Concepts—a hilarious and fascinating discussion of Verne and the other early sci-fi thinkers. Zvi Har'El lists any site that has anything to do with Monsieur Verne, including a link to Mysteries of the Nautilus at EuroDisney.
WEB http://www.math.technion.ac.il/~rl/JulesVerne

▶ THE AUTHOR

Complete Jules Verne Bibliography Part of the comprehensive Verne site by Zvi Har'El, these pages give a chronological and complete guide to the many categories of Verne's writing. Some surprises are in store; for example, that Verne wrote plays and operas. Sections of this site are under construction, but should be complete in a short time. The most important categories, like Voyages Extraordinaires (his novels), are up and running.
WEB http://www.math.technion.ac.il/~rl/JulesVerne/biblio

Extraordinary Voyage (North American Jules Verne Society) Strap youself into your lunar module for a flight to the home page of the North American Jules Verne Society. Membership fees get you a newsletter six times a year, and a chance to aid the society in their mission to promote interest in and research on Jules Verne and his works.
WEB http://www.enterprise.ca/~anash/najvs.html

Jules Verne, from Prominent Men and Women of the Day A contemporary account of Verne from a popular nineteenth-century book, this brief article provides fascinating insight into the man beyond the birth and death dates. He is referred to as the most popular of French writers, "with the solitary exception of Victor Hugo." It's a highly enjoyable and chatty look at a scientific savant "who is a Parisian to his fingers'-ends."
WEB http://www.4j.lalne.edu/CyberSchool/Classes/CyberCraft/Projects/Completed/MenWomen/Verne/Verne.html

Jules Verne Stamps Collectors and those who are merely Verne-lovers will enjoy a look at some of the multitudes of postal stamps bearing Jules Verne's image and celebrating his work. They come from far-off places like France, Monaco, Cameroon, and Upper Volta,

but none, inexplicably, have been issued from the Lunar Post Office. They're awfully ungrateful up there.
WEB http://www.math.technion.ac.il /~rl/JulesVerne/stamps

Les Voyages Extraordinaires An excellent annotated bibliography to the novels of Verne, collectively titled *Les Voyages Extraordinaires*. If the book has been made into a movie, as many of them have, a link to the Internet Movie Database page is provided. Posthumously published works, many of which were almost entirely rewritten by Verne's son, are listed here as well, along with short stories and articles.
WEB http://www.xnet.com/~djk /JulesVerne_Works.shtml

Life and Works of Jules Verne A nutshell bio and bibliography. The author of the page provides reviews and commentary on Verne's most famous works. Don't miss the pictures of Verne—he looks like a cross between Santa Claus and Rutherford B. Hayes. Must be the beard.
WEB http://avery.med.virginia.edu/~mtp0f /flips/jules.html

▶ THE WORKS

Around the World in 80 Days (1873) In fact, as readers will discover, the famous journey of Mr Phileas Fogg of No.7, Saville Row, Burlington Gardens, does not take 80 days, and if we explained why we'd ruin the story for you. But the trip is worth reading about nonetheless, written as it is in Verne's frenetic, hilarious style. Others think so, too, which is why there are so many versions of the classic book online. One click for a world tour? Seems like the best deal going!
WEB http://www.datatext.co.uk/library /verne/world/chapters.htm • http://www .literature.org/Works/Jules-Verne/eighty

From the Earth to the Moon, and A Trip Around It (1865, 1870) With Verne, sometimes it seems like travel only goes in three directions: around, down and up. Go up here, and then around, with the jolly members of the Gun Club. Actually,

you may just want to watch the activity, since their plan involves being shot out of a large cannon. Yeah, that'd work. Neil Armstrong was just too heavy.
URL ftp://wiretap.spies.com/Library /Classic/moon.jv

Journey to the Center of the Earth (1864) Professor Hardwigg and his nephew Harry acquire some dubious directions to the center of the earth, by way of a crater in Greenland. Do they make it? Why aren't they driven back by the extreme heat at the earth's core? Oops, that's the twentieth century talking. Join them and their book for an amazing journey.
URL gopher://gopher.vt.edu:10010/02 /153/1

The Mysterious Island (1874) A hot air balloon, caught in a nasty storm, crashlands on a deserted and, frankly, mysterious island. Fortunately, the passengers are daring explorers who conjure up a classier sort of *Gilligan's Island* and then plan their escape. Will they get away? Who is the mysterious benefactor helping them in their struggle to survive? A classic adventure story.
WEB http://www.math.technion.ac.il /~rl/JulesVerne/kravitz

Round the Moon (1870) This sequel to *From the Earth to the Moon* follows the wacky members of Gun Club as they complete their victorious scientific experiment. Classic Verne, and very funny stuff.
URL ftp://wiretap.spies.com/Library /Classic/round.jv

Twenty Thousand Leagues Under the Sea (1870) Before Nautilus came to be associated with fitness, it meant the mysterious disappearance of oceangoing vessels around the world, and Captain Nemo, the human enigma. Get to know him, and remember that most of what Verne predicted about submarines has come true.
WEB http://etext.lib.virginia.edu/cgibin /toccer?id=VerTwen&tag=public &images=images/modeng&data=/lv1 /Archive/eng-parsed&part=0

SCI-FI LITERATURE A-Z

WHEN IT COMES TO SCI-FI literature the Internet has no respect for convention (sci-fi conventions are another matter entirely). Like an alien being from a superior planet, the Internet takes what sci-fi it wants and repurposes it to strange and exotic ends in accordance with a logic beyond previous comprehension. H.G. Wells, creator of the *Time Machine*, architect of *War of the Worlds*, and a reasonable candidate for the title Father of Science Fiction is paid scant attention. Aldous Huxley who penned *Brave New World* is only marginally acknowledged. Ray Bradbury anybody? These masters are given homes online, but they are not the tech-enhanced funhouses afforded even the lamest SF TV show. In keeping with this advanced logic, Thomas Pynchon is herewith afforded SF status.

▶ CLICK PICK

HyperArts Feeling bad about not being able to finish *Gravity's Rainbow*? Don't. One member of the Pulitzer Prize board actually called Thomas Pynchon's book "unreadable," "turgid," "overwritten," and in parts "obscene." Another academic remarked that she had tried more than once but had only gotten a third of the way through the 760-page book. But it's your pride at stake here. Download Tim Ware's hyper-concordance to help you along when lost your place... or your mind, before your bookmark becomes permanently stuck on page 202. Also available is a Web guide to *V.*, links to FTP sites, and the Pynchon mailing list. **WEB** http://www.hyperarts.com

▶ J.G. BALLARD

Don't Crash: The J.G. Ballard Interview The subtitle of this interview, "Psychosis, euthanasia, apocalypse, and other fun ideas" sums up J.G. Ballard before he even says a word. But it's an insightful interview that follows, covering virtual reality, Ronald Reagan, and Ballard's vision of the future. "I could sum up the future in one word: boring." **WEB** http://www.kgbmedia.com/wsv /ballard.html

J.G. Ballard A thoroughly over-academic take on the "intriguing structures" Ballard works with, this article goes so far as to compare his stories to "the novel's traditional machinery." You know, that lecture you ignored in high school? But it can't be denied that literary criticism of Ballard is a challenging temptation—it's got to be better than trying to find hidden themes in Dickens—and this essay is readable, if a little precious. **WEB** http://www.ualberta.ca/~ckeep /hfl0093.html

J.G. Ballard: What I Believe Message to the creators of this site: OK, so now we know that you can use frames. But did you know that each frame is supposed to say something different? This site is a hypertext version of Ballard's powerful statement of self, a credo that acknowledges the absurdity, beauty, tragedy, and treasure of human life. The site's authors have linked many of the operative words in the statement to Ballard-related quotes and sites. They claim that this is to celebrate Ballard's principle of connectedness between disparate objects. It is a thought-provoking, and, in the end, very affecting presentation. **WEB** http://www.cnw.com/~miki/index.html

▶ IAIN BANKS

A Gift from the Culture This Iain Banks story first appeared in *Interzone* in 1987 and was subsequently reprinted in the short story collection *The State of the Art*. Happily, there are no copyright problems here, since *The Richmond Review* has given permission for the story to be posted online. But what do we care? Dig in: "Money is a sign of poverty..." **WEB** http://www.demon.co.uk/review /library/banks01.html

alt.books.iain-banks "The Minds ensure your every physical requirement. You don't need to work. If you're not in Contact what exactly do you do all day every day for your very long life? Would there be a luddite reaction?" There are many people out there willing to consider those kinds of what-ifs raised by Banks's books, people out there who are more than happy to answer (and debate) these kinds of cultural questions. Could it be said that this newsgroup has a subculture?

USENET alt.books.iain-banks

Culture Shock Banks fans everywhere (at least those with the full online access) ought to be dancing with glee because this site is great! If it's Iain Banks, it has to be listed here. A sampling of the many choices includes a complete directory of Banks books, half a dozen interviews, a guide to the Culture…The list could go on, but fans simply must come here and see for themselves.

WEB http://tigger.uic.edu/~pillbox/cs /shock.html

Dark Station—Iain Banks A site noir which is both artistically and elegantly arranged, not to mention comprehensive. Not only does it link to every Banks-related site imaginable, including newsgroups and mailing lists, but it contains a well-rounded selection of places of interest to those intrigued by the futuristic themes Banks writes about. This includes utopian societies, artificial intelligence, and the future of humanity. It's not to be missed.

WEB http://www.netlink.co.uk/users /sonance/banks/banks.html

▶ BEN BOVA

Linkoping Science Fiction Archive: Ben Bova Mars is much more than a candy bar when it comes to the fiction of Ben Bova. If you're shopping for a new series to read or just want to know which Bova book to read next, stop here for in-depth reviews. They're hardly recent, but not at all outdated.

WEB http://sf.www.lysator.liu.se/sf_archive /sf-texts/books/B/Bova,Ben.mbox

▶ RAY BRADBURY

The Martian Chronicles Study Guide Readers having trouble with *The Martian Chronicles* are probably trying to read it as a coherent novel, rather than the set of linked short stories it is, according to this helpful study guide. It contains historical notes, very brief synopses, and "thought-provoking" questions.

WEB http://www.wsu.edu:8080/~brians /science_fiction/martianchronicles.html

Ray Bradbury This site is a must on a Bradbury site-seeing trip. If you'll step this way, please, you'll see a biography and a bibliography, photos of the author of *Fahrenheit 451*, and even a nauseating recipe for liquid pizza. In the library, pause briefly to read several stories and excerpts from the master, including "Pendulum" and "A Sound of Thunder."

WEB http://www.on-ramp.com/johnston /bradbury.htm

▶ ANTHONY BURGESS

99 By Anthony Burgess If you like Burgess, you might like to know what he reads. Here is his list of the best 99 novels published between 1939 and 1984. The selection ranges far and wide, from Chinua Achebe to Herman Wouk.

WEB http://www.bookbroker.com/99.htm

Anthony Burgess Read a classic and (frankly) incomprehensible excerpt from *A Clockwork Orange*, then follow links to a bio, a glossary of Nadsat (the mix of English and Russian argot that makes the novel near-incomprehensible for the first few chapters—or at least until you get the hang of it), and several other sites regarding Mr. Burgess and his oeuvre.

WEB http://www.empirenet.com /~rdaeley/authors/burgess.html

Anthony Burgess Reading A Clockwork Orange Many authors are the best readers of their own work. They know where the nuances lie, and how the rhythm should flow. When they speak their characters' lines, they speak them as they should be spoken, with proper emphasis. In the case of Nadsat there is only one man who really knew: Malcolm MacDowell. Here, however, you can listen to Burgess himself having a go at it. **WEB** http://town.hall.org/Archives/radio /IMS/HarperAudio/070494harp_ITH .launch.html

▶ EDGAR RICE BURROUGHS

Edgar Rice Burroughs Looking for a science fiction cause to champion? Want something to shout about in a unique, ululating manner? Harlan Ellison has recently rescued Oak Forest Canyon in Sherman Oaks, Calif., from developers and wants to create a 24-acre park dedicated to the memory of Edgar Rice Burroughs. ERB is said to have frequented the little canyon—the inspiration for Tarzan—while riding on horseback and picnicking there. Ellison, however, needs donations to make his ERB shrine a reality and here's where you can help. The site also includes information on joining the Burroughs Bibliophiles, a list of magazines devoted to the creator of John Carter of Mars and Carson Napier of Venus, and links to Burroughs books online. **WEB** http://www.tarzan.com

From Africa to Mars: The Political, Social, and Moral Commentaries of Edgar Rice Burroughs This site is devoted to the notion that Burroughs' fiction goes beyond the good vs. evil tale and that there is "a serious underpinning to his works which gives his fantastic tales more weight than one might glean in a cursory reading." Robert Greer offers an in-depth analysis of Burroughs' characters, settings, and interweaving of social and political commentary in the Mars and Tarzan serials. He attempts to identify the parrellels between Burroughs' fiction and the ideals, fears, and political beliefs that concerned the author and many other Americans during the early twentieth century. Communism and socialism and the "social injustices" rising from these ideologies are explored as potential foundations for much of Burroughs fiction. Delving into the distinct social and political cultures developed in each of the 11 Martian tales makes for a very insightful site. **WEB** http://www.wowdesign.com/erb

The Mars Series: E-text Edgar Rice Burroughs has sold 25 million copies of his novels, which have been translated into 56 languages. Better make that 57—his heroic tales are now in hypertext. If you're a sucker for the Burroughs formula—daring adventure, bold hero, strange cultures, lovely heroine, subhuman bad guys—you'll want to click through the planetary adventures found in *A Princess of Mars*; *The Gods of Mars*; *Thuvia, Maid of Mars*; and *The Warlord of Mars*—four of Burroughs's most famous Martian tales. **WEB** http://www.cs.cmu.edu/afs/cs.cmu .edu/Web/People/rgs/literature.html

▶ MADELEINE L'ENGLE

Madeleine L'Engle Home Page Well, lookie here. Ah do believe that that logo at the top of this Texas page is a crumpled clock. Could it be... a wrinkle in time? This fan page, while it claims to be under construction, seems to have let its building permit expire. But that doesn't matter much, because the bibliography of Madeleine L'Engle is excellent, and the brief discussion of the interconnectedness theme in her works is worth examining. **WEB** wwwvms.utexas.edu/~eithlan/lengle .html

Wheaton College L'Engle Archive Aside from being a library catalog of the Wheaton College collection of *A Wrinkle in Time* and L'Engle's manuscripts and papers, this gopher is a source for an excellent, though brief, autobiography of the author. Naturally, it's a place to find a super-extensive bibliography, too, down to the letters she wrote. The last entry in the menu links to a couple of different Web resources, such as Children's Literature Web Guide.

URL gopher://gopher.wheaton.edu:70
/11/Wheaton_Archives/SC/findaids/sc03

▶ ROBERT A. HEINLEIN

alt.fan.heinlein This newsgroup is never so much off topic as terminally on tangent. Well-rounded posters take the ball and run far, far away with it. Thus, a discussion on the scientific accuracy of Heinlein's use of relativity veers off into a debate on advanced particle physics, making the original posters sorry they ever broached the subject. A chat about the upcoming *Starship Troopers* movie heads off into the murky land of copyright law. Ah, at last, a newsgroup with a brain, even if one needs a doctorate to grok the fullness of the discussions. The newsgroup FAQ is helpful, too, particularly for those in search of background info on RAH.
USENET alt.fan.heinlein
FAQ: WEB http://www.crl.com/~jgifford
/rah_faq.html

Excerpt from The Rolling Stones The cars of the late twentieth century were "unbelievable museum pieces" and pieces of junk, according to Heinlein's account, set sometime in the future. It's entirely believable that this historical "How could they be so dumb?" essay will be written in the not-too-distant future, just as today we mock the wooden submarine and the wax wings of Icarus. This funny excerpt is a good introduction to the thoughts of the "Grand Master."
WEB http://shark.imall.com/~jlp/stones
.html

Index—Heinlein Resource List This Will Hester fellow is serious: no blather, no official connection, and definitely no Church of All Worlds sites. So what's here? An index to the best of the Heinlein-related Web, including FAQs, reviews, interviews, and newsgroups.
WEB http://fly.hiwaay.net/~hester
/heinlein.html

The Notebooks of Lazarus Long "Always store beer in a dark place," is just one of the dozens of hilarious quotes from *Time Enough for Love* that make up The Notebooks. Amuse yourself for a while reading the others, then thank the kindly Heinlein fan who typed them all in.
WEB http://pages.zoomnet.net/~terri
/llong2.html

Robert A. Heinlein Archives Not your typical index. This page catalogs an odd assortment of Heinlein ditties including the ubiquitous FAQ—but that's where the similarity to a normal index ends. There's a Mark Twain essay Heinlein once cited, a fascinating account of the painful genesis of the *Puppet Masters* movie, a Heinlein interview from 1973, and a long paper on Federal Service in Starship Troopers round out the eclectic list.
WEB http://www.crl.com/~jgifford
/rah_docs.html

This I Believe, by Robert Heinlein A statement of belief not even tangentially religious, although it is strongly spiritual. Heinlein's "I believe" is old-fashioned "bootstraps" philosophy, including the usual accompaniment of belief in human resolve and determination, and a firm confidence in charity. Plus, it's well-written.
WEB http://www.channel1.com/users
/rmaddox/believe.html

▶ L. RON HUBBARD

The L. Ron Hubbard Literary Site Seek not, ye sci-fi fans, for an objective viewpoint of the guru here. Master storyteller and Scientology pedagogue Lafayette Ronald Hubbard, if the information presented by his literary agent is to be believed, was nothing short of the Messiah. So why do we get the feeling that hidden behind the can-ya-believe-it bio is the biggest nerd in school? You decide. Anyway, there is a lot of good stuff here. Many of L. Ron's books are available at a 20 percent Internet discount—the intros and first chapters are entirely online, and there's beautiful artwork from the books throughout.
WEB http://www.Authorservicesinc.com

ALDOUS HUXLEY

Aldous Huxley "Claim the right to be unhappy" with the opener on this page, an excerpt from *Brave New World*. Then, pop that soma and peruse a bio of Huxley, born in 1894 to a distinguished scientific and literary British family. Huxley Links at the bottom of the page are extensive and include quotes, related movies, academic papers, and censorship of Huxley's works.
WEB http://www.empirenet.com/~rdaeley/authors/huxley.html

Island Web Does the idea of a psychedelic utopia appeal to you? Help these "hyper dimensional cyber elves" build one at Island Web, an interactive community based on ideas in Huxley's last novel, *Island*. While such LSD-loving druggie froth seems hopelessly '60s, it's always interesting to see what an author can do to help justify anything.
WEB http://www.island.org

SOMA Web We're all feelin' goooooood at SOMA Web, where the topic is Huxley and the soma scatters like pebbles (well, not really). Follow those swirling colors in your head, man, to a comprehensive bio of Aldous Huxley, and a happy little bibliography. Then follow some links to, like, elsewhere.
WEB http://www.primenet.com/~matthew/huxmain.html

GEORGE ORWELL

Animal Farm Test "All animals are equal," but they still have to take tests to prove it. Find out if you're more equal than others by taking this test.
WEB http://rehoboth.co.dekalb.k12.ga.us/~tucker/Eng_Writers_ORWELL.html

George Orwell He died at age 46, but managed to produce many important works, including *1984* and *Animal Farm*. There isn't too much on the Web about Orwell (perhaps his fans are a bit technophobic?), but this page has collected the best links plus a famous quote about a boot and a human face.
WEB http://www.empirenet.com/~rdaeley/authors/orwell.html

Newspeak and Doublethink Homepage The year 1984 has come and gone, but was Orwell's vision of the future so far-fetched as we were all led to believe? The author of this page thinks that newspeak and doublethink have never been so prevalent as they are today. He cites political correctness, employee drug testing, affirmative action, and other common "whipping boys" as evidence that Big Brother is getting bigger. He is also convinced that the government is spying on him through the microphone in his telephone. Even Orwell would run from this nutty, if not amusing page.
WEB http://aloha.net/~frizbee/index.html

THOMAS PYNCHON

HyperArts (Thomas Pynchon) Thomas Pynchon probably loves the Net. Why wouldn't he? It encourages polyphony, produces paranoia, and allows for the transmission of information quicker than you can say "Trystero." It also has a page devoted to Pynchon's works. Web Guides to *V.* and *Gravity's Rainbow* are the stars here, along with related "Pynchonalia" (including a link to a Pynchon mailing list) and an FTP site.
WEB http://www.hyperarts.com

Pynchon List "Welcome aboard, gee, it's a fabulous or-gy / That you just dropped in on, my friend—/ We can't recall just how it start-ted, / But there's only one way it can end! / The behaviour is bestial, hardly Marie-Celestial, / But you'll fit right in with the crowd, / If you jettison all of those prob-lems, / And keep it hysterically loud!" A sometimes scholarly discussion of Pynchonalia.
EMAIL waste@waste.org *Type in message body:* subscribe pynchon-l

San Narciso College—The Thomas Pynchon Home Page Thomas Pynchon probably loves the Net. Why wouldn't he? It assists polyphony, produces paranoia, and allows for the transmission of information quicker than you can say "Trystero." And it also has a page or two devoted to Pynchon's works. Read two Pynchon FAQs, consult a brief biography, and marvel at impressionistic, rebus-like accounts of Pynchon's major works—*V.*, *The Crying of Lot 49*, and *Gravity's Rainbow*.

WEB http://www.pomona.edu/pynchon /index.html

► KURT VONNEGUT

alt.books.kurt-vonnegut Either Vonnegut's fans don't care to discuss him here, or they have given up on the ham-and-cheese-ducking that's all too common in this newsgroup. The pace is pretty slow, but when genuine discussion takes place, it ranges from Vonnegut's books to potential CD-ROMs and movies. Where to find recordings of Vonnegut reading his works is also frequently discussed. Patience is rewarded, but what this newsgroup needs is more activity.

USENET alt.books.kurt-vonnegut

FAQ: WEB http://www.blarg.net/~geocool Vonnegut/abkvFAQ.html

Kurt Vonnegut Ignore the swirling, salt-water taffy colors; they lend nothing to the page. But this site, which carries some original content, including reviews of online Vonnegut stories (and links to them) and a short Vonnegut FAQ, also attractively acts as the starting point for a survey of the Vonnegut Web. Rather than merely listing links, the best are presented in an elegant tabular serving tray. Don't miss taking the link under "Information on a Couple of Novels" to "Slaughterhouse Five," which is actually an excellent biographical article about Vonnegut.

WEB http://www.empirenet.com/~rdaeley /authors/vonnegut.html

Kurt Vonnegut Would you let this guy mind the baby? He looks sneakier than Woody Allen in a sorority house. But this home page is packed with Vonnegut-related links. Of particular interest is the link to an online Vonnegut story

called "Sun Moon Star."

WEB http://www.cas.usf.edu/english/boon /vonnegut/kv.html

Sound Files (excerpts from Slaughterhouse Five) It's unclear who the heck is reading the *Slaughterhouse* excerpts in these fairly gigantic sound files, but it could be Vonnegut. And who, conceivably, could do it better than the author himself? If you want to make certain you're hearing the voice of Vonnegut, follow the link from his name at the top to a sound file of a lecture he delivered at Michigan State University.

WEB http://town.hall.org/Archives /radio/IMS/HarperAudio/1376_harp _00_ITH.html

► H.G. WELLS

Study Guide for H.G. Wells' The War of the Worlds Sometimes even grownups miss their *Cliff's Notes*. This college-level study guide to Wells's novel is both thought-provoking and comprehensive. It contains chapter summaries and such popular discussion questions as "What methods does Wells use to make these events seem realistic?"

WEB http://www.wsu.edu:8080 /~brians/science_fiction/warofworlds .html

The Time Machine In 1898, Herbert George Wells posited a fourth dimension: time. Our consciousness moves across it like any other dimension, why not our bodies? he asked, before sending his anonymous Time Traveler on his way. The rest is history—or is it?

WEB http://www.literature.org/Works /H-G-Wells/time-machine

The War of the Worlds Home Page The year 1997 marks the centennial of the serial publication of *The War of the Worlds*, and little Woking, England (where the book is set) is having a party. There are walks, newspaper stories, and schedules (diaries, to the British). Do you feel like making a pilgrimage?

WEB http://www.dircon.co.uk/mjbstein /warhome.htm

PART 5

Cyberpunk

MAINFRAME

IT'S A LITERARY MOVEMENT. IT'S A subculture. It's cyberpunk. Forget definitions. Suffice it to say cyberpunk usually involves patent leather, cyborg mentality, ego, and a strong urge to free information by any means necessary. The foundation was laid in literature, years before the Internet was a glimmer in the eye of some secret government military agent, but it's now inextricably enmeshed with the Web. The pages that align themselves with the term are some of the most accomplished on the Web. What "real" cyberpunks may find lacking in many cases is a sense of rebellion. A select few sites, however, are sure to put fear in the hearts of the NSA, and tears in the eyes of the devoted. But you don't have to be a cypherpunk, a haqr, a phreak, a wizard or a raver—spend a few minutes at these pages and you'll be able to successfully fake your way through a chatroom debate on Artificial Intelligence, Virtual Reality, or the Electronic Frontier Foundation.

whose aim is to "promote create spaces situations in which people can create behave express experience in ways unavailable in currently existing places. uphold dignity creativity." This is one of the few pages that is true to the cyberpunk spirit, i.e., it is interactive, very strange, and promotes illegal activities. With a table of contents that includes "Pain Of Existence," "Corporate Skip Raiders Manual," and "Isolation In Velocity," this is one page you have to experience to understand (if you're lucky). Find out all you'll ever need to know about interactive fax performance and hacking into the telephones at King's Cross Station, then jump into half a dozen dadaesque slide shows complimented by Joycean train-of-thought poetry. Meaningless, beautiful, revolutionary? All of the above? One warning: depending on your tastes and sensibilities, Cybercafe will either blow your mind or just give you a ripping headache.
web http://www.cybercafe.org

▶ CLICK PICK

Evolution "Weird dancing in all-night computer-banking lobbies. Unauthorized pyrotechnic displays. Land-art, earthworks as bizarre alien artifacts strewn in State Parks. Kidnap someone and make them happy." Culture hacking from Hakim Bey is only the beginning. This site is a strange, delightfully frustrating grab bag of post-modernism and self-promotion, a true cyberpunk scene—aesthetic, enlightening, convoluted, industrious. Features range from the resume-cum-online-exhibition of the site author's laudable graphic design, to Robert Pearson's computer generated poetry, to *FutureCulture* archives. Jack your brain at the door.
web http://www.uio.no/~mwatz/futurec

▶ MOTHERSHIPS

A Rational Thoughts Cybercafe is not just a Web page, it's an organization

alt.cyberpunk FAQ What's all this about cyberpunk anyway? After a quick visit you'll be an expert on the genre. The concise, well-written, and well-categorized listing of the elements of cyberfiction, films, and TV available here covers every angle, and then some. Perhaps the most eerie and intriguing element is the blurring of the lines between cyberfiction and fact, which seems to be a constant companion to most of the questions answered and discussed.
web http://bush.cs.tamu.edu/~erich/alt.cp.faq.html

Aud's Cyberpunk Pinups Madness reigns at one of the most utterly meaningless sites on the Net. It's a brown-acid-dipped everlasting gobstopper! See teddy bears in bondage! Suffer virtual addiction! Help drag queens search for Sid and Nancy at sad, small fairs in Worthing! Send email death threats! Confess your crimes to Scotland Yard! Discover who you were in a former life! Seek the truth that only the *Planet of the Apes* can give! And on and on and on and on and on… it never ends, no matter how long you suck on it. You'll never need another page.

WEB http://www.sirius.com/~rik/aud.html

Cyber Noodle Soup This elusive ezine is mostly substance with a dash of flash— no haqrs, no attitude. Read another Gibson interview and be surprised that he still holds your interest. Check out the Cyberpunk Timeline that takes the human race from 1928 and the first use of the word "punk" to the 1996 release of *Escape Velocity*. Take in the hellfire and brimstone, and dismissive chuckles, that K.W. Jeter's *Blade Runner 2* has wrought in the community. And wonder at the zine's obsessive fixation on *Johnny Mnemonic*. Was it a destructive force that corrupted the purity of the genre and gave the masses a misleading, tawdry introduction to a genuine literary force? Or just a dumb movie that doesn't warrant a second thought, much less a thesis paper?

WEB http://www.teleport.com/~jaheriot/cns.htm

Cyber: Technology and Culture A huge archive of articles, essays, fiction, author profiles, manuals, manifestos, interviews, and news clips on technology and culture: "666 and 700 Club," "Beating Standard Drug Tests," "Clinton on Technology," "Easterwood: Cybersoma," "Fiction that Bleeds Truth," "Guide to VR FTP sites," "Industrial Thresholds .html," "Private Assault on the IN," "Rupert Murdoch Buys Delphi," "Stalin and Lysenko," "Unbelievable Slop," "Wallace: On The Tendency Of Vari," "Zimmermann:PGP," and much, much more. You want information feed? Choke on this!

WEB http://english-www.hss.cmu.edu/cyber.html

Cyberpunk A beginner's guide. Read the FAQ section and learn what they mean by the words cyberpunk, cyberculture, and cyberspace. There's a *Blade Runner*

page. Inside, click onto the *Blade Runner* file and read discussions on *Blade Runner* issues. Was Deckard a replicant or not? Read about it here. Endless links to cyberpunk literature.

WEB http://www.cs.uidaho.edu/lal/cyberspace/Cyberpunk/cyberpunk.html

Cyberpunk Documents Links to Bruce Sterling's *Hacker Crackdown*, William Gibson's *Alien III* script and *Agrippa*, and *Cyberkind Magazine*, a magazine composed of cyberpunk nonfiction, short fiction, poetry, and art. Plus, a nice quote from Richard Nixon.

WEB http://www.umd.umich.edu/~nhughes/cyber

Cyberpunk Handbook Parody on the cyberpunk genre. Bruce Sterling gives a sparkling foreword of the above-mentioned book written by R.U. Sirius, founder of *Mondo 2000* magazine, St. Jude, and Bart Nagel. Excerpts from the book are included. Find out how easy it really is to look like a cyberpunk. All you need are black leather pants, boots, mirror shades, and a laser pointer. Link from here to The Web of Deceit (R.U. Sirius's page) where you can read his latest book *How to Mutate and Take Over the World*.

WEB http://www.dnai.com/~mvsirius/cyberpnk.html

CyberPunk Research Labs Less cyberpunk than cyberdelic, this tongue-in-chip rendition of what's hip in cyberspace could prove almost as entertaining as it is confusing, if only you can stick with it long enough to figure out what they're talking about. It's not characterized by the nihilistic melodrama of most cyberpunk obsessionals, just a healthy dose of flippancy and a deep love of the bovine. The most substantive stuff (downloadables from the likes of William S. Burroughs and Charles Manson) is at Cafe So-Sigh-lty. Just follow the "MeMOry-BaNK oF PatRIaRchs" link to the cow icon, then click in the Egyptian icon's Delta of Venus—and if these directions are making you shake your head, you've already started to feel the effects of CRL.

WEB http://nation.org/~crl

Linenoiz e-zine This ezine, aimed at serious cyberpunks, is kind of cool in content even if its format is pretty mundane. It looks like other zines, but it doesn't really think like them. Mostly it's an exchange of opinion and philosophy from your fellow cyberdenizens on all things cybercultural. If you like the current issue, you can check out past issues or, if you're feeling really brazen, express your own views for a future issue. Fiction, non-fiction, reviews of software and movies, even links to other cyber-oriented pages are all covered here from the nihilist cyberpunk point of view.

WEB http://www.magi.com/~vektor /linenoiz.html

Mark/Space An enormous virtual village far too unwieldy to describe in detail here. What makes this space different from other cyberworlds is that it's not just an overblown link index, it's a wonderful amalgamation of culture-glossary, encyclopedia, art gallery, library, music store, ezine, research project, and marketplace. Cyberpunk is more of a spirit here than a solid entity, but with a little searching you'll find pockets of concentration. One such pocket is the Cyberpunk Author section, a simply fantastic A-Z of authors, with booklists and external links. Many author pages also include synopses of major works, and cross-reference links to other parts of Mark/Space. For example, the Rudy Rucker page also connects to Artificial Life, CyberCulture, Hackers, Physics, Science, Science Fiction, Slipstream, and Virtual Reality. Some advice: Mark/Space is kind of like Disneyworld; you can't do it all in one day. Bookmark it and explore at your leisure.

WEB http://www.euro.net/mark-space /index.html

Mirrorshades Conference Here's the zine which seeks to define and present the cool household words (and con-

cepts) of today and of tomorrow… and tomorrow… and tomorrow… The Mirrorshades Conference covers the full spectrum with interviews and articles on the ever-mutating cyberscene, approached from the perspective of adult contemplation rather than the usual obsessive adolescent hysteria of the cyberpunk post-apocalypse. Here, cyberpunk has no precise meaning. The Mirrorshades Conference claims to be a source for science fiction writers' story ideas, collecting information from every subject (art, music, film, virtual reality, etc.). Judge the process for yourself in the Mirrorshades Postmodern Archive. Read Bruce Sterling's email and find out why he released a copy of his book, *Hacker Crackdown*, on the Internet. You'll have the opportunity to join in special events and discussion groups, even sign up as a HotWired VIP (it's free—go for it); this is the all-round, plugged-in place to see what's going on in cyberpunkspace.

WEB http://www.well.com/conf /mirrorshades

Net-Tribes: Cyberculture on the Web Can't tell cyberhip from cyberhype? Virtual communications encompass the Net and all netizens in the vast haze of negativity known as cyberculture. You can be there, too, especially if you stop here first to pick up the necessary soft- and hardware to experience 3-D by machine. Next, check into the multimedia section, which offers links to cool music, movies, and games you can play with (maybe even understand), now that you're up to speed.

WEB http://www.eerie.fr/~alquier/cyber.html

Unofficial Cyberpunk Page Fuzzy on the whole cyberpunk phenom? Get the low-down on high-tech, from the authors who coined the term (most notably William Gibson) to every movie sporting elements that might even loosely be considered cyberpunk. Check out some links to other cyberpunk hangouts, games, and ezines; spend enough time here and you might even come away with a couple of new "cobbers" (a friend

in cyberslang; one of many new words you'll learn.
WEB http://www.wwmatrix.com/Cyberpunk

Xanner A solid ezine with a strong academic tendency—low tech enough for most newbies, but high theory so they probably won't want to read it in the first place. Starts off with novel, zine, and movie lists (not HTML'd, for shame!), it goes on to offer a chunk of Gibson stuff including a parody of *Agrippa* and a *Neuromancer* opera. Then there are post-modern theory papers aplenty, with titles like "Virtual Boundries" and "After the Deluge-CP in the '80s and '90s," and sociological essays on virtual communities. The Hackerek section contains serious stuff and targeted humor ("How to Hack a Book"). If you're looking for tech, you'll find science and science fiction here, with reports on portable hardware and gaming systems, and musings on neural computer connects and biochips. Other articles cover VR and Matrix, and there are links to FAQs for various films and artists that you've probably been sick of for years.
WEB http://edge.stud.u-szeged.hu /xan_cnts.html

▶ FICTION

Chatsubo The alt.cyberpunk .chatsubo WWW archives! It's a compilation of cyberpunk stories (computer/hi-tech prose) from regular people (i.e., non-professional writers) and from *Linenoiz*, a cyberpunk mag. Links to cyberpunk publishers, such as Del Ray and Bantam Books, as well as other cyberpunk fan home pages.
WEB http://www.magi.com/~vektor /chatsubo

Cyberlit If you cruise by here expecting startling graphics alongside digitized splatter-punk fiction, put the mouse down slowly, cowboy. However, if you're curious about what happens when an English literature Ph.D. candidate takes on sci-fi then perhaps you'll appreciate Joe Steinbach's learned commentary. Drifting somewhere between the writings of William Gibson and modern social theorists (with a dose of techno-future anime), Steinbach considerssome fascinating postulates relating to the Neuromanticism of cyberpunk, its gender biases and its relationship to the rapid computerization of our culture. Take advantage of his bibliography for further challenging readings in fiction and theory.
WEB http://omni.cc.purdue.edu/~stein /stein.htm

cybRpunk Ever wanted to create an un-kinder, harsher future in the comfort of your own home? The armchair William Gibson in you will find everything you could dream of to craft an exciting piece of cyberfiction right here. A variety of "dark futures" (from World War III to corporate takeovers of governments) are presented for incorporation into your own fantasy apocalypse. There are even machine-speak technical tips to enhance the accuracy of your tales. You'll be raking in the digicash in no time.
WEB http://w3.one.net/~wronk/cybrpunk .html

Jayhawk—the series by Mary K. Kuhner A gross of cyberpunky scenarios (or chapters) comprising tales of our forlorn, war-torn future. While you may find a brief peek into the complex and ugly world of Kuhner's characters worthwhile (an exposition of the story and its people is provided to get you on track), the full work is incredibly long and not particularly innovative.
WEB http://www.klab.caltech.edu/~flowers /jayhawk

Scenarios and Stories Still searching for an outlet for your natural gift of pessimistic fantasizing? Well, tether your angry avatar right here, and start opining on the demise of civilization, using the odd assortment of population and Internet growth charts and other sundry information given in the hope that you might be the next cyberpunk visionary. Once you've pieced together their information and your inspiration, get your first taste of glorious "publication" right here—they're always looking for new writers.

WEB http://www.is-bremen.de/~mhi /scena000.htm

Writing About Cyberpunk Wreak havoc as the author of a world-gone-technomad universe and receive college credit to boot. Logically enough, some University of Texas professor had the brilliant idea that a course on cyberpunk belongs in a cyberspace classroom. Required readings and written assignments (for example, reviewing relevant Web sites or creating a little cyberfiction of your own) are posted online for the whole "class" to read, and give feedback. If you're looking for a crash course on the entire cyberpunk movement, this is the perfect way to get it!

WEB http://www.en.utexas.edu/~tonya /Cyberpunk

▶ GAMING

Christian Conkle's Cyberpunk Devoted to those infamous futuristic role playing games, with an obvious bias toward *CP2020*, this place provides a discussion forum and scenario description for the games. If you're already a player, or thinking of becoming one, you may find interesting and convenient the incredibly complete listings of cyberware, vehicles, and weapons available to your *CP2020* characters as they navigate the twenty-first century. Christian has also provided a tech-chic section so you won't commit any apocalyptic faux pas.

WEB http://odin.cc.pdx.edu/~psu00866 /cyber/cyber.html

Cyberpunk 2020 Check out R. Talsorian Games's official site for the role-playing game of the (next) century. The big news here is the online catalog, where you can order the game or its companion books without searching further, so the main reason for a visit is to spend money. The few *CP2020* links take an obvious backseat to merchandising, which is actually fine since there are so many unofficial fan pages offering more

in the way of game information, advice, and fun. Just come here to get the game itself.

WEB http://www.best.com/~rtg1 /cp2020.html

Cyberpunk 2020 Web Archive An impressive and attractive fan-maintained shrine to that fabulous paragon of cyber-fantasy role-playing, *CP2020*. From essays and dissertations on the whole cyberpunk culture (yawn) to the ever-mutating rules and game specs (including highly detailed and technical roles, ammo and weaponry tables), if it's or related to *CP2020*, it's here. The key piece that makes this puzzle fit together like no other is the heavy player input and the myriad new scenarios to spice up your old characters and game techniques. Full of cool stuff to enhance your *CP2020* game!

WEB http://falcon.cc.ukans.edu/~heresy /cyber/index.html

Cyberpunk—The Daemon If you can navigate around the somewhat daunting spelling and grammatical errors, you will find a tremendous amount of past, present, and future information on *Cyberpunk 2020*, a role-playing game for bleak, machine-infested futurists. Learn what "has" transpired between today and 2020 that's doomed us to such a dark, unfriendly future. Choose the type of character you'd like to be and/or weapons you'd use, and become a "player" in this most un-playful encounter.

WEB http://www.excaliber.com/thdaemon /index.htm

rec.games.frp.cyber "Firing full auto, an Ingram (base dm code 7M) becomes 17D, since the standard armor type in the genre is an armor jacket that reduces to a 12D. 12D in anything means you fall over!!" No, that's not the official statistician of the NRA speaking, that's the kind of rules hashing you'll find in abundance in a newsgroup devoted to cyberpunk fantasy role-playing games. Threads on the *Shadowrun* and *Cyberpunk 2020* games dominate

this group, followed by discussions of game mastering tactics and comparisons of which system is superior. Veiled advertisements for new technofuture role-playing and computer games also appear regularly.
USENET rec.games.frp.cyber

Welcome to The Dark Future The role-playing game *Cyberpunk 2020* is the focus here. Get the low-down on what's going to go down in the timeline section—this is some heavy current/future events class. The corporations battling to slice up the world and have a piece a la mode are detailed here, so you can start boycotting their products now. Other useful tidbits are lists of available bio-enhancements to help your character even out the odds in the new and frightening order to come. You won't be bored, but depression and confusion are the names of this highly addictive game.
WEB http://www.wolfe.net/~cipher/index.html

]=[/·\C]<3RZ 0N I _Y

2600 : The Hacker Quarterly Although it doesn't really have anything to do with science fiction, this section couldn't maintain cyberpunk cred without mentioning *2600*, the premier haqr mag. Read about the ongoing computer crime sagas that would make it onto *NYPD Blue* or *Cops* if only the general public knew what a tone dialer was. Get reports, both official and amusing, on HOPE (Hackers On Planet Earth), the New York con where the elite meet to phreak. Find out more about a dog named Walter than you ever wanted to know. Discover that the Secret Service is up to some really bad things (*quel suprise!*). Sometimes *2600* takes itself a bit too seriously, but otherwise, it's a valuable resource both for the hacker and the hack-curious. If you want to join the Daughters of the American Revolution or you plan to run for Congress, you may want to think twice about logging on here—you never know when Big Brother is watching…
WEB http://www.2600.com

WILLIAM GIBSON

NEUROMANCER WAS WRITTEN ON a typewriter. More than ten years later, Gibson is only now beginning to explore the online world. But what he lacks in hardware he more than makes up for in boundless imagination, revolutionary ideas, and late-stage capitalist *Weltschmerz*. The Vancouver, B.C., writer was largely responsible for inspiring a culture, creating a new literary genre, and changing the dimensions of our perception. He was also largely responsible for *Johnny Mnemonic*, but he'll pay for that on Judgment Day. When Gibson coined the term "cyberspace," he meant it to represent "a virtual reality simulation with a direct neural feedback." We haven't yet caught up with his great expectations, and quite a number of these fan pages will attest to just how far we have to go. But don't be discouraged—take a look at the freakshow extravaganza created by Gibson himself.

▶ STARTING POINTS

The Yardshow More than a mindful, this is a bucket o' images, stories, toys, and brain candy. Most features are pieces of dadaesque virtual performance art. Eclectic amalgamations of pictures and hypertext take you from Gibson's Desert Island Discs, to a photo exhibit of toy robots, to an interview about email: "If I were online, watching ongoing commentary on my work, I'd probably feel the way it feels when you sit in the back of a theater in Burbank, after one of those recruited audience screenings, and listen to them talk about your movie. And that's never a good idea, even when they like it." Without an index, and with features bearing vague titles, such as "gravel" and "a life deferred," there's no way of knowing in which direction you are going.
WEB http://www.vkool.com/gibson

▶ THE AUTHOR

An Interview with William Gibson "I sometimes suspect that we're seeing something in the Internet as significant as the birth of cities. It's something *that* profound and with that sort of infinite possibilities. It's really something new, it's a new kind of civilization." Remarks like this make for a great read (or listen, if you have the patience for a huge audio file!). Gibson's left-of-center, bottom-to-top, sideways views of politics and education are edifying, sometimes electrifying. The only problem is that this interview is far too short to reveal anything of real depth and as such, will leave fans wanting much more.
WEB http://www.algonet.se/~danj /gibson1.html

EFF "William Gibson Publications" Archive This small but pithy collection of publications is a link—real, not virtual—between the books that launched a genre and the man who wrote them. The William Gibson revealed here is smart and funny, determinedly himself, relishing the contradictions between the futuristic world he creates in his work and his somewhat old fashioned life.
WEB http://www2.cibola.net/~michaela /gibson

Gibson.html This site doesn't move the William Gibson information-ometer much past count zero, but it's a reasonable introduction to the culture that surrounds the cyberpunk phenomenon that Gibson helped spawn with his books. With its eclectic selection of links (the Timothy Leary Homepage, Amnesty International, The Official Lego Homepage, and alt.cyberpunk) and snippets of lyrics, poetry, and prose, this site is a window into the diverse concerns of one William Gibson proselyte. A walk in someone else's world is always a trip worth taking.
WEB http://www.vt.edu:10021/J /jfoley/gibson/gibson.html

Morningside William Gibson Back in 1983, William Gibson wrote *Neuromancer*, the original cyberpunk novel. If you have a RealAudio player, you can catch the CBC's interview with the unexpected progenitor of cyberspace. Originally aired in May 1995, Gibson discusses his script for the then upcoming film *Johnny Mnemonic*. The movie has since been criticized for rehashing '80s motifs that flounder in the '90s. Listen in and decide for yourself if cyberpunk has outgrown Gibson.

web http://www.radio.cbc.ca/radio /programs/current/mside/gibson.html

Neuromancer: The Third Attempt!

Inspired by the novels of William Gibson and the cyber movement, these pages ask us to ponder, along with the site's author and architect, Neuromancer, such mind-bending questions as whether or not the Internet has a shape, and if so how its shape could be calculated. Neuromancer also diverts us with "The Adventures of Web-Space Man," a non-interactive and possibly autobiographical story about a guy who without the Net was just an ordinary person... not an immortal with unlimited knowledge. There are also links to other cyber-ish sites.

web http://www.studentaccess.com/hp /wemacs

William Gibson Homepage

Are you unable to place the face or attach any kind of identity to the name William Gibson? Are people dropping his name into cocktail-party conversation wherever you go? Are you beginning to feel like a social outcast, or that you've really missed out on something? Help is at hand in the form of the William Gibson Homepage, a primer on the putative godfather, if not father, of cyberpunk. Thumbnail sketches of the man and his work will help you to bluff your way through your next encounter with a Sprawl Trilogy fanatic, and might even entice you into reading the books for yourself.

web http://www2.cibola.net/~michaela /gibson

William Gibson Information

If you are already familiar with William Gibson, visionary science fiction author and social-critic-by-default, you won't find much here that's news to you. But for Gibson virgins, this site offers some basic nuts and bolts information about the man and his books, and will help you decide if you want to become intimate with the seminal cyberpunk. So that you can't possibly go wrong, detailed images of his books' covers (front and back) will ensure that you recognize them the next time you're in your local bookstore.

web http://ee.oulu.fi/~thefinn/gibson /gibson.html

▶ AGRIPPA

Agrippa In 1992, William Gibson wrote a poem based loosely on the death of his father. It became the text of a multimedia project called *Agrippa: A Book of the Dead*. The text was put on a floppy disk, which was part of a pricey limited release package that included special "reader" screens containing light-sensitive etchings by Dennis Ashbaugh. The etchings slowly changed from one form to another when exposed to light, until they finally settled into a final form. After the poem was read, the text was erased from the disk. Got all that? Well, it doesn't matter anyway, because all that's available here is a bootleg copy of the text submitted to a Usenet group. An intriguing work that will make you long for the real real-time experience.

web http://bush.cs.tamu.edu/~erich /agrippa

PHILIP K. DICK

PHILIP K. DICK DIED IN 1982, LONG before the movement he fathered was even given the name. Best known for the book on which the phenomenon known as *Blade Runner* was based—Dick left behind a wealth of short stories, novels, and films that changed not only the genre of science fiction, but the way we look at machines and humanity. He forced his readers to rethink their definition of sentience, their notions of servile technology, and the very nature of reality. His rather alarming precognition of our post-modern evolution has garnered tremendous online appreciation. There is an enormous number of fan pages, information resources, and academic articles dedicated to Dick and his legacy.

STARTING POINTS

Philip Kindred Dick FAQ Born a twin, treated for agoraphobia, addicted to amphetamines, prone to paranoia and mystical experiences—a fascinating and often troubled life paired with unbounded imagination made Philip K. Dick one of the most compelling sci-fi writers of the century. This FAQ is more than a collection of bibliographical lists and external links, and it doesn't stop at answering obvious questions. It takes 18 sections to cover his complete cross-media works, and encompasses a photo library, a bulletin board, quotes from the author and comments from his contemporaries, a short lexicon of Dick lingo, a flurry of facts you would never think to ask about, even pop song references. A nice change from the rubbish often found on amateur fan pages.
WEB http://www.users.interport.net /~regulus/pkd/pkd-int.html

MOTHERSHIPS

alt.books.phil-k-dick Although it's plagued with spam, like so many other discussion groups, this forum recently boasted some serious-minded questions and answers about various items of PKD obscurity. Unfortunately, the ratio of good stuff to garbage is not favorable. Unless the fans get cracking, the bad could easily drive out the good here.
USENET alt.books.phil-k-dick

alt.fan.philip-dick Philip Dick's works were among the most visionary science-fiction novels written, and they've earned the late writer quite a cult following. These self-proclaimed Dickheads spend a great deal of time worrying about the infrastructure of Dick-related Usenet traffic (Should the group be cross-indexed with alt.books.philip-dick? And what about that alt.fan.blade-runner splinter group?), so much so that they almost obscure the more substantive traffic—postings about Dick's epilepsy, critical reviews of his novels, and birthday wishes (Dec. 21) from tender-hearted fans.
USENET alt.fan.philip-dick

Meaning in the Man in the High Castle When it comes to the ending of *The Man in the High Castle*, author Philip K. Dick was, we learn here, just as full of questions as his audience. He says, "I was unable to end it the way I wanted… perhaps you have put a finger on it when you point out that there is no evident way in which all the strings could be tied together in the end… and, there's no real ending…I like to regard it as an open ending." In these pages, possible interpretations of the novel's denoument are examined in scholarly fashion. A collection of Philip K. Dick quotes, notes on the *I Ching*, and a bibliography all serve to make this a must see for all those fans inclined toward literary analysis.
WEB http://lockwood.pacificnet.net/~laura /tmithc.html

Philip K. Dick This profile of the prolific sci-fi writer gives an adequate biographical overview of the author and thumbnail sketches of some of his many writings. A small collection of somewhat arbitrary

quotes from the novels and a selection of some of the author's nonfictional musings on his life and work help to convey a sense of what he was all about. That, along with a good link list, makes this a good springboard for further explorations of Philip K. Dick.
WEB http://dove.mtx.net.au/~jrowse/pkd/dick.html

Philip K. Dick at the Iliad A genuinely useful site, which offers bright, tight bios and bibliographies, plus a list of Philip K. Dick books for sale, with titles, prices, and publishers. This is a great resource for people whose local libraries can't satisfy their reading needs.
WEB http://host.interloc.com/~iliadbks/pkd.html

Philip K. Dick, Cyberpunk Essentially a long, thoughtful, critical essay on PKD—the author, his oeuvre, and his place in the movement now known as cyberpunk—this is a first-rate piece of writing and thinking, and even the somewhat tedious bits are worth slogging through for their info value.
WEB http://www.clas.ufl.edu/anthro/cyberanthro/pkd-wept.html

PKD And Blade Runner "All I can say is that the world in *Blade Runner* is where I really live. That is where I think I am anyway. This world will now be a world that every member of the audience will inhabit. It will not be my private world. It is now a world where anyone who will go into the theatre and sit down and watch the film will be caught up and the world is so overpowering, it is so profoundly overpowering that it is going to be very hard for people to come out of it and adjust to what we normally encounter." You'll find this and other profoundly overpowering comments here, in Dick's last, short interview before his death.
WEB http://madison.tdsnet.com/bladerunner/philip.html

PKD Short Stories A thorough and apparently complete accounting and referencing of PKD's short stories, this page sorts the works chronologically and notes the collection in which they were eventually republished and the golden age magazines in which they first appeared. A must-see for the compulsive fan.
WEB http://www.users.interport.net/~regulus/pkd/pkd-030.html

The PKD Short Story Guide Still a work in progress, whose goal is to provide bibliographical notes plus critical analysis, this page has made headway toward the former but still needs to get its act together on the latter. It's an admirable project, and it's worth a couple of clicks to see if it comes to fruition.
WEB http://www.umich.edu/~ryandhoz/pkdick

The PKDictionary of Terms Intelligently written and filled with its subject's dry and sometimes dark sense of humor, this short but very useful PKD dictionary keeps all the author's coinages in one handy place—from Land-o-Smiles brand cigarettes to NEXUS-6 androids—for reference while reading, arguing about, or communing online over his books.
WEB http://www-leland.stanford.edu/~kma/pkdict.html

The Unofficial Philip K. Dick Homepage A good place to go for a general overview of the man and his work. One of the best sections is the bibliography of critical works on the author—an excellent, smart resource for library surfing.
WEB http://www.geocities.com/SunsetStrip/4589/pkd.html

BRUCE STERLING

ONE OF THE MOST PROACTIVE members of the cyberpunk community, Bruce Sterling's literary contributions, most notably his near-future tour de force *Islands in the Net*, are only part of his influence on the communication generation. His activism and vision have helped shape a movement and a culture, and his presence on the Net is vocal indeed. In cyberspace, Sterling talks about everything from telecommunications censorship to the virtual military to the technological power plays in burgeoning political regimes. There aren't any Bruce Sterling fan pages, per se, but a great deal of his own writing is available online, including dozens of copies of *The Hacker Crackdown*, a nonfiction novel about Big Brother and the EFF.

▶ STARTING POINTS

Bruce Sterling On-Line Resources
"I'd like to see us put a Library of Congress beside every canister of nuclear waste. Let's airmail the Library of Congress to the year 20,000 AD." This is an excerpt from a speech Sterling gave to the Library Information Technology Association under the premise "Information *wants* to be free." Sterling sees cyberpunk as a literary movement, rather than a synonym for computer criminals, and calls his creations "part of the flow of knowledge." With any luck, these documents will be delivered to our descendants along with the rest of our literary heritage. Find digital direction and freedom between the legislative lines.
WEB http://riceinfo.rice.edu/projects/RDA /VirtualCity/Sterling/sterling_res.html

▶ THE AUTHOR

Bruce Sterling's Agitprop Disk In his presentation to the House Subcommittee on Telecommunications and Finance in 1993, Bruce Sterling spoke to the House as Mr. Bob Smith, an NREN network administrator from the year 2015. He ended a litany of disasters potentially in store for the New World Wide Web Order with this statement: "Thanks in part to the advances that you yourselves set in motion, violent conflicts between virtual and actual communities have become a permanent feature of the cultural landscape in 2015." This fantastic collection of etexts, articles bibliographies, internet manuals, and speeches is wrapped up in an unsightly little grey gopher, just for you.
URL gopher://gopher.zilker.net/11/bruces

HotWired and Bruce Sterling HotWired is full of interviews, articles and short stories by and about our cyberpunk goldenboy. Read his philosophical waxings on the virtual military, Prague's Velvet Revolution, the National Security Agency's position on Clipper, the Happy Bear attitude of the Commonwealth of Independent States, the draconian terrorist bill and the ensuing engineered disasters that virtually assure its confirmation. Use the Hot Bot search engine and the keyword "Sterling" and off you go.
WEB http://www.hotwired.com/wired /scenarios/sterling.html

▶ HACKER CRACKDOWN

The Hacker Crackdown The year is 1990, the weapon is the computer, and the crime is the hack. You've covered your tracks with digital decoys, picked the legislative locks, and accessed America's records. But The Man is onto you: the FBI, CIA, IRS, and other unwanted acronyms wait for you. The jig is up. It's the story told in *The Hacker Crackdown*, a chronicle of the search to destroy those meddling kids and their technowizardry. This etext by Bruce Sterling non-fictionally chronicles the pursuit of computer hackers and the Feds' hamhanded attempts to plug the holes in the national telecom grid.
WEB http://www.lysator.liu.se/etexts /hacker • http://sirius.umd.edu/pages /crackdown.html

PART 6

It Came From Comics

JAPANIMATION

THE FIRST THING YOU NEED TO know is this: There are two kinds of Japanese cartoon—*manga*, which covers Japanese comic book art, and *anime*, which covers television shows or movies. *Otaku* worldwide nod sagely, but if you don't happen to be a super-devoted fanboy, brace yourself for a world where a character's personality can be defined by his blood type, where schoolgirls save the world as often as superheroes, and where Tokyo is destroyed and rebuilt as often as in Godzilla movies. The second thing you need to know is that there is almost as much manga in cyberspace as there is cyberspace. This frenzied corner of the Japanese psyche has expanded like a mushroom cloud and is so phenomenally popular online that the following pages promise only the finest cybermanga. Every site here is a winner.

▶ STARTING POINTS

David's Anime Resources and Info That domain name does not lie. This is one of the best anime/manga sites on the Web. It has the most comprehensive, easily navigable, and generally enormous index in the virtual world, which includes not only the expected fan pages and commercial links, but anime search engines, anime guides, convention info, subtitling and dubbing info, shopping guides, and a nice section offering information about Japan. And here's the kicker: The site's author has a nice little collection of anime all his own, with an Astro-boy page offering information, loads of images, and an episode guide, a few choice pics of other series, and a series of articles such as "Anime and Opera," and "You've been watching too much anime when..." (When you awake from surgery and your first words are "Where is Ranma Saotome?!?") It's happened. It happens.
WEB http://www.best.com/~gaxiola/Anime

▶ MOTHERSHIPS

Animes and Mangas: An Introduction A great intro page offering all the basics on manga and anime. Nicely illustrated, too, with an overarching inclination toward *Saint Seiya*. A link list at the bottom, also Seiya-heavy, puts newbies on the track to proper obsession.
WEB http://www.student.isoe.ch/stud94_95 /markulin/pages/animes.htm

The Bioregulator If things go according to plan, this page will eventually be a fantastic hubsite containing multimedia, merchandise, and chat rooms. It's all presented in the form of a virtual space station, and framed with a formula anime plot featuring mad scientists, invulnerable AI robots, and a battle between good and evil etc. Although the frame-story and impressive graphics are already in place, about 85 percent of the actual features are under construction or simply nonexistent. It looks like *DS9* after a Dominion attack.
WEB http://www.intraversal.com/straight /bio/regulator.html

Dokuritsu Fun If you can pull yourself through the sticky mass of text laid out by the site's verbose and only occasionally amusing author, you'll find some worthwhile features on *Dragon Half*, a relatively on-target anime introduction, reviews, and lots of links. The site's creator also writes and illustrates several comics which he plugs here. You'll find a lot of big, barely covered cartoon breasts, too, if that kind of thing interests you.
WEB http://compassnet.com/~doki

Hitoshi Doi's Anime Page Hitoshi Doi is surely a magician, because while his page looks about as exciting as a *Garfield* cartoon in greytones, in actuality, it packs some serious heat. You'll find lots of exclusives—manga newsletters, anime cell collections, and extensive info on Seiyuu and music. But the real meat of the page is the comprehensive fan pages that go far beyond the expected, offering virtual encyclopedias on *Sailor Moon, Idol Project, Aozora Shoujotai, Voogi's Angel*, and *Saint Tail*—everything from A-Z dictionaries to relationship charts to animation staff information. And check out his anime page-within-a-page, which has encyclopedias for dozens of Shoujo series and OAV's. Furthermore, be sure you don't leave the site without visiting Hitoshi's collection of UFO catcher dolls. These little critters are so *kawaii*, you may find yourself going into diabetic shock.

WEB http://www.tcp.com/doi/doi.html

Jim's Anime Page Attention anime-*otaku*! You'll eat this *oishii* site right up! In addition to the expected reviews, links and multimedia on kawaii girls and menacing mecha it offers a guide to subtitling your own Japanimation, release dates for manga and laser disc anime, and a program called Shodouka which lets you read home pages with kanji characters without a Japanese word processor. Pretty cool.

WEB http://www.geocities.com/Tokyo/3947/index.htm

L.J. Newt's Anime Gallery The site features a coloring contest, an arcade full of downloadable games, a multimedia grab bag, a rotating spotlight on one lucky anime a month, and a chunky link list. Some sections are under construction, but when the site gets on its virtual feet, it's sure to pack a kick.

WEB http://www.amaranth.com/~csmith

Manga Glossary *Ketsuekigata* means "Blood type." In Japanese pop culture, blood type is thought to be related to personality. Character profiles of both anime artists and characters often include blood type along with stats such as weight and age. The manga glossary's rough guide to blood types: A = nervous, introverted, honest, loyal. B = outgoing, optimistic, adventurous. AB = proud, diplomatic, discriminating. O = workaholic, insecure, emotional. There are dozens of terms explored here, like

industry terms (*gensaku-sha* means story-writer), and genre terms (*shoujo-manga* means manga targeted for girls and *yaoi* means men loving men—also popular with girls). Many definitions are furnished with links to pages and articles. The site also features an extensive history of manga. If you want to understand the Japanese language and culture better, the site offers links to culture guides and Japanese language pages.

WEB http://ftoomsh.socs.uts.edu.au/~axolotl/Manga/gloss.html

Ming's Anime Page Pics, links, and most importantly film clips from *My Neighbor Totoro, Future Boy Conan, Laputa, Nausicaa, Kiki*, and a number of non-Miyazaki titles as well, including lots of *Sailor Moon* stuff. The best thing about this site is its links, not just to anime resources, but to useful pages for English-speaking anime *otaku*, such as A Kana Guide to reading Japanese, Common Japanese Phrases, Japanese words used in anime songs, Japanese-English dictionaries, proverbs, and idioms.

WEB http://looney.physics.sunysb.edu/~daffy/anime.html

Otaku Cafe Some *otaku* have some deep prejudices against American comics. Just take a gander at the "Why Manga is better than Marvel" article served up at the Otaku Cafe. Some of the claims are justified: "Manga does not make the brainy assumption that its primary target audience consists entirely of grade school children." But others are just a wee bit deluded: "Manga derives its plots from human nature and the world around us; American comics derive their plots from the *National Enquirer*." American comic artists lack the sense of realism required to create stories about bands of scantily clad female cops in cyberarmour battling sex-crazed tentacled demons with the help of small flying piglets who change into pandas when you splash cold water onto them." The rest of the fare includes fun, tasteful reviews, convention info, and links.

WEB http://osf1.gmu.edu/~jweston/otaku/otaku.html

rec.arts.manga There are a few threads on the definition of sojo manga and whether Akemis's renditions of KOS characters are better than Matsumoto's, but this group is mostly about commerce—buying, selling, trading, and translating. Look here for offers on original artwork, WTB's (Want to Buy) for Thundercat Toys, requests for *Marmalade Boy* translations, and lots of manga/anime trading.
USENET rec.arts.manga

Rei's Anime and Manga Page Not your average fan page. Prepare yourself: you'll have to read! Rei has created a site "dedicated to non-Japanese (or deprived *nisei*) who are looking for a deeper understanding of a wide variety of Japanese comic books and animation, whether as fans, researchers, the merely curious, or as fellow artists and writers…" It begins with an article explaining both aspects of Japanimation, and then, among reviews, artist profiles and in-depth overviews of particular anime/manga, offers analytical articles (insightful, though sometimes a bit apologetic) on anime/manga gender relations and the prevalance of psychic themes. When your eyes start to lose focus, you can link to pic-happy pages listed at the bottom.
WEB http://www.mit.edu:8001/afs/athena.mit.edu/user/r/e/rei/WWW/Anime.html

Steve's Anime Page It's almost an index. The 667 links to other Japanimation pages would tend to classify it as such. It has a couple of nice image galleries of its own and two short video clips that sometimes download.
WEB http://www.netspace.org/~stv/anime.html

Tokyo Cool Manga Messe Don't be thrown by one of the coolest front pages ever—this site is under heavy construction. But even with very little functioning at the moment, it still deserves a visit. What is working is excellent, especially the interviews and profiles. The Comic Market section is also notable for its images of the costume play—a flesh and blood Saint Tale, freaky!
WEB http://www.inter-g7.or.jp/g2/manga/home.html

UK Anime Directory Home Page As big as Giant Robo, as big as Iori Yagami's ego, as big as *Akira*'s mile-high, milk-bleeding stuffed animals! The first feature is the U.K. Anime Directory, a great resource offering reviews, links, and purchase info for hundreds of U.K. releases. Then there's *Animejin*, an anime fanzine with news, industry info, and reviews on everything from Sci Fi to Superdeformed to good ol' Sex & Violence. Some of the best material comes from the official blurbs set before the reviews ("She's Half Dragon, Half Girl… And Every Inch A Babe!"). But it's not all breasts and brawn, the zine also covers such dramas as *Wings of Honneamise* and *The Cockpit* which tells the story of several Axis pilots in WWII. A Robotech Chronology takes us from Zor's birth to the Robotech Nursing Home and Maximum Security Prison. Finally, the site houses the *Star Blazers* Episode Guide, which is incomprehensible to anyone but a *Star Blazers* mega-*otaku*: "Space Net [Absolute Death! The Wishing-Star of Orion, Hell-Star] General Krypt uses a space net to stop the Star Force, and ecto gas." Right…
WEB http://spodbox.linux.org.uk/~clueless/anime/directory

Ukyou's Anime Not satisfied merely to offer a few descriptive words and kick us to specific fan pages, this site has three huge image galleries covering fan art, anime/manga images, and scans for dozens of series. It also offers freeware to animize your computer, and a home page for Magic Knight Rayearth which includes—among the expected multimedia—merchandise, fan fiction, scripts, and song lyrics, some of which sound like they were random-generated from bad seventies songs: "Walking towards the unstoppable future / Embracing the wish that I can't give away / The color of the ocean is painted red / We're now in freefall / I want to be taken by the wind just the way it is / With the feeling that I can't lose / I cleared the hurdle I could never jump over / but…, Using our true power together… but who's? / The colors on the map of the heart won't fade / shine the light over your head!" Yeah, uh-huh.

WEB http://tsunami.tisl.ukans.edu/~ukyou

FANZINES

Sushi & Hamburger This tasty little magazine is heavy on the sushi and light on the beef, but promises to cover Western comics soon. At the moment, it's a delicate mix of manga and anime. The site authors press together lots of lightly sugared sticky reviews on a thin paper of article abstracts, stuff it with original fiction and international animation news, then roll it in sound clips, images, and pop music picks. On the side you have a small bowl of random hyperlinks that are alternately spicy, or pungent or nonexistent each time you dip into it. And if you enjoyed your meal, the chef offers another (less virtual) recipe at the bottom of the page, for you to enjoy at home. A genuine feast for the eyes.

WEB http://www.geocities.com/Tokyo/1629

COMMERCIAL

Anime Planet Looking for that model of Sazabi from "Char's Counterattack"? Been scouring the video stores for the Super-Deformed *Spirit of Wonders*? Feel like blowing your raise on the laserdisc series of *JoJo's Bizarre Adventure*? Thinking about trading your car for your friend's impossible-to-find symphonic version of the *Akira* soundtrack? Dying to see what *Bastard* looked like back in the manga days? Well, fangirl, your dreams have come true. You can order videos, laserdiscs, CDs, merchandise, and manga online. Sub and dub, domestic and imports, and possibly the best collection of manga available on the Net. Great selection, reasonable prices, and best of all, you never have to leave your basement!

WEB http://www.neosoft.com/~planet

AVI As well as sharing a name with a computer animation format, AVI is the producer of such illustrious titles as *Techni Muyo*, *Armitage III*, and *Pretty Samy*. Its Web site is, as expected, heads above the pitiful fan-produced pages, with cybaroque graphics, illustrated episode guides, sound files, character profiles, and info on the series' Seiyuu. There's also an impressive CD library with sound clips from *Techni Muyo*, *El Hazard*, *Ninja Mono*, and *Burn-up W*. You can only take the studio tour with shockwave, but it's worth it—go ahead! The whole page can also be explored in VRML. If your PC can take it, download today.

WEB http://www.anime-int.com

Manga Video This site has a few things going for it. First there's a splashy feature on the most hyped movie since *Waterworld*—*Ghost in the Machine*. And in the U.S. and U.K. mirror pages you'll find catalog info and, more importantly, vid clips for some of the best anime movies ever made. At first glance, the U.K. page looks bigger than the U.S. site, but it isn't—really. They're almost identical, except that the U.K. page has some short, boring profiles of anime directors. The rest of the site is dreary—a pretty lame showing for the hottest Western distributor of anime in the world. On a side note—even though it's not anime, anyone who claims to have any kind of interest in animation should take a look at the feature on *The Secret Adventures of Tom Thumb*, a Brothers Quayesque mix of animation and pixelation (animating human actors frame by frame) that will freak out and fascinate even the most hardcore anime fans.

WEB http://www.manga.com/manga

Viz Communications, Inc This terribly dull commercial page supports the company that brings us the English versions of popular titles including *Ranma 1/2* and *Crying Freeman*. Are they responsible for getting 20-year-old women to dub the voices for 6-year-old boy characters? Are they responsible for making sometimes subtle Japanese dialogue read like excerpts from the last year of *Dynasty*? We don't know, but what we do know is that this site is great if you want to buy products you're already interested in, but does nothing to actually interest you in anything else. The online newsletter doesn't have any images in it. Perhaps this a vainglorious attempt to be ironic?

WEB http://www.viz.com

▶ CROSS SERIES

Anime Shrine A cool little page with a few links and some really nice image archives for *Vampire Princess Myu*, U*rusi Yatsura*, *KOS*, and more.

WEB http://faraday.clas.virginia.edu/~lw4n

Endymion's Sanctuary Now this is what *otakus* expect, nay, what they should demand from fan pages. One of the few big pages that lives up to its promises, this site offers beautifully designed pages for *Kimagure Orange Road*, *Tenchi Muyo!*, *Ranma 1/2*, *Nibbunoichi*, *Maison Ikkoku*, and *Ah! My Goddess* and features sizable picture galleries, song libraries, and links.

WEB http://www.lynx.bc.ca/~roneng/index.htm

Feq's Animae Page A large, if nevertheless somewhat shallow, page with resident images, short synopses, and links for many animated shows, most of which are anime. Features on *Ranma 1/2*, *Bubble Gum Crisis*, and *Robotech*. *Record of the Lodoss War*, *Urusei Yatsura*, *Bastard!*, and *Silent Mobius* also get some attention.

WEB http://students.vassar.edu/~jamarin/animae.html

Gallery of Cute A sizable, well-produced collection of enormous, *kawaii* portraits culled from dozens of series. The image of Myu is followed by a handful of links to *Vampire Princess Myu* sites, a pic of Sasami-chan is followed by links to *Techni Muyo!* pages, and Pai links to *3e3 Eyes* shrines. There's no directory, so you have to delve farther and farther into cuteness to reach your object of

desire. Getting there is half the fun.

WEB http://toybox.iac.gatech.edu/~ctydingc/kawaii/kawaii.html

The Herbster's Anime Info Page Another page offering basic plot and character info, links and a few pics for several popular animes/mangas, including *KOR*, *Maison Ikkoku*, *Oh! My Goddess!*, *Record Of Lodoss War*, *Laputa: Castle In The Sky*, *Video Girl Ai*, and *Irresponsible Captain Tylor*.

WEB http://www.oanet.com/homepage/goldbug/anime.htm

Japanese Animation Low on graphics, but with some worthwhile content, the Japanese Animation Web site features several OAVs (original animation videos), including *Kimagure Orange Road*, *Bubblegum Crisis*, *Super Catgirl Nuku Nuku* and *Compiler*. Some fan pages offer in-depth overviews of the series, with dramatis personae, individual episode synopses and images. Others are less lush. There are also the collected texts of *Undocumented Features*, an extremely popular anime-inspired fan fiction series.

WEB http://www.cs.ubc.ca/spider/edmonds/home.html

Jason Ball's Anime Page Synopses and big juicy pics for *Akira*, *Plastic Little*, *Wings of Honneamise*, *8Man After*, *The Running Man* (often undeservedly overlooked), and *Vampire Hunter D*. Reviews tend to sugarcoat—*Vampire Hunter D*'s "impeccable" plot?

WEB http://www.prism.gatech.edu/~gt5546b/anime.html

Ken's Anime Page You get a pic and a collection of links for *Ranma 1/2*, *Bubblegum Crisis*, *You're Under Arrest!*, *Oh! My Goddess!*, *Vampire Princess Miyu*, *Project A-ko*, *Techni Muyo*, and *Dragon Half*. Worth a look just for the Miyu pic (no, fanboy, not nude).

WEB http://www.asuaf.alaska.edu/~fskrh/anime.html

Leo's Anime and Manga Page Nice image galleries and an impressive col-

lection of links mostly dedicated to *Bubblegum Crisis*, topped off with downloads of anime scores and theme songs. Covers a wide area, but is not exactly groundbreaking.
WEB http://www.iinet.com.au/~vincent/LAH.html

Otaku Anime Fan Center This page is a lot like the roads in Costa Rica—nice scenery, but potholes that could sink the *Lusitania*. When the flashing "under construction" signs come off this very well designed page, you'll find image galleries, synopses, and character profiles for the usual all-stars—*Oh! My Goddess!*, *KOR*, *Project A-KO*, *Magic Knights Rayearth*, *Vampire Princess Miyu*, and *Sailor Moon*. Right now the best you can hope for is a nice collection of links to other pages.
WEB http://www.exit109.com/~the3dman/otaku/oafchome.sht

Poopsie's Anime/Manga Page Poopsie has set out image galleries and links for *3x3Eye*, *Akira*, *Ako*, *Oh! My Goddess!*, *Battle*, *Angel Alita*, *Dragon Ball*, *Devil Hunter Yohko*, *Dirty Pair*, *Guyver*, *Macross*, *Magic Knight Rayearth*, *Ranma*, *Sailor Moon*, *Tench Muyo*, and *Vampire Princess Miyu*, as well as a big index.
WEB http://www.tiac.net/users/poopsie/anime

▶ DIVERSIONS

alt.binaries.pictures.anime This is a cool place to find and request images. It's best if you have a range of tastes, as you're never guaranteed to find anything that you're looking for in particular. A warning: 9 out of 10 pages claiming to house enormous galleries (especially of X-rated images) are scams—commercial pages offering CDs or what have you. And speaking of X-rated, yes alt.binaries.pictures.anime offers plenty of *hentai*. Porn often sneaks in too, but it really isn't the main focus of the group, and submissions sometimes get flamed.
USENET alt.binaries.pictures.anime

Anime Song Lyrics You know, romping love is a carp in a pond. Or so the lyrics to one of *Ranma*'s opening songs. Get lyrics to dozens of your favorite series, in Japanese and (usually) English, along with a big, dazzling image from the show. No true *otaku* should be without this valuable resource.
WEB http://home.pacific.net.sg/~mlchoy/index.html

Kiki's Anime Image Service Images, images, images! Not just for *Ranma* and *Bubblegum Crisis*, but for *Marmalade Boy* and *Villgust* and other harder-to-find titles. If it ain't here, you just dreamed the whole thing. You'll find not just a dinky collection of cover scans, but pages and pages of pics for each anime, with specs on resolution and colors. Sadly for one-handed typists, the images aren't hentai heavy, but at least you can image surf at work without locking the office door.
WEB http://www.xmission.com/~matatabi/home.html

Matts' Anime Page Yet another page under major construction for now it has an impressive collection of *Ranma* art, but Web masters promise 10 to 12 full galleries covering a wide range of anime ASAP.
WEB http://ourworld.compuserve.com/homepages/chiahead

Tareme Paradise An enormous collection of image galleries, with lots of hentai (sexually explicit anime).
WEB http://www.st.rim.or.jp/~yuichi_m

Yoshitaka Amano—Artwork A talented artist offers a collection of his work in this online gallery. Yoshitaka's images may lean a bit towards anatomical realism, but they are as wildly fantastical as any anime you'll find. There is a delicacy to the images, and an amazing attention to detail. When you're tired of half-naked schoolgirls with no noses and dewy eyes the size of satellite dishes, take some time to discover Amano.
WEB http://www-sunlab.cit.cornell.edu/Info/People/hnguyen/hiten/amano.html

▶ INDEXES

Anime and Manga Resource List Tell your personal assistant to hold your calls and cancel your afternoon appointments. You'll find comprehensive, well organized and huge links to anime, manga, hentai, fan fiction, ecchi, clubs, conventions, movies, OAVs, images, soundtracks, merchandise, and more. Anything and everything having to do with Japanimation, including lots of stuff you never knew existed and lots more you'll be sorry about.
WEB http://csclub.uwaterloo.ca /u /mlvanbie/anime-list

Anime Center This is a chunky page, but you won't have to wade through an endless sea of links to find what you're looking for. A great place to go if you know what information you need.
WEB http://www.engin.umd.umich.edu /~rwisnk/anime.html

Anime & Stuff A darn impressive collection, but it so pales in comparison to the Anime Web Turnpike that it actually tells surfers to go there instead. In flashing letters. Twice! Still, if you're looking for a collection of links you can sift through in say, a day, instead of an average non-smoker's lifetime, this is a great jumping-off point.
WEB http://server.berkeley.edu/Anime

Anime Web Turnpike This is the biggest, scariest thing you'll ever see. The indexes cover conventions, commercial pages, fan art, galleries, and alphabetical listings for every anime/manga ever produced. So whether you've got to find the laserdisc of *Wings of Honneamise*, want to submit your *Bubblegum Crisis* fan fiction to the proper page, or just need a couple of naked pictures of Mink, Turnpike will take you where you need to go.
WEB http://soyokaze.biosci.ohio-state .edu/~jei/anipike/series.html

Johns Anime and Manga Links
Although this page will soon play host to several very well-produced fan pages (*Genesis Evangelion* is up and running),

at the moment it is of best use as an index, a fantastic index, with hubsites, anime homepages, galleries and archives, databases and search engines, organizations, companies, and every series home page online. You can also launch Shodouka from here.
WEB http://www.hkstar.com/~gotoh /anime/anime.html

SUPERHEROES

WITH AN ALCHEMY THAT TAKES sci-fi pulp and turns it into gold, comic book writers have been able to create a gilded alternative universe of their own. While comics themselves are incalculably diverse, comic book fandom in cyberspace is not. Pages devoted to the Uncanny X-Men and their progeny multiply online like Madrox the Multiple Man, while the Silver Surfer rates only a few pixels. Sure, Dr. Strange could kick Night Crawler's butt, but that doesn't mean he gets a home online. On the Net, sci-fi comic choices are at once plentiful and limited. So where is the place to begin? If you have something to say, enter the rowdy, barroom newsgroup rec.arts.comics .misc and let your fingertips fly.

▶ STARTING POINTS

The Dark Knight The Batman mythos has survived the blitzkrieg of marketing madness: mutant powers, radiation experiments, intergalactic appointments, and any other symptom of the "bigger, better, more" hedonism found in most comics. While the movies and TV fetishize his uniform, his weapons, his girlfriend, his enemies, and his car (Batman himself is practically an afterthought), the comic functions primarily on the main character. Similarly, the Dark Knight home page cuts through the franchise forest and focuses only on Batman in the comics. You'll find well-written bios on the major players and a walkthrough of the numerous Bat-titles for newbies. There's even a forum for fans of the Dark Knight to engage one another in real-time. Wonderful for starters and old timers alike. Big warning: Be sure to type the suffix "ca" and not "com" or you'll get a lecture on chipmunks.
WEB http://www.darkknight.ca

▶ MOTHERSHIPS

alt.comics.fan-fiction "'Bloody Hell!' screamed St. Jean, 'this American ale is 'bout as smooth as a porcupine's ass!' The heat in the room seemed to match the temperament of the Aussie—hot and bothered." So begins "Boys' Night Out," a work of fan fiction based on characters from Marvel Comics. Although the group isn't very active, if you're interested in fiction based on comic book characters, it's worth checking out now and then.
USENET alt.comics.fan-fiction

DC Comics Like many other company Web sites, DC is primarily interested in previewing products rather than offering free resources for fans. Still, you can glean some news of DC's latest offerings. Currently, *Batman: Legends of the Dark Knight* and *Sovereign 7* are previewed. Also, digital trading cards can be downloaded here.
WEB http://www.dccomics.com

DC Heroes If you ever watched the *Superfriends* animated series as a child, you know that Aquaman was always the guy who summoned the dolphins. His limited role prevented you from knowing what a Superfriend he really is. However, this Web site takes the *Dungeons and Dragons* approach to flesh out Aquaman and a host of other DC super-heroes, from A (Abra Kadabra) to Z (Zatanna). Equipped with vital stats and some sort of power rating, this site is good for those interested in comparing superheroes' batting averages. By the way, according to this home page, Aquaman's fatal vulnerability is… yes, you guessed it—no water.
WEB http://copper.ucs.indiana.edu /~rmaple/table.html

Fizban's Guide to DC Comics This charming tour gives vital stats on key figures of the DC Universe, from Azrael, Batman, the Flash, Green Lantern, Superman, and Wonder Woman, among others. Just click to learn more about your favorite hero. There is also a smaller, underdesigned villainous counterpart to this superhero page. Take a look for a

quick dalliance in the DC universe.
WEB http://expert.cc.purdue.edu
/~fizban/dc/dc.html • http://www
.santarosa.edu/~sthoemke/x/x.html

MAWORLD1 While a little content-shallow in itself, this Web site is good for all sorts of Marvel Universe links. Most notable are the Spider-Man and X-Men links, but you'll also find Daredevil, Avengers, Power Pack, Silver Surfer, and Hulk links.
WEB http://www.teleplex.bsu.edu/pages
/bneely/index.htm/maworld1.htm

rec.arts.comics.misc Rant city. This is a gathering ground for mavens and manifesto-writers whose seething obsession is sequential art, graphic novels, and similar euphemisms for comic books. It's one of the largest groups on Usenet, and growing every day. The newsgroup gets upwards of 300 posts a day: unlike most Usenet communities, rec.arts.comics.misc is vertically integrated, which means that, in addition to a roiling mass of fanboys (and a very few fangirls), there are owners of comic-book shops, indie zine publishers, fan-convention organizers and a few professional artists and writers who read RACM regularly. One notable celebri-poster is Peter A. David, perhaps the most successful comic-book writer of modern times, plotter of *Spiderman 2099* and *The Incredible Hulk*, among other series. Have a theory about how one of your fave heroes will die, be crippled, or come out of the closet? Post it to the Net and watch discussion accrete to it like iron filings to a magnet. Some of the responses can be pretty hostile—keep your asbestos leotards on—but others will be lyrical and imaginative. The densely literate Sandman has fans pouring over source material ranging from Frazer's *Golden Bough* to the Dead Sea Scrolls, as they try to find all of Neil Gaiman's canny references. Mainstream superhero comics tend to generate long threads where vets will reminisce about the "good old days, when Purple Penguin was a Real Hero," or argue about rec.arts.comics.misc's greatest bogey-

men. Retailers and first-in-line fans post advance reviews of what to buy and what to avoid. Dave Van Domelen is perhaps the most prolific review generator. His "Rants" regarding different series and his "Timed Release Capsules" generally cover the spectrum from underground to Archie. Here, knowledge of abstruse trivia equals status—gender is not an issue. Be prepared to read this group nightly if you wish to keep up.
USENET rec.arts.comics.misc

▶ BATMAN

The Bat Trove "A tour of Batman's past, present, and forever." The title of this site should be "everything but the comics." This tour accomplishes its objective mostly by using the words of other people. Archived here are articles from *Life*, *Time*, and *People* magazines. A link to Pathfinder offers media spotlights on the original *Batman* and *Batman: The Animated Series*. Worth taking a look at, especially for the information-starved, although with one major exception. Feel free to ignore the anachronistic link to the *Batman Forever* home page.
WEB http://users.aol.com/JimD19713
/batman.html

The Dark Knight Companion "B" is for Batman. "A" is for Azrael. "T" is for "Two-Face…" This "encyclopedia-like page is devoted to chronicling the life and times of the Caped Crusader," as its mission statement makes clear. The Companion does a good job at it, with cross references among characters that weave between Bat titles and stretched across numerous story lines (*Knightfall*, *Knightquest*, *Knightsend*, etc). However, since brief descriptions are given to each subject, anyone seeking something more substantial might be hard pressed to find it here.
WEB http://www.rvgs.k12.va.us/Other
/Mac/Batman

▶ CAPTAIN AMERICA

The Star-Spangled Site 2.0 The miraculously fit Captain America did not

become so after mail-ordering the Thigh-Master, despite whatever rumors may be circulating. This Web site asserts that a "super soldier" formula he imbibed in the 1940s did the trick. All sorts of intimate knowledge is revealed at this cybershrine for Ol' Cap.
WEB http://www.sigma.net/capt_am /index.htm

▶ FANTASTIC FOUR

Unofficial Fantastic Four Web Presence Surely among the most fortunate of cosmic radiation victims, the Fantastic Four and their radiation-triggered powers are among the most well-known in comic history. Unfortunately, links here to the history of the FF are problematic, and the biographies are not much good. The most valuable parts of this Web site are the marvelous issue summaries of every FF comic since issue one, and the picture archive for those of you who like pretty colors. This site isn't exactly one-stop shopping, but it's worth a look.
WEB http://www.ocf.berkeley.edu /~arlen/ff.html

▶ FLASH

Flash: Those Who Ride The Lightning "A comprehensive listing of those heroes and villains who draw superhuman speed from the other-dimensional field known as the 'speed force.'" You know immediately that this home page will not feature Samba the Human Slug, or any of his close friends for that matter. Instead, Max Mercury, the Flash, Johnny Quick, Speed McGee, and similar dashing denizens of DC can be found accompanied by bio info. While a speculative guide to footwear for these fleet footed fellows would have been nice to see, this Web site is still a worthwhile site for DC fans with a need for speed.
WEB http://www.arts.uci.edu/Individ uals/Staff/Kelson/flash/index.html

▶ GREEN LANTERN

The Unofficial Green Lantern Page Kyle Rayner, the current Green Lantern representative to the Green Lantern Corps., "can make or do almost anything he desires from a power ring given to him by Ganthet." He might have even made the flashing ring animation on this Web page, which tends to be hypnotic if stared at for longer than five seconds. Aside from a migraine and a sudden urge to do evil, staring at the ring is about all you can glean from the first page. Click the biographies link to follow the Green Lanterns, past and present, then move on to the picture gallery for eye-popping images of the green-clad guy.
WEB http://www.unlv.edu/~lauv/gl

▶ THE INCREDIBLE HULK

The Incredible Hulk—Earth's Mightiest Mortal It's not easy being green, especially if you're the Incredible Hulk. While his free-spirited rages have lead to some success, most notably the hit comic title and a TV show, there have been some down times in his "Hulk Smash!"-ing career. For instance, the Hulk once became a deranged idiot and was banished by Dr. Strange to an inter-dimension nexus point known as the Crossroads of Reality. From this Web page, a Hulk crossroads of sorts, you can fan out and learn about the Hulk's powers, his foes, and his past.
WEB http://www.netside.com/~chl3 /index.html

▶ IRON MAN

The Iron Man Armory "When Multi-Billionaire Industrialist Tony Stark, Inventor Extraordinaire, Dons His Solar-Charged Steel-Mesh Armor, He Becomes A High-Tech Warrior—The World's Greatest Human Fighting Machine!" greets any visitor to this Web site for Iron Man a.k.a. Tony Stark. Unlike some billionaire playboys, who might be inclined to spend their money on Ferraris and call girls, Stark chooses to fight crime. He is in fact Marvel Comic's answer to DC Comic's Bruce Wayne, a billionaire willing to trade his tuxedo in at any moment to fight evil in a self-made high tech suit. As this site points out, the comic is pure

science fiction, rife with techno jargon: inertial dampers, magno-hydraulic pseudomusculature, repulsor rays, cryogenic suspension, and the like. While Iron Man Armory will not bombard you with as much techspeak as the name would indicate, it does give you a history lesson of Iron Man's origins. It even draws cursory parallels between Iron Man and American jingoism and politics. Check out the 1977 ad for Hostess cupcakes featuring Shellhead himself.
WEB http://www.missouri.edu/~c549108/index.html

▶ JUSTICE LEAGUE

Justice League FAQ Because of continuity problems, this FAQ focuses only on the Justice League after the "Crisis on Infinite Earths" storyline. It runs, in fact, like a history, providing information on membership status's, allies, affiliations, and their appearances dates and titles. For those who are unclear about "The Crisis of Infinite Earths" storyline, there is a link to a Crisis explanation, not to mention other Justice League resources. Dense, like molasses.
WEB http://members.aol.com/myke4/jlafaq.html

▶ LEGIONNAIRES

Encyclopaedia Galactica Let's get this straight. Steve Rogers ingests a "super-soldier" formula and becomes Captain America, blessed with super-human agility, endurance, strength, and, incidentally, rugged good looks. Chuck Taine, on the other hand, imbibes "super-plastic fluid" to become Bouncing Boy, enabling him to expand his body into "a spherical form and... bounce harmlessly off of any surface." Do you believe in bad karma? Written entirely in Brainiac 5 character, the medical logs of the Encyclopaedia Galactica give you well-written, info-dense bios on Bouncing Boy and the other major characters of the Legion of Super-Heroes. Sun Boy, Ultra Boy, Matter-Eater Lad, Cosmic Boy, Star Boy, (writer's block at DC or a cry for help?) among others, are covered.

However, this absorbing Web page doesn't merely drop references, colorful graphics and harp fanboy-style on character powers. Instead, it provides a complete context for the characters and the DC Universe. The impressive chronology of the DC universe is a resource in itself. Beginning ambitiously with the Big Bang, it provides in-depth explanations of key events with a degree of nuance and continuity reminiscent of *Star Trek*. Moreover, the common galactic tongue, Interlac, is explained with a chart of its alphabet. Often enjoyably dense and involved, Encyclopaedia Galactica is informative and engaging.
WEB http://www.onu.edu/~stu3131/encygal.html

▶ SPIDER-MAN

The Spider-Man Home Page This unofficial Spidey home page offers a dossier on the web crawler that would make an FBI agent weep with admiration. Not only are visitors privy to the latest goings-on of this superhero, but a host of Spider-Man background info is offered as well. Under the Spider-Man Resources menu you'll find several Spider-Man FAQs, an explanation of his powers, a brief rundown of friends and foes, a Spidey pictorial history, fan fiction, and info on animated and live TV shows. Want to know what's on everyone else's mind? Subscribe to the Spider-Man listserve. The site is quite well-rounded but it does fall short of encyclopedic. A few pages might be skinnier than you'd like—the episode lists, for example, don't have dates or descriptions—but you'll still come away with an eyeful.
WEB http://minuteman.com/spiderman

▶ SUPERMAN

The Fortress of Solitude Tower of Thoroughness is what this Supershrine ought to be called. Only the Superman from 1986 is covered here, which is at the point when DC decided to revamp the Superman titles to ensure absolute continuity. Whether you missed an impor-

tant issue or whether you're simply starting a Superman collection from scratch, this Web site will be a valuable asset. Major story lines are listed as well as plot summaries for significant story arcs. In the Superman library, you'll find interviews with the talent behind Superman at DC Comics and a speculative piece by science fiction writer Larry Niven on the physics of sex with Superman and its effects on his social life. Another must-see is the Man-of-Steel chronology, which will impress the curious, the meticulous, and the anal retentive. Barring the Rogues Gallery, which is unfortunately largely unfinished, this Web site has much to offer.
web http://www-scf.usc.edu/%7Ed silvers/supes1.html

Lois and Clark on the NET With considerably more sex appeal than its '50s predecessor, *The New Adventures of Lois and Clark* has garnered a considerable following. On the Internet, Fans of *Lois and Clark*, or FOLCs, distribute images, article transcriptions, and current events regarding the show. Of the Web pages that track this show, this is one of the best out there. Complete with description, episode guide, multimedia, and cast info, you can find out the past credits of Justin Whalin a.k.a. Jimmy Olsen or learn how Teri Hatcher broke into acting. FOLCs appear to be a well networked bunch, and this Web site has the links to prove it. Chat rooms, discussion groups, online fan clubs, and newsgroups can be had via the FOLCs links page.
web http://paradise.net/%7Ejose/lc/lc.html

Lois & Clark: The Media Archive If you're tired of half-naked pics of Terri and Dean, this site offers transcribed newspaper, magazine, TV, and radio articles and interviews on the show and its cast. Also, the site links to related sites, multimedia archives, mailing lists, and newsgroups.
web http://www-cs-students.Stanford .EDU/~carolynt/lc

Superman Homepage With so many versions of Superman floating out there like debris from Krypton, how do you choose the quintessential Man of Steel? Is it George Reeve's Superman (who looked like he should be pumping gas), Chistopher Reeves's WASPy Man of Steel, *Lois & Clark's* Chippendales Superstud, or DC's dashing inked wonder? Well, if you liked them all, check this site out. Superman is covered in multiple media. The richest is the comics page, a who, what, when, where, and why of the Kryptonian's life, told through a FAQ and a chronology of the *Superman* comics since 1933.
web http://web.syr.edu/%7Eajgould /superman.html

WATCHMEN

The Annotated Watchmen This abridged version of Alan Moore's dark, gritty series from DC is intended for second-time readers who may have missed the highly detailed nuances the first time around. A critical eye is placed on the rotund Nite Owl, enigmatic Dr. Manhattan, deranged Rorschach, and the rest, with explanations and emphasis on key panels. Also note that a timeline and character guide is available for those who need a quick overview.
web http://darwin.clas.virginia.edu /~jbf9a/watchmen.html

X-MEN

Generation X-Treme! Douglas Coupland's pop-intellectual summation of the twentysomething generation, *Generation X*, has been cleverly lifted by Marvel to appeal to the teen boy demographic. The result is the *Generation X* comic book, a hot addition to the wildly successful X-series, and this Web site, which is devoted to the mutant team. Although hampered by bad use of graphics, this home page does offer bios for the team members, as well as a link to Stan Lee Presents Generation X, the complete online version of the first issue.
web http://www.geocities.com/Paris/5690

The Mutant Pages Perusing this home page is like surfing in a tsunami. Infor-

mation flies in front of you, to the left of you, to the right, and sometimes over your head. Despite the orderly menu selection, this home page is disorganized and only sporadically informative about the Marvel Universe's mutants. Brief yourself with the X-tinction Agenda Issue Guide, the X-Cutioner's Song Issue Guide, the guide for the New Mutants, or some other storylines that you may have missed. If you'd like to obtain all appearances of the time-traveling Cable, his past (or rather future) appearances are followed in The Cable Guide. Also worth skimming is The Angst Guide, which, like a John Hughes film, posits that teenage angst is what makes the world go 'round. Each character's past is analyzed to determine his alienation and is then rated numerically to determine his angst. Check out the many resource links.
WEB http://www.santarosa.edu /~sthoemke/x/index.html

Professor X's Power Links Brilliant, determined, eloquent, chrome-domed Professor Xavier is the Jean-Luc Picard of the Marvel Universe—except Prof. X came first. This Web site, adorned with his intense visage, seems as authoritative as the Professor, with extensive links to mutant home pages. You'll find links to commercial and noncommercial pages, character home pages, comics newsgroups, chat rooms, and forums.
WEB http://www.uky.edu/Classes/CJT745 /ProfessorX.html

Stan Lee Presents Generation X Comprised of the up-and-coming gifted youngsters, the Generation X mutant team is reminiscent of the now extinct New Mutants. Marvel and Marvel maven Stan Lee uploaded the entire first issue to hook Net-savvy kids. It's a good idea, except that the constant scrolling is a pain.
WEB http://www.st.nepean.uws.edu.au /stuff/genx

The Uncanny X-Page Every tourist needs a guide, and every netbound mutie lover needs the Uncanny X-Page.

It is the ideal resource to ease a comic newbie into this alternate dimension of comic fandom. Besides links to other fans' character pages, this well-designed Web site links you to many FAQs, mailing lists, a handful of Telnet X-Men simulations, and fan fiction. All is accessible from a convenient table of contents at the top of the home page. Top-notch.
WEB http://www.students.uiuc.edu /~m-blase/x-page.html

PART 7

Sci-Fringe

FANTASY

TELL A FANTASY FAN THAT SHE'S inhuman. She'll thank you. Mention that her unusual almond-shaped, silver eyes are otherworldly, and she's sure to know exactly which world. But while a lot of fantasy deals with alien planets and unearthly creatures, it is fundamentally about culture—elaborately constructed worlds, languages, glorious quests, and the relationships between the characters caught up in the adventure. The Internet has made the realm of fantasy more vital than ever, and fans have taken to it like a Pern dolphin to a pink ocean in the sunset of a distant moon. Is it escapism, dissatisfaction with reality, or a love of the soap opera-style plot twists? Is it a childlike love for fairy tales, or a penchant for bloodletting in leather? Or is fantasy a way to broaden creative skills and free the imagination?

▶ CLICK PICK

Fantasy Forum The unfortunate choice of title for this active section of America Online almost makes it sound like the forum is a late-night refuge for lonely singles over 18. But *this* Fantasy Forum is really just a place of celebration for all fans and purveyors of fantasy fiction, including books, authors, TV shows, and occasionally movies. From *I Dream of Jeannie* to Tolkien to Dungeons & Dragons, this forum has become a catch-all for both the barely relevant and the absolutely mandatory. The treasure here, though, is the beautifully envisioned, bustling group of message boards. Tens of thousands of posts are collected under topics ranging from peer reviews of fantasy books to "Children of the Night." A gaggle of fan clubs also host boards here, gathering for live chat or role-playing at scheduled times weekly. Castles, knights, dragons, fairies, and even the occasional elf have all found a home in this must-see fantasyland.

AMERICA ONLINE *keyword* fantasy→Fantasy

▶ MOTHERSHIPS

Danne Lundqvist Fantasy Authorguide Thanks to Danne of Sweden, we all can sleep a little easier knowing that we can find information on the Internet about all of our favorite fantasy writers, whether they've written just one master work or a wildly popular series like Pern. He's linked to the bibliographies of every author you can think of, and created comprehensive link indexes for 23 of the biggest and best.
WEB http://www-und.ida.liu.se /~e95danlu/fantasy.html

The Fantasy Book List Now, you all know that life will not end because your favorite author (whomsoever he or she may be) simply won't finish that long-promised next novel in the best serial you've ever read. But doesn't it feel that way? When you're feeling blue and desperate for new installments, there's more to do than just sit around imagining the movie version of the series. The Fantasy Book List holds information about hundreds of fantasy authors and their books. This includes recommendations, brief summaries, and links to author home pages. But if you really can't stomach the thought of reading any other author's books, you might enjoy learning about the source mythology behind your favorite fantasy fiction. Cheer up!
WEB http://www.mcs.net/~finn /home.html

Internet Speculative Fiction Database Some sites evolve casually, collecting links, quotes, and miscellany like cat hair on a sweater. The ISFD is not one of those sites. Its home page has been constructed with the precision of an engineer, promising bibliographies, and awards databases. Unfortunately, despite the initial impression, there seems to be some underlying chaos as the database moves over into HTML from its origins as ASCII. Unlike similar

sites, this one is searchable by author, title, series, or year, which redeems it somewhat. For starter information, this is the place.
web http://www.cu-online.com /~avonruff/sfdbase.html

▶ NEIL GAIMAN

A Gallery of Dreams Available through FTP or WWW, this is an enormous collection of Sandman images covering the entire wacky family, as well as images of Neil, fan art, even cover and trading card scans. Some members of the Endless get a lot more press than others, of course, but the most popular siblings, Dream, Death, and Delirium, will keep you in wallpaper for weeks. Anyone who hasn't taken a close look at McKean's covers lately is advised to do so.
web http://joffre.newcastle.edu.au /sandman.html

A Page of Dreams A very cool index page that begins and ends in Sandman links and image galleries, but also contains lots of links to poetry, fiction, artwork and music about dreams, dream analysis, dream journals, precognitive dreaming, and lucid dreaming. There's even a link to the Bill Gates Fountain of Dreams.
web http://lucien.berkeley.edu/dreams .html

All Good Things This site holds A&E's online cover article about *The Sandman*, the series' demise, and its legacy. It provides an analysis with journalistic objectivity, certainly a change from the usual fawning praise of fan pages. Whether this is a benefit or a detriment is up in the air. It doesn't spend an inordinate amount of time on exposition, but the tone is one of an insider addressing outsiders, and although he has praise enough for the comic, he isn't really swept away by it. On the other hand, it picks up on things that a fan may gloss over or simply miss in her enraptured state. You decide.
web http://www.daily.umn.edu/ae /Print/ISSUE28/cover.html

Comics "Most of his dreams are set in one vast, dark house, but he never dreams of the same room twice." Finally, a page recognizes some of Neil's other works, including *Books of Magic*, *Death*, and his and Dave McKean's first collaborative graphic novel *Violent Cases*. For these and several other comics, the page offers cover scans, bios of the artists and writers, and more.
web http://stahlw00.stahl.bau.tu-bs .de/people/rhildebrandt/comics.html

The Dreaming With the death of Morpheus, our boy is very busy these days—his plate holds the *Sandman* and *Death* movies (let's cross our fingers), two new novels, a new collection of short fiction, and a possible second season of his fanbloodytastic BBC series *Neverwhere*. It's hard to keep up with him, but the site authors make a good go at it, covering everything that's going on with Gaiman in the real world (new projects, print interviews, chat transcripts, articles, cons), the fictional (resident fan fiction and e-text short stories, image galleries), and the fanatical (*Sandman* fan pages, bios, and Vertigo resources). The page even has a "Soft Places"-type category, which links to Shakespeare, Tori Amos, T.S. Eliot and other things that bleed into the edges of the *Sandman* universe.
web http://www.holycow.com/dreaming

Gallery of the Endless The Gallery of the Endless offers descriptions of Destiny, Death, Destruction, Dream, Desire, Despair and Delirium culled from Gaiman's introductions to the characters in "Season of Mists," as well as the site author's musings on the dysfunctional family. Each member gets their own group of images, including The New Dream (or The Anthropomorphic Entity Formerly Known As Daniel). As we all know, the family is even more out of sorts than usual since the change— Dream's like the second wife at Thanksgiving dinner where everyone can't stop talking about how delicious dead Judy's gravy was.
web http://www.primenet.com/~carr /endless/endless.html

Heart of The Dreaming One of the best sites on the Net, period. In a large virtual world built on the Realm of the Dreaming, you flit around, visiting different places on the map—Lord Morpheus's Castle, The Shores of Nightmare, The Soft Places, The Houses of Mystery and Secrets... In each region McKeanesque artwork leads you to a number of thematic features. Play an interactive game with the Corinthian where winning is a matter of life or death. Interrupt Cain and Abel's argument to be regaled with a tale of mystery. Read an interview with Gaiman, or Lot or Nero. And finally, be sure to share your fiction, poetry, or dreams with the rest of the wanderers.
WEB http://www.av.qnet.com/~raven

Index—Neil Gaiman "Neil Gaiman is always wearing black clothes. Neil Gaiman is almost always wearing sunglasses and a black leather coat. Neil Gaiman writes [wrote] *The Sandman* for DC Comics. Neil Gaiman writes a lot of other things, including songs for the Flash Girls. He has a garden." A short collection of useful resources concerning the strange man unwittingly responsible for letting the Goth culture live way past its comedic usefulness.
WEB http://sunspot.health.org/flash /people/neil.html

Magian Line "While we're at it, I should also clarify that this is NOT a Sandman club and it's NOT a fan club... Neil casually mentioned (in Rocknet, on CompuServe) that he was working on a record with Alice Cooper. I gasped and wheezed, and said 'how the heck can we keep track of all your projects, Neil?' He mused aloud about how he probably should have some way of getting news about what he's doing out to readers. I said 'Me! Me! I'll do it!' He said 'Do you really want to? Think about it, don't just say "yeah yeah, yummy yummy" (that's a direct quote, folks!) and I said 'yeah yeah, yummy yummy!'" Well, it's a lovely story, but apparently the site author's been very busy—though surely not as busy as Neil—as an issue hasn't come out since December 1995, save the article about the filming of the BBC series. But if you want a sublime time capsulesque series of articles and interviews, not just about his *Sandman* stuff, but about all the other wonderful things Neil's done, this is the place to go.
WEB http://sadieo.ucsf.edu/Magian /magian.html

The Magician's Study Part of the illustrious *Sandman* page The Heart of Dreaming, The Magician's Study should be your first stop on the InforGaiman Highway. The page is an enormous index linking to live appearances, annotations and FAQs, interviews and reviews, bibliographies, news, and about 10 million fan clubs and Sandman/Gaiman fan pages. Some of the best things available through this site are the short stories and hard to find essays by Neil on everything from Sim City to H.P. Lovecraft, to Snow White. And be sure to check out the pages on similarly brilliant illustrator Dave McKean, who is breaking ground online with his interactive comic book at Wall Data and multimedia project at Petalhead.
WEB http://www.av.qnet.com/~raven /magick.html

Sandman Annotations A fantastic resource for fanatics who want to dissect the comics piece by piece, catching all the inside jokes, artistic details, and, of course, all the millions of literary and historical references (don't feel bad if you didn't get them before, Neil had to look up most of them too). Some of the information here is of little use—"The Corinthian, we learn, is a sick bastard."—especially considering the level of knowledge of anyone interested in the annotations to begin with. But most of the time it's fascinating: "...DC's Hell has no set continuity at this moment. The Demon, at least, has stayed out of Hell since *Season of Mists* concluded, but a major plot device in *Hellblazer* depends on the triumvirate being intact and stable," or "Haroun Al Raschid: 763-809, ascended as the fourth Caliph of Baghdad in 785... He is a protagonist in the *Arabian Nights*, and represents the ideal

ruler in Arab stories." It adds a whole new level of meaning and enjoyment to the comics.
WEB http://www.holycow.com /dreaming/annot.html

▶ ROBERT JORDAN

Adam's Wheel of Time Page If you're a friend of the dark from Illinois, Wisconsin, or Indiana, you belong on Adam's mailing list, so he can send you information about the social events he plans for the Midwest Darkfriends group he just started. Not from the heartland? Don't despair, because Adam has also assembled a pretty good index, character summaries, and "miscellaneous tidbits," along with some of the Wheel of Time questions on his mind these days. Email him the answers if you know if Lan already knew Logain, or what "Rods of Dominion" are.
WEB http://www.mcs.com/~orion/wot /index.html

Bill's Repository of Robert Jordan Fandom Few fans bother to question why they, or anybody else, simply must read Robert Jordan. Bill does on this page, and his answer boils down to details. Robert Jordan invests a lot of words into his characters, the land they live on, and the "rich tapestry" of the story. This has been his critic's biggest bugbear, but Bill says that "every word… is there for a reason!" His homage to Wheel of Time fandom, like Jordan's novels, contains volumes of content including a long introduction to the author, an art gallery, and lots else. Proving that even Darkfriends have a sense of humor, he has also archived Wheel of Time Humor ("Beavis and Butt-head go to Rand-Land and are made Dreadlords: huh, huh, huh… Balefire's cool… huh, huh, Yeah-Yeah, Cool, Yeah…") and created an insane set of Robert Jordan Madlibs.
WEB http://www.cs.unc.edu/~garrett /jordan/jordan.html

FAQ—rec.arts.sf.written.robert-jordan What can I read until I get my hands on the next Robert Jordan book? How many books will eventually make up the Wheel of Time series? What's the next book called and when is it coming out? Jordan junkies have just one thing on their minds, and this FAQ contains some info on every aspect of the exquisite obsession known as fandom.
WEB http://cegt201.bradley.edu/~jsn /faq/rasfwrj_faq.html

FAQ—The Wheel of Time Want to know what those chapter icons are? Curious about what the Seanchan are up to? Can't figure out if Verin is black, brown, or purple? And what's the deal with Saldaea? This FAQ gets down and dirty covering the details of the Jordan series. It includes a WoT timeline, a list of unresolved plot threads, explanations of the elements from Norse, Chinese, Japanese, and American Indian mythologies Jordan has sprinkled throughout the series, and inconsistencies in cover art. Plus, each element of the FAQ is backed up by a fan vote of confidence.
WEB http://www.cc.gatech.edu/ftp /people/viren/www/jordan/FAQ.html

rec.arts.sf.written.robert-jordan Apparently, Robert Jordan's books are as addictive as the Net. Threads here tend toward the hundred-message-long length, focusing on the latest RJ book. When we visited, focus was on A Crown of Swords, the seventh in the series. Fervent members of Jordan fandom are compelled to post their own personal reviews and interpretations of The Wheel of Time novels as they read and reread their copies and lie in wait for the next addition.
USENET rec.arts.sf.written.robert-jordan

Robert Jordan Because reading Robert Jordan provides even more problems than solutions to the fantastic conundrums in which the characters find themselves—kind of like an otherworldly soap opera—the Robert Jordan board in the Fantasy Forum is one of the busiest. Who killed Asmodean? Hundreds of people with apostrophes in their names have weighed in on that one. Same goes for discussion of Crown of Swords: a rip-off? Slow? The best yet? Also, the Robert Jordan Fan Club has a pretty loyal following, although most of the action takes place at real-time chat meetings.

AMERICA ONLINE *keyword* fantasy→ fantasy→Message Boards→Robert Jordan

Some More Robert Jordan Fandom

Seems like Karl-Johan has written as many papers about his favorite author as the author has written books. Many of them have been Webified and posted here, and their titles include "The Rand-Mat-Perrin Tripod" and "White Tower Conflict." That ought to be enough to satisfy any yen to perform an in-depth examination of *WoT*, but if not, Karl-Johan has kindly provided detailed plot summaries of "the books so far" and a complete index to other sites.

WEB http://www.dsv.su.se/~k-j-nore /jordan.html

The Waygate: Wheel of Time Archive

"Elder Hage will be with you and will translate the directions on the guide-posts into URLs," intones the introduction to this site. It's refreshing to see a little fantasy creep into the typical index. Once Hage gets around to translating, he carefully outlines each of several *Wheel of Time* topics, particularly focusing on fandom on the Tel'aran'rhiod, which "infidels" call the Usenet. Because this is the official archive of the Robert Jordan Usenet, there are plenty of resources here that can be found nowhere else, such as the advanced Dreamers' "loony pet theories" on plot twists, and *WoT* filks for all the songs on the album *Flood*, by They Might be Giants. (Which, by the way, is a terrible thing to do to a good album.) This is a crazy tour, but fortunately Elder Hage makes an excellent guide.

WEB http://www.cc.gatech.edu/ftp /people/viren/www/jordan/jordan.html

Wheel of Time Graphics Page

Most RJ fan pages tend to be somewhat color-less, but this one more than makes up for their dismal lack of graphics. Many of the oddly beautiful chapter icons have been posted here with the full permission of Tor Books. They look like potential tattoos or desktop wallpaper, and include ravens, dragons, and, of course, the wheel-and-snake. Beyond these emblems, at the bottom of the page, are full-color cover shots for each book, a map of the continent where it all happens, Rand-Land, and a picture of Robert Jordan at a booksigning.

WEB http://www.az.com/~reddraco /wot/newwot.html

The Wheel of Time Index

All other Robert Jordan sites bow down before this one, the master index and the first place any fan (or potential fan) should begin. Pam Korda, who is also the FAQueen, keeps this page, which she claims links to everything Wheelish on the Web. She's not kidding. Join her ASAP.

WEB http://student-www.uchicago.edu /users/kor2/WOT/WOTindex.html

Wheel of Time Survey

Wheel of Time fans are an eclectic lot, with about as many opinions as answers. After all, why would fans of finality like a series with so many open questions? Will Rand clean the Ways? Who will Rand end up with—Aviendha, Egwene, Min, Elayne? This survey represents the average fan's chance to be heard in the storm of debate. Vote for Favorites, Least Favorites, and General Questions, and then review the results of others before you. So far, *The Lord of Chaos* is most folks' favorite book, and a majority believe Rand will die. But frankly, with not too many voters registering their opinions, it's anybody's game.

WEB http://www.imperium.net /~dennisr/survey.htm

The Wheel Turns

Speculation about favorite books being made into movies always rages among fans while they're waiting for a new book to come out, and Robert Jordan fans are certainly no exception. This particular *WoT* fan hosts a page, complete with pictures, of the actors he and others have suggested could play Rand and the rest of the gang. He'll be disappointed if the real thing ever comes out, because it's doubtful that Audrey Hepburn would be available to play Min. And Lea Thompson as Aviendha? Oh, please. Still, it's a fun game to play, and the result is an interesting cast of characters, indeed. Other points of interest available from the home page include an article about RJ from Book Page and a few links to other sites.

WEB http://www.wiw.org/~seth/jordan .html

WoT Concordance (Version 2.0 ToC) Whatever you need to know about the environment in which the *Wheel of Time* books take place, it's here. Geography, clothing, food, sword forms, the One Power, and tons more subjects are covered in the Concordance, which was originally written for fans who participate in *WoT* role-playing clubs. Each bit of data is referenced to the relevant book. However, it does not overlap with anything discussed in the Usenet FAQ, such as specific character information, plot details, speculation, or prophecies.

WEB http://www.d.umn.edu/~knovek /wotc/wotcToC.html

Yet Another Robert Jordan Fandom Page A cry has gone out across the Internet: "Dude! 'Who is this Jordan guy?'" Well, he's James Oliver Rigney, Jr., and Darkfriend Aaron has created this page to honor him. "Well, what sort of stuff is out there?" Plenty of links to dictionaries, tidbits, funnies, and newsgroups, plus the home pages of what seems like every Jordan fan around.

WEB http://pantheon.cis.yale.edu /~abergman/jordan.html

> ## C.S. LEWIS

alt.books.cs-lewis Frequent posters swear that this newsgroup's not dead, but since they're spending all their energy doing that, there's not much discussion of C.S. Lewis going on. A lot of the posts run something like this: "I loved the Narnia series!!!" "Wow, so did I.

Wasn't it great?" Not much depth to the pool. But serious debate does take place, especially about the Christian aspects of Narnia and, of course, in Lewis's sacred works. Douglas Gresham does drop by occasionally, so it's possible to catch an interesting thread.

USENET alt.books.cs-lewis

Aslan's How Now Lucy and Edmund won't have to climb through a bunch of dusty fur coats to get into Narnia— Aslan's How is billed as Narnia's home page. The creator is particularly inspired by the Christian allegory in the Narnia series, and provides plenty of images, character descriptions, and brief plot summaries for each of the books. Don't miss the link to a home page just for everybody's favorite lion: it's hiding under the "Mere List of Narnia Characters."

WEB http://www.wsu.edu:8080/~langc /aslan.html

C. S. Lewis and the Inklings No, it's not your cousin's awful garage band. The Inklings, with Lewis as their spiritual center, were a group of 20th century Anglo-Irish Christian fantasy writers. This particular scholarship page splits its time about evenly between Lewis and "the rest." Plenty of pictures and links round out the original content by the Bowling Green professor who created the page. His own contributions include a review of Shadowlands, and "Lewis Redux: A Postmodern Dialogue."

WEB http://www.bgsu.edu/~edwards /lewis.html

CSL FAQ by Doug Gresham For those who missed out on *Shadowlands* (a "deliberately inaccurate" but "emotionally spot-on" portrayal of C.S. Lewis's life), Douglas Gresham is Lewis's stepson, the son of Lewis's beloved wife Joy. He's still quite alive and is very active in the Net community. Gresham's FAQ is a trove of inside information, written by a man in the unique position of having been there. Why was Clive Lewis called Jack? Which are the best biographies? Is Narnia a Mobius strip? These burning issues and

plenty more are addressed here.
WEB http://ernie.bgsu.edu/~edwards/faq1.htm

Into the Wardrobe: The C.S. Lewis WWW Site

This is the site to see if you only have time for one. It's by far the most comprehensive, and even uses frames successfully. A brief Life Outline contains a biography, with the dates of major works built in; the tenor of Lewis's works is highly dependent on time. A three part bibliography lists everything Lewis ever wrote. In fact, if Lewis had published a grocery list, it would be here. Thirteen related essays, speeches, and parodies are gathered together, and the Photograph Album is the most complete source of images available in one place. Mailing lists, newsgroups, clips of Lewis speaking, links elsewhere, and even Douglas Gresham's email address are all here under sensible categories. It's a proud effort.
WEB http://www.cache.net/~john/cslewis/index.html

ANNE MCCAFFREY

A Dragonlover's Guide to Pern Fandom

It is theoretically possible to be a Pern fan without participating in the special brand of Anne McCaffrey fan club known as a Weyr, a Crafthall, or a Hold. But what fun would that be? Weyrs blur the line between book and reality through role-playing, fan fiction, and fanzines containing anything that's Pern (and not Terran). This basic guide to the structure, creation, and membership of these clubs is written by a dragonrider who has been a Weyr leader and member for years. Her advice on becoming Pernese is hilarious. Avoid cutesy names, she warns: "You'll be wondering whatever possessed you to saddle yourself with such a ridiculous thing. Just try writing a serious story with a character named K'mart, rider of blue Woolworth."
WEB http://www.sfrt.com/sfrt3/pern.htm

alt.fan.pern Serious dragonlovers only! The permanent devotees of this newsgroup are equally enamored of Pern, dragons, and their goddess, Anne McCaffrey. So, when's the next book coming out? How strong are Lessa's psychic powers? And if a lizard is the size of a cat, how can it fly? Someone here will know the answer to all of these questions and any others imaginable. If no one does, at least visitors are sure to find a welcoming Weyr, as long as they don't mind attending a hatching or two.
USENET alt.fan.pern
FAQ: WEB http://kumo.swcp.com/~quirk/afp-index.shtml

Anne McCaffrey "In the hour of the Sheep, Year of the Fire Tiger, star Sign Aries with Taurus rising and Leo midheaven," also known as April 1, 1926, Anne McCaffrey was born. The detailed biographical material on this page is entirely provided by McCaffrey herself. She discusses why she began writing about dragons—they "seemed to have had a very bad press," and quips that "2,000,000 words later, I'm not allowed to stop" writing about them. We also discover that she has seven Maine Coon cats and a horse named Pi. At the end is a complete bibliography, along with related resources.
WEB http://www.wwwebguides.com/authors/society/authors/mcaff.html

Anne McCaffrey While the links collected here to the PernWeb are not particularly numerous and some are dead, there is one redeeming feature: a lovely, quality .GIF of the dragon lady herself, posed for publicity for an Irish con.
WEB http://arrogant.itc.icl.ie/Anne McCaffrey.html

DragonWeb An excellent companion to A Dragonlover's Guide to Pern Fandom, DragonWeb is like a road map for dragonriders and their trusty steeds. Which commercial service is friendliest to its Weyrs? Where are the MUSHes and MOOs, and what are they, anyway? And where's that Web site for Weyrfest? The site's creator also promises that soon, in the Archives, he will gather together fanwritten Pern files, but not fan fiction

since McCaffrey doesn't permit it online.
WEB http://voyager.abac.com/lensman
/pern

Pern Images While at first glance this doesn't look too exciting, it contains the largest, most detailed scanned Pern images anywhere on the Web. Brekke, F'nor, plenty of other characters, and more firelizards than you can count are presented in illustrations from the books, several in full color. Almost 30 images are here with little obvious description, so to see a thumbnail preview of the pics, click on "aaindex01pern.gif." Full descriptions reside under "aapern.txt."
URL ftp://ftp.nmt.edu/pub/graphics
/dragons/pern

Pern Weyrs Grab yourself a dragon and mosey to a Hatching! Then, pick a Weyr from the large, competing selection here. It all depends on where on Pern you want to live, and what the scenario is. There's plenty to do when you're a dragonrider (or a dolphin, or...)
AMERICA ONLINE *keyword* fantasy→
fantasy→Message Boards→Pern Weyrs

J.R.R. TOLKIEN

alt.fan.tolkien Tolkien connoisseurs are all around us. Paul suggests that Sibelius's 7th is great to listen to "when you get to Weathertop." Sean, though, prefers Led Zeppelin. Plenty of fans are happy to offer explanations when someone asks why Gandalf warns Frodo not to use the ring again, when Frodo hasn't used it yet. Occasionally, a new fan asks for recommendations on what to read next, but woe to the fool who suggests that what he's read already is "self-indulgent, intellectual masturbation." This is alt.fan.tolkien, not alt.complain.tolkien, and consequently the posters are much more interested in debating the finer points than in hearing criticism of their idol.
USENET alt.fan.tolkien

Aragorn's Tolkien Links On this page, decorated with pictures of the likes of Tolkien and Frodo, Aragorn has gathered the best links to all kinds of Tolkien-related sites, from Rings of Power to the Oxford Tolkien Society. He also hosts some original content, particularly a page of charming verses and hobbit ditties from *The Hobbit* like "Chip the glasses and crack the plates!"
WEB http://paul.spu.edu/~aragorn
/tolkien.html

Audio Excerpts: Tolkien Reading Lord of the Rings If you love a man who speaks Elvish, you'll adore these audio excerpts. Follow along with Sam, Frodo, and Gollum as they trek to Mount Doom and experience the battle at Pelennor Fields like it's all new again. Megabytes of fantasy joy!
WEB http://town.hall.org/Archives
/radio/IMS/HarperAudio/020294
_harp_ITH.html

Computer Games Based On Tolkien's Works Just reading the books is never enough. Even seeing the movies doesn't satisfy a dedicated Tolkien fan. Fortunately, there are plenty of computer games— strategy games, role-playing, text-based, MUDs, action, and others—that take place exclusively in one of Tolkien's worlds, and a fellow fan has listed them here. Screen shots, availability information, and a brief review of every game (if he has played it) are listed.
WEB http://www.lysator.liu.se/tolkien
-games

Electronic Tolkien Encyclopedia Project When an author's works pass into the classics oeuvre, as Tolkien's have, they become academicized. This yields a deeper, more literary examination, which generates journals and articles and theses. Real glory comes when these articles and theses along with specific topical entries are collected into a coherent volume like the ETEP. Under such subject heads as "The Art of J.R.R. Tolkien" and "Family Trees," the compilers have grouped the best of submissions by fans and scholars alike. For those who already know Tolkien well and want to go deeper, this just may be as important as the One Ring.

WEB http://www.chem.lsu.edu/cbury /ETEP/Default.html

The Hypertextualized Tolkien FAQ
Some of these questions really belong in an NAQ—for Never Asked Questions. Does anybody really care which date on our calendar is Bilbo and Frodo's birthday? (OK, we admit it, we wanted to know.) But the interface is far better than 99 percent of FAQs, and the detailed biography of Tolkien is worth a peek from even the most cursory of admirers. Plus, there are any number of tidbits about Tolkien's hobbits, elves, dwarves, and other Middle-Earth creatures, as well as links to other Web sites.
WEB http://www.daimi.aau.dk /~bouvin/tolkienfaq.html

The J.R.R. Tolkien Information Page
It's safe to say that if this site doesn't list it, it's probably not about Tolkien. Many other Tolkien sites point to this Information Page as the master index, and that seems indubitable, since there are at least 100 links listed here in categories from Language Resources to Parodies. It'll be a frequently visited bookmark for any wannabe resident of Middle-Earth.
WEB http://www.lights.com/tolkien /rootpage.html

J.R.R. Tolkien Page Congratulations to Bruce Jewell, a true and creative fan of J.R.R. Tolkien. Instead of simply indexing the various and sundry Tolkien shrines on the Web (although he does that, too), he has gotten permission to take what he considers to be the most original and best and build his own temple around it. We are treated to Tolkien's Oxford, a virtual tour of his alma mater and subsequent home. That's not all, though, because a complete explication of the etymology of TengWar, with pictures and fonts, is here, along with Tolkien-related documents and scanned images from the 1984 Tolkien calendar.
WEB http://203.0.168.99/wwwsites /tolkien

rec.arts.books.tolkien Besides a lot of cross-posting with alt.fan.tolkien, this newsgroup is home to plenty of its own discussion about *LOTR* movies, books, and the nitty-gritty of Tolkien fandom. What would Frodo have done if...? What do elves look like? How does *Lord of the Rings* translate into Quenya ("Heru i Million")? The fan group here tends to be more diverse in its level of devotion than the alt. newsgroup, but there are just as many of them and the action is just as happening.
USENET rec.arts.books.tolkien

Tolkien and Classic Fantasy Pippin thinks that Gandalf is a Christ figure. Silquendi, the elf, wants to share the news about what the Tolkien Club is up to on weekend nights. Plenty of people want to discuss Ralph Bakshi's animated version of *LOTR*, even if they claim that they don't. Clearly, the Tolkien and Classic Fantasy Board is hopping with orcs, hobbits, and wizards who love their Tolkien. In fact, although Classic Fantasy is tacked onto the title, only a silent minority of the folders have nothing to do with Frodo and friends.
AMERICA ONLINE *keyword* fantasy→fantasy →message boards→Tolkien and Classic Fantasy

The Tolkien Language List Tolkien, himself a linguist, provided plenty of grist for the constructed language mill with the many dialects, alphabets, and whole languages which he created for the *Lord of the Rings* series. TolkLang is a mailing list comprising devotees of Elvish, Quenya, and their many cousins. The archive Web site contains a good selection of posts, the weekly digest, Elvish poetry, and other resources related to both the list and the languages. It's a recommended stop before joining the list.
EMAIL tolklang-server@dcs.ed.ac.uk ✍ *Type in message body:* subscribe *Info:* **WEB** http://www.dcs.ed.ac.uk/misc /local/TolkLang

▶ DRAGONS

Alt.fan.dragons Page Have you ever... conquered a major city just so you could brag about it in bars to your friends?

been tempted to kill your best friend because they approached your hoard? listed your occupation as anything like "Queen of the Tree People," "High Druid of the Stuff," "Owner of the Plushy Shop"? Ever seen your breath on cold days, and thought "wow, I'm smoking"? Ever wondered why your tongue isn't forked? Well, you're not alone. The Draconity Test sampled above is only one of the features offered at this site. Gather around the hearth with other dragophiles. Take a look at the sketch of the week, read a little fan fiction, join the Soaring Heart and Soul Publications Project, take the Dragon Census, drink a few pitchers of mead, and flirt with the serving wench.
WEB http://icecube.acf-lab.alaska.edu/~fxdlk

Dragon's Flight So green and scaly, you can almost feel it breathing! Apart from a selective index, this page holds one of the largest dragon image galleries online. A feast of eye-candy for those with a reptilian aesthetic.
WEB http://www.gnomes.org/rethan/dragonf/dragonf.htm

Jae's Dragon "The Knights of Inyensarh mounted their steeds and had tried to fight the Dragons and their horrible masters but they were no match for the acid breath and fire of the Dragons and the arcane spells of the Drashij. The other factions of the Jaliea refused to intercede, on the grounds that allying with the rest of the human world would threaten their positions of neutrality, though the Drakshij threatened their existence. No matter the appeals, no matter the rewards offered the rest of the ring refused to help, or aid Inyensarh in anyway, it was as if a collective knife named the Drakshij were being held to the ring's throat." Fan fiction is only one part of this well-produced site. Fire-breathing dragons also lead you to an impressive image gallery, a comprehensive set of links, a fan fiction archive, and a not-very-dragonistic set of VRML downloads.
WEB http://dragon.sedona.net

L'rac's Lair "You have entered a large cave over ten times as tall as yourself. You hear a deep rumbling noise and peer around. Lying in a corner of this cave is an enormous, and yet relatively small for its species, bronze dragon. You instinctively reach for the hilt of your sword and pull it from its sheath. The dragon's many-faceted eyes look you over, whirring in the green of anxiety. L'rac walks in and welcomes you to his weyr." And ooo, look L'rac has Dragonimation! One of the beefiest dragon pages out there, L'rac (unfortunate name, no?) offers individual pages for Pern, Mirkwood, Dragonlance, and of course, penguins. Yeah, penguins—got a problem with that?
WEB http://www.hooked.net/users/lrac/lraclair.html

▶ DARK CRYSTAL

The Unofficial Dark Crystal Home Page *The Dark Crystal* is one of Monica's favorite films, and she was bummed that it had no Internet presence. So, to her computer she went, and now the world has this beautiful Web page to visit and learn from. She's collected sound and graphic files, a list of *Dark Crystal* books and other related media, and even a 1982 article from American Cinematographer.
WEB http://www.fairfield.com/wyvern/darkcrys

When single shines the triple sun... "*Bougez! Bougez, bougez, bougez.*" How's your French? Just one of the sounds collected at this site devoted to Jim Henson's fantasy masterpiece. The usual stuff, though—information about *Dark Crystal*, images, and related links.
WEB http://www.phlab.missouri.edu/~c619888/darkcrystal.html

▶ DRAGONHEART

Dragonheart A superb little Shockwave preview is the only thing here worth your time and effort, because it takes far too much time and effort to play the interactive adventure game, which

appears to be in temporary disrepair. If it's not in disrepair, it is frustrating enough to make you want to go back to 1961 and sabotage the set of *Dr. No*, and relegate Sean Connery to a life of anonymity and failure.
WEB http://www.mca.com/universal _pictures/dragonheart/index.html

Dragonheart The mixed fan reviews are an indication as to why this is such a dead area. If you're looking for information on the film with the friendly dragon, you might be better off looking somewhere else.
AMERICA ONLINE *keyword* fictional→ Science Fiction→Message Boards→ Science Fiction Films→List Topics→ Dragonheart

HERCULES

Hercules: The Legendary Journeys Universal Channel's site is devoted to that hulking hunk of a hero, Hercules, who stands up for mere mortals everywhere. You'll find descriptions of demi-gods and mortals, a broadcast schedule, and an episode guide for the show, which features Kevin Sorbo as the son of Zeus.
WEB http://www.univstudios.com/tv /hercules

Vicki's Tribute to Hercules In a mere 12 episodes, Hercules did more than most do in a lifetime—he killed the Nemean lion, destroyed the Lernaean Hydra, captured the deer with the golden horns, captured the wild boar of Erymanthus, cleaned the Augean stables in one day, drove away the Stymphalian birds, captured the Cretan bull, captured the man-eating mares of Diomedes, fetched the girdle of Hippolyta, stole the cattle of the triple-bodied monster, Geryon, won the Golden Apples of the Hesperides, and brought back the three-headed dog, Cerberus. Vicki's page is devoted to that dutiful demi-god and defender of innocents, as portrayed on the TV show *Hercules: The Legendary Journeys*. She's collected episode lists, a guest star guide, an assortment of .WAV files, a photo gallery, and a rundown of the act-

ing history of *Hercules* star Kevin Sorbo, who's greatest previous success was as a corporate shill.
WEB http://oscar.teclink.net/~vbird /hercules.html

XENA: WARRIOR PRINCESS

alt.tv.xena At the moment, this group is split between posts arguing about whether the characters and/or the actresses are having sex with each other, and posts flaming the people who spam up the group arguing about whether the characters and/or the actresses are having sex with each other. Occasionally a discussion breaks out about the whooshing noises that accompany everything from swordplay to simply turning-your-head-really-fast. Some people think it's annoying and unrealistic. Duh. Yeah, the Action Pack is really beginning to lose that gritty cinema vérité feeling.
USENET alt.tv.xena

Buumzer's XENA: Warrior Princess Episode Guide This episode guide is thorough in its expositions, but hasn't caught up to the viewing schedule yet. You'll find close to 20 synopses, a handful of one-line descriptions, and only a few episodes with no info at all. The site also promises that Xena/Hercules crossovers, as well as the princess's appearances on *The Legendary Journey*, will be chronicled in due time.
WEB http://www.erols.com/psnook /xe_guide.htm

Chris Boem's Xena Page This guy has a serious thing for Lucy Lawless. With those blue eyes, those strong thighs, and the ability to mortally wound 100 men with only an attitude and a metal frisbee, who can blame him? CB offers an impressive index, a superb collection of images, and a few sound clips.
WEB http://www.angelfire.com/pages2 /xena/index.html

Logomancy: Xena Fandom Bigger than Raimi's production budget, bigger than Kevin Sorbo's hair, bigger than Lucy's… horse. This is the most comprehensive

Xena page on the Net, and it's more than comprehensive, it's original. Apart from all the multimedia, the FAQ, the links, the bios and the info on clubs and mailing lists, the Logomancy also offers two pages, Panhellas and Pantheon, on ancient Greek culture and mythology, respectively. The site also holds a great deal of fan fiction, graphic novels, articles, art, and poetry:

WEB http://www.duke.edu/~mero /xenatop.html

Tom's Xena Page Desktop toys, articles, and an index of links are just the appetizers here. The real meat comes from the multimedia libraries that would have fit nicely into Zeus's pad on Olympus. Well over 500 images are filed here, ranging from enormous, crystal clear JPEGs to small thumbnail gifs "perfect for chatting." The sound archive is not quite as enormous, but you're sure to find your fave quote nonetheless. Gabrielle actually gets more clips than anyone else, including leather-bound Lucy herself, but Autolycus, that dashing King of Thieves, still gets the best lines: "Of course the trick in killing someone with an apricot is really in the wrist… so for situations like that I use a muffin." Don't miss the link to the *Army of Darkness* page, another of Tom's sites that honors Sam Raimi's camp genius.

WEB http://www.erols.com/psnook /xe_idx.htm

Xena "In 1983, in a small village east of Macedonia, Dr. Araham Hasson discovered the Xena Scrolls… Papyrologists were quick to challenge the discovery, but AMS carbon-14 dating and chemical analysis of the ink quickly authenticated the find, and the Xena Scrolls became one of the oldest known papyrus writing…" This is part of an introduction to the Xena Scrolls, a very imaginative offering from MCA which creates a fictional correspondence between members of the Xena Restoration Society (XRS) debating their various findings on the forgotten heroine's history. A fun read. Everything else you expect to find

on this official site is here, station lists and air dates, multimedia, and cast and crew info. There's even a forum dedicated exclusively to the pumped princess, equal parts discussion group and Lucy love-fest, and posters range from young femmes happy to see an enormously popular TV show with a strong, sexy, self-sufficient woman at the center, to middle-aged men with sword fetishes.

WEB http://www.mca.com/tv/xena /cast/oconnor.htm

Xena: Warrior Princess "The Top Ten Reasons Xena Kicks Butt!—10) That warrior yip. 9) Leather and steel. 'Nuff said.8) Makes Gabrielle do all the walking while she rides the horse. 7) Not much for girl talk. 6) She's got that bitchin' aerobee. 5) Has no problems with permanently disposing of society's riff-raff. 4) Gabrielle might be an amazon princess, but Xena is their queen. 3) How many sword-swinging women do you know that are babes to boot? 2) She's the only one who has started Herc's motor since his wife died. 1) Geary and Chris say so." Geary and Chris, and most of the other contributors to the Creative Mayhem part of this Web site, have the rapier-sharp wit of 14-year-olds. But don't let that keep you away from the rest of the page, which offers character profiles, an episode guide, background on Xena's origins, and more.

WEB http://www.byu.edu/~simpsont /xena.htm

Xena: Warrrior Princess Page "If you like the sight of blood so much keep talkin'," "Kill 'em all!," and "Don't you ever touch my horse again," are only the beginning. Besides these and other characteristic sound quotes, you'll find an FAQ, a series overview, viewing schedule, and links. There is even a Gabrielle Tribute page in honor of everyone's favorite comparatively diminutive sidekick.

WEB http://www.realnetnw.com/~dmd /xena.html

HORROR

THERE'S PLENTY ON THE NET TO satisfy a sci-fi fan's hankering for horror, whether it takes the form of novels, movies, cult classics, or short stories. If your pleasure turns to pain, check out the *Hellraiser* havens on the Net. If it's a taste of blood you want, sink your teeth into dozens of Anne Rice sites. And if you want self-pitying remorse with your A-positive, feed on *Forever Knight*, still undead and kicking online. If you like your horror with plenty of gore, Sam Raimi's *Evil Dead* trilogy has opened the portal to something really nasty on the Web. If you prefer your tales of terror with more inspired imagery (not to mention the cephalopod-like Cthulhu), explore H.P. Lovecraft, the man and the Mythos. Whatever your tastes, there are dozens of horror hubs to cater to your every evil impulse.

▶ CLICK PICK

The Dark Side of the Net Catering to those with a morbid streak, the Dark Side lists resources that range from pre-Raphaelite paintings (their skin so pale you can almost see the bite marks on their necks) to lists of gloom-and-doom newsgroups. But the meat of the Dark Side is its collection of Gothic tales. With contributions from postmodern dean Robert Coover ("The Dead Queen"), modernist stalwart Joyce Carol Oates ("The Goat Girl"), and gorecore forefather H.P. Lovecraft ("The Outsiders"), the library furnishes more than a dozen examples of the English language's capacity for manufacturing unease and fear. The oldest story in the collection, Edgar Allen Poe's "Black Cat," contains a description of a keening cat horrifying enough to make even a plastic mouse quiver: "with a cry, at first muffled and broken, like the sobbing of a child, and then quickly swelling into one long, loud, and continuous scream, half of horror and half of triumph, such as might have arisen only out of hell, conjointly from the throats of the damned in their agony and of the demons that exult in the damnation."
WEB http://www.cascade.net/dark.html

▶ MOTHERSHIPS

alt.horror Who'd win in a fight between Freddy and Jason? Is Dean Koontz a genius or a hack? What horror film had the best shock ending—Brian DePalma's *Carrie* or John Boorman's *Deliverance*? This newsgroup covers the horror genre in all media. Occasionally, discussions will delve into the esthetics and artistic merit of a particular work, but more often than not the focus is on the ever-popular combination of blood, guts, and gore.
USENET alt.horror

The Cabinet of Dr. Casey When you open Dr. Casey's cabinet, you'll find a site exclusively devoted to the genre in all of its gory incarnations, from literature to television to movies. There are archives of horror movie posters, audio, and graphics; horror reference material, a timeline, and an atlas of the macabre; interviews with the head honchos of horror; and links to horror sites and newsgroups on the Net.
WEB http://www.cat.pdx.edu/%7ecaseyh/horror/index.html

The Dark Side of the Web A Caligari's Cabinet of links to the more horrifying hollows on the Web.
WEB http://www.cascade.net/darkweb.html

DarkEcho's Horror Web A home spun in one corner the Web for those who tend toward the darker side of fiction. Among the finds are a weekly electronic newsletter for writers and fans of horror fiction, featured interviews with writers, reviews of recent offerings in the horror genre, and dark links to similarly slanted sites.
WEB http://w3.gwis.com/~prlg

De Web Mysteriis A World Wide Web guide to the Cthulhu Mythos. Who's Cthulhu? Well, no one who has seen him or his spawn has lived to tell about it. According to the myth, all we have left are the visions of artists after He appeared to them in dreams… some expressed in words and some expressed visually. This site links to the alleged visionaries and their visions, including Cthulhu chief H.P. Lovecraft, Robert Bloch, and Brian Lumley.
WEB http://www.eerie.fr/~alquier /cthulhu.html

Great Horror Movies In addition to the list of great horror films here, you'll find a weekly review of a bad one, too. The monthly forum also addresses such hard-hitting and horrid questions as "What's the weirdest way you've seen someone get killed in a horror movie?"
WEB http://www.sccs.swarthmore .edu/~dansac/movies/horrornet.html

Horror at Arnzen's Arbor Vitae Got a beef with Barker? Want to chat with Douglas Clegg? Care to shower S.P. Somtow with cybercompliments? Arzen's site makes it easy to get in touch with your favorite horror writer by email. Also available—information on the Horror Writer's Association and a list of links to horror literature, TV, and film pages.
WEB http://darkwing.uoregon.edu /~mikea/horror.html

Horror Films: A Bibliography An index of horror, terror, and macabre cinema.
WEB http://slaughter.net/horror

Horror Forum The horror area of AOL's Fictional Realm, better known as the Realm of Shadows, where something is always stirring in the chat rooms and discussion boards devoted to classic horror films, slasher movies, horror writers, vampires, werewolves, and other creatures of the night.
AMERICA ONLINE *keyword* horror→Horror

Horror Haven An archive of one man's obsession with horror films. Find the facts on films from all areas of the genre, including Old Classics (*Franken-stein*), New Classics (*Halloween*), Die Laughing Classics (*The Incredible 2-Headed Transplant*), Gore Fest Classics (*Dead Alive*), and the Grim Remnants (*Pumpkinhead*).
WEB http://www.magicnet.net/~tkearns /horror.html

Horror in Literature Lurking within Dr. Casey's Cabinet, the Horror in Literature page provides the horror addict with excerpts from recent novels, author's bibliographies, and the top 100 horror books.
WEB http://www.cat.pdx.edu/~caseyh /horror/book.html

Horror in the Movies We all know that if characters in horror films practiced a little common sense, the genre might be lost forever. Along those lines, this page offers up the Horror Movie Character's Survival Guide which presents such tips as "Do not take (or borrow) anything from the dead," "If you're running from a monster, expect to trip or fall down at least twice, more if you're female," and "Stay away from certain geographical locations…: Amityville, Elm Street, Transylvania, Nilbog (God help you if you recognize this one), the Bermuda Triangle, or any small town in Maine or Massachusetts." In addition to some good humor, Horror in the Movies provides links to horror movies trailers on the World Wide Web, a horror star's list, and FAQs for *Hellraiser* and *Friday the 13th*.
WEB http://www.cat.pdx.edu/~caseyh /horror/movie.html

The Night Gallery Dedicated to horror sights and sounds and all things rude and repulsive, The Night Gallery is a comprehensive horror site. The Horror Digest keeps you abreast of all the latest thrillers, writers, and monsters. Masters of Terror archives biographies of the site maintainer's favorite horror film actors (including Karloff and Lugosi). If it's the blood-curdling shrieks that keep you hooked on horror films, take a listen to

the Scream of the Week. Be forewarned, you may have to wade through some horrid, though not directly horror-related pages, like The Rude Things in My Fridge and Fartology. If that's not scary enough, try to flee and be cast down to the Unofficial Brady Bunch Homepage.
WEB http://www.wbm.ca/users /kgreggai/indexa.html

Three Idiots' Guide to Horror Three idiots who have nothing better to do than watch splatter films all day long share what they have learned with you. Should you desire to become as engrossed in the genre as they are, they've made easy to avoid dry films with reviews of movies and videos, and even a few books and hot links thrown in for good measure.
WEB http://www.horror.com

▶ CLIVE BARKER

A Story With No Title, A Street With No Name You've read Clive Barker, you've loved Clive Barker... now here's your chance to write like him, and have your contribution posted on the World Wide Web. Clive started the story (it's only three paragraphs) and the continuation has stretched across five episodes, with two branches. Be like Clive.
WEB http://kspace.com/KM/spot.sys /Barker/pages/piece2.html

alt.books.clive-barker Brad wants to know what people think of Barker's latest book, Sacrament. Amy and Nicholas (the former keeper of the World Wide Web of Lost Souls) go back and forth on Nicholas' perceived greed. Jake wants to know what "Jesus wept" at the end of Hellraiser means. All told, this newsgroup is well-focused, well-written, and filled with indidual and opionated voices. Drawbacks? It's a spamfest, so much of the discussion is disrupted by those who complain about that particular Hormel product (spamming, themselves, to nine or ten newsgroups!) Clive's admirers must pay a visit to this group—it's a necessity.
USENET alt.books.clive-barker

Animal Life Here's a whole Clive Barker short story, absolutely free. Who says being a netizen has no benefits? It's an odd tale about an earthquake and a talking dog named Duffy, but don't let that deter you from being the first on your block to read it.
WEB http://www.darkcarnival.com /jan96/animal_life.html

The Books of Cyber-Blood Of all the cyber-coined words, this has to be the cyber-strangest... does cyberblood run through cyberveins? Where were we? Oh, yes, this unofficial Clive Barker Web site. It's a very nice one, even if the introductory text is a little, well, cyber-gothic. There are extensive Hellraiser and Lord of Illusions links, but plenty of the sites listed here relate to Clive's written words or the man himself. A lovely, if cyberbloody, collection.
WEB http://www.afn.org/~afn15301 /bocb.html

The Clive Barker Anthology Don't miss this guide to all the books everyone's favorite scary Liverpudlian has written. It treks the gory trail from The Books of Blood to Everville—providing plot descriptions, excerpts from the book jackets, and photos of the covers so potential readers of the books can easily find them.
WEB http://www.siue.edu/~pbute /clive/clive.html

Clive Barker Biography From his early start in the fringe theater of London to his recent children's book The Thief of Always, this bio-in-brief outlines the career of creepy Clive. You'll also find a literature bibliography, a filmography, and various other horrific pointers.
WEB http://www.cat.pdx.edu/~caseyh /horror/director/barkbio.html

Clive Barker Lost Souls The official Clive Barker fan club, the Lost Souls post a newsletter and provide an extensive calendar of book signing sites for the real live Clive. A gallery of Clive's art provides visual stimulation. Plus, horror fans will find interviews with Barker con-

ducted by the Lost Souls under the Confessions topic, ongoing online contests (when last seen, the Damnation Game,) and fan fiction. Joining the Lost Souls costs $25 for the year, and will bring bountiful joy in the form of *Lost Souls Magazine* and the *Lost Souls Newsletter*, a signed 8X10 from Barker, and even a Lost Souls Club Pin. The best part of this site, though, is the Lament Configuration, a ring of sites put up by Clive Barker fans, and linked together by unified icons.
WEB http://www.clivebarker.com

Clive Barker Quote of the Week The title says it all. On a recent week, the quote was as follows: "I don't want sanity if sanity is what comes out of the television. I don't want sanity if sanity is a world without miracles, a world without the possibility of transformations. I don't want sanity if sanity is politics, economics and mortgages, and learning to live with the neighbors." Visit again for other words of wisdom.
WEB http://www.afn.org/~afn15301 /clivequote.html

Clive Barker, the True King of Horror If Clive is the king, then this is his kingdom. The first thing visitors to this fan page will see is an excellent color picture of Barker posing ominously with one of his paintings. Major news is highlighted next, followed by biographical information and Barker's mailing address. After writing a letter or two, visitors simply must follow the blinking signs to Clive Barker pictures and links.
WEB http://users.aol.com/barnabas01 /barker1.htm

Hell's Handbook A page from the journal, known as *The Devil's Handbook*, as well as a look inside the mind of Clive Barker, who began all this craziness with one novella, *The Hellbound Heart*.
WEB http://www.extratv.com/pres3 /hellbk.htm

The Hellbound Heart Encyclopedia Fans of one of Clive Barker's scariest books will appreciate this guide to *The Hell-*bound Heart*. Characters, things, places, and times are all listed in extensive detail, complete with sound clips and photos of Barker artwork. Return to the home page for similar guides to the *Hellraiser* series.
WEB http://www-personal.umich.edu /~rexerm/hell/encyc/HBH.html

The Hellbound Web Your complete guide to Hell on the Net. In addition to an all-encompassing *Hellraiser* link list, this site contains much original information. The Complete Hellraiser Encyclopedia has entries from the Angel of Suffering to Ways to Summon the Cenobites. Hellraiser Connections traces the relationship of the films to various corners of popular culture, such as the music of Nine Inch Nails ("Sanctified" is an account of Dr. Channard's experiences with Julia in *Hellbound*), *Star Trek: Deep Space Nine* (*Hellraiser* actors Andrew Robinson and Terry Farrell both have major roles in the series), and *A Clockwork Orange* (In *Hellraiser*, the Cottons live at 55 Lodovico Street and the system uses the "Ludovico Technique" on Alex in order to suppress his violent nature). Audio, image, and movies galleries round out this site.
WEB http://www-personal.umich.edu /~rexerm/hell

Hellraiser FAQ Answers the questions on the tongues of *Hellraiser* hounds everywhere, filling in the gaps that some scripted, but unfilmed or cut scenes left in the minds of fans. What's the address of the house? What does the hall of mirrors mean? Who is the person who writes "I am in hell… help me"? How were the four films originally intended to be played? This insider FAQ also provides trivia from the film foursome. For instance, skinless Julia and Frank were played by different actors than their human twins, and Butterball's glasses hide his eyes, which are sewn shut.
WEB http://www.cat.pdx.edu/~caseyh /horror/hellraiser/index.html

Hellraiser Homepage "Is it the pain? Is it the suffering? Tell me, what brings you

to this place? Is it your curiosity? Or is it for the pleasure? The pleasure that you get as your flesh is being torn apart. The pleasure you get as the blood runs down upon your body. Is it the fascination? The fascination with the darkness of your mind, the darkness of your soul. Now, I will give you more of what you want, more suffering, more Hellraiser..." Quite a build-up for a simple list of links. But they're the best links. So, no tears please, it's a waste of good suffering.
WEB http://pages.prodigy.com /hellraiser/hell.htm

Hellraiser IV: Bloodlines It turns out the Cenobites are aliens—now there's an original idea for a movie in the middle of the 1990s! Pinhead stills and trailers from the fourth in the series, straight from Miramax.
WEB http://www.miramax.com /dlpages/hellradl.html

Hellraiser IV: Bloodlines There's one thing you can say for ol' Pinhead: he's persistent. First, you couldn't keep him in Hell. Now, he stalks a family through four generations of terror. This page provides a plot summary for the 200-year quest, the latest of Pinhead's exploits.
WEB http://www.transatlanticent .com/hellraiser.html

The Hellraiser Page What is it about the Hellraiser movies and their explorations of the further regions of pain and suffering that attracts so many? For the owner of this site, the atmosphere, the riddles and questions from the past, and the dignity with which the Cenobites inveigle their victims. For like-minded fans of the films, this page provides several links that focus on those features.
WEB http://www.mds.mdh.se /~ent94fcg/hell.htm

Interview with Clive Barker This in-depth article, while a little too preciously written, is an enlightening window onto the world Clive Barker inhabits. And what a world. This brief conversation with the British Barker touches on "physics, evolutionary consciousness,

and alchemy." Somehow this is all synthesized into an impressive profile of a nice Liverpudlian bloke named Clive, who just happens to like S/M.
WEB http://cgi-bin.iol.ie/hotpress /archive/iss13951/clivebar.htm

Kaleidospace Spotlight: Clive Barker Clive's the artist-in-residence in Kaleidospace, but don't expect a focus on only his surreal drawings and paintings. You'll also find collaborative fiction, a biography, and video clips from Candyman. And of course, there are eerie images like "Susannah Becomes a Dragon"—guaranteed to send delicious shivers down your spine.
WEB http://kspace.com/KM/spot.sys /Barker/pages/piece1.html

The Lament Configuration How to explain the box? It's like a Rubik's Cube with an incredibly dark side. The puzzle box featured in the Hellraiser films is called Lemarchand's box, constructed by a master craftsman. The movies refer to it as the Lament Configuration, which is a way to raise Hell, literally. The riddle associated with the box is that if you solve the seemingly impossible puzzle, your any whim and pleasure will be satisfied. You will be taken to the boundaries of your pleasure, and beyond. It's the beyond you should be worried about. You'll also find an explanation of the Elysium Configurations—a lattice of light which counters the effect of the Lament Configuration.
WEB http://www.hooked.net/~faust666 /index.html

Lord of Illusions Trust nothing but your fear... and your QuickTime movie player, when you download these clips from Lord of Illusions.
WEB http://www.dnx.com/reeltalk /promo/lordofillusions.html

Lord of Illusions Scott Bakula takes a quantum leap into the body of Harry D'Amour, a New York private detective on the case in the latest from the Lord of the B-movies, Clive Barker. This MGM/UA site includes the transcript of

an online conference with both Barker and Bakula.
WEB http://www.mgmua.com/lord

Movieweb: Lord of Illusions "Between what can be seen and what must be feared / Between what lives and what never dies / Between the light of truth and the darkness of evil / Lies the future of terror." Between hype and hoke, Clive Barker introduces his latest horror/thriller here. Movieweb houses a cyberarchive of sights and sounds from the film.
WEB http://movieweb.com/movie /lordillusions

Original Clive Barker Artwork Scary. Disturbing. Just plain gross. Barker's artwork is all this and what's more, it's really good. If Barker weren't so talented in other areas, he could surely make it as a sci-fi illustrator alone. Don't miss the screaming naked man with what look like exploding nipples all over his body. It'll keep you awake all night.
WEB http://ns.utech.net/users 10004/barker.htm

OUTline's Interview with Clive Barker Clive Barker came out publicly in *Ten Percent Magazine* in early 1995, although many of his fans were entirely aware of his homosexuality before that. It's hard to miss in his work, filled as it is with alternative sexuality and homo-erotic situations. This well-written interview deals mostly with Barker's sexuality as it relates to his work.
WEB http://www.suba.com/~outlines /september/clive.html

The Ritual Alk of Pinhead An ode to everyone's favorite Cenobite chief in verse.
WEB http://www.theshaman.com /pinhead.html

UnderScope Magazine's Interview with Clive Barker UnderScope, a media review zine, conducted this apparently brief interview with Barker a few months back. It goes beyond the usual background and plumbs the daily habits of the man who won't use a typewriter and yet can scare modern audiences to death. Also included in the article are Barker's views on censorship, music, and the horror genre.
WEB http://www.hallucinet.com /underscope/clive.html

The Unofficial Clive Barker Home Page Unofficial fan sites are often better than official sites. We don't know why that is, we just know that this Clive Barker site will eventually go further to establish that rule, although, like the official site, it's massively under construction. Soon to come are links to books, movies (some already in place), a personal history, stories, and poetry. Clive Barker really is a modern, twisted version of the Renaissance man, and this site focuses on him with the wide-angle lens he requires.
WEB http://www.cs.uidaho.edu /~bald9464

H.P. LOVECRAFT

A Cthulhu Hymnal A collection of odes, songs, hymns, psalms, ballads and rhymes in honor of the great old one, from "Be Bop Cthulhu" and "Cthulhu of Ages" to "We're Slimey, We're Squishy" and "Who's the Elder God We Fear?"
WEB http://www.physics.wisc.edu /~shalizi/cthulhu-hymnal.html

alt.horror.cthulhu The primary news-group for Lovecraft lovers includes discussion of the Cthulhu Mythos, as well as Cthulhu collectibles and role-playing games which have sprung up around the frightful, fictional creature.
USENET alt.horror.cthulhu
FAQ: WEB http://www.primenet.com /~dloucks/hplpage.html

alt.necronomicon Although someone finally got around to correcting this misspelling in the name (it was alt.necromicon for much too long), the traffic to this newsgroup, theoretically devoted to discussion of the notorious *Necronomicon*, remains sparse.
USENET alt.necronomicon

Beyond Books: H.P. Lovecraft in the Movies Despite the contention on this page that Lovecraft is rolling in his grave over film adaptations of his eldritch work because "some things man was not meant to view," this site makes it easy to find the nearly 20 movie versions made, from *The Haunted Palace* (1963) to *In the Mouth of Madness* (1995) and send ol' H.P. a-spinning.
WEB http://www.teleport.com /~beyond/HPL/index.htm

Chronological List of Lovecraft's Tales A complete and chronological list of the more than 100 horror tales of Lovecraft as well as a list of books in which you can find them. There's enough here to keep you frightened for years.
WEB http://www.primenet.com /~dloucks/hpltales.html

Cthulhu for President Home Page Why vote for a lesser evil when you can vote for the great old one? this page asks. Taking a tongue-in-cheek approach to the tentacled terror, this site includes a policy and platform page and vends Cthulhu fish and bumper stickers.
WEB http://www.cthulhu.org/jmc

Cthulhu on the Web Links to everyone's favorite fiendish cephalopod on the Web, from the *Call of Cthulhu* and the Cthulhu Hymnal to "Cthulhu is My Friend" and Cthulhu for President.
WEB http://www.contrib.andrew.cmu .edu/usr/lw2j/list.html#cthulhu

H.P. Lovecraft Brief bios of Howard Phillips Lovecraft, one of the twentieth century masters of the Gothic tale of terror, and a briefer list of links.
WEB http://marlowe.wimsey.com/~rshand /streams/scripts/lovecraft.html

H.P. Lovecraft Image Gallery The very visual fiction of H.P. Lovecraft inspired countless artists to delve into the darker sides of their creativity and sometimes into madness. This site displays the more hard-to-find H.P.-inspired images. Some of the works on digital show include *The Great Cthulhu, At the Moun-*

tains of Madness, and *Wormskull.*
WEB http://crow.acns.nwu.edu:8082/hpl

H.P. Lovecraft Page One fan's hyper-homage to H.P. Lovecraft, consisting of the photos he took of Lovecraft's grave and the Phillips' house in Providence, the burying ground in Arkham, Mass., and the Pickman family monument in Salem.
WEB http://www.lehigh.edu/pv02 /public/www-data/hpl.html

H.P. Lovecraft Page Best known for his Cthulhu Mythos series describing ordinary New Englanders' encounters with horrific beings of extraterrestrial origin, Donovan Loucks professes that Lovecraft's voluminous correspondence in fact may have been his greatest achievement. Loucks' site includes quotes from those many letters regarding the fictional tomes mentioned in Lovecraft's works, a bestiary of the creatures of the Cthulhu Mythos, a travelogue and photos from Loucks' trip to pay tribute to the master of terror, and a page dispelling misconceptions surrounding the man and the Mythos.
WEB http://www.primenet.com/~dloucks /hplpage.html

The Lovecraft Ledger This page, posing as a fictional front page with the headline "Rhode Island Recluse Rattles Readers!," is actually a cyberad from Del Rey for a new collection of classic stories from Providence's most prolific master of the macabre, *The Dream Cycle of H.P. Lovecraft: Dreams of Terror And Death,* the sequel to *Bloodcurdling Tales of Horror and the Macabre.*
WEB http://www.randomhouse.com /delrey/lovecraft

Lovecraft's Necronomicon As with anything written about the fictional *Necronomicon,* this page should be taken with a proverbial grain of salt. But fans of Lovecraftian fiction may find the supposed references to the *Necronomicon* eerily entertaining.
WEB http://marlowe.wimsey.com/rshand /streams/scripts/necronomicon.html

▶ ANNE RICE

About Anne Rice Many fans of Anne Rice fiction are as enchanted with her as they are her characters. This site is devoted to Anne Rice, the public persona. Rice seems to welcome her fans into her life with rather open arms, with information on her house on First St. in New Orleans, her biography, and her opinions on Hollywood, anonymity, her critics, and her mainstream appeal. Even the trivia gets personal: Anne's favorite candy is a Symphony bar.
WEB http://www.personal.psu.edu /users/l/m/lms5/aboutar.html

alt.books.anne-rice From the FAQ: "a.b.a-r, where the women are women, the men are occasionally women (don't ask), and the chickens are frightened." The members here alternately refer to themselves as Anne's Children, Rice-cakes, the Great Family, and Darling Dears and discuss everything from the sexual undertones in Rice's vampire novels to sexual overtones in her erotic fiction to offerings of their own speculative fan fiction.
USENET alt.books.anne-rice
FAQ: **WEB** http://www.nwceter.com /ar/faq.htm#2.

The Anne Rice FAQ The more fervent fans of the Vampire Chronicles may not want to discover that Anne doesn't really believe in vampires, but it's all here in hypertext. She does, however, allow for the existence of ghosts and witches. In addition to providing information on Anne Rice resources on the Web, this FAQ also answers such questions as "Why doesn't Anne write about characters who aren't white?" (she says she's not sure what they would think or feel) and "Are all of Anne's vampires gay?" (They are, by nature, bisexual.)
WEB http://www.nwcenter.com/ar/faq.htm

The Anne Rice Home Page All things Anne Rice. Whether you're drawn by the lure of LeStat or you've followed the adventures of the Mayfair witches, you're sure to find something to suit your fancy. Vampires and mortals alike can sink their teeth into info on all books by Rice, including those written under the names A.N. Roquelaure and Anne Rampling.
WEB http://vader.nkn.net/dave/rice.html

Anne Rice Links As the title says, links to Queen Anne on the Web as well as non-Ricean vampire sites.
WEB http://users.aol.com/barnabas01 /annerice.htm

Anne Rice Mailing List If you are looking for a place to discuss your fear that your reclusive neighbors are actually vampires or if you are looking for general discussion of the blood-sucking creatures, this is not the list for you. However, if what fascinates you is specifically the work of Anne Rice (including her Vampire Chronicles), then you've found a home. With 600 members, the mail load may be heavy, but if you're a true Rice scholar, that's just what you're craving—besides blood, that is.
EMAIL listserv@psuvm.psu.edu ✍ *Type in message body:* subscribe annerice <your full name>

ARBOOKS Mailing List The mailing list set up to discuss all of Anne Rice's fiction, but focuses on the Vampire Chronicles, specifically the sexual orientation of LeStat.
EMAIL listserv@psuvm.psu.edu ✍ *Type in message body:* subscribe arbooks <your full name>

Commotion Strange *Commotion Strange* is Anne Rice's newsletter to her fans, complete with her own frequent use of caps and her typos (or what she refers to as her "unique spelling"), and you'll find a few issues posted here. More timely information includes news about the mistress of vampires herself, such as the answering machine she has set up to leave messages to her flock of fans; the latest on the books, and interviews with, and essays by, Rice.
WEB http://ecosys.drdr.virginia.edu /~jsm8f/commotion.html

Guide to the Children of Darkness
Focusing on Rice's Vampire Chronicles, the pages contain vampire family trees, vampire law, the Talamasca, LeStat's comments on the series, and letters from a vampire. All a self-respecting bloodsucker could need, really.
WEB http://www.maths.tcd.ie/pub/vampire/intro.html

The Web of Anne Rice Those caught up in the web of Anne Rice's writing will want to check out this guide to the Goth queen on the Web. An FAQ; vital stats, the newsgroups, and mailing lists; information on all of her series including The Vampire Chronicles, The Beauty Series, and *The Lives of the Mayfair Witches*; and an image gallery from the movie version of *Interview With The Vampire*.
WEB http://www.nwcenter.com/ar/index.htm

> **AMERICAN GOTHIC**

American Gothic "Never thought *X-Files* would be reduced to just an opening act," writes one early fan of the short-lived series directed by Sam Raimi. If you've never been to the forum, you can follow the life of the series with the posts: First, anticipation. Second, celebration of the genius of the show. Finally, desperation and anger over the "bad news" of the program being dropped. Discussion still continues about—surprise—the show coming back to CBS.
AMERICA ONLINE *keyword* fictional→tv→Message Boards→Current Television Shows→List Topics→American Gothic

American Gothic Sam Raimi, the man wholly responsible for bringing the *Evil Dead* films into the world, brings us a truly creepy television show that is part *Needful Things*, part *Rosemary's Baby*, part *Village of the Damned*, part *Ghost*, and part *Twin Peaks*. But the strangest thing about *American Gothic* is that Shaun Cassidy is the creator/writer/producer. Da doo run run run da doo run run. This is one of the two official pages for the show, and it's a hum dinger.

Character profiles with images, two interactive mystery games, and a forum with surpassingly heavy flow. Most of the posts are desperate, last-minute panic attacks from the shows would-be saviors, but there are also interesting discussions on the nature of evil, and weird threads between people who may or may not actually believe they are the characters in the show.
WEB http://www.mca.com/tv/gothic

American Gothic A great collection of character profiles, images and quotes.
WEB http://qld.nationale.com.au/~ricky/AG.htm

American Gothic Apparel T-shirts, caps, and mugs with the *AG* logo, Merlyn's famous last words and Lucas's creed: "Conscience is just the fear of getting caught." Could be worth big bucks someday—if the series stays canceled.
WEB http://www.art-vision.comamgothic.shtml

American Gothic Mailing List You know, it's not nobody that makes anybody do anything they don't wanna do in the first place. It's Sheriff Lucas Buck, that's Buck, with a "B," gets the lions share of the attention on this mailing list, naturally. Apart from the rants to save the show, most of the mail comes from people who either want to be him or be with him in the biblical sense. There's even a group of women called Buck's Broads who have pledged themselves to eternal damnation in his arms. This is a very high flow ML, and it rarely goes off topic. People discuss the new relationship between Caleb and Matt, ponder the exact nature of Lucas's powers (is he just a really nasty mortal, an actual demon, or the devil himself?), and note the sexual tension, subtle and otherwise, between all of the characters all of the time—Lucas and Gail, Gail and Matt, Matt and Selena, Selena and Lucas, Lucas and Matt? Gail and Selena? Selena and Caleb!—it's an equal opportunity smolder-fest. From the looks of it, this short-lived show is going to garner cult status akin to *Twin Peaks*.

EMAIL majordomo@stargame.org ✍ *Type in message body:* subscribe agothic

CBS: American Gothic It's too late for salvation (probably). By the time you read this, *American Gothic* will most likely be over—too dark, too strange, and too unsettling for prime time consumption. But *AG* lives on, online. This other official site is quite nice, although apart from a tail-end episode guide it hasn't been updated since the show debuted. The page has sound clips, videos, and a number of excellent images. There's even an interview with Raimi and Cassidy. "Yeah, I think [Lucas is] a very powerful individual. But I think the thing for [him] is not to use any of his powers. And the real victory for Lucas Buck is to take an individual and destroy them, bring them down to their lowest level from the weaknesses within themselves. That's really a great victory for him. To take someone who has the sin of pride and use it against themselves to bring about their fall." **WEB** http://www.cbs.com/ag

The Trinity Guardian This newspaper is indebted to the Fulton County Sheriff's Dept. (Lucas Buck, Sheriff) for its kind support. Who isn't? A great read, with top stories on the precious few summer episodes, a chamber of commerce section updating fans on the campaign to save the show, a society page that offers info and snapshots for all the happenings in Trinity (i.e., an episode guide), and a gossip column where you can hear about a dozen quotes from each episode of *American Gothic*. Just remember, folks, all guilt is relative, loyalty counts, and never let your conscience be your guide. **WEB** http://www.best.com:90/~owls /AG/coc.html

WWB—American Gothic A surprisingly large index for such a quiet little town. You can also download the theme song and Merlyn's maddeningly irritating chant from the first episode: "Someone's at the door, someone's at the door, someone's at the door…." There are lots

of links to "save the show" pages as well. With a little bit of luck, and a big fat miracle, the show could come back in the fall. What kind of deal would you make with the Devil's right-hand man to see a permanent resurrection? Everything has a price, my friend. **WEB** http://www.global.org/bfreed /heckifiknow/gothic.html

▶ THE CRAFT

The Craft What do you get when you combine *Teen Witch*, *Clueless*, and a second-hand copy of the *Big Book of Wicca*? You get *The Craft*, of course. It was a big budget movie, but it may someday become a cult classic like *Faster Pussycat! Kill! Kill!* It has that whole sexy-women-in-cool-outfits-doing-bad-things-to-bad-men thing going for it. This is a typical promo page with images, sounds, character synopses, production notes, and videos. **WEB** http://www.spe.sony.com /Pictures/SonyMovies/features /craft.html

▶ THE CROW

The Crow A cult movie in the making even before Brandon Lee's mysterious death, *The Crow* has had an obsessive following since its comic book days. This enormous fan page covers both *The Crow* and its 1996 sequel, *The City of Angels*. The script to the first film is only one of the items you can pick up on the page for the original—there are bios on the cast and crew, quotes, sound bites and pics, trivia and goofs, and soundtrack info. The sequel page has less information, understandably, but offers a collection of articles on the upcoming release, and gives a brief plot synopsis. **WEB** http://www.machnet.com/crow

The Crow: City of Angels "People once believed that when someone dies, a crow carries their soul to the land of the dead. But sometimes, just sometimes, the Crow can bring the soul back to put the wrong things right. I thought that Eric was the last. I never imagined there

would be another…" Vincent Perez (*Cyrano DeBergerac*, *Queen Margo*), Mia Kershner (*Exotica*, *Love and Human Remains*), and Iggy Pop (you had better know who he is!) star in the new incarnation, which promises to be a blast, even without the undertow of morbidity caused by Brandon Lee's tragic death. This is an excellent site, with a page dedicated to the cast and crew, a slew of video clips and images (check out the tattoo page, now that's devotion!). But the best thing here is the Crow BB, where fans pay a small tribute to the original, argue over the sequel's potential, share their feelings on Lee's death, and reveal their own experiences with undying love. Some fans get just a wee bit dramatic: "His eyes are like a dove's and as blue as the raging sea. His skin is as white as the wings of an angel and his hair is as dark as the shadows in a heart filled with despair. His voice is the whisper on the wind, while his spirit is the weeping willow by the lake filled with blood. 'Why,' I ask, 'do you cry?' When he turns to me, I know that I'm looking into the face of love."
WEB http://www.thecrow.com

In A Lonely Place—The Crow Homepage This is the most comprehensive *Crow* page on the Net, covering the comic and both films in disturbing, dark detail. Get images and plot synopses for the first graphic novel *Inertia*, and info on the newest release *Dead Time*. Coverage of the original movie includes sound files, the original script and all the changes that made it into the finished product. Coverage of *City of Angels* is not so comprehensive, with only a handful of downloadable vids, but there are other places online for a better fix. The best features here are the enormous image archives, not only from the original film, but from the comics as well, and lyric sheets to the entire soundtrack which includes such luminaries as The Cure, NIN, Violent Femmes, Rage Against the Machine, The Rollins Band, Pantera, and, of course, Jane Siberry.
WEB http://pulsar.cs.wku.edu /~nothing/crow.html

Mashua's Madness Crow Page "In a world without justice, one man was chosen to protect the innocent. There is a legend that when a soul can't rest, a crow can bring that soul back from the dead, to seek justice and make the wrong things right." While this site gives better coverage to the sequel, with animated images, overview and plot synopses, articles, and cast and crew info, it also houses an excellent photo gallery of the original.
WEB http://iccu6.ipswich.gil.com.au /~jmac/crow1.html

▶ **DARK SHADOWS**

Dark Shadows "The original *Dark Shadows* is a fun show to watch. I like seeing if I can catch the camera messing up from time to time. I remember when it hit a mirror and you could see everyone in the background… LOL." This commentary on the *Dark Shadows* and a little more is available in this surprisingly quiet America Online forum.
AMERICA ONLINE *keyword* fantasy→ Message Boards→Light From a Tube→List Topics→Dark Shadows

Dark Shadows For those so inclined, this is a wonderful place to be weird. Talk to other bizarros and creatures from the dark side at this meeting place for devotees of the spooky vampire soap *Dark Shadows*. Take the Bat Quiz or get a free Internet I Ching reading. Of course, there are also mundane episode summaries, a still-photo archive, fan fiction, and a shop-op for collectibles and videos.
WEB http://www.epix.net/~jphill /shadows.html

Dark Shadows Less baroque than Barnabas would have liked, this is still one of the better *DS* pages out there, mainly because of a creative set of links to bat quizzes, *DS* action figures, online I Ching, and the weather in Bangor. There is also a sizable amount of multimedia, including images from the oft-ignored 1991 resurrection of the show, which starred Ben Cross. It really wasn't such a bad show—no fake British accents, no

rubber bats on strings.
web http://users.aol.com/barnabas01
/dark.htm

Dark Shadows Home Page Apart from a couple of sound clips and some very amusing Top Ten Lists (Top Ten Pet Peeves of Barnabas Collins) and life lessons (If things go wrong, get sedated), this is a resource guide to all things fanatic, and mostly offline—convention reps, newsletters, books, videos, and a handful of links to other pages.
web http://www.natural-innovations
.com/boo/ds.html

Dark Shadows Supernatural Page For the somewhat dim, this page offers background on the general sources that the characters were based on. For instance, Barnabas was based on—don't tell me, don't tell me, it's on the tip of my tongue... Dracula? And Adam was based on, hmm, let me see now, uh, was it, could it be... Frankenstein? For those who already know to put their socks on first, the page offers a little quiz on the literary allusions in *DS*. What lofty tomes did *Dark Shadows* rip o... er, pay homage to? *The Picture of Dorian Grey*, *Wuthering Heights*, *The Cthulhu Mythos*, and many more. There are lots of little media gifts on this page, and a nice piece of fan fiction. But the only truly terrifying thing is the background music, another 1982 Samsung electric organ tinkling out the theme song endlessly—it won't hypnotize you, but it might make your ears bleed.
web http://members.aol.com/darkk
shad/super/natural.htm

IFDS The International Friends of Dark Shadows have a dream. "The museum will be housed in a large warehouse. The outside will have a full size cut-out billboard with Collinwood painted on it... We can simulate night and storms all the time..." And so on and so on ad infinitum. The Project Team has applied for not-for-profit status, and hopes to open museum doors in 1998. If you take *DS* this seriously, by all means, visit this appropriately elaborate fan page and

donate some of that long-held family fortune to the immortal preservation of your beloved program.
web http://www.europa.com/~ifds

▶ EVIL DEAD

alt.cult-movies.evil-deads Discussion here extends beyond the *Evil Dead* movies to include talk of other Sam Raimi (*Darkman*) and Bruce Campbell (*Briscoe County*) projects, both joint and solo.
usenet alt.cult-movies.evil-deads

The Army of Darkness DOOM Page Be Ash and protect the town of Arthur and make your way back to S-Mart in this version of DOOM. But don't rev up your chainsaw yet—it's still in production. In the meantime, you can meet the DOOM team, check out the project outline, and keep up to date with the latest status reports on the game.
web http://sch-www.uia.ac.be/u/maes
/aoddoom.html

The Evil Dead If you think you're having a bad day, strap a chainsaw onto that stump of an arm and check out these shots of Ash after a group of teenagers unleashed an evil spirit in the woods of Michigan. Consider it a not-so-gentle reminder that unless you're being dismembered, it could always be worse.
web http://xray.chm.bris.ac.uk:8000/naj
/evildead.html

The Evil Dead Homepage What is Ash's last name? What the hell is a "fake Shemp"? And what is with the alternate endings to *Army of Darkness*? Calm down, take a deep breath, try not to awaken the unspeakable evil in the forest, and look up the answers here. An FAQ, the Rumor Pit (Will there be an *Evil Dead IV*?), the latest from the mouths of Sam Raimi and Bruce Campbell, and even the logo from the fictional S-Mart make this one of the more comprehensive sites devoted to some of the campiest horror movies ever.
web http://members.aol.com
/roysteeth/edindex.html

Exit 13: Evil Dead Fans of the cult classic movies will take this exit off the information autobahn to fill up on .GIFs, .JPEGs, and .WAV files from all three films, *Evil Dead*, *Evil Dead 2: Dead by Dawn*, and *Army of Darkness*, with separate multimedia galleries for each. They'll also find a comprehensive list of links to other *Evil Dead* and Bruce Campbell sites.
WEB http://www.daze.com/exit13/evil

Robert's Evil Dead Fan Page Fans of the one-two, Raimi-Campbell punch thrown in the Evil Dead trilogy can vote for their favorite *ED* flick here, get Bruce Campbell's email address, and send or browse through tidbits of trivia on the Raimi movies. Those who haven't yet experienced the unwittingly slapstick gore fests which are the *Evil Dead* can check out the plot summaries before they decide to make it a Blockbuster night. (Three Stooges fans are in for a treat.)
WEB http://www.europa.com /~rew1977/dead/dead.htm

► FOREVER KNIGHT

alt.tv.forever-knight Less debate and discussion than simple Q&A (What's the name of the vampire dog in "Blind Faith"? When is LaCroix referred to as The General?). There's also a fair amount of merchandise info, but on the whole the most interesting thing you're likely to find out here is that Nigel Bennet did a commercial for Oatmeal Crisp. Mmmmm good, pour on the O Negative!
USENET alt.tv.forever-knight

The Cousinly Page Let's face it, LaCroix is inarguably the coolest character on the show. Denounce his utter lack of politics. Spit upon his moral structure. Chastise his parenting technique (he killed both his kids, sometimes more than once!). Make fun of his receding hairline. But evil is cool, and you know it. LaCroix accepts what he is and enjoys it. He knows self-pity is for suckers. He owns a chic nightclub and a radio station, which is a lot more glamorous than being a cop. He has a voice that could slip into the airtight vault at the coroners' office, thaw the dead, and have them whispering Anaïs Nin poems to each other within five minutes. He has something that no one else in the entire city of Toronto seems to have—a sense of humor. And finally (spoiler alert), he's the only one who didn't commit suicide, get murdered, or die tragically in the end, and as we all know, the last one standing wins the game. The Cousins are LaCroix groupies who, in the realms of almost-role-playing and fan fiction, are vampires that don't need therapy. This page holds tons of Uncle LaCroix's quotes, all his radio monologues, and details the Cousins' nefarious activities.
WEB http://www.glue.umd.edu /~sdragon/cerk.html

Dee's Forever Knight Page "He was brought across in 1228. Preyed on humans for their blood. Now he wants to be mortal again." Who would have thought that a show more aptly named "Vampire Cop" could have garnered this much obsessive attention? This is a properly cyberoque page with in-depth bios linking to actor homage pages, several site indices, and impressive image and sound galleries, though they don't have much from the last episode. To have lived in the most glorious cities in the world at their height of decadence and splendor, and then to die in 1996, in Toronto—now that's tragedy.
WEB http://www.realnetnw.com/~dmd /fk.html

The First Unofficial Forever Knight Page An amazing collection of features that borders on the obsessive. OK, forget borders, it takes a flying leap without a bungee cord. You'll find the Show Premise, Background, Episode Guide, Known Vampires (a list of supporting characters on a liquid diet), Cast & Crew, Soundtrack, Special Effects, TPTB Addresses, Fan clubs, Conventions, and Links to Other Web sites. There's also a prominent feature on Saving the Show. If you haven't seen the last episode yet, don't read any further… Forget about saving the show, people! Take a hint!

Everybody's dead! Not just undead but dead dead! Well, except for LaCroix. Maybe he'll get a spin-off. It's over! Deal with it!
WEB http://www.hu.mtu.edu/~gjwalli /fktoc.html

Forever Knight A realm for the obsessed. Fans of the vampire series are so gung-ho that they're begging and pleading with each other for ways to contact the show's stars! The usual stuff—episode guides and questions regarding what else the performers do, is also there, however. Enter at your own risk.
AMERICA ONLINE *keyword* fictional→ tv→message boards→current television shows→list topics→Forever Knight

Forever Knight If you take the show seriously (and I mean *seriously*) this is the page for you. In the cemetery, you'll find dramatic character descriptions in Nick's voice—"Janette: Isn't she more beautiful than heaven can attest to?" But then again, this is hell. Nothing here knows a boundary—including half the Anne Rice Universe. Unfortunately for NatPackers, Perkulators and other mortal groupies, this page is vampire-exclusive. Each blood-sucker has a separate fan page. The best lair belongs, naturally, to LaCroix. It houses images, some of his more memorable monologues, and several pieces of fan fiction that lack the calm amusement usually inherent in the character, e.g.: "It was easy to shock the peasants before. I'd murder a young girl, or bare my fangs, and all would go into frantic screams. Now, mortals meticulously employ what Dr. Freud called 'defense mechanisms'; you'd like to believe it's all props. Well, do I have a surprise for you! It is called emptiness. You have carried it throughout your lives, but now I will make you face it. Primitive urges pave the way to your doom. See the darkness and look into it! Feel the coldness emanating from my breath, the stench of rotting flesh!…" Someone got up on the wrong side of the coffin this morning.
WEB http://www.ualberta.ca /~dtzatzov/knight.htm

Forever Knight Official Site This is an official Sony Pictures Entertainment page, so while it's full of useful information, it's also somewhat aloof, and you won't find the aroma of singed obsessiveness that permeates the more devoted of the fan-generated projects. You'll find a good range of show topics, biographies, background and fan clubs, but there's a decided lack of style.
WEB http://www.spe.sony.com /Pictures/tv/forever/forever.html

Forever Knighties This tribute includes the standard images, sounds, and links to fans and zines. In terms of quality, it's pretty much middle of the road, with a decent if unspectacular smattering of information, as well as a helping of absurdly huge images of the show's various actors. But the Knighties are more than fans, they are a fan faction. There is an entire world of *FK* not-quite-role-playing going on in cyberspace, and the Knighties are supporters of Nick, the hero, whose amount of existential angst is rivaled only by the number of women he almost sleeps with/brings over in any given season. Knighties have allies in the NatPack and the Perkulators, fans dedicated to Natalie and Tracy, respectively, and enemies (in a mocking, yet deeply caring sense) in The Cousins, who follow LaCroix and try to make life interesting (i.e., chaotic and dangerous) for everyone else—fan-fictionally and virtually speaking that is. There are a dozen other factions—even Screed has a page!
WEB http://www.intex.net/~perridox /knight/knight.html

Mr. Happy's Forever Knight Page There are tons of exclusive features on this page. There's the Question of the Week (Q: What would you be willing to give for a fourth *FK* season? A: I have a sister that I would gladly trade for a fourth season), soundtrack clips and lyrics, events updates, surveys, a transcript of live chat with Geraint (Q: Why was the show Forever Night canceled? Geraint: I would say that it's because it was aired simultaneously on USA Network and first run syndication and the numbers individually weren't strong enough. I think it's called cannibalism. In a way, the audience ate itself!), and images organized by *FK* factions, including the "Unnamed Faction." Apparently I wasn't the only one who thought LaCroix should have kissed Nicholas goodbye (nudge, nudge).

WEB http://mtl.net/solidarite/mrhappy /fk.htm

Sci Fi Channel: Forever Knight Some people at the station are worried. They're beginning to question Nick's mental stability. Listen to recorded conversations where he reveals to Natalie that he believes himself to "be" a small bejeweled figurine called the Black Buddha, where he asks LaCroix to take him to see an exorcist, and finally, to a terribly disturbing conversation he has with himself, in which he calls himself schizoid and mumbles something about King Crimson. Then sit down and throw back a pint or two, and check out some cast photos.

WEB http://www.scifi.com/fknight

VWB—Forever Knight So the series ended (and we mean ENDED). Don't reach for that stake just yet, you still have a lot to live for—the show is immortalized online. There are dozens of links to fan pages, mailing lists, newsgroups and media archives. Come on over to the other side—the hours are great, you get to meet lots of interesting people (Caesar, Rembrandt, Hitler), you may even get a hell hound for a companion!

WEB http://www.global.org/bfreed /heckifiknow/foreverknight.html

▶ FROM DUSK TILL DAWN

From Dusk Till Dawn RealAudio interview with the film's writer, the quirky Quentin Tarantino. Tarantino talks not only about writing *From Dusk Till Dawn*, but also about success, fame, his fans, and what's ahead.

WEB http://www.bitesite.com /new/fromdusk.html

From Dusk Till Dawn If your idea of a good movie is one in which two psychotic criminal brothers running for the border in a hijacked RV to keep Texas' finest from catching them, end up in a Mexican Bar called The Titty Twister, chock full of vampires, you're not alone. This site was set up by one of *From Dusk Till Dawn's* biggest fan(atic)s and is loaded with movie clips, still images, and sound bites from the Rodriguez-Tarantino creation.

WEB http://www.hooked.net/users /cpatubo/fdtd.html

Movie Target: From Dusk Till Dawn Blood is thicker than salsa in this Mexican vampire film from director Robert Rodriguez and writer-actor Quentin Tarantino. This multimedia site contains articles on the films, behind-the-scenes photos, video clips, and a look at the special effects crew. If you're looking to this movie for the familiarity of the cape-and-nape style of European or Ricean blood suckers, this site will straighten you out.

WEB http://www.hooked.net/~clayton /movies/from_dusk_till_dawn

Mr. Blonde's From Dusk Till Dawn Page Follow the Gecko Brothers, Seth (George Clooney) and Richie (Quentin Tarantino), as they gallivant across the Southwest and south of the border in movie clips and images of *From Dusk Till Dawn*. Mr. Blonde also provides the script of the Tex-Mex horror pic, and a transcript from MTV's interview with the propagator of *Pulp Fiction*.

WEB http://osiris.sunderland.ac.uk /~cb3gha/dusk1.htm

One of the From Dusk Till Dawn Pages Available in a PG- and R-rated version, both renderings of this site house audio and video from the vampires-meet-gangsters movie; the censored version simply excludes expletives and extra-violent and sex scenes. Both pages also include an original *From Dusk Till Dawn* Internet game.

WEB http://www.tyrell.net/~rosiefan /index.htm

The Rendezvous From Dusk Till Dawn Style A rendezvous with the fiendish film from Tarantino and Rodriguez consists of an image gallery, the complete script, and sounds from Seth, Jacob, and Santiago.
WEB http://www.li.net/~kirkg/dusk.htm

▶ HALLOWEEN

Halloween Until 1978, Halloween was just another holiday. After the masked murderer named Michael Myers came home on the big screen, it became a horror classic. This site contains info on all the *Halloween* movies and even includes the *Halloween* wanna-bes.
WEB http://ourworld.compuserve.com/homepages/Garrick_Bernard

Halloween Homepage This home page dedicated to escaped murderer Michael Myers goes beyond a basic rundown of the series of seriously scary films. It includes a news section, interviews with Daniel Farrands and Ellie Cornell, *Halloween* soundtrack info, and a fan forum.
WEB http://www.webbuild.com/~jrnyfan/index.htm

▶ KINDRED: THE EMBRACED

The Haven A hush must have come over this unholy haven when FOX first announced the cancellation of *Kindred: The Embraced*. But now the fans behind this *Kindred* site are screaming to get the show back. While patrons plead with the network head, this page continues to display an explanation of The Embraced, a chat room, and histories of the *Kindred* clans.
WEB http://www.azstarnet.com/~ong/kindred

Kindred: The Embraced A list of links to all the Web sites that remain in the wake of the *Kindred* cancellation, a continuing source of disappointment bordering on damnation for many.
WEB http://www.global.org/bfreed/heckifiknow/kindred.html

Kindred: The Embraced "Embracing" is the process by which a human becomes a part of the Kindred. Lest you think we're talking an ordinary hug here, a Kindred embrace occurs by removing—usually drinking—all the human's blood so that she dies and replacing her blood with Kindred blood. This comprehensive site explains in detail not only the Kindred and their embracing, but also includes information on individual characters, bloodlines, and the haven.
WEB http://www.kindredemb.com

▶ NIGHTMARE ON ELM ST.

A Nightmare on the Doctor's Street A collection of the good doctor's pages devoted to Freddy Krueger and the nightmare series, including his tribute to the first movie, the Freddy's Nightmares TV series page, and a Freddy Krueger musical page. A must-download: the haunting children's song. "One, two, Freddy's coming for you…" Sweet dreams.
WEB http://www.cofc.edu/~chandlec/freddy.html

A Nightmare on the Web A funhouse for Freddy fans featuring encyclopedias for each of the six films in the Craven series, images and sounds, links, and pages of *Nightmare* nuances—a map of Springwood, Ohio (a nice place to live), Nancy's diary, and the eternal Freddy vs. Jason debate.
WEB http://www-personal.umich.edu/~rexerm/nightmare/index.html

▶ TALES FROM THE CRYPT

Tales From the Crypt The official home of the Cryptkeeper, complete with an episode graveyard, the Cryptkeeper family album, and the laboratory where the HOBO crypt cam, helliday songs, and coming attractions are kept. With RealAudio and the right browser it's a full sensory experience—you'll see scary Java-animation, hear the Cryptkeeper narrate your journey through the crypt, and smell the aromatic scent of burning human flesh.
WEB http://www.cryptnet.com

CULT

HOWEVER YOU DEFINE IT, "CULT" is actually what distinguishes us from the beasts of the field. Were we interested exclusively in culture that was good for us, then our appetites would be no more advanced than those of dogs. We would scarcely qualify as having free will. For many, "cult" can be defined as the accompaniment to vital moments during rites of passage: *The Rocky Horror Picture Show* was the first time you heard the word "transsexual"; *Naked Lunch* was the book that made you realize at age 16 that there was more to words on paper than Stephen King; *The Toxic Avenger* was the first movie you had to leave Blockbuster for; and *Twin Peaks* taught you how to tie a cherry stem with your tongue. In their own weird way, these cult phenomena, and the subcultures they produced, have become institutions. God only knows what will cross the line tomorrow.

▶ CLICK PICK

Shock Cinema Run for the hills! The previously print-only guide is now online, and it's got hundreds of reviews in its library. That's great for B-movie fans, since the *Village Voice* wrote that Shock Cinema has "some of the best bizarre film commentary going... with sharp, no-nonsense verdicts." Some of the latest reviews include assessments of Pia Zadora in *Voyage of the Rock Aliens* and Timothy Leary in *Energy!!! The Movie*. If you're not looking for something specific in the archives, check of the best of the bizarre with Shock Favorites, such as *Love is a Dog from Hell* and *Blood Freak*. Demented art films, queer cinema, and musical misfires included.
WEB http://members.aol.com/shockcin /index.html

▶ MOTHERSHIPS

Alf's Cult Television It may not seem like *The Simpsons*, *The X-Files*, *Red Dwarf*, and *Mad About You* have anything in common, but they do: Alf loves them all. His home page, divided into four separate sections (one for each program), is a useful resource of links, sounds, and images from his favorite shows. But if *Mad About You* is cult, Murray is moonlighting as a short-order cook.
WEB http://www.loom.com.au/home /alf/cult_tv

alt.cult.movies Sex against a wall. Sex in swimming pools. Incestuous alien elbow sex in the bed of a handbuilt bisexual monster. Do the discussions on alt.cult.movies consistently revolve around cinematic interpretations of carnal acts in somewhat strange places? Not usually. The director's cut of *Natural Born Killers*, Ed Wood's *Plan 9 from Outer Space*, and *La Jetée*, the short that *12 Monkeys* is based on, are examples of more typical fare.
USENET alt.cult.movies

Cult Movies Charles Manson is apparently a favorite film subject, as demonstrated by the extensive list of his films collected under the Strange Videos section of Cult Movie magazine's home page. Smart businesspeople, they only put portions of the publication online, but their teaser is good stuff—an interview with artist Dave Stevens, as well as a look at the new Vampirella. (Literally. It's just a picture.) Subscription information is posted, as well.
WEB http://www.primenet.com/~orpheus /cult

Cult Movies FAQ Not your typical FAQ collection, but then again, is there anything typical about cult cinema? This is a hearty mail-order directory, with catalog, contact, and ordering information from hundreds of film and memorabilia distributors, including Far East Films, Video Oyster, and Something Weird Video.
URL gopher://wiretap.spies.com:70 /00/Library/Media/Film/cultmov.faq

The Cult Shop John Carpenter, Joel and Ethan Coen, Peter Jackson, Sam Raimi, Robert Rodriguez, Quentin Tarantino, and Kevin Smith are the featured directors at The Cult Shop. The site is also neatly divided into sections on actors—Bruce Campbell and John Turturro, for example—and the films themselves. The Cult Shop includes in-depth looks at the movies, with links to outside resources such as the Internet Movie Database. Many of the people and pictures here, though certainly more mainstream than, say, *I Spit on Your Grave*, are hard to find elsewhere online.
WEB http://lasarto.cnde.iastate.edu /Movies/Cultshop/movies/coen.html

The Cult TV Episode Guide *The A-Team*, *Absolutely Fabulous*, *Acapulco Heat*… These are just the first three listings in this incredible database of cult television shows' episode guides. Search for a specific series, or scroll through the alpabetized list of boob tube gems. That will take you right through to *The Young Rebels*, *The Zoo Gang*, and *Zorro*. It's a site for cult television fans to worship fervently.
WEB http://www.ee.ed.ac.uk/~jmd/CultTV

Cult TV Net Directory Just about every television program with a cult following has some sort of tangible presence on the Web. This Aussie site features many links to your favorite shows—including *Forever Knight*, *Highlander*, *X-Files* and *Lost in Space*—and a few you'd like to forget.
WEB http://www.ar.com.au/~jriddler /index.html

Phantom of the Movies "Dear Phantom: I am looking for a copy of the 1972 flick *Son of the Blob* to buy." The elusive Phantom answers your cult classic questions, and gives you reviews of recent film and video releases. The Phantom welcomes fans of true classics (1959's *The Great St. Louis Bank Robbery* is a feature) as well as Anime-niacs with reviews of *Ghost in the Shell* and news of the *Star Blazers* trilogy release.
WEB http://www.phantom.nyc.pipeline.com

Silicon Heaven Awooga—it's Silicon Heaven, and its creator, Chris, will help you out with more than tips on Windows 95. He's dedicated the site to cult and sci-fi television and movies, with special emphasis on *Doctor Who*, *Highlander*, *The Avengers*, and *Red Dwarf*. You'll find trivia quizzes, drinking games, fan fiction, and links for the taking.
WEB http://www.cityscape.co.uk/users/ij88

▶ DAVID LYNCH

Actors' Oeuvres For all the oddness in *Twin Peaks*, the show managed to include some show-business luminaries among its cast, including acclaimed film and stage vets such as Joan Chen, Piper Laurie, and Richard Beymer. And don't forget the fistful of new pin-ups the show created—Madchen Amick, Lara Flynn Boyle, and especially Sherilyn Fenn. This document offers a complete list of all known roles of the actors who appeared in *Twin Peaks*.
URL ftp://lutetia.uoregon.edu/pub /twin-peaks/oeuvre.actor(A-L).tp

alt.tv.twin-peaks For such a strange TV show, a rather normal group. Discussion revolves around posters of the female stars, the show's music in various software formats, and some of Lynch's other movies. Lots of talk about theories makes the debate lively and intelligent.
USENET alt.tv.twin-peaks

The Black Lodge Birds, traffic lights, psychic visions—*Twin Peaks* had it all. A list of symbols and motifs is only one of the resources you can find at this UK-based site. A must-see is the shooting script from the film, including unreleased scenes.
WEB http://www.city.ac.uk:8080/matthew /twin-peaks

David Lynch Sexy. Suggestive. Smart. Surreal. David Lynch's artwork comes across in the same stimulating way as his big screen projects do. California's *HotLava* magazine's short feature on Lynch, the artiste, showcases a small collection of his impressive photograph-

ic pieces and drawings.
WEB http://www.hotlava.com/13/lynch

The David Lynch Home Page Did you know that David Lynch turned down the opportunity to work on *Return of the Jedi*? Yep. Instead, the now influential director went to work with Francis Ford Coppola on a project called *Ronnie Rocket* that didn't get off the ground. Learn more about the man behind the myth from this developing Web site.
WEB http://www.scit.wlv.ac.uk/~cm4298 /dlynch

David Lynch Info Page He has a taste for low/middle frequency noise, dark and rotting environments, distorted characters, a polarized world (angels vs. demons, Madonnas vs. whores), and debilitating damage to the skull or brain. Is it any wonder David Lynch's films are so powerful? Facts about his career as a director, editor, actor, producer, and even composer abound.
WEB http://www.xmission.com/~jonyag /TP/Cast/David.html

The Director's Cut He's known as the "Czar of the Bizarre." He has an affinity for chocolate milk shakes. And, he's one of the most powerful, affecting filmmakers of a generation. The director of *Wild at Heart*, *Eraserhead*, and *Twin Peaks* has his life summed up in a nutshell.
WEB http://netspace.net.au/~scorsese /lynch.htm

Directory of Fan Fiction "Passion Play" and "Vanished" are some of the stories written by *Twin Peaks* fans. These and others on reserve here.
URL ftp://lutetia.uoregon.edu/pub /twin-peaks/Creative

Twin Peaks Episode Guide Remember Sept. 30, 1990, the broadcast date for the now-famous Episode 8 ("May the Giant Be With You")? This site lists all 29 episodes, with titles, airdates, plot summaries, casts, directors, and writers. If you continued watching long enough to see the final show, in which Nadine regains her senses and Donna confronts

her parents about Ben, this document will make your dreams (and your nightmares) come true.
URL ftp://lutetia.uoregon.edupub/twin -peaks/episode.guide

Log Lady Intros "Where does creamed corn figure into the workings of the universe? What really *is* creamed corn? Is it a symbol for something else?" A collection of the introductions spoken by the odd but prescient Log Lady character.
URL ftp://lutetia.uoregon.edu/pub /twin-peaks/log.lady.intros.txt

Lynch Stuff Brian's got "stuff online" for *Blue Velvet*, *Dune*, *Twin Peaks*, and *Fire Walk With Me*. His collection of audio clips—and a few links—is small, but useful.
WEB http://brian.homecom.com/~brian /lynch.html

Online Guide to Eraserhead Have you noticed the number 13 trend in the movie? Do you have problems understanding *Eraserhead* in general? Well, this Lynch devotee has written a "book" to explain the cryptic 1976 film. Henry's life with Mary and the baby might just be more comprehensible when you've filled your head with this info. Then again, maybe not.
WEB http://users.aol.com/RayWolf1 /eraser.htm

Twin Peak Quotes Cooper: "Well, my symptoms suggest the onset of malaria, but I've never felt better in my life." Promo dialogue and even entire scenes from the show that was so weird it made your teeth ache.
URL ftp://lutetia.uoregon.edu/pub /twin-peaks/twinQuotes

Twin Peaks Billed as the "Ultimate *Twin Peaks* Reference Page," this site is maintained by Jon Yager, who admits in his introduction that "over the years [he] has become obsessed with the show, and with the other works of David Lynch," and that he's planning on using his Web site to "spead the 'gospel' of

Twin Peaks." If only the page lived up to his description. It does contain a number of links, and Yager's enthusiasm is admirable, but ultimately this is little more than the same collection of links available at other *Peaks* sites.

WEB http://www.xmission.com/~jonyag /TP/Twin-Peaks.html

Twin Peaks Allusions Want to know how David Lynch and Mark Frost came up with the name "Twin Peaks?" Try these explanations on for size: "Supposedly a fairly obvious sexual reference, I hadn't heard it used before, *SPY*'s *Separated At Birth?* book (1988) commented on the "Twin (widow's) Peaks" of Bob Eubanks and Butch (Eddie Munster) Patrick... Also, Blake Edwards's 1962 thriller *Experiment In Terror* features Lee Remick as a bank clerk terrorized by a psycho into stealing from her employers. She lives in Twin Peaks (in San Francisco) and the psycho's name is Red Lynch!!" As this excerpt indicates, this is a document long on archivist's perseverance, with mini-essays on everything from Dale Cooper's name to Ben Horne's Civil War fantasies.

URL ftp://lutetia.uoregon.edu/pub /twin-peaks/allusions

Twin Peaks and the Films of David Lynch A truly dedicated fan has created the ultimate David Lynch tribute Web site. While the director's biography is handled by a link to the Internet Movie Database, the author has included loads of information on every Lynch project, including his musical work "Industrial Symphony #1: The Dream of the Broken Hearted." There are thorough descriptions of each film, as well as clips and images.

WEB http://www.mikedunn.com /index2.html

Twin Peaks FAQ Who is the dwarf? What did the letters under the fingernails mean? Who killed Laura Palmer? Helpful, and yet sometimes elusive answers from Lynch's painfully suspenseful movie and television series. For example, the aforementioned dwarf "it would

appear is the 'embodiment' of Mike/Gerard's left arm and as such, is a link to the old Mike that hunted with BOB." Not for the cynical.

WEB http://www.city.ac.uk/~cb192 /twin-peaks.faq.html.2.4

Twin Peaks Final Episode An archive of the messages that flew across the wires in the days following the broadcast of the final episode of *Twin Peaks*. Was McLachlan's acting bad? How many inside jokes were there? And did you see the guy humping the deer?

URL ftp://lutetia.uoregon.edu/pub /twin-peaks/final.episode

Twin Peaks FTP Archive "Welcome to Twin Peaks. It's one of those picturesque rural towns that reminds you of time-honored American traditions, like peace and order and homemade cherry pie." But fans know better than that. This quote is from the *Twin Peaks* press kit, just one of the resources available from this huge FTP archive. Fan fiction, images, quotes, sounds, and a timeline are also available.

URL ftp://lutetia.uoregon.edu/pub /twin-peaks

Welcome to Twin Peaks "Are you looking for secrets? Is that what this is all about? Well, maybe I can help you." A good general site, with series information and FAQ, rebroadcast schedules, cast biographies and filmographies, and an image gallery.

WEB http://pogo.wright.edu /TwinPeaks/TPHome.html

▶ WILLIAM S. BURROUGHS

The Unofficial William Burroughs Home Page What better graphic to use as a bullet on a William Burroughs Web page than a big, black gun?!? A few excerpts from Burroughs's work are available on this fan page. There's also an "FAQ"— actually a file of Burroughs's recorded works, film and video appearances, audio samples used in songs by artists such as Ravi Shankar, and an interview by Corso and Ginsberg.

WEB http://www.peg.apc.org/~fire
horse/wsb/wsb.html

William S. Burroughs Kerouac
described him as "Tall, 6 foot 1,
strange, inscrutable because ordinary
looking (scrutable), like a shy bank clerk
with a patrician thinlipped cold
bluelipped face." This, and other biographical facts from a great Web site
devoted to beat generation writers,
including Allen Ginsberg and Gregory
Corso.
WEB http://www.charm.net/~brooklyn
/People/WilliamSBurroughs.html

William S. Burroughs "Yen pox"—ash
of opium after the opium has been
smoked. "Pop corn"—someone with a
legitimate job, as opposed to a hustler or
thief. Learn the definitions of words from
Burroughs's tale of heroin addiction,
Junky, and tune into information on his
novels, movies, and spoken word
recordings.
WEB http://studwww.rug.ac.be
/~fvcauwel/burrough.html

William S. Burroughs His writings?
Condemned as degenerate and porno-
graphic. His themes? Drug addiction,
secret conspiracies, homosexuality, and
death. His impact? Undeniably immeasurable. This collection of links will
point to you places around the world
featuring various tidbits on William S.
Burroughs's controversial life and
works. Quotes, sound bytes, images,
and interviews can be accessed from
this central Web.
WEB http://www.primenet.com
/~dirtman/wsb.htm

William S. Burroughs at the Iliad "A
heroin-addicted, gun-crazed, bisexual
eccentric who accidentally shot his
wife…" Who else could it be but "genuine literary genius" William Burroughs?
You can order any of his works from this
Web site, or you can just use it as an
extensive catalogue of the many things
he's done.
WEB http://host.interloc.com/~iliadbks
/burrous.html

William Seward Burroughs "The evil is
there waiting. And always cops: smooth
college-trained state cops, practiced,
apologetic patter, electronic eyes weigh
your car and luggage, clothes and
face…" Burroughs wrote in his remarkably influential *Naked Lunch*. Quotes
from the story, links to other Burroughs
sites on the Web, and the tale of the
home page creator's introduction to the
author's work are featured here.
WEB http://violet.umfacad.maine.edu
/~gokcen/burr.html

▶ **ROCKY HORROR**

**A Virgin's Guide to the Rocky Horror
Picture Show** So, it's your first time, and
you want to be prepared. That's OK; it's
a big step, and it's something you'll
remember forever. This helpful guide will
help get you through the experience as
painlessly and with as little humiliation
as possible. We're talking about seeing
Rocky Horror for the first time in the
theater, of course. The user-friendly document lets you know what you should
bring (rice, water guns, toast), what to
expect ("People will be yelling things at
the movie!"), and what to do. For example, "Comments on the Criminologist's
neck are good. (He doesn't have one.
That's the joke.)" Sure, it's cheating, but
you'll thank us later when unprepared
virgins have to suck a cast member's
toe. Feet get really sweaty in size 13
heels.
WEB http://www.keithnet.com/insanity
/virginsguide.html

alt.cult-movies.rocky-horror Discussion of the movie from fans and cast
members from around the planet. In
how many languages can you say
"elbow sex"? What kind of household
products are best for simulated sex?
Enter at your own risk!
USENET alt.cult-movies.rocky-horror

Charles Atlas Club From Japan, a wacky
site complete with lips that drip blood
and a dancing Riff-Raff. The Rocky Horror Fanatics Association, as the sponsoring club is known, has put something on

the Web that most *RHPS* fans have probably never before seen: images of *Rocky Horror* from Japanese television. The members of this "club" have collected a series of screen grabs from when the cult classic was mentioned on Japanese TV programs; they've even got an image from a Fuji Xerox commercial starring Tim Curry. There's also a library of information for every single recorded *RHPS* disc, including something truly horrific: an *RHPS* karaoke sampler. **WEB** http://www.ifnet.or.jp/~kei-t.

Cosmo's Factory "I am looking to play the part of Riff Raff in just about any cast near or reasonably close to Pomona, California. I look remarkably similar to Richard O'Brien's Riff Raff. Thin. Long Blonde Hair. Hollow Face…" No matter what *RHPS*-related thing you're looking for, this is the one place you're guaranteed to find it. Song lyrics, the movie script, the script of the play, and tons more. There's even a *Rocky Horror* trivia game. Cosmo tops it off with a full set of information about *Shock Treatment*, the sequel that follows Brad and Janet through an interesting adventure in a Denton TV studio. Most useful at this site is the searchable database of fans. **WEB** http://wl.iglou.com/cosmos factory/cosmosfactory.html

Graceland's Rocky Horror Site Although it has nothing to do with Elvis, this home page rocks. This Columbus, Ohio cast has assembled a great collection of *RHPS* materials. In their vault, find biographies on the movie's actors, scripts, pictures, and sounds from the film. There are even guitar tabs. You're welcome to join them, just remember their No. 1 rule: "NO F%$#ING RICE AT THE CAST!!!!" **WEB** http://pages.prodigy.com/rocky /index.html

Official Rocky Horror Picture Show Web Site In the beginning, God said, "Let there be lips!" And there were, and they were good. This beautiful, but slow (read: graphics heavy) site features a list

of theaters currently playing Brad and Janet's awfully big adventure. There's also background information on the film, its weekly performances, the fan club, and memorabilia. **WEB** http://www.rockyhorror.com

The RHPS FAQ What's a virgin? Only a virgin would ask. What's with all these errors in editing? What parodies of *RHPS* exist? The WWW version of the FAQ is a veritable universe of information. The play, the movie, and *Shock Treatment* are all summed up and analyzed. Find out if the casts ever get paid, and why the performers do it. Expect light-hearted answers: When addressing the question of what one should wear to a *Rocky* screening, the author writes, "Nothing—or at least as little as possible. Well, lots of black is usually good. As is lingerie. As are fishnets. Basically, the weirder the better." **WEB** http://faq.rhps.org

The Rocky and Bullwinkle Horror Picture Show A parody to end all parodies. Canadian Joe Blevin has taken the adventures of Brad and Janet with the Transylvanians and turned them into a cartoon free-for-all. For example, Eddie's emergence from the deep-freeze unit is replaced by the following: "Suddenly, a large refrigeration unit opens like a drawbridge. A little boy breaks through a wall of ice on his tricycle. The boy has glasses and red hair and is dressed in short pants and a t-shirt. Real kick-ass rock music starts to play. The boy takes off his bicycle helmet and gets off the tricycle." Freaky. **WEB** http://www.er.uqam.ca/merlin /jb191854/bullwink.txt

The Rocky Horror Picture Show "Michael Rennie was ill *The Day the Earth Stood Still*, but he told us where to stand," sing the lips. "On our feet!" shouts the irreverent audience. For a guide to audience participation, visit this site—a nice-looking illustrated version of the annotated script (with gems like "…Coooooming!" "So's Brad! No he isn't! Now he is.") Lots of pictures and

links (Tim Curry in *Muppet Treasure Island!*), too.
WEB http://www.cs.wvu.edu/~paulr/rhps/rhps.html

Rocky Horror Picture Show Sound Clips
"It's not easy having a good time," moans the pleasure-seeking Dr. Frank N. Furter. He should know, since he's the one who gets fried with a beam of pure anti-matter and winds up dead in a pool, wearing knock-off Frederick's of Hollywood and non-waterproof mascara. But you'll have fun with this collection of sounds taken from the film. As Magenta says, "We're all lucky." But not as lucky as the bannister.
WEB http://www.clandjop.com/~jday/rocky/rocky.html

The Rocky Horror Purity Test Have you slept with more than one cast member at once? Have your parents shown up at *Rocky* without you knowing about it? There's no explanation of the scoring here, but it seems that the more "yes" answers you have, the more of a *Rocky* die-hard you are.
WEB http://newton.math.grin.edu/~hamilton/rhps/purity.test

Sweet Transvestite's Pelvic Thrust "A wedding? (I always cry at weddings...) Let's throw some rice! It's raining in the movie? Let's shoot water at everybody! And we don't just throw things, we also sing and shout." The author's short essay about the movie includes the thing that makes the movie so enjoyable—the crowd interactivity. Scripts, including annotated audience participation versions, and links to other *Rocky* sites on the Web make up most of this home page.
WEB http://www.lancite.net/~denis/rhps/e_rhps.html

Zenin's Rocky Horror Archive Did you ever really want a picture of Barry Bostwick and Susan Sarandon in their underwear? Here's your chance. Zenin's amassed a major library of *RHPS*-related materials—sounds, images, text files, archives of newsgroup postings. The major drawback to the site? There are hundreds of images with absolutely no description. You just have to try and find one you like.
WEB http://www.best.com/~zenin

TROMA

ILL ZOMBIE MUTANT PSYCHO WEB masters conquer cyberspace? After making some of the joyously worst movies of the past 20 years, Lloyd Kaufman's Troma Film Studio has finally created a masterpiece: a Web site.

Tromaville, as this corner of the Web is named, is the only place online to find information about Troma, its films, and characters. Designed like a small town, complete with a movie house (of course), it includes information on every Troma production to date, from *Adventure of the Action Hunters* to *Zombie Island Massacre*, with a brief synopsis of each of the hack-and-slash, peek-a-boo, sci-fi cheapies.

Key to the success of the Tromaville Web site is its interactivity. Troma loves its fans—without them, it wouldn't have survived as an independent film company for the past 22 years. As a reward, it gives them the chance to join the mutant party. Learn how to become a Tromoid! Get sex advice from the Tromettes and Tromen, a select group of scantily clad love slaves! Enter a script-writing contest! If Troma likes it enough, it'll get used—and you'll get $50! Better yet, send in your photo for the chance to join the galaxy of Troma stars!

Low-brow of a just-high-enough quality has long been Troma's hallmark, but lately, there has been a worrying trend toward larger budgets and, potentially, respectability. One critic has dubbed *Sgt. Kabukiman, NYPD* the *Citizen Kane* of Troma movies; after many years, Blockbuster Video has finally made the decision to carry the old Troma classics including *The Good, the Bad, and the Subhumanoid: Class of Nuke 'Em High III*; and with a Web site of this quality is the Troma trip towards the mainstream now unstoppable? Well, so long as movies like *Tromeo and Juliet* are sold on the strength of their computer sex, Kaufman's empire will remain a cult favorite only.

Launch pad

Tromaville
http://www.fxmedia.com/home

Tromaville, UK
http://www.troma.co.uk/main.html

PARANORMAL

WHAT'S BETTER THAN THE *X-Files*, *Aliens*, *Close Encounters of the Third Kind*, and *Poltergeist*? Real-life paranormal phenomena, alien abductions, UFO sightings, and hauntings, happening to real people, maybe even to you. The supernatural side of cyberspace is inhabited by hundreds of sites devoted to exploring that hazy area where science fiction and science fact meet. We've explored all the nooks and crannies of the numinous Net and found the best pseudoscience sites, from paranormal pages and haunted hallows to alien arenas. And for you conspiracy nuts, er, theorists, there are bunkers full of secrets exposed online. Whether you take this stuff as seriously as the site authors, or use it for entertainment purposes only (just like the Psychic Friends Network), you'll find the answers you need.

▶ CLICK PICK

AUFORA Web Did you see flashing lights? A big saucer in the sky? Have a close encounter of the first, second, or third kind? Report it to the Alberta UFO Research Association. Besides the sighting report form, AUFORA Web contains news from that other world of ufology, a guide covering everything from crop circles and cattle mutilations to Area 51 and the Roswell incident, an explanation of AUFORA's investigation procedures (including explanations of CE1s, CE2s, and CE3s), and a picture archive. Most importantly, AUFORA Web not only provides links to all the UFO sites, newsgroups, and commercial service forums, but it also rates them. You'll realize the hundreds of unidentified flying resources that are out there.
WEB http://ume.med.ucalgary.ca/aufora

▶ MOTHERSHIPS

alt.paranet.* Believers, skeptics, experts, and amused bystanders jump among the family of paranet news-groups—alt.paranet.abduct, alt.paranet.paranormal, alt.paranet.science, alt.paranet.skeptic, and alt.paranet.ufo—in ongoing discussions about the possibility of aliens and a world beyond. Discussion on these groups tends to be more scientific and serious than its newsgroup counterparts.
USENET alt.paranet.*

alt.paranormal A well-trafficked newsgroup, despite the fact that most who believe in the paranormal either (a) focus on specific interests, like psychic activity, witchcraft, or alien abduction—which have their own newsgroups—or (b) are members of the somewhat more "serious" alt.paranet groups. Alt.paranormal mostly has dilettantes talking about personal experiences and dabblers asking querulous or curious questions. The gender ratio is fairly even, and the environment relatively flame-free.
USENET alt.paranormal

The Anomalist A twice-yearly periodical reporting on anomalies not only in science, but in history and nature, as well. Created by writers, scientists, and investigators, rather than believers or skeptics, expect a balanced publication with justified questions and criticism. Not the place to report Batboy sitings or musings on when the Venusians are going to return Elvis.
WEB http://cloud9.net/~patrick/anomalist

Committee for Scientific Investigation of Claims of the Paranormal Home to the *Skeptical Inquirer*, a publication devoted to debunking everything from alien abductions to floral health remedies, this site also lists events sponsored by CSICOP and reprints articles about the organization. One question: If the committee's mission is one of investigating scientific and pseudoscientific events, why didn't its members choose the name Scientific Committee for Investigation of Claims of the Paranormal, which would have permitted the

acronym SCICOP? Sounds a little suspicious.
WEB http://iquest.com/~fitz/csicop

Dark Side of the Web: The Paranormal Links to the supernatural side of cyberspace; from "The Apparition" by John Donne to the Ultimate UFO Page.
WEB http://www.cascade.net/dpara.html

Encounters Forum Associated with the Fox network's *Encounters: The Hidden Truth*, this forum sets out to prove that the world is not an empiricist prison, and that things happen every single day that simply cannot be explained by reasonable scientific minds. The most common phenomenon is alien abduction, generating roughly a dozen messages daily. The subscribers seem dead serious about their lunch dates with aliens, as one man says, "When my wife started coming up with memories and dream recollections that made me suspect she was a possible abductee, I couldn't ignore it any more. Funny how a thing like that turns your thinking around." *Encounters* also covers ghosts, spiritualism, possession, and announcements of spoon-bending parties. The staff of the *Encounters* television show frequents this forum looking for stories (strange kangaroo behavior in Australia, sidewalk-eating blobs from the sky in San Francisco). Maybe you'll see your communion re-enacted right after *Married, With Children!*
COMPUSERVE *go* encounters

Fortean Times: The Journal of Strange Phenomena One of the more creative paranormal magazine sites, *Fortean Times* has press clippings of reports on UFOs, creationism, and other concepts that are a little hard to swallow. An image archive of "20 years of Fortean Photo-Highlights"; short stories; and tables of contents for the current and back issues. Oh, and did we mention the page also houses excerpts from the *FT Book of Weird Sex*? Well, you're probably not interested in that kind of thing.
WEB http://alpha.mic.dundee.ac.uk/ft/ft.cgi?-1,ft

The Fringes of Reason Links to the weirdest of the weird on the Web, from the AquaThought Foundation (communicate with dolphins and transform your brainwaves) to the Nostradamus FAQ (also called "conversations" with Nostradamus) to Gopher Abduction. Also available are links to the skeptic's point of view on each supernatural subject.
WEB http://www.physics.wisc.edu/~shalizi/hyper-weird/fringe.html

KeelyNet An Australian archive of articles devoted to the paranormal, UFOs, and the vibratory physics of John Keely.
WEB http://zeta.cs.adfa.oz.au/KeelyNet

Obi-Wan's UFO-Free Paranormal Page Obi-Wan, the other white meat! This is not your usual paranormal index; it excludes UFO and EBE sites, and focuses on ghost pages, fortune-telling sites, and online journals of the paranormal.
WEB http://www.lido.com/ghosts

Obscure Research Labs Billing itself as "the world's only organization devoted to the acquisition of Total Knowledge," Obscure Research Labs specializes in UFOs, time travel, paraphysics, and misinformation tracking, as well as links to a variety of Web resources on these topics.
WEB http://140.249.8.212/orl

Paranormal Belief Survey Do you believe that the Loch Ness monster lives? Do you think the government regularly engages in widespread conspiracies? And most importantly, do you believe that Elvis is still alive? Participate in this survey and make your beliefs and/or paranoia known. The latest results reveal that more than 90 percent of people believe in the existence of extra-terrestrials, but only 5 percent think the King lives on.
WEB http://galileo.metatech.com/surveys/paranorm/paranorm.htm

ParaScope An online forum dedicated to exploring and exposing the mysteries of the unexplained and unexplainable, from conspiracies and UFOs to paranormal phenomena and cover-ups. Contributors, both amateur and professional, search for concrete answers to some of life's most puzzling mysteries, fostering an atmosphere where cyberbelievers can explore ideas and concepts ignored or ridiculed by the mainstream media. The Matrix area covers conspiracies and scandals. Enigma covers paranormal phenomena. Nebula contains aliens and UFOs. And Dossier offers "evidence" in the form of government reports, corporate memos, and more.

AMERICA ONLINE *keyword* parascope

PAW Resources for the paranormally-inclined organized by preternatural pages covering tarot, astrology, palmistry, ouija, occult resources, and parapsychology.
WEB http://www-scf.usc.edu/~siddique /PAW.HTML

Scientists Confront Pseudoscience Imagine a kid going to the library to research the legend of the Loch Ness monster and coming home with reports of eyewitness accounts, photos of the monster rearing its head, articles about the legend, and absolutely nothing that suggests that there might be a scientific explanation for Nessie. Two skeptics imagined just that and in 1990 compiled a bibliography for librarians who need information to balance claims of monsters, faith healing, UFOs, creationism, cult archaeology, and other pseudoscience topics.
URL gopher://gopher.lysator.liu.se:70 /00/information/Skeptical/Bibliography

Unexplained Phenomena Strange things happen, and sometimes they happen within earshot of people who subscribe to CompuServe. For instance, 1,700 head of cattle might disappear from a heartland farm or a 17-year-old girl in Palisades Park might suddenly begin to speak fluent Egyptian. What can account for these mysterious events? Well, according to CompuServe's Unexplained Phenomena message board, the answer is simple: aliens! Whether disparaging the "growing abductee mentality" or quoting ufol-

ogist Richard Hoagland on "large semi-transparent structures on the moon," visitors to this forum have a robust interest in the inexplicable, and they're not ashamed to admit it. This is not just a place for speculation on the extraterrestrial and/or paranormal (for that, see CompuServe's Encounters forum). There's also plenty of entertaining chat about the Kennedy assassination and unorthodox techniques for scuba breathing.
COMPUSERVE *go* issues→Libraries *or* Messages→Unexplained Phenomena

Weird Science Radical research on anomalous physics is being recorded on Bill Beaty's home page. Quoting William James, this site states, "Round about the accredited and orderly facts of every science there ever floats a sort of dust-cloud of exceptional observations, of occurrences minute and irregular and seldom met with, which it always proves more easy to ignore than to attend to... Anyone will renovate his science who will steadily look after the irregular phenomena, and when science is renewed, its new formulas often have more of the voice of the exceptions in them than of what were supposed to be the rules."
WEB http://www.eskimo.com/~billb /weird.html

The WWW Virtual Library: Paranormal Phenomena Archive X is devoted to maintaining a record of the supernatural sightings and experiences of cyber-surfers. Submit or scroll through ghost stories and folklore, angel encounters, channelings, near-death experiences, and UFO sightings. Leave your email address and you'll be notified each time new experiences are posted.
WEB http://www.crown.net/X

▶ HAUNTINGS

A Spectre Search Some folks turn to *Zagat's* or *Fodor's* or even AAA to decide how to spend their dining and entertainment dollar. Others use the Spectre Search, a directory of haunted dining and lodging in the U.S. For an unexpect-

ed (and undead) guest at dinner, try the Crier in the Country Restaurant in Glen Mills, Pa. Going to Florida? Forget Disney World and its Haunted Mansion. Stay at the Artist's House in Key West and find out what a real haunted house is like. Or try the Captain Lord Mansion in Maine and keep an eye out for the Captain's widow who floats across the floor in the Lincoln Room and on the stairs. Don't worry about the rates—the extra spirits in your room stay free. A great resource for those who take their ghost stories with a dash of salt.
WEB http://web2.airmail.net/spectre1 /source/page0.html

alt.folklore.ghost-stories Keeping the oral tradition alive in the age of cyberspace, talk here tends to focus on the spreading of supernatural tales. You'll also find plenty of discussion of ghost-story-like movies and ghost mythos surrounding the making of them.
USENET alt.folklore.ghost-stories

alt.folklore.ghosts-stories FAQ Posted to several ghastly newsgroups, this FAQ offers a rundown of rules (don't steal stories for your own personal or professional use), elementary lessons on famous hauntings and spooky spots (The Amityville Horror, the Brown Lady of Raynham Hall, Winchester Mansion, the Tower of London), and erudition on various urban folklore and legends.
WEB http://www.lib.ox.ac.uk/internet /news/faq/archive/folklore.ghost -stories.html

The Ghost Pages Become a ghost links research assistant. If you've seen a ghost, be prepared to provide not only the who, when, and where of the sighting, but also answers to such questions as "What color was the ghost?" "Did it glow?" and "Did it try to communicate with you?" All you'll get in return, however, is the satisfaction of helping one researcher with his work. But take note: he is "only interested in ghosts, not others of the spirit world."
WEB http://www.murlin.com/~webfx /ghost

Ghost Stories R Us A rather small collection of personal encounters with phantasms of all shapes and sizes. Add your own experience electronically.
WEB http://www.azc.com/client/page /fright.html

Ghosts What's the difference between a ghost and a ghoul? A poltergeist and a psychopomp? This haunting hubsite contains a guide to the undead, with such entries as radiant boys (also know as *kindermordernin,* boys murdered by their mothers), spunkie (a goblin or trickster ghost), and golem (an artificial human made by magical means). Also available are an index of hauntings, a ghost bibliography, and links to other sites of the supernatural.
WEB http://star06.atklab.yorku.ca /~peterpan/ghost.html

Ghosts Now *Enquirer*-esque articles such as "I've Been Haunted By A Ghost Since 1922," "Fireman's Ghost Rescues Family From Killer Blaze," and "Phantom Pilot Haunts Airbase for 50 Years." Message boards keep the spectacular story ideas coming.
AMERICA ONLINE *keyword* wwn→Ghosts Now

The Ghostwatcher Do you ever hear strange sounds coming from your closet or worry about what may lurk underneath your bed? June does. Help her get a good night's sleep. Through the magic of the CU-See Me cam, you can keep an eye on the platform under her bed, inside her trunks, and on strategic points in her basement while she gets some shuteye.
WEB http://www.flyvision.org/sitelite /Houston/GhostWatcher/index.html

The Phantom's Closet Ghost hunter Richard Senate invites you into his closet and provides you with a list of everything you'll need when in hot pursuit of the undead and the best places to search for the specters. What you do with the ghost when you catch it is up to you. They make a great baby shower gift; who needs another Gund Bear?

WEB http://www.phantoms.com
/~phantom/ghost.htm

The Shadowlands Ghost Pages Real
ghost stories sent in by real people. Real
ghosts? You be the judge. Also available
are pictures of the infamous Brown
Lady, the Amityville House, and several
unidentified flying objects—and we're
not talking spaceships.
WEB http://users.aol.com/shadoland2
/ghost.html

What Is a Hopping Ghost The Chinese
honor their dead, and for good reason.
They believe an unsatisfied soul can
become a ghost and make life unbearable
when, in some cases, they literally
become hopping mad. This page
answers questions on one of their more
animated apparitions making star appearances on the Hong Kong movie scene.
WEB http://www.resort.com/~banshee
/Misc/hopping_ghost.html

Where the Ghouls Are Skeletons in the
closet. A one-page listing of the most
noteworthy haunted houses according to
international "authority" on the topic,
Dennis William Hauck, from Chatham
Manor in Fredericksburg, Va. to The
White House.
WEB http://www.obs-us.com/obs
/english/books/pg/pg527.htm

▌ UFOS & ALIENS

Alien Exploratorium A cyberclearing-
house of alien "intelligence," including
stories of mass abductions and abductions at the White House, a rundown of
types of aliens from the Greys to lizard
people, as well as government conspiracy and cover-up theories. Note: information on alien autopsies and cattle mutilations, however implausible, is not for the
faint of heart.
WEB http://area51.upsu.plym.ac.uk
/~moosie/ufo/aexplo.htm

Alien On Line Download the MPEG
movie of the alien autopsy of the
Roswell girl and decide for yourself if it's
real or a ruse. The two image galleries

also contain stills of UFOs and EBEs.
WEB http://www.crs4.it/~mameli/Alien
.html

Aliens, Aliens, Aliens Put your question
about whether or not there's intelligent
life out there to rest with one visit here.
After perusing some of the posts of visitors to this page, like "Aliens rule. I want
too be abducted, and lose my virginity to
some extraterrestrial chick," your new
question will be, "Is there intelligent life
down here?"
WEB http://www.xensei.com/users
/john9904

alt.alien.research A newsgroup devoted to the development and debunking of
evidence of UFOs and aliens. Let the
surfer beware.
USENET alt.alien.research

alt.alien.visitors The group that epito-
mizes the kook ecosystem is almost
equal parts True Believers, scientists, Net
bystanders, and Kookwatchers—existing,
if not in harmony, then in synchronicity.
Discussion of crop circles, the "Greys"
(insectoid ETs whose activities have been
documented, sort of), Erich Von Daniken,
and biblical proof of aliens sits side by
side with utterly hilarious posts mocking
the UFO party line. One ongoing, somewhat paranoid thread concerns whether
alt.alien.visitors is now "moderated," i.e.,
screened for improper—or overly revela-
tory?—posts. The conclusion anyone
might draw from actually reading
alt.alien.visitors is: No. If you're a True
Believer or scientific, watch for the posts
of Earl Dumbrowski, an even-headed,
empirical researcher and enthusiast of
UFOs. If you're more inclined to see the
whole thing as a gas, watch for the posts
of the so-called Hastings UFO Society,
which claim to be channeled onto the
group by a psychic named Madame Thel-
ma. The posts, documenting the activities and beliefs of a UFO club somewhere
out in hooterville, are so strange and well
written that you might just believe—for a
second—that the society exists, before
you fall down laughing.
USENET alt.alien.visitors

Contact Project An entertaining simulation of first contact that asks netsurfers to help decipher a message from an alien civilization. The message, a jumble of letters and numbers, looks like the alien telegraph operator fell asleep at the switch, but you can give it a try anyway, and post your comments about the experiment on a message board.
WEB http://sunsite.unc.edu/lunar/alien.html

The EBE Page The Extraterrestrial Biological Entity Page is actually a list of links to more than 200 sites categorized by The Roswell Incident, Area 51 at Groom Lake, unidentified flying objects, abductions, crop circles, Internet resources, off-the-net resources, multimedia, and personal experiences. Bulletin boards of discussion in each area are also up for the posting.
WEB http://sloop.ee.fit.edu/users/lpinto/index.html

Faking UFOs The cybercharlatan's guide to making people think they've seen a UFO. Some of these might actually work if you have a lot of time on your hands. Roel van der Meulen provides how-tos for creating close encounters using hanggliders and balloons as well as instructions for leaving crop circles. Wacky antics and emotional breakdowns are sure to follow!
WEB http://www.strw.leidenuniv.nl/~vdmeulen/Articles/UFOfake.html

Internet UFO Group IUFOG is not a formal UFO investigative organization. Instead, it is an attempt to organize WWW and traditional authors of UFO and EBE pages into one cohesive cybermovement. It appears the effort was not in vain. Some must-reads: "The Ten Most Compelling UFO Cases in History," "Cosmic Conspiracy: Six Decades of Government UFO Cover-ups" (from OMNI), and "Stupid Government Tricks." The IUFOG site also includes a database of research, events, and sightings; a media page of clippings and press releases; and a library of books, periodicals, and zines.
WEB http://members.aol.com/iufog/index.html

Skywatch International A pilot in California reports two large, bizarre red lights hovering "at 245 degrees, 45 degrees up" which fade sequentially. The same night, an anonymous female caller reports that multiple observers see two bright red lights hovering in night sky. Across town, a man also reports two bright red lights hovering together "35 degrees to the left of Venus" which move in formation to the left and disappear. Is it a bird? Is it a plane? No, it's one of hundreds of sightings maintained by the National UFO Reporting Center. At Skywatch International, you'll find the center's monthly reports with accompanying maps as well as a gateway to a galaxy of UFO and EBE information, including photos of UFOs, government documents, and another "authentic alien autopsy." Jonathan Frakes is on the case.
WEB http://www.wic.net/colonel/ufopage.htm

Smitty's UFO Page Smitty's site focuses on the Groom Lake area and the reputed deceit which has taken place on that area of land in Nevada—whether the deceit was on the part of the government or the the conspiracy theorists depends on which side of the galaxy you're on. Smitty recounts his personal experiences at Area 51 and provides 3D-rendered views of the Nellis Bombing and Gunnery Range.
WEB http://www.schmitzware.com/ufo.html

UFO Base If you canceled your subscription to *The Star* and haven't been to a supermarket checkout stand lately, get your UFO sighting fix here. *Weekly World News* headlines include "Jupiter Sends Distress Signal to Earth," "Teacher Kidnapped by UFO in 1880," and "Man Posing As Space Alien Conned Gals Into Sex."
AMERICA ONLINE *keyword* wwn→UFO base

UFO Folklore Whether it's up-to-the-day UFO news and press releases, Freedom of Information Act documents, or speculation about the vaults at Wright-Patterson Air Force Base, cattle "moo-tila-

tions," and the MJ-12 documents, each piece of evidence at this site is treated with appropriate skepticism until it is proven fact. Among the more interesting tidbits of trivia in this comprehensive collection of extra-terrestrial information is a U.S. law on the books in 1969 that specifically prohibited astronauts from making contact with aliens.
WEB http://www.qtm.net/~geibdan /framemst.html

UFO Sightings by Astronauts The supposed beliefs and/or encounters with UFOs and alien life forms of NASA astronauts from James Lovell and Frank Borman to Neil Armstrong and Buzz Aldrin.
WEB http://www.cs.bgsu.edu/~jzawodn /ufo/astro-sightings.html

UFO-L Biblical references to UFOs, the recent disappearance of the Mars observer, lost Soviet probes—what on earth can it all mean? This bunch approaches the idea of extraterrestrial life thoughtfully and seriously. A relatively flame-less list for the curious and the almost-convinced to figure it all out together.
EMAIL listserv@brufpb.bitnet ✍ *Type in message body:* subscribe UFO-L <your full name>

UFOs and E.T.s A random assortment of spaceship and spacemen sightings and images, with a notable absence of alien autopsy pics.
WEB http://www.io.org/~dnewton/ufo.html

The Ultimate UFO Page Ufology 101. Touting itself as a rational approach to ufology, TUFOP includes articles exploring whether the alien autopsy film is a scam, the complete Roswell primer, and a survey you can complete electronically to help them out in their UFO/alien abduction research.
WEB http://www.serve.com/tufop

Unexplained Phenomena: Crop Circles A cyber-resource guide to the crop circle phenomenon, in which geometrically intricate circles appear mysteriously in farmlands. Eighty percent of sightings occur in England, but circles are also reported in Australia, Italy, the U.S., Norway, and Canada. This site points you to the answers which have been formulated to explain the circles and the more puzzling questions that still remain. Like, who are the circle makers? What explains the sound and light which sometimes accompany the appearance of the ancient symbols? And why in the world would aliens want to spend all of their time in a wheat field in Devonshire?
WEB http://www.vuw.ac.nz/~broche /crop.htm

World Wide Web Virtual Library: Unidentified Flying Objects It's like a cyber-card-catalog for all the spots on the Net with information on objects of extraterrestrial origin. And when they say worldwide, they mean it. Linked sites include every page from A Summary of UFO Activity in Belgium and an overhead photo of Area 51, to John's Close Encounter and NASA astronauts who've seen UFOs.
WEB http://ernie.bgsu.edu/~jzawodn/ufo

▶ **CONSPIRACY**

50 Greatest Conspiracies of All Time This site is amazing! Absolutely incredible! Filled with enough conspiracy-related reading and images to waste dozens of hours. In fact, come to think of it, you probably will spend all your time on it, rack up huge phone bills, and not finish any of your other work. And it seems quite likely that your wife would then have an excellent excuse to divorce you and get the kids. AT&T and Sprint would then drain every last dollar from your savings. And, the guy who sits next to you at work would be in a perfect position to take your job. Not that you should be paranoid or anything. This site was created to advertise the book *50 Greatest Conspiracies of All Time*, and includes descriptions of the prize winners (from Kennedy to Jonestown to the Freemasons, and more); offers weekly conspiracy reports; houses an archive of dozens of conspiracy-related interviews and articles; sponsors a "find Oswald"

contest; and even links you to the CIA home page.
WEB http://www.webcom.com/~conspire

alt.conspiracy From the murder of JFK (by the Mafia? The pope? The CIA? Elvis?) to the ineffable workings of the Secret Persuaders, alt.conspiracy is perhaps the most "serious" of the "kook" newsgroups. It has the highest ratio of True Believers to kook-watch and flamer types. Which isn't to say there aren't flames here: Everyone's got an agenda or an idiosyncratic belief, and most of them contradict. Wanna watch irresistible forces hit immovable objects? This is a good place to do it. The "NY News Collective—All the News That Doesn't Fit" posts reprints of articles condemning government activities. The Maoist Internationalist Movement is another regular rant-posting group. Meanwhile, on an individual basis, Brian Redman keeps flames high with his "Conspiracy of the Day" posts, lengthy digressions on topics ranging from the International AIDS Conspiracy to, yes, the assassinations of JFK and Martin Luther King. Lengthy threads include discussions of the redesign of U.S. currency, the national debt, and ongoing talk about standby subjects like skinheads, the anti-Holocaust movement, and Waco.
USENET alt.conspiracy

alt.conspiracy.area51 Rumor has it that the U.S. military pulled its support from the blockbuster *Independence Day* when the director refused to remove all mention of the now more infamous Area 51. In this newsgroup there's a lot of distrustful discussion of the block of government land north of Las Vegas rich in UFO lore. Visitors here believe that everything imaginable—captured aliens, underground bases, alien-government collusion—has existed on the shore of Groom Lake, and that the U.S. government, as always, is covering it up.
USENET alt.conspiracy.area51

Deep Black Magic Devoted to "exposing over forty years of U.S. government

research into Extra Sensory Perception and the psychological 'technology' of individual mind control using drugs, hypnosis and abuse," this site focuses on research into psychokinesis (mental manipulation of solid objects), and remote viewing (acquiring information at a distance in space or time). Tom Parker began accumulating research since he found out he had friends who were involved in it, and he's not afraid to name names. But be careful when you log on here. The NSA may be watching you.
WEB http://ourworld.compuserve.com /homepages/T_porter/govtesp.htm

The Government Psychiatric Torture Site Check out MRI scans of Brian's brain, taking great care to notice the "inexplicable foreign objects" there. To Brian, these are clear signs of psychiatric torture perpetrated by the federal government. Brian exposes supposed proponents of these mind games and their torture techniques, explores the unanswered questions of Jonestown, and shares the stories of fellow victims. A side-note to would-be flamers—whatever the actual cause, he certainly has enough problems without your comments, don't you think?
WEB http://www.webcom.com /designr/MK-resistance

Mind Control Forum Homepage Ed claims he's a captive of the mind-control "cabal's" microwave anti-personnel projects. His remote controllers talk to him through radios, televisions, automobiles, trains, airplanes, sometimes even using his own voice, and hail from areas like Minot AFB, North Dakota, the Florida Keys, and somewhere on the grounds of Nellis AFB in Nevada (Area 51 territory). Ed's forum provides archives of his and other's experiences with psychiatric torture (check the pic entitled "brain implant being removed"), news in the field, and other resources.
WEB http://members.gnn.com/fivestring /index.htm

PART 8

Sci-Fi Games

VIDEO ARCADE

WHILE PAC-MAN, THE RAVENOUS, simplistic little dot, never asked, "What is my motivation?" today's games have not run short of reasons for players to blast, paralyze, or otherwise maim each other with modern weaponry. As Duke Nukem 3-D, you have no choice but to wage war on aliens who've blown up your ride. *Command & Conquer*, compels you to take out the Brotherhood of Nod, a cult whose members are armed to the teeth and who aren't in the mood to pray. "Shallow are the plots!" Yoda might say. He'd certainly be correct, if it weren't for the fact that most people simply don't care. If they'd wanted plot, they would have rented *Yentl*. For insights into death matches and other fun things, go to DoomGate for the gamut of Doom resources. Then visit Motaro's MK Page, which breaks down the excellent plot(!) of *Mortal Kombat*.

▶ CLICK PICK

The Happy Puppy Games Onramp
This is one BIG-framed, animated, Java'd, and pumped puppy. There's an online magazine, multimedia downloads, and a shop chock full of happy puppy merchandise, but the site functions mainly as an index. The biggest, friskiest gaming index in the known universe. Hundreds of links to game pages, reviews, software companies, cheats/patches, zines, Mac games, PC games, demos, and many other indices, just for starters! Grab a comfy chair, wrap your hands with Ace bandages, set up an IV drip with Chef Boy'ardee and Zot soda, and play.
WEB http://www.happypuppy.com
PICTURE: web http://www.vidgames.com

◀ MOTHERSHIPS

Anime Video Games List What could be more perfectly suited to video games than anime, manga, and sentai? They're the perfect blend of blood, sex, and sci-fi with some of the highest quality graphics on this or any supernatural plane. This list of anime games is part of the FAQ for rec.arts.anime, and notes Japanese/American software and hardware compatibility, basic info and regional availability of the games on the international market, release dates and reviews for new games, and even a list of action games subsequently made into animation series or films.
WEB http://www.math.uio.no/faq /games/anime-faq.html

History of Video Games Page Atari Pong, the progenitor to many a modern video game, first appeared in 1975. Learn Atariana and more at this well-designed site that has an inexplicable picture of *Sesame Street*'s Grover astride a toilet on its home page. This oft-visited page tracks the history of video games; simply choose a hyperlinked year from 1972 to the present and you'll find a list of games that debuted that year. You can then easily link to that on- or off-site game site.
WEB http://www.sponsor.nct/~gchance

Video Game FAQ Kind of like a window of an electronics store, the opening screen shot of this site features lots of TVs turned on to the likes of Sega, Nintendo, and Genesis. But the Video Game FAQ is not all about image. As the title suggests, FAQs are on offer for almost every video system and game imaginable. Bone up on the backgound of all your favorite sci-fi games; it may work wonders on your gameplay.
WEB http://www.flex.net/users/cjayc /vgfa/index.html

Sailor Moon Support Site-Video Games WWW Sites No, *Pitfall* was not forgotten and you can still use your ColecoVision. Just because the graphics are better, doesn't mean it's forgotten, and you can find those special games here. This site's got more links than the food chain, so don't be shy about your fetish with *The*

Legend of Zelda or your shame at your Level 1 status on *Super Mario*. The blood and guts of *Street Fighter*, the speed of *Pole Position*, and the reality of *Doom* are at your fingertips, so get clicking. A part of the huge, wet-eyed collection of anime and video games known as *SailorMoon*, this site offers over a hundred links to sites for Japanese and U.S. hardware/ software companies; electronic gaming magazines; home pages for Sega Saturn/Genesis, Sony, Nintendo SNES/SFC/Ultra 64, and IBM/PC; sites for games such as *Killer Instinct*, *Mortal Kombat*, and *Virtua Fighter*, and other gory gaming pages.
WEB http://www.hkstar.com/~chimo /html/game.html

Video Gaming Information The graphic design of this site may leave a lot to be desired, but what matters is that you can read the page; you'll find a great list of resources for all the biggest video game companies, magazines, FAQs, and games. It's possibly worth the migraine.
WEB http://weber.u.washington.edu /~mosaic/vidgames.html

Warbirds Video Game Pages Warbird, whoever he is, has compiled a comprehensive list of codes, cheats, and facts for Sony Playstation's many games including *Alien Trilogy*, *Tekken*, and *Novastorm*. You'll also find a less voluminous but still helpful section devoted to the Nintendo system.
WEB http://users.aol.com/warbird0 /videogames.html

▶ SATELLITES

Arcade Games Forum Discuss coin-gobbling games, new and old, from *Kiss Pinball* to *Primal Rage!*, put in your bid for the arcade game you'd most like to see (the posts so far feature a few semi-original ideas such as *Highlander* and lots more for uninspired combos (anyone up for *Mortal Kombat vs. Streetfighter*?). Add your "Fighting Game Rumor Humor" to the high-brow collection which already contains posts such as "grabmythingality," "retardoality,"

"constipatality," and "nipples."
AMERICA ONLINE *keyword* video games→ Bulletin Board→Arcade Games

Classic Video Games Ah, the early eighties—headbands, break-dancing, *Webster*, *Flashdance*, valley girls, the Go-Gos and of course, video games. You whiled away the hours shoveling quarters into *Q*bert*, *Donkey Kong*, *Centipede*, *Dig Dug*, and *Pac Man*. This page gives you links to newsgroups, FAQs, archives, museums, auctions, and even classic advertisements. You can almost smell the cheese fries.
WEB http://sharkie.psych.indiana.edu /rynersw/vids/vids.html

Coin-Ops Library topics include the latest 3-D technology, combos and fatalities, while the message board seems a bit on the skinny side—mostly people in search of codes. The libraries are particularly well-stocked in the *Star Gladiator* and *Mortal Kombat* departments.
COMPUSERVE *go* vidgam→Libraries *or* Messages→Coin-Ops

Coin-Ops Cheats FAQs, hints, cheats, and walkthroughs for all the biggies—*Street Fighter*, *Bloodstorm*, *Virtua Fighter*, *Mortal Kombat*, and more. You're not in luck if you're looking for classic-game action, however; you'd be better off browsing the genre-specific forums.
AMERICA ONLINE *keyword* video games→ Hints, Pics, Sounds: Arcade Coin-Ops

rec.games.video.arcade Ground-zero for discussion of coin-operated and home-system videogames, ranging from the practical (cheat sheets) to the technical (maintenance, retro-fitting, and pirating) to the philosophical (are you addicted? what are the best games of all time?). The most useful information is quickly incorporated into FAQs that are posted on the newsgroup (coverage of hot new games is practically simultaneous with their release) and archived.
USENET rec.games.video.arcade
FAQ: WEB http://www.cis.ohio-state .edu/hypertext/faq/usenet/games /videoarcade/faq/faq.html

The St. Louis Coin-Op and Video Game Museum Frightening as it may be, the video games you spent your lunch money on are now relics. This virtual tour of the St. Louis Coin-Op and Video Game Museum offers text and images for pinball games, sports coin-op games and, of course, video games such as *Qix, Pole Position, Q*bert, Dig Dug, Phoenix, Missile Command, Galaxion, Millipede, Tron, Space Invaders, Berzerk, Joust,* and the whole *Pac-Man* family (make sure to take a gander at the transparent *Ms. Pac Man* game, the eighth wonder of the world). All you need now is some black rubber bangle-bracelets or a pair of parachute pants. Nostalgia in your early twenties? Such is the price of the technological revolution.
WEB http://sharkie.psych.indiana.edu /rynersw/vids/coinop/coinop.html

▶ DESCENT

Descent Chat Come here if you're itching to wage war. This channel is almost always awash with *Descent* players ready for a network game. You can also type "/dcc chat Descender" and then "/msg Descender files" to get a list of files for downloading and relevant instructions.
IRC #descent

Descent Conference The denizens of CompuServe's Action Games Forum are nothing if not friendly—just stop by and you're sure to get an invite to talk. This is a membership forum, although visiting gamers are allowed.
COMPUSERVE *go* action

Descent on AOL Can't get enough of your favorite game? You'll find official *Descent* news and demos you crave at the Interplay Forum.
AMERICA ONLINE *keyword* interplay

The Descent Weenie's Tactics Site Is your roommate repeatedly whipping you in multiplayer mode? Frustrated by your inability to sneak up on the bad guys? This site can help with a compilation of every last tip, tweak, and secret the author has come across.
WEB http://www.msn.fullfeed.com /agiesler/descent.htm

Descent WWW Information DoomGate is the dominant *Doom* information source; so it's no surprise that they also have one of the best *Descent* pages as well. The site has cheat codes, information about playing *Descent* over the Internet, and more.
WEB http://doomgate.cs.buffalo.edu /descent

Level Alpha This is a central resource for *Descent* players, with an emphasis on Level editing.
WEB http://www.eskimo.com/~stickman /descent

Official Descent FAQ This official FAQ answers technical questions such as whether *Descent* is compatible with Windows 95 (don't worry—it is).
WEB http://www.interplay.com/website /descent.faq

Prepare for Descent A semi-official home page endorsed by Parallax and Interplay software, this page features lots of screen shots and some "official" Interplay-provided cheat codes. See how fun and enlightening cheating can be.
WEB http://tech.eitc.edu/students /toddbelc/descent.html

Descent Thought *Doom* was the ultimate action game? Think again. In addition to *Doom*-like tunnels, mazes, and 3-D mapped worlds, *Descent*'s action takes place in 360 degrees. Instead of crawling around on your feet, you're in a spaceship, shooting monsters, soldiers, and other foes. With the appropriate third-party software, such as IHHD, KALI, and MILK, you can play anyone in the world over the Internet. You'll find a few basic hints here, including how to beat the boss on Level 7, and notes on how to order additional information. Interplay's *Descent* site may seem limited in comparison to the game's unofficial pages, where you'll find cheat utilities, editors (DEVIL), and ranking systems. You'll find access to all of them here, plus information on *Descent 2*.

WEB http://www.interplay.com/website/descent.html

▶ DOOM

DoomGate It's in your face, literally. The fast-paced, 3-D game is exalted here, with a legion of listed links. *Doom*, *Doom II*, and *Ultimate Doom* are available, as well as links to related sites. *Doom*-heads are anxiously awaiting the impending launch of the www.gamers.org site, the new home of DoomGate, the uber-resource for the game.

WEB http://doomgate.cs.buffalo.edu

▶ GALACTIC COMBAT

Galaxy Harboring a secret desire to control the universe? Each player gets the chance to control their own personal empire of planets. The objective of the game is to wipe out the other players by capturing their planets and destroying their ships. Technology (allowing ships to fly faster, fight harder, and carry more cargo) plays a major role in the game. Twice each week, a player mails in orders for his ships and planets to the moderator, who processes the orders and mails back the results. The game is free and lasts between 50 and 70 turns. More than a dozen games are usually in progress at any given time

WEB http://www.iquest.net/galaxy

EMAIL galaxy-web@indyramp.com ✍ *Write a request*

Info: **URL** ftp://ftp.pbm.com/pub/pbm/galaxy

MegaWars I You're facing a seemingly infinite assault of enemies. Thankfully, you don't have to go it alone, you've got your own personal Han Solo—friends can play on your team. Two teams of up to five players battle for control of the galaxy—confronting each other and the evil Acherons who roam through this game. As soon as you choose to "Play *MegaWars I*," you'll be asked to join either the Coalition or the Empire—at which point you select a ship and enter the game. Beginners can help their side immediately by capturing neutral planets, marked by the "@" symbol on the map. Neutral planets have the pesky habit of firing back, but they're generally easy to subdue if your ship's in good shape. Friendly bases are marked by "$$," friendly planets by "++." Beware of the "//" and "--" on the map! Those are enemy bases and planets. They're here for you to destroy. As you earn points, you'll rise in rank and obtain more powerful spaceships. Check out the Multiplayer Games Forum (a link is available from the *MegaWars I* main menu) where you'll find a message board devoted to *MegaWars I*, and a file library with chronicles of battles, help text files, macros, and front-end software for various platforms.

COMPUSERVE *go* mega1

MegaWars III And you thought *Mega Wars I* was a struggle. The galaxy in the third incarnation of this game gets even more complicated. In phase 1 of this game, your objective is to battle ships and enemy bases. In phase 2, you develop your colonies to earn the title of Lord Emperor of All the Galaxies. You'll find *Mega Wars III* optional front-ends for PCs, especially for use on CompuServe, in the Multiplayer Games Forum Library. Also in the Library are final scores from past wars, reference texts, and commentary. On the Multiplayer Games Forum Message boards, players discuss the front-end programs, scores, and tactical maneuvers.

COMPUSERVE *go* mega3

Phoenix In the course of about 30 turns (each consisting of up to 200 orders), players compete with each other to take control of, at least half the galaxy. Each player controls a space empire and issues orders for his or her ships, factories, and other units. Ally with others or go it alone in this intense game of diplomacy, exploration, and trade. Once a week, a player mails in orders for ships and planets to the moderator ($2.50 per turn), who processes the orders and mails back the results. A graphical interface for the game is being developed, so you'd better work on your hand-eye coordination.

WEB http://www.den.com

EMAIL info@den.com ✍ Email for automated info

Support: URL ftp://ftp.den.com/pub/phoenix

Stars! Another competitor to *VGA Planets*. *Stars!* lets you design your customized race before the game starts, then allows you to compete with other empires while you develop your technology. Mineral management is an important part of the game. Up to 16 players may play. Requires Windows.

WEB http://beast.webmap.com/stars%21

▶ MARATHON

Bungie Software You'll know you're at the home of *Marathon* when you see an animated Major Hunter running straight at you only to be blown away by an unseen shot. Bungie Software created *Marathon*, and they've made their home page a friendly place to visit, with chat rooms for both *Marathon* and *Marathon 2: Durandal*, along with an FTP archive and a set of cheat programs.

WEB http://www.bungie.com/Default.html

Bungie Software Bungie maintains a decent-sized presence on AOL—there's plenty of talk about *Marathon 2*, demos are even available for downloading. This is a good place to hang out if you're looking for advance news from inside the company—Bungie first announced *Marathon 2* here!

AMERICA ONLINE *keyword* bungie

Marathon Central The debut of *Doom* for the PC seemed like a major blow to the Mac. "You don't even have the best games any more!" cackled DOS advocates. Mac's true believers, however, had faith in the future: "Just wait for *Marathon*," they said, smiling and subtly caressing their mouses. The wait was well worth it. *Marathon* improves on the basic *Doom* model in three important ways: a real 3-D map instead of *Doom's*

trumped-up 2-D, intelligent aliens who can hear you coming and fall into ambush positions, and, perhaps most impressively of all, a plot. *Marathon* fans have taken to the Net in numbers that rival *Doom* players. Just as Doom-Gate serves as a central site for *Doom* information, the *Marathon* pages at AMUG (Arizona Macintosh Users' Group) coalesce dozens of individual home pages into one authoritative reference. Definitely start your Marathoning here—you may never need to go elsewhere.

WEB http://www.amug.org/~marathon

Marathon Files Another enormous FTP site containing *Marathon* maps, pictures, tips, and editors.

URL ftp://www.ese.ogi.edu/pub/mac/entertainment/marathon

Marathon Hyper-Archive The Marathon Hyper-Archive indexes and describes all the files available from AMUG's two *Marathon*-related FTP archives. AMUG is more or less the definitive site for all things *Marathon*, so this is the best place to start if you're looking for something specific.

WEB http://www.amug.org/~marathon/files
URL ftp://ftp-2.amug.org/pub/contrib/marathon • ftp://ftp-2.amug.org/incoming

▶ MORTAL KOMBAT

Mortal Kombat 3 Visitors have to pass a test to get beyond the opening screens of this graphically superior site. This is a site for people who love *Mortal Kombat*—no pussyfooting allowed. If you like the ruthless, blood thirsty world of *Mortal Kombat*, you'll feel right at home here.

WEB http://www.gtinteractive.com/mk3

The Mortal Kombat Web Compiling the latest news from newsgroups, strategies for fighting (when is your opponent most vulnerable? Try a high punch as they begin the descent at the tail end of their jump), pictures, sounds, technical information, and even voices from the

game. This is a very hot spot for *MK*ers. The sponsor of the site does seem to have a preference for female fighters (Jade, Kitana, and Sonya are well represented), but the quality leaves something to be desired.
WEB http://icarus.uic.edu/~osengb1

Motaro's MK Page Curious about the world which gave birth to *Mortal Kombat*. This page lays the groundwork for *Mortal Kombat*, explaining how an age-old competition of honor was corrupted by the evil warrior Shang Tsung. Lots of codes are on offer, with links to the entire *MK* family, from the original to the *Ultimate*.
WEB http://greg.simplenet.com/mk

Pictures from the MK Bugs A graphically illustrated set of helpful hints for players with an appetite for *MK* blood. Learn, among other things, the trick of the "nut punch."
WEB http://www.mit.edu:8001/people /jevans/mk/bugs.html

Rat's MK Information Page The reassuring silhouette of a rat lurking against a sunrise adorns this page of *Mortal Kombat* links. Rat deserves an extra dose of respect for this compliation— this page has been around for a while and is considered 'old school' among cyber *MK* aficionados.
WEB http://rat.org/mk/mkinfo.html

▶ VGA PLANETS

alt.games.vga-planets Invitations for and conditions of new games are discussed at this active newsgroup. One case in point is this request from Ross in the U.K.: "What we would like to do is get a team game going with someone, using host 3.2(1) with all the new features such as ion storms, etc., enabled. What we need for this is, obviously, another team to play against, but also an independent host, who would allocate five races to each team, and could then play in the game themselves as a sort of spoiler type race. Anyone interested?" So far no one has taken up Ross's offer, but plenty of other Planeteers have checked into the newsgroup for other reasons—to ask if a cloaked ship can attack an enemy ship and to debate which of the races is best. (Johan believes that the "Privateers are one of the worst races when given to someone who cannot handle them, while they are one of the best races in the hands of a relative expert.") Still other players have gone to the newsgroup's FAQ to pick up addresses for the latest shareware for the *VGA-P* game, host, and client, and to read up-to-date news on *VGA-P* Websites. And some, however, are way too busy playing the game to bother with either the newsgroup or the FAQ!
USENET alt.games.vga-planets

Carsten's VGA Page *VGA Planets* is alive and well in Osnabrÿck, Germany, thanks to Carsten and his excellent Web page. Besides a link to the alt.games .vga-planet newsgroup, this site also offers an invaluable list of ongoing games and players (future opponents, perhaps?). The site also carries Dreadlord's famous players manual—it's directed at beginner and intermediate players and talks about the various races, planets, credits, and strategies (which the author has based on Sun Tsu's *The Art of War*). German-speaking players might appreciate the additional links here to five exclusively German-language *VGA-P* sites. Vielen Dank, Carsten!
WEB http://brahms.informatik.uni -osnabrueck.de/~gcwilhel/english /Planets

VGA Planets While most of the hard core VGA-Players cruise the Internet to pick up their games and software, there are still good places to arrange games and talk to other *VGA-P* fans on commercial serivces like AOL and CompuServe. While the sites are dominated by gamers looking for players, you'll find copies of the front end and utilities as well.
AMERICA ONLINE *keyword* pcgames→ Software Libraries→planet

COMPUSERVE *go* pbmgames→Libraries *or* Messages→VGA Planets

VGA Planets Home Page Meet the mastermind behind the game. Tim Wisseman and his friends at BMT Micro and Dan and Dave software have assembled an informative *VGA Planets* Web site. Read an introduction to the game which explains its goals and what you need to get started. Or cruise over to the *VGA Planets* Information Pages for news briefs and game reviews. Scan a list of Commonly Asked Questions for answers to such questions as, "What will the next version look like and when will it be released?" (Tim will be working on the new version through 1997) and, "How do I make torpedoes in space?" (You have to build them from base materials and leave enough room on the ship for your crew to construct them). And if you just can't start your day without a little VGA Planets, you'll be happy to know that the Web site also sells game-related merchandise—who wouldn't want to sip chocolate hazelnut from a brand-new *VGA Planets* coffee mug? **WEB** http://www.wilmington.net /vgaplanets

VGA Planets SubPage This page prefers to leave the "fun, tricks, fancy backgrounds, and sexy layout" to the actual game, so don't expect anything but the facts when you visit the site. So what does this straight-forward, visually unexciting page have to offer *VGA Planets* fans? Three things that the author, Timo, says he couldn't find at any other site. First, there is a large catalog (500 K) of tactics, hints, and tips culled from the alt.games.vga-planets newsgroup. Second, Timo offers the latest Climate Death Rate formula that helps you calculate the best way to distribute your clans on different planets. And finally, the Web site provides an impressive list of ship names—1,000 monikers, some of them jazzy (Iskenderun), some of them romantic (Balya). Pick a name and set sail for Planet VGA. **WEB** http://www.chem.vu.nl/0 /Studenten/kreike/vgap.html

ROLE PLAYING

WHETHER YOU'RE STEERING your battleship through an asteroid field, swinging your sword through a dragon's lair, or shadowrunning through a sewer, remember one simple rule: "It's just a game." As you dissolve into the virtual landscape, cyberspace will suck you in and spit you out with a lizard's tail and chain mail armor if you aren't careful! Role-playing games reach a zenith with online capabilities, offering a wealth of gaming resources that narrow the boundaries between reality and fiction. First, find your favorite lane on the information superhighway, then craft your character and choose your weapon, from broadswords to lasers, before entering an IRC and another world.

▶ CLICK PICK

Role-Playing Games The infinite possibilities of a role-playing game require a meticulously crafted resource hub. All the sights, sounds, and stories give rise to entire alternate universes. The array of adventures must be broken down if one is ever to decide which path to choose— and this page has done that. Equipped with a search engine, resource library, and shareware, this Web site offers descriptions of many of the Net resources available to RPG players and links to several FTP sites and Web sites where you'll find netbooks, character sheets, adventure modules, and FAQs about fantasy role-playing. The games will only get better, as this site keeps you up to date on the latest upgrades, outgrowths, and overhauls to rules, roles, and rights on every situation your character may face.
WEB http://www.mcs.com/~duff/rpg

▶ MOTHERSHIPS

Fellowship of Online Gamers The AOL chapter of the Role-Playing Game Association Network. FOG members can participate in various RPGA Network events, FOG activities, and contests. They can also use the FOG's private message board, library, and conference room.
AMERICA ONLINE *keyword* fog

Havoc Headquarters Havoc Headquarters is an environment for RPGers. Its a large, well designed cyan and steel-grey domain with different rooms storing different resources. For example, the East Wing is the Entertainment arm of Havoc, where Games are stored, and the West Wing houses Arts and Music. The artwork isn't very impressive, but after the deluge of anime, its easy for drawings to look amateur.
WEB http://www.zone.ca/~havoc

Leanthar's Realm Leanthar's realm is a pretty site with up-to-date, well-organized links to a range of gaming sites, subdivided into categories that include Role Playing Sites, Gaming Companies, and Gaming Tool Sites.
WEB http://www.cybergate.com/~leanthar/leanhome.htm

Morph's RPG Page Well designed and packed with role-playing guides, aids, and resources for AD&D, Cyberpunk 2020, Storyteller, and RIFTS games. It also features one of the most impressive indexes to online role-playing materials on the Net.
WEB http://www.teleport.com/~morpheus/rpgs.html

Role-Playing Games Directory This Web page is devoted to advertising openings for email-run, role-playing games. Most games are free and human-moderated.
WEB http://http://www.pbem.com/pbem-news.html

Role-Playing Games Forum Use this forum to conduct play-by-message and play-by-conference campaigns—from medieval fantasy to cyberpunk systems. Games are announced in the Playing/Recruitment section of the message boards and then played in the section dedicated to the genre, such as Fantasy, Horror/Occult, or Heroes. Each game's messages has a header abbreviating the title of the campaign, and you'll need to read those messages to follow the game. Games are also held in the two conference rooms dedicated to the forum—players meet at a preset time and play using real-time chat. Logs of these adventures, and the completed message-based games, are then put in the gaming library according to genre, where they are preserved for members to download. You'll also find lively chat about running the games in the GameMastering and The Crossroads messaging sessions. Look in the various libraries to find artwork and game statistics for player characters, submission guidelines from role-playing game publishers, and programs for your home computer to help you create characters or track combat information. *The Crossroads Gazette*, an electronic gaming magazine written by and for forum members, is full of reviews, regular gaming columns, and news from game publishers. And like the forum, the newsletter caters to all kinds of role-playing games.

COMPUSERVE *go* rpgames

Role-Playing Gaming Forum The Forum offers info about and links to live (i.e., chat room) and message-based RPG games. Check the Game Schedules for when and where games are being played. You should be able to find games for almost any role-playing system here—and, if not, just start your own and post an announcement. The General Information message board contains posts from game seekers and GameMasters. You'll also find descriptions of ongoing games in the Live Game Descriptions and the Message-Based Game Descriptions folders. For a general overview of live games, select the Live Games folder, which contains How to Play Live Games, the Live Game Schedule, a Live Games Updates message board, and a link to the Dungeon, where many live games take place.

AMERICA ONLINE *keyword* rpg

Star Frontiers Mailing List How has the culture of Yast been shaped? Well, if you factor in the break from the theocratic government of Hentz, the grammar of the official Gnarsh language, and the harsh desert environment, you may start to get some idea of the kinds of people you have to deal with in *Star Frontiers*, the old TSR role-playing game involving space themes. Talk to other game players on this mailing list and consult the archives.

EMAIL majordomo@uidaho.edu ✍ *Type in message body:* subscribe frontiers <your email address>
WEB http://kuoi.asui.uidaho.edu/~kamikaze /StarFrontiers/frontiers_list.html

Star Sythe Empire Command The Sythe leaders used to control multiple empires, but those empires fell to pieces, and the rubble lay at the feet of the high and mighty Sythe. Now they want to take back the universe, and they're using IRC channels to do it. Join the fight, help destroy the four races of the Quadrant, and decide whether the KyrAx poses any threat to you, the universe, or standard rules of capitalization.

TELNET groucho.dal.net:6667
IRC #sse
WEB http://www.nmia.com/~hawke/sse

Steel Harbinger While visiting her father's lab, Miranda Bowen had a terrible accident. A dormant alien pod sprung to life, then attacked and infected her. As a result, this sweet young thing was forced to live part time as the Steel Harbinger. Find out how she suffers, and can make you suffer, at this gorgeous site.

WEB http://members.aol.com /steelharb/index.html

The Unofficial AnimeMUCK Home Page This home page for the virtual world of Japanese animation includes a technical manual for MUCKs, registration and contact information for the MUCK, and the Hitchhiker's Guide to AnimeMUCK— Fodor's and the Lonely Planets have nothing on this stellar travel guide.

WEB http://gpu.srv.ualberta.ca /~cmadill/am-hp.html

Usenet Complete Role-Playing Games List! If you're new to role-playing, get a copy of this list. It divides RPG games by gaming system and genre and defines many of the most commonly used terms in role-playing games. **WEB** http://www.cqs.washington.edu /~surge/gaming/rpgs

The Wanderer's WWW Page A huge index of role-playing materials. The Wanderer is particularly fond of Forgotten Realms, but he's also collected links to Shadowrun home pages, Tolkien information, a library of medieval studies, spell books, and much, much more. Don't miss the section of his site dedicated to favorite characters—anyone can submit the stats and histories of favorite characters. **WEB** http://crpp0001.uqtr.uquebec.ca /www_wanderer/RPG.html

CHAT

rec.games.frp.advocacy Not sure which game to buy? Ever thought about changing game systems? Or are you just so happy with the game you have you want to tell the world? This is the place for the great debates: *Hero* or *GURPS*? *Ars-Magica* or *D&D*? *Cyberpunk 2020* or *Shadowrun*? Gaming systems and materials are compared and rated in this forum for the highly opinionated. You'll learn the pros and cons of just about any gaming system out there. Just be careful—it's a free-for-all in here! Take your Vorpal Blade (or your Ingram, Elder Sign, or battle armor). **USENET** rec.games.frp.advocacy

rec.games.frp.announce Look here for announcements of new games, netbooks, FTP sites, gaming conventions, and live-action games. Discussions of specific role-playing games should be directed to their appropriate newsgroups. The rec.games.frp.* FAQ, which is posted here and to other frp newsgroups, covers the full extent of role-playing. Part 1 explains the structure of the frp* newsgroups and gives posting guidelines. Parts 2 and 2a answer frequently asked

questions about role-playing games, explain such terms as "munchkinism" and "Monty Haul," and provide some background on important role-playing-game figures, such as Gary Gygax and Steve Jackson. Stackpole's Defense Part 2b is also called "Stackpole's Defense of Gaming" and addresses parental concerns about role-playing games as well as pointedly answering charges against RPG gaming put forth by various religious organizations. Part 3 lists FTP archive sites containing role-playing-game-related materials. Parts 4 and 5 offer addresses for mailing lists and digests on the Net dedicated to RPGs. Part 6 is a directory of non-Internet BBSs of interest to role-playing gamers, and Part 7 describes the various netbooks. **USENET** rec.games.frp.announce

rec.games.frp.misc The catch-all discussion group for role-playing games without their own newsgroup. Talk about *Runequest*, *Call of Cthulhu*, *Star Trek*, *Toon*, and *Macho Women with Guns* here. Discuss rules, evaluate supplemental material (published either by the gaming company or good gamester Samaritans on the Net), and swap story ideas. If you're not sure which newsgroup to post to about a role-playing game, start here. **USENET** rec.games.frp.misc

ARCHIVES

Arthur Shipkowski's Semi-Ultimate Roleplaying FTP List Links to some of the major role-playing archives on the Internet. **WEB** http://nspace.cts.com/html/RPG /FTP_Sites.html

Monster RPG Archives Material for several role-playing game systems, including character sheets, GameMaster-assistant programs, home-brewed rules, archived threads from Usenet newsgroups, and original RPG fiction. **WEB** http://www.funet.fi/pub/doc/games /roleplay • http://www.funet.fi/pub/doc /games/roleplay **URL** ftp://ftp.csua.berkeley.edu /pub

rec.games.frp.archives The fantasy role-playing discussion newsgroups generate volumes of information: digests of interesting threads, netbooks, stories, and even binaries of useful programs for role-playing games are posted here.
USENET rec.games.frp.archives

PUBLICATIONS

Apocrypha Can a GM be objective? How can graphics enhance a campaign? Read the Digital Dwarf and find out. What are possible future histories of the world? This zine is filled with ideas for the RPG GameMaster.
WEB http://www.webcom.com/~apcrypha

Arcane Home page for the role-playing print magazine *Arcane*, the U.K.'s best-selling independent role-playing magazine Find out what's in the current issue, subscribe, and consult their list of links to role-playing sites online.
WEB http://www.futurenet.co.uk /cgi-passwd/passwd_login.pl /entertainment/arcane.html

WORLD BUILDING

Unlimited Adventures Unlimited Adventures (UA) is a product from Strategic Simulations, Inc. that allows RPG enthusiasts to create their own worlds. This forum offers UA owners a chance to download additional modules for free, participate in discussions about world building, and add fantasy artwork to their worlds.
AMERICA ONLINE *keyword* unlimited adventures

World Building So you have visions of a new world and you need instructions on how to build it? This site features dozens of articles on game design, world construction, and methodology.
WEB http://www.hut.fi/~vesanto/world .build.html

World Design Discuss the creation of fictional settings for gaming worlds.
EMAIL world-design-request@hops .wharton.upenn.edu ✍ *Type in message*

body: subscribe
WEB http://www-marketing.wharton .upenn.edu/~loren/Links/world-design

The World Wrights' Web An excellent repository of world building info, including a dictionary of design terms, an essay on the artwork, an analysis of legendary artifacts in games, an examination of secret societies and conspiracies, a list of links to related sites online, and much more.
WEB http://www.galstar.com/~dbolack /WWW/welcome.html

INDEXES

Networlds in the Net The Net is filled with visions of alternate realities, many of them created in the form of role-playing games. This site links to dozens of these worlds —from a version of *Vampire: the Masquerade* in New York City to a page dedicated to *RuneQuest* Campaigns online.
WEB http://www.hut.fi/~vesanto /link.networld/networlds.html

Role-Playing Game Internet Resource Guide This index of role-playing sites online is organized by game system, genre and type, gaming stores, and mega-archives.
WEB http://www.common.net/~shadow /rpg_index

Surge's RPG Archive and WWW References From *Storyteller* archives to the *HERO/Champions* FAQ to a *DragonQuest* page, this huge list of online RPG resources goes on, and on, and on.
WEB http://www.cqs.washington.edu /~surge/rpg.html

Woodelf's RPG Index A large index of RPG sites on the Internet sorted by game systems —from *AD&D* to *Ysgarth* to *World of Darkness* to *GURPS*. There are also links to gaming societies, organizations, personal home pages, ezines and mags, companies, online stores, and other RPG indexes.
WEB http://dax.cs.wisc.edu/~woodelf /RPG/RPG.html

PART 9

New Worlds

FUTURISM

IN THESE INSECURE TIMES A COM-
promised vision of the future backed
up by a couple of good degrees can
be parlayed into a great career. Sci-fi
movies, TV, books, and games might
satisfy our desire for escapism, but
when we need a pin-striped, board-
approved and academically qualified version of the shape of things to come, we
turn to the futurists. And whether we
think of them as geniuses or charlatans,
philosophers or pariahs, some of us pay
them big bucks. One futurist finds herself worshipped by corporate America.
The books of another transformed the
thinking of House Speaker Newt Gingrich, and the work of yet another provides the intellectual rigor behind *Wired*
magazine. All find support for their
thinking on the future's onramp, the
Internet. And in this instance the medium truly is the message.

▶ CLICK PICK

Alvin Toffler in MicroTimes Not the first,
nor the last, but certainly the big daddy
of all futurists, Alvin Toffler became a
household name in the early '90s when
Newt Gingrich deemed *The Third Wave*,
co-written with Toffler's wife Heidi, an
important and prophetic book. The Tofflers have an uncanny ability to get it
right and have presaged many of today's
social trends in such books as *Future
Shock*, and *War and Anti-War*. *The Third
Wave*, written in 1980, has particular relevance: it addressed the advent of a third
wave of social change—the move to a
post-industrial, high technology, informa-
tion-based economy. It's hardly visionary
today, but 15 years ago the suggestion of
a non-industrial America was considered
mildly blasphemous. Toffler also explains
his association with Newt Gingrich and
the Progress & Freedom Foundation. An
excellent introduction to the ideas of the
Toffler team, of which the male usually
gets more of the credit on the Web.
WEB http://www.microtimes.com/toffler
.html

▶ MOTHERSHIPS

alt.future.millennium The future's so
bright you gotta wear shades. While this
'80s anthem doesn't quite ring right in
these somewhat cynical times, it might
be the theme song of this often spiritual
newsgroup. Alt.future.millennium is
home to anyone interested in the dawn
of a new millennium and all that comes
with it. Individuals from all religious
belief systems are invited to contribute;
as one helpful weekly contributor intelligently puts it: "for those who have faith
in (…), no proof is necessary; and for
those who have no faith in (…), no
proof is possible." Although one particularly popular string is a debate over
something from many millennia ago—
The Sphinx—most postings do pertain
to the not-too-distant future.
USENET alt.future.millennium

alt.society.future Predictions are popular as posters try to guess at what's to
come. They don't appear to be looking
too far down the road. One string is a
debate on the coming election; no revelations here. But one posting titled "ism-
schisms" points to the more challenging
quandaries that lie ahead for modern
society. Then again another person has
proposed a new calendar for the future
in which every month has 30 days,
except December, which would have 35.
"New Year's Eve should not be a day of
the week, but an 'unattached' day
between the end of the last week in the
year, and the start of the first week of
the new year."
USENET alt.society.future

Great Thinkers and Visionaries While
this is merely a page of links, it's a good
place to start in on some of the present
day's most respected thinkers, scientists, and futurists, as well as a few
geniuses from previous eras—names
you may have heard like Albert Einstein,
Leonardo da Vinci, and Isaac Newton.
Present-day mental leviathans include

Noam Chomsky, George Gilder, and Stephen Hawking.
WEB http://www.lucifer.com/~sasha/thinkers.html

The Luddite's Dictionary One Luddite has paradoxically posted to the Web this brief riff on technological terms. "Artificial Intelligence—The ability of computers to think like humans; see Fuzzy Logic. Cellular Telephone—A device that transforms solitude to servitude." You get the point.
WEB http://140.174.234.4/Luddites.html

The Magna Carta for the Knowledge Age This tome, released by the Gingrich-related Progress & Freedom Foundation in August of 1994, was the work of four of today's intellectual giants: Ms. Esther Dyson, Mr. George Gilder, Dr. George Keyworth, and Dr. Alvin Toffler. Toffler's ideas on the three waves of civilization set the tone, and the four describe the Information Revolution already upon us, explaining what it portends, and how societies and governments should respond. As national boundaries fall, dynamic relationships develop, and conflicts become rare, we are primed for an age when, "The powers of mind are everywhere ascendant over the brute force of things." This is an excellent analysis of both what was, what is, and what will be, by four people who should know.
WEB http://www.pff.org/pff/position.html

The Neo-Luddite Reaction Your movement's not in great shape when your best known advocate is the Unabomber; the timing of his 18-year crusade is telling, as it parallels the rise of the computer and the resurrected popularity of Luddism. As much as it seems a contradiction, Luddites are futurists as well—though their vision of the future is a decidedly stripped-down one. Even more paradoxical is the fact that some of them are using the Web to spread the Luddite word. This list of links shows how they differ from the Luddites of the Industrial Revolution, what exactly they renounce and espouse, and what others have to say about them.
WEB http://www.cudenver.edu/~mryder/itc_data/luddite.html

NewHeavenNewEarth Links Yet another page of links; this exhaustive listing, supplied by NewHeavenNewEarth, can take you to hundreds of sites, most with a spiritual bent. Among the often New Agey references you'll find a good bit of philosophizing on the future.
WEB http://nen.sedona.net/nhne/like-minded.html

Panelists at the Aspen Summit '95 A good resource. This one's a list of experts that the Progress & Freedom Foundation was able to gather for the 1995 Aspen conference. Among them you'll find many of cyberspace's great visionaries, including John Perry Barlow, Esther Dyson, Kevin Kelly, and Jeffrey Eisenach.
WEB http://aspen.pff.org/cyber/guests/guests.html

Rights, Camera, Action Consider yourself warned: this is a long-winded essay. It's worth it if you can find the time, and should be of particular interest to anyone who cares about the implications of wired interconnectivity on social structures, in particular the underlying legal issues with regard to the Web. It's written by U. Mass. Amherst Professor Ethan Katsh, and it was first published in the *Yale Law Journal* in May, 1995.
WEB http://www-unix.oit.umass.edu/~eleclaw/ylj.html#FN8REF

▶ MCCLUHAN

Hot & Cool McLuhan Connection A helpful McLuhan resource that includes a bio, sound files, photographs, and links to other sites on McLuhan, the man who coined the term: "the medium is the message." Take the Millennium link to see cartoons dealing with technology and culture. The best will be published in the McLuhan Connection's forthcoming book, *The McLuhan Millennium*.
WEB http://www.magic.ca/mcl-prj/index.html

Marshall McLuhan In the beginning there was the word. Then there was Gutenberg. And then there was Marshall McLuhan. McLuhan's writings on the power and future of language, such as *The Medium is the Message* and *Understanding Media*, have served as the springboard for much of today's thinking about media and the information age. If Nicholas Negroponte is the apostle of *Wired* magazine, Marshall McLuhan is its patron saint. McLuhan's long career and prodigious oeuvre were nurtured by the University of Toronto, and it's here that his legacy lives on in the form of The McLuhan Program in Culture and Technology, an entire program devoted to examining both old and new media in the context of McLuhan's work.
WEB http://www.mcluhan.toronto.edu

The McLuhan Probes McLuhan's influence on modern media is well-documented. Institutions like the center at the University of Toronto and The Herbert Marshall Foundation are doing their best to ensure his continued relevance. The Foundation, thanks to his wife Corinne McLuhan, holds the electronic rights to her husband's work and hopes to raise enough money to make it electronically accessible to all. The Probes themselves are a series of beautifully designed scrims upon which McLuhan's writings have been posted.
WEB http://www.mcluhan.ca/mcluhan

McLuhan Quote-a-Rama McLuhan's words of wisdom are manifold, seemingly inexhaustible. This page, part of Webcorp's larger site, will throw up a new and profound quote every time you reload. Handy for that monthly *Wired* magazine masthead. (Head elsewhere within this site for more amusing fare; although it's not future-related, it's well worth the trip.)
WEB http://www.webcorp.com/cgi-bin/quote-o-rama

THE TOFFLERS

Alvin Toffler: Still Shocking After All These Years This interview, published in *The New Scientist* in March of 1994, is yet another good introduction to Alvin Toffler from the man himself. He weighs in on technology, the relevant implications of chaos theory, and the future of international conflict.
WEB http://http1.brunel.ac.uk:8080/~ph92szh/toffler.html

Alvin Toffler with Peter Schwartz The Tofflers maintain that with the Third Wave will come social change as profound as that of the Industrial Revolution. They were also among the first to really consider as a current *cause célèbre* the gulf between the information haves and have-nots. Here Alvin Toffler talks with Peter Schwartz, a fellow futurist and co-founder of the Global Business Network. Toffler's concerns for the future—whether he's talking about education, biology, or war—are a bit worrying, to say the least.
WEB http://www.netropolis.be/dialectrique/docs/toffler.html

Toffler at the Masters Forum If the man's own words haven't been clear enough, try this page in which the writer tries to distill a talk by Toffler given at The Masters Forum in Minneapolis as part of Tomorrowday, an annual conference on the future. Other speakers included Gary Hamel and Nicholas Negroponte. While it's a spotty read, it does convey Toffler's ideas simply.
WEB http://www.skypoint.net/members/mfinley/toffler.htm

▶ NEGROPONTE

Inc. Interview In this ongoing email interview from 1994, Negroponte responds to questions posed by *Inc.* magazine's Jeffrey L. Seglin on topics ranging from *Being Digital*, which he was then writing, and the Information Age's haves and have-nots, to the MIT Media Lab.
WEB http://www.inc.com/incmagazine/archives/15940741.html

Letter to Negroponte Sapiens vs. Cyborgs. This unidentified correspondent and philosopher fancies himself a notable thinker on par with Toffler and Marshall McLuhan. The writer heralds the advent of the cyborg's virtual world and calls for a "respectful eulogy" for humans. For a brief, one-sided discussion on the demise of mankind, digitality, and sensuality, it's worth reading this posted letter directed at Negroponte. **WEB** http://www2.eff.org/~erict/Personal /Prose/letter_to_negroponte.html

Nicholas Negroponte Home Page This is a concise introduction to Negroponte, relating his early years as an MIT graduate student and professor to his later experiences founding the Media Laboratory, serving as the senior columnist of *Wired*, and writing *Being Digital*. It has two links of interest; the first to every column he's ever written for *Wired* (lately a showcase for ideas such as digital pants and digital paper); the second to a series of pictures of the maestro with his own best friend and so-called collaborator, his droopy-eyed dog. Great minds look alike. You'll also find his email address. **WEB** http://nicholas.www.media.mit .edu/people/nicholas

Review of Being Digital Don't have the time to read the book and want to bone up quickly on just what it might contain? It isn't mere commentary or prediction; "it's about the relationship between man and his latest 'phenomenon' of being." Review this read at Negroponte's publisher's site. **web** http://www.randomhouse.com /knopf/nick.html

Wired Interview—Being Nicholas A man of considerable ego, talent, and arduous but seminal prose, Negroponte is one of cyberspace's most prominent thinkers and doers—he spearheaded the MIT Media Lab and was an early contributor to *Wired* magazine's pockets. In this authoritative and wide-ranging piece from the magazine, Thomas A. Bass finds out what makes Negroponte tick. **WEB** http://vip.hotwired.com/wired /3.11/features/nicholas.html

▶ POPCORN

Faith Popcorn With a name like Faith Popcorn you're bound to stir up some interest. But it's her understanding of trends, more than her name, that's really getting people to listen. She and the Brain Reserve, the company/think tank she founded, have been in much demand since her notions of the future, promulgated in such books as *The Popcorn Report*, started hinting at where mainstream America was headed. Cybercomm and Media Marketing "are very proud to present" the comments Popcorn made at a conference hosted by The Flemish Centre for Quality Assurance in Antwerp in October of 1995. Not the best writing, but it does convey the pop in her corn. **WEB** http://www.cybercomm.be /popcorn.htm

Faith Popcorn—Top Trends of the Nineties Popcorn's prescience has been applauded throughout the international business world. While she works for mighty corporations, her ideas really pertain to all of us—how the typical person will lead their lives in the years ahead. Here she lists the top 10 trends of the present decade. **WEB** http://www.bible.org/reg/illus2 /ill205a7.htm

Suck on Faith Popcorn Not everyone loves Popcorn, as this article in *Suck* lets on, alleging that she's more of a master marketer than a master forecaster. **WEB** http://www.suck.com/daily /dynatables/96/05/29

▶ GILDER

George Gilder George Gilder is yet another official future guru whose status was confirmed when *Wired* placed him on the cover of their March 1996 issue. While his politics run to the right, his predictions for the future are anything but conservative. He's advised and addressed many a media mogul, futurist, and president—of both countries and companies. This *HotWired* site is an excellent place to start if you want to get giddy about Gilder.

WEB http://www.hotwired.com/wired/4.03/gilder/index.html

SAFFO

Paul Saffo Lucky is the man who gets to spend all his time examining the future. Saffo has been at it for more than 25 years at the Institute for the Future, a consulting firm he founded. On the subject of the Web, his favorite tagline is "Context over Content." We'll leave it to you to figure it all out—it's outlined in this *HotWired* feature, as is Saffo's forecast for the Web. Take the "context" link to get a clearer definition of Saffo's emphasis on context over all else.

WEB http://www.hotwired.com/club/special/transcripts/10-16-04.saffo.html

HUBBARD

Coming Attractions In this essay, Barbara Hubbard outlines her visions for the future. She sees the eventual emergence of a "genuinely universal species" and compares the period ahead for mankind as radical a period as the one which saw aquatic animals evolve and emerge from the sea to live on the land. A world in which nationalist structures will disappear and the future, the higher frontier, will be determined by "cooperat[ion], free enterprise, and self-selected groups of pioneers." And what is the stage for all this progress? Space, of course.

WEB http://www.millennial.org/pubs/ffn/1_6/future.htm

The Revelation—Barbara Marx Hubbard A futurist of the first order, Barbara Marx Hubbard has been doing her thing since the late 1960s. Read about her accomplishments here; it says she was nominated for Vice President of the Democratic party in 1984: the question is by whom? Get to know the woman Buckminster Fuller once described as "the best-informed human" in the field of Future Studies.

WEB http://www.nataraj.com/npweb/nataraj/rev.html

Trajectories Interview: Barbara Marx Hubbard Hubbard founded the Committee for the Future and now serves on the board of the World Future Society. Although this interview, by fellow-futurist and Trajectories publisher Robert Anton Wilson, is more than seven years old, her ideas still have resonance. Particularly interesting are her views on procreation as overpopulation forces modern man to expend his creative juices "not on progeny, but projects; the creative urge now wants to synergize genius, not genes."

WEB http://www.nets.com/raw/ihub.html

WILSON

Robert Anton Wilson The author of *Schroedinger's Cat* and *The Illuminatus! Trilogy* first started publishing *Trajectories: The Journal of Futurism and Heresy* in 1988. It's been home to many a futurist theory or interpretation, whether it's completely off-the-wall or just mildly conceivable. Read articles he contributed, like "The Future of the Future" or "Medard Gabel and the World Game."

WEB http://www.nets.com/raw/raw.html

ZUBRIN

Dr. Robert Zubrin Not a futurist in the vein of Heidi and Alvin Toffler, Zubrin, a member of the board of directors of the National Space Society, is nonetheless laying out a future of interest to all, especially sci-fi fans. He invokes the American frontier mentality and the attendant air of exploration and creativity in making the case for the investigation and settlement of Mars. Only with such a frontier experience can mankind hope to avoid a new Dark Ages and further the vitality and creativity that resurfaced in the Renaissance and found its apotheosis in America. Or so Zubrin argues.

WEB http://cmex-www.arc.nasa.gov/MarsNews/Zubrin.html

THINK TANKS

The Center for Utopian Studies The world's no Garden of Eden yet. With cynicism on the rise, and the heady claims of communism dispelled, the notion of an achievable Utopian society has given way to realities and less ambitious matters. But the desire for a Utopian state has not completely disappeared. On the Web, not surprisingly, individuals, groups, and foundations are enthusiastic about what technology offers to societies of the future. In fact, this center doesn't exist anywhere but on the Web though its Web master is a doctoral candidate at Ohio University. The virtual community the site has spawned, as well as the resources it provides, are impressive. Links to utopian theoretical essays, architectural manifestos, fictive writings, Utopia-inspired artwork, even games, are all available here.

WEB http://oak.cats.ohiou.edu/~aw148888

EFF Forum The "digital revolution" is transforming our lives, traditions, and institutions. We may need an entirely new way of thinking regarding law, medicine, advertising, even personal identity. That's precisely the ambitious mission of the Electronic Frontier Foundation—not only to catalog those new concepts but to exert some critical control over them. This forum functions as an EFF storefront. For instance, after one woman complains that a new policy at her husband's company violates his electronic privacy—"The company may audit, access, and, if necessary, disclose any transaction such as phone usage, voice mail, and email messages, using corporate resources"—forum members respond, explaining that the company has not only the right, but the obligation to manage its electronic resources.

COMPUSERVE *go* effsig

The Foresight Institute This institution is a nonprofit educational organization formed to help prepare society for anticipated advanced technologies. Their primary focus is on molecular nanotechnology which will allow people to assemble objects and materials with atomic precision. Consider this: "Today's manufacturing methods are very crude at the molecular level. Casting, grinding, milling and

even lithography move atoms in great thundering statistical herds. It's like trying to make things out of LEGO blocks with boxing gloves on your hands. Yes, you can push the LEGO blocks into great heaps and pile them up, but you can't really snap them together the way you'd like. In the future, nanotechnology will let us take off the boxing gloves. We'll be able to snap together the fundamental building blocks of nature easily." Carrying on the ideas first laid out by Richard Feynman, the Foresight site make for mind-blowing reading. Excellent and informative links, too.

WEB http://www.foresight.org

The Millennium Institute It's not surprising that many of today's visions of the future focus heavily on ecological sustainability, given that 80 percent of the world's crude oil will be gone in less than 25 years and one-third of the world's species will disappear in the next 15 years. At least those are the numbers supplied by the Millennium Institute. While worrying, the knowledge of such numbers demonstrates the great benefit of these forward-looking institutions to redirect our best scientists, thinkers, and shapers of society and allow them to seek out answers to anticipated problems. Under the banner for justice, peace, and environmental sustainability, the Millennium Institute fights the good fight with such notable advisors as Oscar Arias, former president of Costa Rica; Nobel Peace Prize Laureate, Jane Goodall; and Vigdís Finnbogadóttir, the president of Iceland.

WEB http://www.igc.apc.org/millennium

The Progress & Freedom Foundation Clubby visionaries convene at this veritable think tank, founded in 1993 by Jeffrey A. Eisenach and George A. Keyworth. The foundation, loosely allied with Newt Gingrich and with a distinctive conservative slant, has very quickly become one of the more innovative and creative idea fonts in the country. Armed with "the American idea that… progress is the belief that Mankind has advanced in the past, is presently advancing, and will continue to advance through the foreseeable future," the foundation brings together futurists, politicians, scientists and other players to guage the present so as to better forecast the future. It's a vast site with many well-considered and articulately argued contributions.

WEB http://www.pff.org

▶ **JUST DO IT...**

Honoria in Ciberspazio One art form that refuses to die, at least in the hands of these creative individuals, is opera. A few enterprising and imaginative folks have put together this romantic, comic, and, most important, collaborative work. At their Web site they invite "everyone who visits these pages to send in rhymed couplets of poetry based on concepts or quotes from the opera's plot, which tells of five humans routinely connecting to the Internet from their separate computers, searching for significant romances, but encountering unreal cyborg-generated "clone" personae portrayed by dancers. Eventually the humans turn away from their clones and frolic together in a romantic flesh-meet (real life meeting) during which the promise of bonding in cyberspace is revealed to them through the character Honoria's insight. Interested in contributing to the opera about Netizens just like you? Send in your couplets and arias and watch as the libretto and opera take shape on the Web.

WEB http://www.en.utexas.edu/~slatin/opera

Futurist of the Year Contest Forecasting and future-telling has paid off for Negroponte, Faith Popcorn, and George Gilder. Why shouldn't it for you? Heineken sponsors a Futurist contest. In an essay of no more than 2,000 words, contestants are free to opine away on what the future bodes. Multimedia files—Quicktime, audio, illustration, etc.—are welcome. Four felicitous futurists will win $2,500 each.

WEB http://www.heineken.nl/futurist/intro.html

Arcosanti If living on an island in the Caribbean isn't quite your cup of tea, another community which aspires to be the model for future societies can be found in the high desert of Arizona. Construction of the nonconventional town first started more than 25 years ago. The town and its surroundings are laid out according to the precepts of Arcology, a concept of the city of the future that fuses architecture and ecology, as conceived by Paolo Soleri. Soleri, a trained architect who left Italy after World War II, worked at Taliesen West with Frank Lloyd Wright for 18 months before setting out on his own. Among his achievements is the Cosanti Foundation, a not-for-profit educational foundation whose major project is Arcosanti. You don't have to just read about the marriage of a sustainable community with conscientious urban planning. If you want, jump in a car, head for Arizona, and you can actually help build the city of the future yourself. Five-week workshops as well as seminars and tours are available.

WEB http://www.arcosanti.org

The Atlantis Project If reading, talking, and writing about the future aren't doing it for you, you might want to give this option a thought—living it. No one is quite sure what fate befell the first Atlantis. In the case of its second incarnation we're a bit better informed, thanks to the idea's very organizers: they went broke. (Seems they can't quite get a handle on that capitalism they so adore.) This crowd, with Libertarian, Objectivist leanings, are presently out of funds but hoping to raise enough to pay off past debts and start anew in the quest to build a new country named Oceania. "This country will be devoted to the value of freedom, and will first exist as a sea city in the Caribbean. As no collectivist nation is likely to sell us the land we need, we will build an island out of concrete and steel." Read the Oceania constitution, their laws, and an FAQ. You can even apply for a passport right now. Some of it's bizarre, some fairly interesting.

WEB http://www.oceania.org

NOSTRADAMUS

FOR THOSE OF US WHO HAVE TROUBLE PREDICTing what we're going to eat for breakfast tomorrow, the idea that physician and astrologer Michel de Nostradame produced a book of prophecies covering events from his lifetime to the end of the world, is difficult to comprehend. Even harder to comprehend is that not everything Nostradamus predicted failed to happen. In the mid-sixteenth century, he wrote:

"Out of Castille, Franco will leave the assembly,
The ambassador will not agree and cause a schism:
The followers of Rivera will be in the crowd,
And they will refuse entry to the great gulf."

During the Spanish Civil War of 1933, Francisco Franco and Primo de Rivera just happened to have been the two main opposing leaders. Coincidence? Many think not. Nostradamus's 100 verses supposedly include forecasts of natural disasters, the deaths of popes and world leaders, comets, and anti-Christs. The good news is that he did not predict the end of the world.

The main problem with the predictions is interpreting them. Nostradamus's prophecies were written in verse in a crabbed, cryptic style—a polyglot of French, Italian, Greek, and Latin. In order to avoid being prosecuted as a magician, he also deliberately confused the time sequence of the prophecies so that their secrets would remain invisible to the non-initiated. Misunderstood by most during his time, the quatrains are still hard to decipher today.

Enter the Net. Online interpretations of the 100 verses written by the seer of seers abound, some more conventional than others. **Nostradamus** provides the original French verses and a complete literal English translation. *In Conversations with Nostradamus*, Dolores Cannon, a retired Navy-wife and regressionist, disproves the concept of linear time altogether and claims to have established communication with the living Michel De Nostradame in the 1500s. Other personal interpretations of the prophesies exist at **Nostradamus Link and Prophetic Insights**. **Mike Herbert's Homepage** is home to the online Nostradamus quatrain search engine. And **Resources for Nostradamus** includes an FAQ, analyses, and links to reference materials like a 1606 French dictionary, a list of popes, and natural disaster information.

Most of Nostradamus's prophesies have been understood only in hindsight. Handy, that. Perhaps online discussion and dissemination of the divinations will help us use them as preventative medicine. Except he didn't predict we ever would.

Launch pad

In Defense of Nostradamus
http://www.sas.upenn.edu/~smfriedm/nostradamus.html

Nostradamus
http://www.newciv.org/~albert/nosty/nosty-index.html

Nostradamus Link
http://www.infobahnos.com/~ledash/nostradamus.html

Prophetic Insights
http://www.concentric.net/~adachi/prophecy/prophecy.html

Resources for Nostradamus Research
http://www.alumni.caltech.edu/~jamesf/nostradamus.html

Mike Hebert's Homepage
http://www.cs.uregina.ca/~hebert

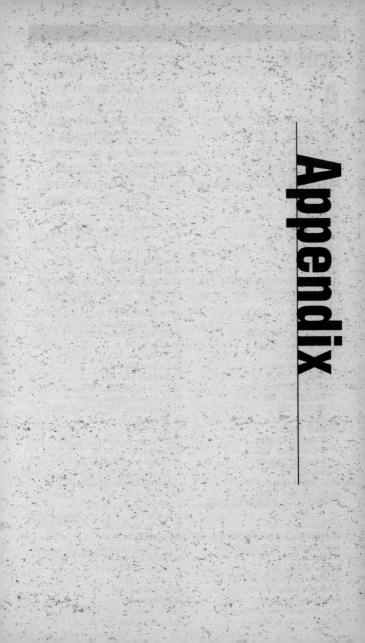

Appendix

INDEX

B

S

WOLFF NEW MEDIA

Wolff New Media is one of the leading providers of information about the Net and the emerging Net culture. The company's NetBooks series includes titles such as *NetGuide, NetGames, NetChat, NetTrek, NetSports, NetTech, NetMusic, Fodor's NetTravel, NetTaxes, NetJobs, NetVote, NetMarketing, NetDoctor, NetStudy, NetCollege, NetSpy, NetSci-Fi, NetShopping, NetKids, NetLove,* and *NetMoney.* The entire NetBooks Series is available on the companion Web site YPN—Your Personal Net (**http://www.ypn.com**). And *Net Guide*—"the *TV Guide*® to Cyberspace," according to *Wired* magazine editor Louis Rossetto—is now a monthly magazine published by CMP Publications.

The company was founded in 1988 by journalist Michael Wolff to bring together writers, editors, and graphic designers to create editorially and visually compelling information products in books, magazines, and new media. Today, the staff consists of some of the most talented and cybersavvy individuals in the industry. Among the company's other projects are *Where We Stand—Can America Make It in the Global Race for Wealth, Health, and Happiness?* (Bantam Books), one of the most graphically complex information books ever to be wholly created and produced by means of desktop-publishing technology, and *Made in America?*, a four-part PBS series on global competitiveness, hosted by Labor Secretary Robert B. Reich.

Wolff New Media frequently acts as a consultant to other information companies, including WGBH, Boston's educational television station; CMP Publications; and Time Warner, which it has advised on the development of Time's online business and the launch of its Web site, Pathfinder.